10,000 SHIPYARD WORKERS WANTED

Shipyard Workers Are Happy and Are Doing a Grand Job!

at SWAN ISLAND · VANCOUVER · OREGON SHIP

★ Here it is—in plain words that every patriotic American can understand:

To win the War, we must build more ships. To build more ships WE MUST GET MORE MEN. These men, whoever they are and wherever they may be—*perhaps you are one*—are entitled to the shipyard employment picture.

PREVIOUS EXPERIENCE NOT NECESSARY

Practically all of the 55,000 employees of the three Kaiser yards never saw a shipyard before. Yet they are the men who have broken record after record in shipbuilding.

Previous experience is not necessary. Training will be given on the job. Willingness to work and a desire to do that work where it will do the maximum good—those are the things that count.

WAGES

Along with the patriotic viewpoint look at the practical side—wages. Here is the pay scale at Oregon Shipbuilding Corporation, Portland; Kaiser Co., Inc., Swan Island, and Kaiser Co., Inc., Vancouver, as contained in the Master Agreement between the Pacific Coast Shipbuilders and the Metal Trades Department, A. F. of L.

LABORERS	**88¢**	per hour
HELPERS	**95¢**	per hour
JOURNEYMEN	**$1.20**	per hour
LEADMEN	**1.43**	per hour
FOREMEN	**1.58**	per hour

IMPORTANT

This message is directed particularly to men in Portland and vicinity who are not working in an essential war industry.

We Will Not Consider for Employment—

1. Any present worker in an essential war industry.

2. Any worker who has been employed since September 1, 1942, in the non-ferrous metal mining, milling and smelting industry, or in the lumber and logging industry in the states of California, Oregon, Washington, New Mexico, Nevada, Arizona, Colorado, Texas, Montana, Idaho, Wyoming and Utah.

Time and a half pay for all time above 40 hours in any calendar week, or above 8 hours in any one day. Day Shift—8 A. M. to 4:30 P. M. with 30 minutes for lunch.

Plus 10% Extra Pay for Swing Shift

Swing Shift 7½ hours work with pay for 8 hours. Hours—4:30 P. M. to 12:30 A. M. with 30 minutes for lunch.

Plus 15% Extra Pay for Graveyard Shift

Graveyard Shift 7 hours work with pay for 8 hours. Hours—12:30 A. M. to 8 A. M. with 30 minutes for lunch.

NOTICE—All shipyard employees must become members of the A. F. of L. having jurisdiction over their particular craft.

WORK DAYS—AND VACATION

Yard employees work 6 days in a calendar week. Every 7th week they have both Saturday and Sunday off.

The vacation agreement provides for one week's vacation (with 40 hours' pay) in a year's period and is given after 1200 working hours.

ENLARGED TRANSPORTATION FACILITIES

BUSSES—150 additional busses are on order; 45 have been received and the balance should be in operation within two weeks.

FERRIES—2 former San Francisco Bay ferries will be in operation shortly, carrying workers from downtown Portland to the yards. Each ferry can accommodate 3500 men.

TRAINS—Direct train service will be started soon from downtown Portland to the Vancouver yards.

All of these transportation services are in addition to present facilities.

10,000 WORKERS NEEDED IMMEDIATELY

The sooner you can come to work, the better. *There is a definite shortage of 10,000 men in the Kaiser shipyards right now.* Time is vital in the job that all of us have to do to win the war. *We need you!* The instructions below on what to do are for your convenience.

UNION EMPLOYMENT OFFICES OPEN EVERY WEEK DAY

LABORERS—Apply for immediate employment at the Labor Temple, 4th and Jefferson.

GENERAL HELPERS—Apply at the International Brotherhood of Boilermakers, Iron Ship Builders and Helpers of America at 1313 S. W. Third, for immediate employment.

JOURNEYMEN—Apply direct to your respective locals at the Labor Temple for immediate employment.

IF YOU CAN COME TO WORK WITHIN 5 DAYS

Telephone WE 2201 or fill out coupon and mail:

—5

Within 5 days from now I can come to work

....
Name   Street and Number   City, State   Phone

....
Age   Trade or Business   Single or Married   No. Children

Do you have living quarters in Portland or vicinity?......
(Yes or No)

Mail to Oregon Shipbuilding Corp., Portland, or Kaiser Co., Inc., Portland, or Kaiser Co., Inc., Vancouver.

DO THIS

If You Can Come to Work Right Now

Telephone WE 2201 7 A.M. to 10 P.M.
(Starting Sunday, September 20)

for information or apply in person to the proper union headquarters given above.

IF YOU CAN COME TO WORK AFTER 5 DAYS

Telephone WE 2201 or fill out coupon and mail:

+5

On ...., 1942, I can come to work.

....
Name   Street and Number   City, State   Phone

....
Age   Trade or Business   Single or Married   No. Children

Do you have living quarters in Portland or vicinity?......
(Yes or No)

Mail to Oregon Shipbuilding Corp., Portland, or Kaiser Co., Inc., Portland, or Kaiser Co., Inc., Vancouver.

Waging War on the Home Front

Waging War on the Home Front

AN ILLUSTRATED MEMOIR OF WORLD WAR II

Chauncey Del French
with
Jessie French

EDITED BY
LOIS MACK
AND
TED VAN ARSDOL

Oregon Cultural Heritage Commission, Portland, Oregon
Oregon State University Press, Corvallis, Oregon

The production of this publication was made possible with funds provided by Kaiser Permanente and individual gifts.

Cover and book design, Corinna Campbell-Sack
Production management, Lois Mack
Cover: photograph, Louis S. Lee; graphic, *Bo's'n's Whistle* logo

© 2004 Oregon Cultural Heritage Commission
    P.O. Box 3588
    Portland, Oregon 97208
    www.ochcom.org

Every effort has been made to trace the copyright holders of material reprinted in the book. The editors and publisher request that any copyright holder not listed here contact the publisher so that due acknowledgment may appear in subsequent editions.

Library of Congress Cataloging-in-Publication Data

French, Chauncey Del, 1890-1967.
Waging war on the home front : an illustrated memoir of World War II / Chauncey Del French with Jessie French ; edited by Lois Mack and Ted Van Arsdol.
    p. cm.
  Includes bibliographical references and index.
  ISBN 0-87071-048-6 (alk. paper)
  1. French, Chauncey Del, 1890-1967. 2. French, Jessie, 1886-1970. 3. World War, 1939-1945—Personal narratives, American. 4. Kaiser Company (Portland, Or.)—History. 5. Shipbuilding—Vancouver (Wash.)—History—20th century. 6. Shipyards—Vancouver (Wash.)—History—20th century. 7. Pipe fitters—United States—Biography. 8. Cleaning personnel—United States—Biography. I. French, Jessie, 1886-1970. II. Mack, Lois, 1947- III. Van Arsdol, Ted. IV. Title.
  D811.5.F728 2004
  940.53'7112—dc22
2004007155

Printed in China

Oregon State University Press
102 Adams Hall
Corvallis, Oregon 97331-2005
541-737-3166 fax 541-737-3170
http://oregonstate.edu/dept/press

Dedicated to Rick Harmon, valued colleague and friend
1952-2004

Contents

Acknowledgments

This book was made possible by the contributions and support of many people over several years. First, I would like to acknowledge Ted Van Arsdol, who initially brought Chauncey's manuscript to my attention.

Thanks to Marjorie Hirsch, Clark College's Archer Gallery director, who pointed me in the right direction to track down the art work. Special thanks to Trisha and Craig Kauffman of ArtSpace Gallery for their enthusiasm and invaluable help throughout the project. Thanks to the many art collectors who generously shared their knowledge and collections: Sue and Phil Augustyn, Mary Barrier, Peter Belluschi, Brian and Gwyneth Booth, Brooks Cofield, Ron Ennis, William and Terri Frohnmayer, Randy Gragg, David Horowitz and Gloria Myers, Claudia and John Lashley, Barbara and Jack McLarty, Douglas Magedanz, Bonnie Mentzer, Paul Missal, Michael Munk, Jimmy Onstott, Michael Parsons and Marte Lamb, Nick and Sue Storie, and Ron Stark. All illustrations are credited in the back of the book.

Special thanks to Louis Lee, Herald Campbell, and Douglas Lynch whose artwork and stories so greatly enrich this book; to Pat Koehler for her critical comments and memories of her shipyard work; and to Rochelle Cashdan for her constructive advice and editorial help. Thanks to the following people and organizations for their assistance in a variety of ways: Carole Van Arsdol, George Champlin, Jim Carmin, Betty Patapoff, Kaiser Permanente Northwest Region, Fort Vancouver Regional Library, Clark County Museum, Vancouver National Historic Reserve Trust, Oregon State Library, Multnomah County Library, Portland Art Museum, Tonkon Torp LLP, and Oregon Historical Society.

Thanks to David Milholland and the Oregon Cultural Heritage Commission, who believed in the project and the value of Chauncey's story, and to the advisory board and staff of the Oregon State University Press. Thanks to the Labor Arts Forum advisory committee and especially to Margaret Bullock for her contributions. Special thanks to Sarah Munro and Corinna Campbell-Sack for all their help and support.

Finally, I would like to express my appreciation to the late Rick Harmon, in part for his copy editing, but mostly for his steady guidance that was always an inspiration.

Lois Mack

Ships by the Thousands

The unexpected Japanese attack at Pearl Harbor on December 7, 1941, ushered in the most dramatic era in the history of Portland, Oregon—and its smaller neighbor, Vancouver, Washington, across the Columbia River. Devastating losses to the U.S. Pacific fleet in those days represented just the start of an era requiring total mobilization of the nation's economic and military resources to meet the challenge from Japan and its Axis partners, Germany and Italy.

Huge new shipyards were built all up and down the U.S. littoral. A labor force of 640,000 was trained and employed—only 2% had ever worked in a shipyard. By the end of the war, shipyards working under government contract through the U.S. Maritime Commission had built a total of 5,777 cargo ships. Revolutionary construction methods of assembly-line production were developed to meet this urgent national need. Prefabrication and welding replaced riveting and dramatically reduced the time necessary to build ships.

The success of the program was founded on a combination of private enterprise (long-time shipbuilding companies and newcomers, such as industrialist Henry Kaiser)[1] and governmental activity, through the Maritime Commission. The U.S. Maritime Commission was created by the Merchant Marine Act of 1936 in order to improve and modernize American merchant shipping. One year before Pearl Harbor, a closer integration of the shipbuilding industry with government was instituted to facilitate and speed up ship production, particularly to aid Britain and its allies through the lend-lease program. The Maritime Commission was divided into sixteen divisions serving three general activities: construction, operations, and general services. A five-commissioner board with specialized expertise facilitated efficient operations during the war.

Officials in Washington, D.C., decided that the building of ships would be a priority for Portland and Vancouver, which are relatively close to the Pacific Ocean. Inexpensive electrical power, required to run the shipyards, was generated by the new dams on the Columbia River, Bonneville and Grand Coulee. Although the area had turned out many ships in World War I, that effort was quickly dwarfed by the huge output in the 1940s, headed by Henry Kaiser under the Maritime Commission.

Maritime Commission shipyards were necessary to augment production of needed vessels and launched more ships than could be built in yards under contract to the Navy. Traditional centers of United States shipbuilding were concentrated on the East Coast—Boston, New York, the Delaware River, and Chesapeake Bay. Ship construction under the Maritime Commission centered at yards located on the West Coast around San Francisco Bay and the Columbia River (Portland–Vancouver), as well as Chesapeake Bay. Other locations included Puget Sound; Maine; Florida; Los Angeles and Long Beach, California; Newport News, Virginia; the Great Lakes; and along the Gulf of Mexico.

Most of the Maritime Commission yards constructed ships—classified as military—that were basically merchant vessels; transports, attack cargo ships, or oilers. Some vessels built at Vancouver were designed purely for military use, such as the tank-carrying ships that effected landings on enemy beaches (LSTs) and aircraft carrier escorts ("baby flattops").

Tens of thousands of workers were needed, and recruiting extended to all parts of the United States. At Vancouver alone, employment reached a peak of more than 38,000 in 1943—including 10,000 women. Giant housing projects were constructed to accommodate the newcomers, and residents faced the need to adapt to major social changes, among which were crowding, wartime shortages of civilian goods, and mixed races in housing and work. Local schools were forced to adjust quickly. Average daily attendance in pre-war Vancouver was 3,200 students. As families flooded in for work in the shipyard, daily school attendance rose to 9,900. Schools were double-shifted and teachers were hired by the hundreds. The federal government supplied funding to meet the crisis.

For the first time, women were employed on a large scale in jobs formerly thought of as the domain of men, and many African Americans migrated to the area to labor alongside whites. This was a striking change for

Henry J. Kaiser (1882-1967) was one of the twentieth century's greatest industrialists. During World War II, his ship-building program built roughly 30 percent of new U.S. merchant shipping, plus fifty small aircraft carriers for the Navy. Kaiser's humanitarian endeavors in establishing the private initiative system of hospitals and prepaid medical care, known today as Kaiser Permanente, are a lasting legacy for today's world.

Louis S. Lee

an area where blacks previously had been scarce and their work often confined to menial labor.

Kaiser's first entry into shipbuilding at Portland predated the Pearl Harbor attack. Oregon Shipbuilding Corporation's yard, managed by Henry's son Edgar Kaiser,[2] began operation in 1941, building ships under the Lend-Lease Act. In early 1942, the U.S. government approved a shipyard site at Vancouver (a short distance above the Interstate Bridge on the Columbia River), and construction started there almost immediately. The shipyard at Vancouver turned out a total of 141 ships—fifty of them escort carriers. Edgar Kaiser took charge of this facility and a new Swan Island shipyard in Portland on the Willamette River, located just south of Oregon Shipbuilding Corporation.

The record of Kaiser yards during World War II was outstanding. Nearly 1,500 vessels were delivered, equal to almost 30 percent of all U.S. Maritime Commission production. The ships were built in two-thirds the time and at 25 percent less cost than the average of all other shipyards. Kaiser's concern for the welfare of his workers was manifested in the unprecedented benefits he

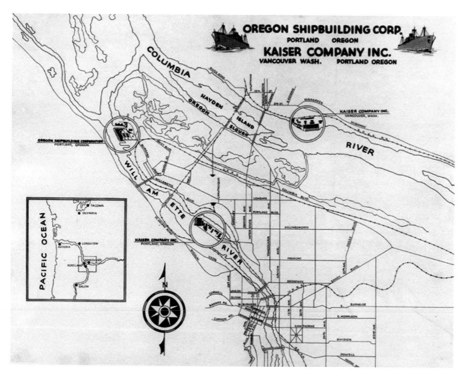

Operations for the emergency shipbuilding program at yards on both coasts and the Gulf of Mexico—including the three Kaiser shipyards in Portland and Vancouver—were funded by the federal government through the U.S. Maritime Commission and executed through contracts with private enterprise.

Chauncey Del French
(1890-1967)

Chauncey French's
writing career included
magazine fiction in *True
Story, Outdoor Life, Motor,
Railroad Magazine, and
Cowboy Stories*. Macmillan
published his book,
Railroadman, to wide
acclaim in 1938.

extended in the form of health care, child care, and subsidized housing. Henry Kaiser was more cooperative with labor unions than many twentieth-century industrialists. He understood that better wages and benefits were returned many times over in more efficient work by satisfied and experienced workers.

Among the large numbers of new workers flooding into Kaiser employment offices not long after the U.S. declaration of war was Chauncey Del French, a former railroadman, auto salesman, and freelance writer for pulp-fiction magazines and other publications. In 1938 French had enjoyed his greatest success when the Macmillan Company published *Railroadman*, a biography of his father, Henry Clay French, that was well received by critics. French claimed to have "a well-filled scrapbook registering the feelings of the great and near-great" regarding the work. Noted author Stewart Holbrook borrowed considerable information on French's father for his book *The Story of American Railroads*. Chauncey Del French also wrote a book about a railroad line between Idanha and Yaquina, Oregon, but a copy of this manuscript has not been located.

A native of Portland, French lived most of his life in Salem, Oregon. He had attended Vashon Military Academy on Vashon Island, Washington, and was preparing to study law at the University of Washington when, as he explained, "the 1907 panic wrecked family fortunes."

French labored first in the woods, then as a freight brakeman on the Oregon and Washington Railroad which became Union Pacific, and later in railroad passenger service. He also worked in fruit orchards in Oregon when he first decided to write stories. Although he encountered what he described as "a blizzard of rejection slips" for eight years, he finally began getting acceptances from editors for his stories.

French apparently began work on his Kaiser memoirs shortly after taking a job at Vancouver in 1942. He and wife Jessie soon moved to a Vancouver Housing Authority[3] project to be closer to work, while retaining their house in Salem. Although at first rejected for a shipyard job, Jessie later was accepted and rose to the position of leadlady. Her experiences were similar to those of many other women who broke through traditional male attitudes and proved their skills. Jessie describes her own experiences in considerable detail.

The writer, as shown in his memoirs, was sympathetic to his African American co-workers at the Kaiser yard, and his story provides an anecdotal description of them. His use of the vernacular in duplicating African American dialogue, as he heard it, has been retained in this book, along with the use of the word Negro, following the custom of that time. Although this style is offensive by today's standards, French authentically renders the sounds and rhythms of everyday speech, including words such as boy, gyp, and Yiddisher.

French's description of his fellow workers underscores the variety of ordinary Americans responding to the nation's call in the war emergency. As Frederic C. Lane has noted in *Ships for Victory*: "actual construction of the world's largest merchant marine was the handiwork of farmers, shopkeepers, housewives, and workers recruited from every walk of life." French's memoir, cultural historian David A. Horowitz has observed, "places the reader inside the work experience of the yards…it is infused with a direct honesty and humor in which people are dealt with in terms of their contribution to the cause of fighting World War II, no matter what their ethnicity, geographic background, or pedigree…it offers an unadorned portrait…what might be called a 'working-class' perspective on events without any overriding political ideology except support for the war effort." After their shipyard work, Chauncey and Jessie returned to their home in Salem. In 1951 French was contacted by the Pacific Northwest Library Association for details of his activities as an author.

He was working at the time for the State of Oregon as a driver's examiner, and his Kaiser manuscript remained unpublished. He said he had

WAGING WAR ON THE HOME FRONT

written magazine fiction stories "too numerous to mention" under the names Chat French, Chet Delfre, and Samuel Del, and he had won three *True Story* prizes totaling $1,500. Among his hobbies were hunting big game, fishing, studying geology, and collecting old books.

French died at a Salem hospital in November 1967 after a long illness. He was seventy-seven; Jessie passed away in August 1970 at eighty-four.

The couple, who had no children, turned over French's manuscript to the Kaiser Company. A public-relations official for the firm provided a copy to Ted Van Arsdol when he was researching a story on the Vancouver shipyard for the *Columbian* newspaper in 1970. The original manuscript was later transferred from the Kaiser Library at Oakland, California, and subsequently to the Bancroft Library at the University of California, Berkeley.

Ted Van Arsdol
Lois Mack

The Artistic Environment

The artworks illustrated throughout this memoir were created in or for the Kaiser shipyards in neighboring Portland and Vancouver during the World War II years, 1942-1945. Though at their most basic these images record day-to-day life in the yards, most were not meant as simple documentation but rather encapsulate the viewpoints, concerns, and aesthetics of their creators. In various ways, they also reflect national trends in American art in the 1930s and 1940s—a period of both economic and social turmoil and unprecedented public discussion about the role of art in American society.

Nationally, with the advent of the Great Depression in the 1930s, the scarce opportunities for artists further decreased. For the general public struggling to meet basic needs, art was a luxury. However, when President Franklin Delano Roosevelt proposed a series of government employment programs to stimulate the economy, several of his advisors encouraged him to include jobs programs for people in the arts. Part of the catalyst for this push to employ artists was the Mexican government's recent support of large-scale public mural projects by such artists as Jose Clemente Orozco and Diego Rivera—projects designed to boost civic pride, a goal Roosevelt's advisors also hoped to accomplish. A pilot project, known as the Public Works of Art Project (PWAP), was established in December 1933 under the Civil Works Administration to provide artwork for public buildings. Although the program lasted only five months, it employed almost 4,000 artists, and its success encouraged the Roosevelt administration to launch a larger program.

The PWAP was followed in the fall of 1934 by the Section of Fine Arts for the artistic decoration of new public buildings, and the Treasury Relief Art Project (TRAP) for the embellishment of small federal buildings such as post offices. Work on these projects was awarded mostly through competitions and commissions. The greatest opportunities for artists sprang from the creation of Federal One under the umbrella of the Works Progress Administration (WPA) in 1935. Federal One comprised four projects: the Federal Art, Music, Theater, and Writers' Projects.

The Federal Art Project (FAP) offered materials and a weekly wage to painters, sculptors, and printmakers in exchange for the work they created. These works became the property of the government and were dispersed to public institutions such as schools, community centers, and libraries. Federal Art Centers were also established across the United States offering free art classes, exhibiting works created by FAP artists, and serving as local community centers. For many recipients, the FAP offered their first opportunity to subsist as professional artists. FAP administrators also hoped the projects would serve larger goals—by making art accessible to the general public the quality of everyday life would be improved and public patronage of the arts increased. Opinions about the efficacy of the FAP were mixed. Many artists earned their first real wages as professionals and received public support and encouragement for their work on the FAP. A number of artists also described feeling a new pride in their work born of public acknowledgment of art as a legitimate career. Though the FAP administrators' goal to increase the public's interest in and support of American artists did not materialize in any long-lasting way, it did make many more aware of art in their daily lives and improved the overall status of artists in society.

American art created in the 1930s and early 1940s reflects a diverse mix of influences. The predominant style of the period was American Scene painting: images of everyday life in rural America depicted in a descriptive and generally realistic manner. This style's widespread popularity reflected both nostalgia for a simpler, familiar lifestyle and a desire to rekindle American pride—battered by the Depression—by celebrating American values.

At the same time, many American artists were working in a modernist vocabulary fully embracing such innovations as the expressive use of color, the primacy of technique over subject, the abstraction of form, and the fracturing and reordering of compositional space. Others chose to use their art to comment upon social conditions of the period, such as labor strikes, riots, conditions for immigrants, and other social ills. The PWAP, TRAP, and Section of Fine Arts stressed American Scene painting and other noncontroversial subjects, but artists who worked on the FAP were given greater latitude. Though many chose a regionalist style, other artists on the project created social realist, abstract, and other forms of contemporary art. Some alternated, creating one type of work for the FAP and another on their own time.

Oregon art of the 1930s and 1940s displays the same diverse mix of styles and subjects. Underlying much of the work is the influence of the Northwest landscape and palette. In his recent explorations of regionalism in the Northwest, Roger Hull, Professor of Art History at Willamette University, has suggested that it took a different form here, resulting in images of the local life and landscape in a modernist idiom. A survey of Oregon art from the period reveals realist images, modernist experiments, and abstract works all created contemporaneously. This eclecticism is also found in the work produced by the artists employed on the Oregon Art Project (OAP, Oregon's branch under the FAP). Although there is a preponderance of images of pioneers and farm laborers, the artworks include a broad array of styles and themes.

Martina Gangle, self portrait

After America entered World War II, funding for the FAP was redirected toward the war effort. Many of the artists employed by the FAP, like their colleagues in the private sector, turned to war work, laboring in the shipyards, factories, and other industries. The works from the 1940s illustrated in this memoir share a common subject—the life of the war-time shipyard—but the artists' motives and methods vary.

Martina Gangle (later Curl, 1906-1994) was born in Woodland, Washington, and started work as a migrant fruit picker at the age of eight. She began taking art classes in 1931 at the Museum Art School in Portland under Harry Wentz, adapting his blend of modernist techniques and regional subjects to her own ends. She was employed under both the Oregon PWAP and OAP, most notably creating a mural of pioneers for Portland's Rose City Park

School. Her primary interest, however, was the working class, often working women. Gangle was a dedicated and longtime member of the Communist Party and committed to addressing the situation of the common laborer. During World War II, she was a welder in the Vancouver shipyard. During breaks and lulls in activity, she recorded images of life in the yard. Her powerful, expressionistic style captured the interactions of the shipyard workers on an intimate and sympathetic scale revealing always their essential humanity.

Arthur Runquist (1891–1971), a committed leftist and foreman in the Vancouver shipyard, also focused on human concerns in his work—what he saw as an artist's primary responsibility. He and his brother Albert (A. C.) (1894–1971) were farm boys who studied art at the University of Oregon.

Albert (left) and Arthur Runquist, photographed in their seventies.

Jack McLarty

Arthur was employed by the OAP and Albert by the Oregon PWAP and briefly by the OAP. Albert assisted his brother with some of Arthur's larger OAP projects such as his murals for the University of Oregon library and Pendleton High School, as did their good friend Martina Gangle. Arthur's work for the OAP followed mostly the American Scene idiom, showcasing farm workers and pioneers in a brightly colored, linear style. Outside the projects, his work, as seen in his shipyard scenes, is painted more freely and in a darker, more muted palette. Figures and objects are essentially massed shapes, details are minimized, and the viewer becomes acutely aware of the paint surface and underlying structure of the composition. Like Martina Gangle,

Arthur Runquist captured his images during slow times on the job, and he focused on the everyday life of the shipyard. His works alternate between those that approach the yard on a human scale (showing men going over plans, talking and resting together) and others that show the workers dwarfed, even threatened, by giant structures and huge machines. A number of his images show accidents and injuries, reflecting the roughness and danger of the work. It is sometimes difficult to identify, with certainty, which brother created the artwork. Both brothers would work on the same piece, and Arthur often signed Albert's work.

Like Gangle and the Runquists, Ralph Chessé's (1900-1991) images of shipyard workers were also captured at off moments on the job. Chessé, an African American, was essentially a self-taught artist, though he briefly attended classes at the Art Institute of Chicago. Primarily working in theater stagecraft and puppetry in San Francisco in the 1930s, he was chosen to create a mural as part of the Coit Tower project under

Douglas Lynch, shown here painting a mural for an Armed Services Lounge on the mezzanine of the old Broadway Theater in downtown Portland.

the federal government's PWAP. Two years later he joined the California Federal Theater project as director of puppetry during the 1930s. When the federal project closed, Chessé directed his energies toward the war effort, working in various industries including the shipyards. He made thumbnail sketches of the people and activities in the shipyard during his spare time, focusing most often on the workers themselves. The image illustrated in this memoir is a simple line drawing and reveals Chessé's ability to capture the character of his subjects and evoke their personalities through small details. Reflecting his background in set and costume design, the women in the picture suggest types rather than individuals.

Art also functioned as part of the visual fabric of the shipyard in the form of posters, magazines, and other forms of graphic art. Douglas Lynch (b. 1913), provided much of the art for the shipyard's magazine, the *Bo's'n's Whistle.* He received his training at the Museum Art School in Portland and the

Louis Lee, Kaiser photographer, considers his work in Vancouver "the best five years of my life." Louis Lee's wife, Dorothy, got a job in the Kaiser payroll department, and they rode to work together during World War II from their home in southeast Portland.

Chouinard Art Institute in Los Angeles, working in a variety of media including oil and watercolor. He was employed by both the Oregon PWAP and OAP, creating linoleum murals depicting a calendar of mountain sports for Timberline Lodge in addition to other projects. After the war, he became a teacher of graphic arts at the Museum Art School in Portland. Lynch's magazine covers and posters for the shipyard were designed to have a gripping emotional impact and are often dramatic or stark. Though printed images, they have a painterly touch, using masses of light and shadow rather than line to create form. They convey opinion directly and play on emotions. Several illustrated in this memoir are designed to motivate workers and stimulate work production by dramatically illustrating the consequences of delays or errors.

In contrast to the images of these artists are those of the two photographers whose works are reproduced here. Both men were hired to document the operations of the Portland area shipyards in detail. To that extent, their photography was primarily documentary. However, it is clear from their images that they did more than record the process of building ships for the war effort. They produced careful compositions, often somewhat eccentric views, clearly influenced by modernist photography. In the period between the world wars, photography saw an explosion of experimentation in techniques, styles, and subjects. A number of artists sought to bring the principles of such art movements as Cubism or Surrealism into photography. The dominant style, however, was that pursued by artists such as Edward Steichen and Paul Strand and the generation that followed them. Their work emphasized complex formal structures, and their images were framed to reveal ordinary objects in a new light, whether through unconventional vantage points, interesting juxta-positions, or extreme close-ups on one part of an object rather than the whole.

Louis S. Lee (b. 1911–2004) was born in America of Chinese parents who had recently immigrated to the United States. He began work at an early age at various restaurant jobs to help support his family. He was given his first camera, an Eastman Kodak, for his fifteenth birthday and was immediately enamored with it. What began as a hobby became a freelance business photographing weddings, birthdays, and other special events in the Chinese community. When Lee heard that Kaiser was opening another shipyard, he applied for work as a staff photographer. He was hired to set up a photography department at the Vancouver yard to document all the activities taking place, from celebrity visits and ship launchings to the materials being used. Lee's images of special events at the Vancouver shipyard are generally straightforward documentary ones, but his photographs of the ships and equipment reveal his fascination with the scale of the machinery, parts, and finished product—something he empha-sized by taking panoramic views or shooting up from below his subject.

As shipyard photographer at Swan Island, Herald Campbell remembers, "I can't believe what I did, but we all did it, we didn't think anything of it. With a camera in one hand, no hand rails or anything, I'd walk out 100 feet or so and take pictures of the hull's daily progress, no safety belts."

C. Herald Campbell (b. 1911) took up photography in 1936. He was fascinated with the photographic process—from loading film to the final im-age—and experimented with all its elements. His first images were rural scenes and portraits, though he later developed a business specializing in industrial commercial photography while serving as the first Alumni Director and Di-rector of Endowment at Reed College. He later taught courses in photogra-phy at Reed. In the fall of 1942, Campbell was hired as staff photographer at Kaiser's Swan Island shipyard. The majority of Campbell's work shown here reveals his artistic experimentation with photography outside of his regular task of documenting ship production. He often used unusual viewpoints (close-ups or odd angles), combining juxtapositions of human gestures and mechanical shapes or distortions of scale to capture his subjects. His images celebrate the formal beauty of the equipment, ships, and people who used and built them, and the interactions of man with machine.

These artists convey in images many of the themes that run through French's memoir. They capture the sense of teamwork, camaraderie, and, sometimes, simple tolerance that made the extraordinary level of production at the shipyards possible. They show the close quarters, rough and often dangerous labor, and mixing of social classes, races, and sexes that characterized the crews. They document the shapes, textures, and scale of the industrial components of the shipyard which both spring from the hands of, and tower over, their human stewards. These images reveal the myriad ways in which individual artists interpreted a common experience. These works inherently suggest the time and place in which they were made, and they embody the varied influences—national, regional, and personal—that shaped the rich diversity of their expressions.

Margaret Bullock
Associate Curator of American Art, Portland Art Museum

Preface

The crash of bombs on Pearl Harbor did much more than expose the weakness of a supposedly impregnable naval base. Following the cry that went up for vengeance in kind, the hard facts of our national unpreparedness were forced into the open. Politicians had kept our Army inadequate and only partially equipped with modern weapons. Our Navy was paper-strong before Pearl Harbor and water-weak after that debacle. We had but a token force of combat planes, few experienced pilots, and almost no heavy bombers.

Our weakness invited the attack; yet our nation—unified by the blood of its sons—declared war on an enemy whose homeland lay so many heartbreaking miles across the Pacific. To wage war across those watery wastes, America had to have ships by the thousands.

America needed tankers to carry oil to our Navy, to the Air Force we were to build, and to our allies. Freighters were needed to carry food, ammunition, and guns. Transports were required to carry the men capable of conveying America's wrath.

In any large-scale construction operation, certain fundamentals must be present to assure success. There must be an experienced, job-tested organization. That organization must have leadership capable of directing and inspiring. Proof that such an organization existed on the West Coast lies in the fact that just forty-seven days after Pearl Harbor, the first of nearly 40,000 pilings was driven into the mud of the north bank of the Columbia River, two miles east of Vancouver, Washington. During the three months that followed the driving of that first piling, the keel of a Liberty freighter was laid and the major portion of a $17 million shipyard had been built. That yard was Kaiser-Vancouver. America was fortunate that one of her sons, Henry Kaiser, could meet all the complex requirements of leadership. He was not unknown. Travel the smooth highways of the West, view the dammed electrical might of its great rivers, or look upon the manmade

During World War II Edgar Kaiser (1908-1981) managed all three Kaiser shipyards in Portland and Vancouver. Edgar Kaiser played important roles in the construction of Bonneville and Grand Coulee dams. Edgar shared the humanitarian views of his father, Henry Kaiser, and it was he who made the key decision after the war to open the firm's pioneering pre-paid health plan to the general public. Edgar guided the Kaiser empire after his father's retirement. He served four U.S. presidents, and, as a business statesman, earned an international reputation for integrity.

(above right)
From January to April 1942, the Kaiser Company transformed a Vancouver dairy farm into a $17 million shipyard.

Louis S. Lee

lakes of stored rainfall—the story of Henry Kaiser, and his organization, had been written in concrete.

The gearing of this organization to the war effort could not have been easy, but it was done. The problems that must have been encountered stagger the imagination. Prior to the war, the Kaiser organization had never built a ship. Its first accomplishment was the revolutionizing of all methods of construction formerly used in shipbuilding. Speed was the need. Taking three vessels from a shipway in the time formerly required to build one ship—that was the miracle.

With the Japanese hammering at the gates of Australia, the Kaiser-built Liberty freighters arrived in numbers—and just in time. These ships also provided the backbone of convoys to Malta and Murmansk[1] and liberty skippers learned the way to London town. When General Douglas MacArthur's[2] divisions started back to Manila, Kaiser-built tanklanders put heavy equipment on any beach the general selected. Kaiser-built tankers followed the fleet and supplied the air bases. Kaiser's escort carriers, the "baby flattops," helped put a plane cover over the convoys in the Atlantic and Pacific. In battle test, they proved themselves worthy of a place in the line of the greatest fleets the world has ever known.

In the mighty armada assembled under Pacific fleet Commander-in-Chief Chester Nimitz,[3] there were other types of Kaiser-built ships. Late in

1944, the Kaiser yards at Richmond, California; Oregon Shipbuilding Corporation in Portland, Oregon; and Kaiser-Vancouver raced to build attack transports for the final blow against Japan. Tankers were built at Kaiser's Swan Island yard in Portland. Liberty ships and turbine-driven Victory freighters were assembled at Oregon Ship. The yards at Richmond and Vancouver built liner-like troopships (C4s) when the war ended. Ship repair was also included in the organization's effort

during the last phase of the conflict. Oregon Ship accepted a side contract to build aluminum pontoons for the army, and the Vancouver yard, in spite of a hurrying schedule of ship deliveries, built two 14,000-ton dry docks for the Navy.

Unfortunately, the scope of this work must be limited to the war effort of the Vancouver shipyard. Peak production at Oregon Ship reached a

Just upstream from the Interstate Bridge, the shipyard site covered 245 acres. The Vancouver yard included twelve shipbuilding ways, fourteen craneway trestles, a multitude of buildings, and eventually an annual payroll of more than $115 million. The Kaiser company main telephone directory listed 124 departments, all necessary to build ships in a hurry.

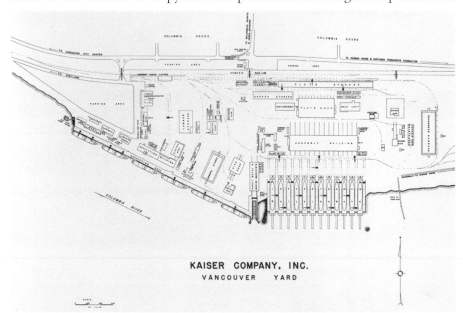

KAISER COMPANY, INC.
VANCOUVER YARD

total of fifteen ships in a month. A ship every other day! At Swan Island, a tanker was delivered each week! Such records were never before approached in the shipbuilding industry.

Ship deliveries to the Maritime Commission, or to the Navy, began in the latter part of 1942. No detail of their outfitting was lacking. When the ships were delivered, they were ready for the crews to come aboard. The machine-like regularity of those deliveries, when they were most needed, was high tribute to labor and management functioning as a team. In that record of teamwork—made under the stress of war—lies the hope of industrial America when at peace.

Honors came to the Vancouver shipyard from the Maritime Commission with nearly the same regularity as the yard's production of ships. Records were made and then exceeded with a casualness that was but part of the morale of those employed. There were many who wore Vancouver-Kaiser work badges. At the peak of employment, in December 1943, there were 38,762 men and women on the payroll. More than 120,000 were hired, fired, or took quit slips during the first three years.

The little people of America—grocerymen, farmers, loggers, school-teachers, barbers, prostitutes, cowhands, housewives, high-school kids, sheep-herders, clerks—those were the craftsmen who actually did the job. It was a real privilege to work with these thousands. The majority of them were the finest type of Americans. Nor was there any part of America unrepresented. The transformation of the little people of peace into craftsmen took place daily for almost four years. The Vancouver shipyard provided full proof that skill at a task is not restricted to sex, color, or age. That is the most unbelievable accomplished fact. The Mabels and the Bills—and the old Black Joes—built America a lot of ships when ships were one of America's most vital needs.

Chauncey Del (Chat) French
Jessie (Jess) French

1

"He hired every danged one of us"

There were only a few skilled ship craftsmen in the Portland-Vancouver area when war was declared. The maximum could not have been more than 10,000 men. Within a few weeks, they were working—or teaching—in a score of local industries. The Pacific Northwest's cupboard of skilled labor was soon bare. Even though, within a year, more than 350,000 people were engaged in shipbuilding, ship repair, and marine supply. America's little people were in denim. They were the home-front divisions the Axis could not count. Those thousands who staffed the various shipyards and allied industries were not impressive as individuals, but their massed effort had an immediate effect on the progress of the war. How this group was assembled, trained, and kept at its peak force is a tribute to American industry.

From Sidewalks of New York to Shipways of the Pacific Northwest

PORTLAND, OREGON, WEDNESDAY, SEPTEMBER 30, 1942

Long before the primary needs of the shipbuilding program were met, it became necessary to canvass the nation for labor. The Kaiser organization met that emergency head-on. Employment teams—recruiters—moved into the Midwest and the larger Eastern cities. Armed with a base pay rate of 95 cents an hour for common labor, these recruiters were able to compete on better-than-even terms with the local industrialists. In the slugging matches that developed, recruiters uncovered an additional potent punch—the use of women in quantity. Man-and-wife teams—sometimes whole families—were hired and sent to the West Coast.

The wail of a former owner of a Midwestern beer parlor provided a perspective on Kaiser recruiting methods: "I had to come out here and get a job. That damn Kaiser man walks into my beer joint and

Heading for the big war job in Portland and Vancouver, a seventeen-car special train carried 500 future war production workers across the country. With local help soon exhausted, Kaiser's recruiters scoured the nation for labor.

1 ⭐

Arthur Runquist gave the title "Riggers Resting" to his 1944 painting of two Kaiser-Vancouver workers. Riggers fastened lifting gear on steel plates and other material, and then balanced and steered the load during the lift. Riggers earned good pay, up to $1.20 per hour.

Arthur Runquist

hires every bum in it. He hires my bartender, too. That mug pusher is a foreman now, and he's getting more dough from Kaiser than he could steal from me!"

At the beginning of the hiring program, many of the workers started toward the West Coast with just their ticket. Some of them—low in funds at the beginning of the trip—found the ticket to be inedible, and they missed a lot of meals before they ever saw a shipyard. Those who came on the "Kaiser specials" (trains)[1] had good meals furnished for the entire trip. There were many workers, too, who attempted a transcontinental trip in an already worn-out automobile. Some of their adventures rivaled those who came to the Oregon country in covered wagons a hundred years earlier.

Most of the recruiters were more than fair with those they hired. The requirement for workers was so great the recruiter could not be choosy. If a man said he was an electrician, he was hired as an electrician. The real transformation often happened after that man arrived on the job. Within a few days, he was doing the work of an electrician and getting paid for it. What the recruiter wanted was someone not ashamed of the sweet smell of his own sweat. Such a person could be taught to build ships.

How the recruiters hired can be pictured by telling the story of a shipwright from Arkansas. There were about two dozen of us waiting in the almost total darkness of an engine room of a tank lander. Some were waiting for lights; some were waiting for scaffolds which the shipwrights were going to erect. Somewhere out on the dock the riggers were fastening cables to a half truckload of lumber. That bundle of planks would be

lifted by a whirly crane and lowered to where the shipwrights waited. Part of that lowering would be done swiftly, as long as the crane operator could see where his load was going. But when the load passed below the first deck, the crane man was guided entirely by the signals from the rigging crew. The load's progress then might be only a foot at a time—or an inch at a time—as the riggers maneuvered the load around obstacles in its path.

With the aid of flashlight, the electrical maintenance man was stringing a network of light bulbs to a master switch. The rest of the workers were relaxed wherever darkness had caught them. Cigarettes glowed, and the conversation turned to what each individual did for a living before the war. One of the riggers had been a logger. His partner came from the oil fields of Texas. One of the machinists had been a barber in Cincinnati. The burner[2] had been

Photographer Herald Campbell tells the story of his first day on the job. He was hoisted up 100 feet in a skip to shoot the progress photos of hull construction. At the end of the shift, the crane operator dropped the skip at the speed of gravity to within ten feet of the ground. If one survived the initiation, then you would be respected.

C. Herald Campbell

3

a schoolteacher. Two of the welders had been in high school. The chipper[3] had been a Boston taxi driver whose traveling stake had been only six dollars. He ran out of money somewhere in Montana and was quite hungry when he arrived in Vancouver. Several of the group, like myself, were local people and had no story, but the tall, high-split boy from Arkansas took time to tell of his hiring.

The use of acetylene torches for cutting steel plate and preparing it for welding was an important step in the shipbuilding process.

C. Herald Campbell

"One of them Kaiser fellers hired me. When I heard he was comin' to Little Rock, I jest thumbed my way to town. They was a passel of us at the hirin' place, an' he hired every danged one of us to do somethin'. When it come my turn to talk to him, he asks me if I ever did any plumbin'. 'Course he ain't ever been up in the hills. He jest don't know what our plumbin' is like. Same way with 'lectricity.

Then he asks me if I can carpenter. I told him I'd jest finished a new hog house an' had whipsawed my own boards. That was the truth, too. I sold them danged razorbacks to a neighbor, an' I'll betcha he had to ketch a lot of them with a 30-30. Anyhow, this Kaiser fellar hires me to carpenter. He tells me I'm to go to Vancouver, an' he gives me his word it's in the United States. I'm to git a ticket out here an' pay it back outen my wages. Shucks, I ain't no great shakes as a carpenter; but I ain't found nuthin' I can't do yet."

Somewhere in the darkness the electrician snapped on the master switch and the engine room flooded with light. The shipwright glanced down at his work badge. "S–h–i–p–w–r–i–g–h–t," he spelled slowly, "Ol' Navy sure has funny words for things. Ain't that a hell of a way to spell carpenter?"

And in the light that flooded the engine room, all of us discovered that the electrician who had hooked up the lights was a woman. Brown hair peeped from under the yellow rim of her hard hat, and there were curved lines where a young woman should have curved lines. All of us could see the wedding ring on her finger as she adjusted a light globe; some of us could see the single-starred service pin worn at her throat and the bronze insignia on her breast.

"I was a housewife—for a month," she said casually. "My husband enlisted before Christmas in '41 so he could join the same regiment his father had

Women were enticed to be war production workers with high wages and national advertising campaigns that were very effective. Full-page ads appeared in women's magazines and other media with slogans such as: "Remember: The more women at war, the sooner we'll win!"

Albert Runquist

served in during the First World War. His dad was killed at a place called Belleau Wood. It's not a very big place, I guess; it don't show on any map of France."

As she walked toward the iron-laddered escape hatch, most of ustook a good look at the marine emblem. Mentally, at least, we were saluting the husband and the wife. Nobody wolf-whistled as she climbed out of the engine room. Once hired, a carpenter from Arkansas, an Indian welder from Oklahoma, a burner from Brooklyn, and a housewife from Kelso, Washington, together with one of the authors of this book, in the engine room of a tank lander found they had many things in common. The first was the necessity of individual adjustment to the job. The housewife may have had shipyard training for only a week or two before going on the ships. The welder from the oil fields discovered he knew but little of welding heavy ship plates.

The yard training program was as complete as it could be made under the stress of war conditions. Thousands of workers were taught fundamental skills to help them function in their chosen craft. Some of the training offered was highly technical but was lifted from textbooks that offered no conception of actual shipbuilding needs or practices. But this was not altogether the handicap it would seem to have been. In the roaring assembly area, in the plate shop, in the hurry-scourged acres of marine pipe, on the scaffold-bounded shipways, and on the vessel-cluttered outfitting dock, America's common government-issue citizens had discarded textbooks. Those people were revolutionizing the methods of building ships.

Housing for the flood of workers that poured into the Portland-Vancouver area became almost nonexistent early in 1942. The first shipment of workers who arrived in 1942 had found empty houses and vacancies in apartments. As the need for living space grew, attics and basements were hastily converted to apartments, and old houses were reconditioned to make them livable. Anything that was roofed could be rented. But the real flood of workers was yet to come. To meet the needs of those people, federal housing authorities moved in and began placing contracts on a scale that adequately pictured the scope of the war effort planned for the area.

There were actually eight housing projects serving Vancouver's workers. Two of the projects were intended for workers of the Bonneville Power Administration; the remaining six served shipyard workers only. These six projects were widely separated but covered 1,800 acres. Each project was a miniature city, with its own stores, fire stations, and police departments. There were seventy-five miles of streets, many paved and all hard-surfaced. In 1943, 50,000 people in Vancouver lived under federal housing roofs, and they were paying $5.3 million a year in rent alone. These figures do not include Vanport or any of the other projects on the Oregon side of the Columbia River.

Early in 1942 Vanport emerged from its blueprints to become Oregon's second largest city and the world's largest war housing project. No detail was overlooked in its planning or building. There were social centers, a half dozen nursery-kindergartens, shopping centers, schools, play areas, a theater, a hospital, a cafeteria, and fire, police, and postal facilities. All rentals were of the apartment-house type, and the maximum tenancy was placed at 40,000 people. During the war years, Vanport operated at capacity.

Thousands of Vancouver's workers lived in Vanport and Portland. Every conceivable means of transportation was used or tried to get these people to and from the job. A ferry service was devised with the object of reducing traffic congestion on the Interstate Bridge, but this project never was satisfactory. It ended when the ferry capsized with the loss of several lives. Later, when gasoline and tire shortages became more critical, a train service was established from the shipyard to Portland. But this service was doomed by its slowness, and by the fact that its terminal was often several miles from the homes of workers.

With the tourist trade eliminated, cabin camps and trailer camps overflowed with permanent guests. There were also the inevitable small shack towns, where jerry-built houses of box crating crowded the mud puddles that

Hudson House was located a quarter mile east of the Vancouver shipyard. The single men's dormitory complex provided accommodations for a cross section of America. Daily brawls were common and the facility earned the nickname, "Hoodlum House." Monthly cost per person for room and board was $53.00. The *Bo's'n's Whistle* reported on February 18, 1943 that 7,000 individual meals a day were being served.

Louis S. Lee

7

were the towns' streets and sidewalks. One of these shack towns, in Portland, flourished and acquired its own temporary store. Only the stress of war conditions permitted such a village to be tolerated at all. A dozen families might share the use of one Chic Sale[4] outdoor privy.

Joining the upriver side of the Vancouver shipyard, Hudson House[5] was built to house the "women-less men." Later, other dormitories were added to care for "menless" women. Hudson House was actually a hotel with guest housing, feeding facilities, and a capacity of some 12,000 persons. A fire that took several lives swept the Hudson House project soon after it was completed. Fire-control walls, omitted in the haste of building the first units, were part of the construction of the rebuilt project.

New hires received a copy of this little book, *How'dy Stranger,* full of helpful information about wage scales, shift schedules, housing, transportation, schools, hospitals, insurance, war bonds, descriptions of principal crafts, and more.

Vancouver's population grew from 18,000 to more than 90,000 during World War II. To accommodate this influx of people, the Vancouver Housing Authority (VHA) built public housing for 50,000 new arrivals. The VHA spent about $65 million in federal funds appropriated through the Lanham Act. Federal funding also provided aid for schools and day-care centers in communities affected by defense industries. Public housing in Vancouver was not segregated. Look-alike houses on look-alike streets confused residents trying to locate their homes in McLoughlin Heights.

When it is remembered that Hudson House sheltered a cross section of all the men of America, it can easily be imagined that it was an interesting place to live. By presidential fiat, no segregation of races was permitted. Order was maintained only by constant, continuous, and strenuous effort on the part of the Hudson House police. The daily and nightly brawls earned the hotel the sardonic nickname of "Hoodlum House."

Columbia House,[6] also built just outside the high-wire fences of the shipyard, was apparently the only overplanned project of the area. Its facilities were never put to their full use. Inadequate and incompetent police protection permitted a full-scale riot shortly after the project's opening. There were also ugly rumors of police graft which no one took the trouble to deny, prove, or investigate. The reasons behind the decision to close the project were never made public. In the later stages of the war, many of the buildings were torn down and moved to Seattle.

On the hills above the shipyard, and less than two miles away from it, a housing project was rushed to completion in 1942. Most of the original houses built here, on McLoughlin Heights, were prefabricated and intended to be permanent. At the start of the building program, it was possible to get electric stoves, refrigerators, space heaters, and electric hot-water heaters. This equipment was installed in all of the prefabs. The tenant supplied the rest of the furniture.

When the supply of electric gadgets ran out at the site, houses were built in long rows. Hot-water coils in the coal cooking ranges made hot water available, and iceboxes (you buy the ice) substituted for the more modern equipment in the earlier houses.

The government called for people to produce their own food to support the war effort. The emphasis was on making gardening a family or community effort, and a national duty. Victory Gardens in the Vancouver housing projects (as shown here) sprouted on little plots of vacant land, from window boxes to backyards and vacant lots. Every type of garden was cultivated, and the surplus was often canned for later use. Nationwide, nearly 20 million Americans did their part to produce vegetables.

After the United States declared war, the draft and increasing demands on war production industries soon exhausted the available supply of white male workers. Consequently, African Americans and women were hired for war work. The U.S. Maritime Commission helped attract labor to the shipyards by patriot appeal, associating the work with national defense and by approving large wage increases.

Martina Gangle

Like Vanport, the McLoughlin Heights project was almost city-size, with schools, churches, child centers, and stores of every kind. Broad, four-laned highways fed traffic into an intricate pattern of curved side streets. Seen from the air, the pattern was beautiful. But to find one's house at night required navigation ability of the highest order. Fog complicated the task during the fall, winter, and spring months.

Whoever conceived the painting of the houses must have had camouflage in mind. But why camouflage was attempted on so small a scale is a mystery that only official Washington could answer. With other great shipyards within a ten-mile circle, a major airport directly across the river, and a dozen key bridges also in that ten-mile circle, it strained the imagination to picture an attack on this residential district.

Regardless of the fact that each house mimicked its neighbor in design, the individuality of the tenant usually expressed itself in the house's appearance. After the first year, lawns replaced the mud of front yards. There were tiny Victory Gardens,[7] too, wherever the soil and the land's contour permitted. Climbing roses began to grace the windows and entrances of many of the homes. Then there were those houses where the filth inside seemed to spill from every door and window. Clean or dirty, the homes were a cross section of America. Between the clean and the dirty, too, there was one common bond—the service flag in the window. The bond was strengthened as the war years passed and the service stars began to turn golden.[8]

The fundamental democracy of the nation was strengthened by an intermingling of its citizens in housing and work. A score of houses might represent a score of different states. The family from Alabama might lose some of its all-Southern viewpoint while living between families from Maine and Montana. The family from Iowa really got acquainted with the family from New York when they shared, borrowed, bought, or traded ration points.[9] The housewives from Michigan and Texas might listen, somewhat unbelievingly, to a local storekeeper explaining that it really only rained part of the time in the Pacific Northwest.

This mingling of viewpoints extended to the schoolrooms and recreational grounds, where there were no color lines observed in either the schoolrooms or on the baseball diamonds. The white kids played with the black kids—freely and willingly—proving, if nothing else, that racial feeling is something taught.

The importation of Negroes in volume, early in 1943, must have posed great problems for those in charge of the housing projects. By direct order of the president of the United States, there could be no segregation. In fairness to all concerned—the blacks who were being brought in, the whites who were already located, and the housing authorities who were charged with the responsibility of proper management—the presidential order did not solve the problem. The presidential order did create situations in the Pacific Northwest which could not have been anticipated in Washington, D.C.

Social equality is something that is won by the character and conduct of an individual—or by a race. It could not be granted, even by presidential fiat, to Negroes in Vancouver and Portland anymore than it could be given to Negroes residing in Atlanta, Memphis, or Waco.

Discrimination because of race was forbidden by a clause in Maritime Commission contracts in accordance with President Roosevelt's order. Although for the most part the yards were not segregated, the reality was that it was very difficult for African Americans to upgrade their jobs.

Ralph Chessé

11

Insofar as McLoughlin Heights was concerned, the matter was handled with a tact and wisdom that satisfied both the black and white residents— and the snoopers who were sent out from Washington. From their inception, all the housing projects had a rule that retained in the hands of the management the actual location of the tenant. The tenant could pick the area in which he desired to live but not the actual house or apartment.

Clean-up crews were made up of women, both African American and white. One worker recalled in the Vancouver *Columbian* on October 23, 1981, that sweepers were wearing out fifty-two brooms a day in 1944.

When the first trickle of blacks began, there were two areas in McLoughlin Heights still under construction. Most of the completed portion was filled to capacity. As the Negro families applied, they were given a list of all available houses. With the choice between a new house located among members of the Negro race and a less desirable one in the white quarter (which included the possibility of dubious welcome), the segregation was actually made by the Negroes themselves. The snoopers did come from Washington, D.C., but their canvass of the Negro tenants revealed only that selections had been made by the tenants.

If all the white and black racial problems could have been handled with equal wisdom, the fundamental democracy of America could have reached new heights under the stress of war conditions. But wisdom, tact, tolerance, and respect for the rights of others are seldom predominant among the masses—

regardless of how much they may be developed in the individual. When the McLoughlin Heights recreational director sponsored community dances, it was not possible (under the no-segregation order) to bar the Negroes from attendance. But the whites could, and did, stay away. The full democracy of the armed services—where black boys and white boys share the same dangers, the same trenches, and the same common graves—that democracy had yet to reach civilian life. It had a long way to go.

The only true measure of the wisdom of importing Negroes to the West Coast was the cumulative effect of Negro labor on the war effort of the area. On the whole, that labor was good. Many Negroes brought highly developed skills with them. This was especially true of painters. Also, many Negroes were first-class electricians and plumbers. Those who had experience with air tools became chippers or grinders. Many Negroes, anticipating postwar jobs, took welder-trainee courses and became valued members of the welding crews.

Most World War II shipyards were not segregated—however, African Americans and women were hired for less skilled jobs.

Arthur Runquist

On the distaff side, Negro women welders made excellent production records, but the majority of the Negro women signed up for jobs they could do without training. Two of the heaviest manual-labor jobs in the shipyard, cleanup and scaling, were favorites with the Negro women. On the shipways, cleanup meant relaying from deck to deck (usually upward) of all small steel. The size of the steel was limited only by what the weakest member of the crew could pick up or drag. A male pickup crew handled pieces too big for the women to move.

After the ship was launched, there was little steel to handle on the outfitting dock. Here the cleanup crews were equipped only with a broom, a dustpan, and a bucket. They not only swept the floors but collected all discarded pipe and pipe fittings, all pieces of wire trim, paper wrapping, and empty crates. When the ship's outfitting reached the stage where insulation of

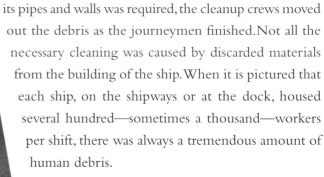

its pipes and walls was required, the cleanup crews moved out the debris as the journeymen finished. Not all the necessary cleaning was caused by discarded materials from the building of the ship. When it is pictured that each ship, on the shipways or at the dock, housed several hundred—sometimes a thousand—workers per shift, there was always a tremendous amount of human debris.

Pile up the papers and peelings of several hundred lunch buckets. Add to that the cigarette butts and empty cigarette cases of several hundred workers, and the worn-out gloves and bits of discarded clothing. The size of such a heap, collected daily, was startling, and it gives a definite idea of the housekeeping required of the cleanup crews. Theirs was one of the toughest jobs in the yard.

Deep down in the ship were tanks that held water, oil, and gasoline. Each tank was designed for the liquid it would hold, and each one needed to be pro-tectively painted for that liquid. Before tanks were painted, all rust had to be removed from their steel. That was the scaler's job. Armed with a scraping blade, a wire brush, a whisk broom, a dustpan, and a bucket, the scaler worked on the tank's inside. The tank itself might be one holding fresh drinking water; it might be a section of the double bottom of the ship; or it might be a huge area for storing fuel oil.

Every bit of rust had to be removed from all walls, floors, and ceilings of the tanks, and the tedious inch-by-inch progress over the steel surfaces took stamina of the highest type. White women and black did that work and did it well. It is not easy to picture the sticky heat of the tanks during the warm-

Practical work clothes for women doing war production were not easy to find. Welders wore special leather clothing, gloves, and hoods for protection.

weather months; nor can the bitter cold of the steel in winter be adequately described.

Ventilation (fresh air from the upper decks), if any, during the scaling and painting process would be brought into the tank by flexible piping. Rust dust rose in choking clouds when a crew scaled a tank, and most of the workers wore "dirt catchers" strapped over the nose and mouth. Scalers didn't last long on the job. They, too, were considered expendable.

The scalers and the sweepers made up the production labor units of what the shipyard called its "unglamorous gals." In a wistful shipyard poem, one of the gals complained that "nobody whistles at us." The lack of such whistles was probably due to the fact that most of these women were middle-aged or older, and that most possessed contours Percheron.[10] These contours were pronounced when the wearer was encased in a pair of heavy men's overalls. Again, a yard nickname, "A.P.&P." meant, in gentle translation, "All Prat and Pockets."[11]

And it really was necessary for scalers and sweepers to dress for the job. Without heavy shoes and extra-warm clothing—except in summer—the woman worker usually caught one cold after another and "sneezed her way to a quit slip." Here it might be added that the shipyard made a subtle differentiation between the woman worker in production and the female office worker—"women with pants on and women without pants on."

Joined to the necessity of wearing work clothing were the trials and troubles of trying to purchase the garments. All prewar stocks of clothing in the Portland-Vancouver area were soon exhausted. Replacements, under governmental control, were made on a population basis—using the 1940 census as a guide. The fact that 50,000 people had poured into the Vancouver area alone made no difference to the blind planners in Washington, D.C. Overalls became precious things. Stores were canvassed in Vancouver and in a 100-mile circle around the city. Any kind of work garment was bought on the spot, wherever found and of whatever size. If it was too big, it could be altered. If it was too small, it could be traded.

Garments were not the only scarce articles. Shoes, especially women's work shoes, were almost equally difficult to get. Lunch buckets, thermos bottles,

Workers voluntarily purchased war bonds through payroll deductions to help with the war effort and their own security.

This pamphlet, "The Ships We Build," produced by the Kaiser Company, describes the different types of ships built at Vancouver and lists those constructed through the end of 1944.

culinary equipment, bedding—anything used by the masses—was bought as fast as it could be placed on the counters.

Throughout 1942 and most of 1943, the 1940 census remained the guide for supplying the needs of the area. The 1940 census for Vancouver listed a total of 18,788 persons. In December 1943 the number of workers employed at the Kaiser Vancouver yard alone was 38,827. Only a small percentage of those employed were original local residents. Most, at all times, were imported labor.

Those who came from other states usually brought only their suitcases. Therefore, their housing had to be complete with furniture, and furniture—particularly beds, tables and chairs—was very scarce. Buyers haunted the "trading posts" where used furniture was sold. Any article that could be used, or repaired for use, was purchased on the spot. Oftentimes the buyer had no use for the article purchased, but it was used as trading stock. Prewar davenos[12] and overstuffed rockers became prized treasures.

Auctions, urban and country, became prime reasons for absenteeism, and the prices bid for simple, homey articles often doubled and trebled their cost when new. Three pieces of home equipment took priority over all others at an auction—and, to keep the crowd, were invariably sold last. These were alarm clocks, electric irons, and electric refrigerators. None of these things had to be in working condition to bring premium prices. In the ranks of workers at Vancouver were men and women who could fix, repair, adjust, or rebuild anything. Better than that, they could and did invent.

One of the fine things to come from the war effort was the encouragement, given by management, of original thinking by the workers. This was highly successful on a national scale. At Vancouver-Kaiser it must have exceeded every hope of management. Whenever a worker had an idea of a better way to do a job, or even a mental picture of a better tool to do it with, he took a form from a suggestion box, wrote out his idea, and put it back in the box. Then his idea or sketch was reviewed by a screening board of

Patricia Cain, (row one, second from left) was an electrician on day shift at Kaiser-Vancouver. Pat was one of many workers, including Chauncey French, who received awards for production ideas from the Labor-Management Committee. A Suggestion Clearing Office established a formal program in September 1942 to increase efficiency for time, safety, and labor-saving suggestions. Within ten months 8,695 suggestions had been received, according to the *Bo's'n's Whistle*. Pat's safety idea was that the whirly cranes flash lights in the direction they were moving in addition to the audible signal that might not be heard in the noisy yard.

engineers for value and practicability. If the idea or sketch met those requirements, the worker was in line for a bond prize of a size depending upon the number of man-hours saved.

Thousands of these ideas were submitted. Some were of a decidedly Rube Goldberg–type conception; but the vast majority of ideas were practical at least in intent. They ranged from simple time-savers to heavy machinery costing large sums.

A sweating cable puller noticed how the cable rubbed on the sharp edge of a bulkhead. This man submitted the idea of a roller that could be clamped on any bulkhead, and his idea speeded the building of ships. When low water in the Columbia River created a hazard to the twin screws[13] of the aircraft carriers at launching, an engineer designed a pontoon to give the stern more buoyancy. It worked, and the schedule of a carrier a week to the Pacific fleet's commander Chester Nimitz was maintained.

In the pipe shop of the outfitting dock, there was need for a small-pipe bender. Pride of the shop, and its biggest tool, was the bender for large pipe. A pipe-fitter foreman supplied the original idea of a small-pipe bender, operated by compressed air turning a drum. It worked, but at first it was not accurate. Much labor and considerable treasure were required to make it accurate. The man-hours saved by the small-pipe bender must have totaled up into the hundreds each week. The savings in nonspoiled pipe alone probably paid for the device many times. These savings and many others came from the minds and hands of men and women who knew what was needed to build better ships faster.

2
"Put him to work"

The U.S. entry into World War II and the swarming of workers into the Portland-Vancouver area reignited memories of my own shipyard experience at the Skinner and Eddy Corporation in Seattle during World War I. It was impossible to forget the roaring chaos of sound caused by hundreds of rivet guns bonding steel to steel. On the job, in order to be understood, we talked to each other by signs or by screaming. Sweat, dirt, deafness, and danger unlimited—that was shipbuilding, as I had known it when I was twenty-six. Did I want to go back to all of that now when I was twice that age?

The decision to leave my white-collar state job in Salem, Oregon, was not an easy one to make. To complicate matters, my wife, Jess, wanted to work, too. We had a home to pay for and a host of bills that kept getting larger as my state pay lagged further behind the cost of living.

When I investigated the possibility of returning to my old craft, I discovered that the new science of welding had almost eliminated the riveter from the shipbuilding industry. So going back to manual labor as a riveter was out. But part of my early training had been in railroad shops. Cutting, bending, and installing pipes for air brakes had formed some of my railroad experience. During rush times, too, I had served as a helper on locomotive steam lines. I knew a little—a very little, I thought—about pipe fitting.

Late in December 1942, I was cleared by the Steamfitters Union in Vancouver as a pipe fitter for work in the Vancouver yard. Meanwhile, Jess was promised a job as a time checker, but it failed to materialize. The supervisor of the time checkers thought she was too old to climb. How little he knew of her capabilities!

Badges were color-coded to indicate a worker's shift. Swing and night shift wages were 10 and 15 percent higher than day shift pay.

Politically and in an artistic
sense, Arthur Runquist was
attracted to the concept of
the working man. The
shipyards provided him
fertile ground to develop
as an artist. His faceless
figures and abstracted
forms take on elements of
the universal that raise the
artwork beyond a
particular time and place.

Arthur Runquist

After acceptance by the union, I and every employee had to go through
the "hiring mill." The actual time of processing took about an hour; the wait
in the line was about twice that long. The usual questions about age, place of
residence, and social-security number could have been expected when applying for any employment. But these forms probed deeper. Uncle Sam wanted
to know that his niece, or nephew, was genuine.

When the case history was complete in the hiring process, the employee was given a badge number. Mine, in the last days of December 1942,
was 43119. Not that many people were employed at that time. While up to
then there had been as many hired as the badge number indicated, labor turn-
over was fast and continuous throughout the shipbuilding program.

The bond desk was the second stop in the hiring mill. Any worker
could refuse to sign up for bonds, but only a few—less than one in a

thousand—did refuse. Hundreds of workers signed up for more than a 10 percent deduction; many took the major portion of their pay in bonds.

The girl at the fingerprinting desk was not very expert, in spite of all the practice she received. She admitted, rather ruefully, that several men employed had told her they had better fingerprints taken from them unwillingly than she had been able to get willingly. She spoiled several cards before she got a set of mine that were satisfactory.

It is easy to understand the discouraged appearance of the girl who operated the photograph gallery after seeing the pictures she took. From her camera came the world's greatest rogues' gallery. No matter how honest a citizen might appear, or how deacon-like his facial contours, the camera in use seemed to discard the cherubic and emphasize the satanic. No crime-steeped candidate for Alcatraz could have been photographed with a more criminal face than mine.

When my hiring papers were complete, there remained about three hours before swing shift went on duty. I used those hours to look over downtown Vancouver, where there were plenty of interesting humans to observe. The bus terminal, every beer parlor, and almost every store of any kind was jammed with people. One man came out of a clothing store with a huge bundle in his arms. "Thirty dollars worth of overalls," he boasted, "an' damn near all of 'em will fit me." His companion had what appeared to be a package containing several pairs of shoes.

Drugstores were packed with women buying cosmetics. No salespeople were needed; the clerks merely operated the cash registers. Men stood in line waiting to play slot machines. In a similar line, both men and women waited to get into a bingo gambling joint. In most beer parlors, the poker tables filled every bit of available space. While the police acted as kibitzers, soldiers and workers watched for someone to go broke. The vacant seat was filled immediately, and usually quickly vacated. Gambling entertainment was expensive in Vancouver.

Many stores—especially food stores—never closed. The buying spree that began with the opening of the shipyard never ceased until peace came to the Pacific Coast. The extent of the buying spree in Vancouver

Vancouver first built Liberty ships, then switched overnight to Navy tank landers, followed by escort carriers, attack transports, and troop transports. Each time the yard geared up for a whole new production, yet still turned out a record-breaking performance.

Arthur Runquist

was limited only by the supply of merchandise. All the desires of the working class showed clearly. Some of them gambled, some bought liquor, and some bought homes and farms.

An hour before the start of swing shift, I reported at the main pipe shop. A clerk took my name and badge number. He instructed me to get a hard hat and to report to the outfitting dock for a crew assignment.

The hat I drew was hard, heavy, and, as I proved many times later, safe. It actually weighed about two pounds. Webbing inside the hat held it in place. It couldn't be "screwed on for a big wind," and it could fall off, or blow off, easier than any other headgear I had ever worn. But it was a head saver on the ships. The dents and scars it acquired caused me to bless it with the same fervency I used to cuss its shortcomings.

When the whistle blew, I expected to go to work. But even though I had checked out a work badge at the timekeeping station, I was still unattached to a crew. Along with a dozen other "new hires," I reported to Jack Larkin. Jack, boss of marine pipe on the dock, was busy. He was to remain so for the duration. He told our group to wait, and an hour passed before any of us were placed. By ones and twos, the others were led out into the rain during the next hour. Then Earl Shea, Jack's second in command, called me.

"Chat French?" he asked. I nodded and stared at his six-foot, two-inch frame. "You have been assigned to install steam heat. It's a temporary deal for a week or so. I'll take you to your crew."

Here, a worker cuts steel pipe with a semi-automatic band saw.

We went out to a ship, onto the dock, and through a maze of tents holding materials. Workers could be seen everywhere throughout the hull. Our progress toward the control cabin of the LST (landing ship tank)[1] was an obstacle course. We climbed over men and equipment, webs of welder leads,[2] and mountains of ventilation piping. The control cabin was piled high with material and fogged with the blue haze of welder smoke. Earl pointed to a man of short stature and said, "Your leadman. Hey! Shorty! This is Chat French. A fitter. Put him to work." Earl turned to me and held out his hand. "Good luck to you," he said. I was on the job as a pipe fitter.

Shorty was hard of hearing, but he was all business. "The tool shack's up on weather deck, forwards," he informed me. "Draw a couple of pipe wrenches and a crescent wrench. I'll get some fittings for you while you're gone."

When I returned with the tools, he had a small box of fittings and was waiting for me. "Did you ever install steam?" he asked.

I shook my head. "Only bigger stuff in a locomotive," I said.

He selected a few fittings and walked over to a radiator. "The steam trap valve goes below, then a nipple to the union, then a nipple to the strainer, then another nipple to the next union. Then cut yourself a piece of pipe to connect to your supply line." That didn't seem any tougher than hooking up an air-brake system under a boxcar. "Okay," I told him, "How does that trap valve install?"

This illustration of bronze valves from the manual, *Marine Pipefitting,* helped with shipyard vocational training.

He picked up one of my wrenches, took the valve apart, and pointed to a couple of projections in its interior. Shorty said, "You'll have to make yourself a chuck to fit in there. The tool shacks don't have anything that'll work. Draw a hacksaw and cut yourself a piece of heavy steel that will fit. All this stuff has to be made up tight."

After much measuring, I decided that my chuck should be four inches long and almost an inch wide. By searching with a flashlight, I found a piece of scrap steel of the required thickness. After more searching, I found a vise to hold the metal while I laboriously sawed out the part I needed. My tool fitted, but its edges needed grinding to make it efficient. By hunting, I found a workman using an air-driven grinding wheel. I borrowed his tool long enough to shape mine.

When I got back to the control cabin, almost two hours had elapsed. It had cost over two dollars for me to make a 15¢ tool. Looking out over the dock, the massed background of buildings, and the forest of shipways[3] in the distance, it was difficult to understand a war necessity that would put $17 million into a plant and then force a worker to use time to make his tools.

Later in the shift I asked the leadman why such tools were not furnished. He waved his hand toward the dock and said, "They've been ordered, but tools of all kinds are scarce. Don't leave the tools checked out to you lying around. If you lose them, you will have to pay for them."

That was good advice. Tools had to be carefully hidden when not in use. It was also wise to keep them close to the job during the shift. Most of the wrenches used were easily portable and could be smuggled out the gates. Throughout the shipbuilding program, there were always dishonest people who would pocket anything that could be pocketed.

My employment swelled our crew to ten—nine men and a leadman. This broke down into six pipe fitters and three helpers. One of the helpers was an old man who was used as a runner for fittings. The two other helpers were youngsters—ripe for the draft and expecting to beat it by joining the Navy. One of the boys was allergic to beans; the crew called him Beans. One of the older fitters, who had served a couple of hitches in the Navy, solemnly assured him that he would get to like beans, that he would even want them for breakfast, and that, further, he would get them for breakfast whether he wanted them or not. Beans became my helper during the time I was on the steam crew.

When I had all the fittings properly assembled under the radiator, I measured the remaining distance to the supply line. It may have been coincidence, but all of the crew and the leadman were there to watch me do it. I was certain my measurements were correct. As I glanced over the group, I knew my status as a fitter was on trial. With my pipe firmly fastened in the chain of the pipe vise, I marked the length to be cut. As I reached for the pipe-cutting tool, an old journeyman watched my efforts to twist the pipe cutter open. He took the tool from me, held it vertical with one hand, started the cutting head spinning, and then rotated the moving head until it was open to the size needed.

"Use a tool when you're ready to use it," he ordered, and "practice that spin in your spare time."

Now, with all those eyes on me, I spun the cutter open, cut the pipe, reamed it, and threaded it. It was impossible to miss the look that went around the group. The nods of approval were open when I screwed the pipe into place and snapped the union halves together. They fitted, and I was as surprised as they were. There were certainly a lot of pipes I cut later that didn't fit on the first try.

When the whistle blew for the half-hour lunch period, I went with the crew to the pipe shop on the dock. There was no time and no place to clean up. The shop itself had an area of 150 by 200 feet. Pipe racks and bins for fittings lined the walls. There was a tool-issuing station, a small room filled with copper and brass piping and fittings, and a tiny office. A single radiator supplied heat, but the warmth of 400-500 men really made it comfortable. The room was crowded when we arrived, but we ate together while seated on the floor. My lunch mate was the ex-gob of World War I.

"Where did you learn to fit pipe?" he asked.

"In a Northern Pacific roundhouse, when I was a kid," I told him.

"First time I've seen a cutter spun open in years," he admitted. "Shorty's going to give you Beans for a helper. Teach him what you can. It'll help get the kid a rating when he goes in the service."

The social consciousness of the Runquist brothers is revealed in their art. War workers take a lunch break during their shift.

Arthur Runquist

"I'll show him what I can, but I don't know too much myself. I felt as if I was sticking my neck out when I hired out as a fitter," I said.

"You'd have been set up right away, anyhow," he assured me. "Shorty's trying to get you permanent, but it's the freshwater system that's short handed. See that little guy over there wearing the greasy black hat? That's Red. He's the foreman of the freshwater crew. He's forgot more about pipe than a lot of guys will ever know."

"If he knows pipe, I'd like to work under him," I said.

He nodded understandingly. "So would I, but I'm checking out in a month to join the Merchant Marine. I'm too old to go back into the Navy." He finished his coffee and stood up.

"Let's go watch the crap game," he said. "We can't get in, but we might get some side bets."

The crap game was a honey. About twenty players—all that could crowd into the semicircle facing a wall of the pipe shop—were on their knees. Onlookers made a solid bank behind them. It was hard to get within seeing distance. Whenever the dice changed hands, it was customary for the new holder of the bones to throw a five or ten-dollar bill on the concrete and offer to "shoot all or any part of it."

Once the point was established, side betting started among the players and onlookers. For every dollar bet by the players on the floor, ten times that amount was won or lost in side bets among the crowd.

It was not possible for me to see all of the players, but one I *could* see was outstanding. He was skillful in his betting, and he rode his luck hard when he won. When he lost the dice, he seemed equally skillful in placing side bets. The players called him Harry, and as I watched, the pile of bills and silver in front of him grew larger with each cast of the dice. The ex-gob[4] by my side nudged me. "The little Jew is cleaning the boys again," he observed. "Nothing crooked about his gambling. He's just one of the best percentage players I've ever seen. He plays poker at Hudson House, and he wins plenty there, too."

"Is the game a regular feature?" I asked.

"Yeah, but there's a rumor going around that all gambling in the yard is to be stopped. Even in Hudson House. Look, one of the brass hats[5] is going to stop and make a talk," he pointed out.

A heavy-set man wearing a huge raincoat and a shiny tin hat climbed upon a pipe bench in the center of the room. He picked up a huge wrench and pounded the top of the table for silence.

"Hey, gang!" he called. "Listen for a minute. Most of you know Bill Blank. He used to work swing shift with us, and he transferred to day shift so he could care for his sick wife. She didn't pull through a major operation, and

Bill wants to take her body back home. The hospital bill, the doctor bill, and the railroad fare will cost plenty. How about a buck for Bill?"

He took off the shiny hat, stuffed a bill into it, and started the hat out into the crowd. The crap game resumed while the hat made the rounds. The hat went down among the players before it got to me. I saw Harry flip through the pile of bills in front of him and select one for his contribution. I couldn't see the denomination of the bill he gave; but when I put in my dollar, there was a ten-dollar bill close to the top of the pile. I will always believe Harry put it in, perhaps for luck. In the confusion following the whistle for the second half of the shift, I missed the announcement of the total amount contributed. But I later learned that the cash amount collected from the three shifts had covered all of Bill's expenses.

First Aid stations on the ways treated accidents and injuries on the job. The two major causes of time-lost injuries were handling tools or materials and eye injuries. Kaiser vigorously campaigned to promote health and safety.

Arthur Runquist

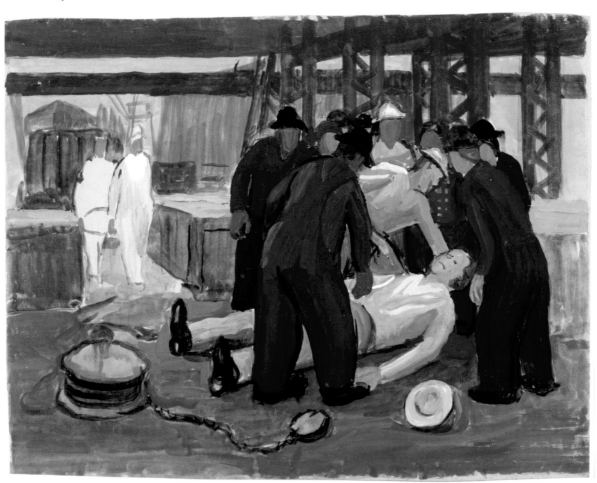

When we got back on the hull, Shorty gave me Beans as a helper. Our work was located in the aft end of the ship—supply pipes to a steam cooker in the galleys. Beans had an armful of tools and was ready to start. "We're going to work in the kitchen on the back end of the boat," he told me as I dug my hidden tools out.

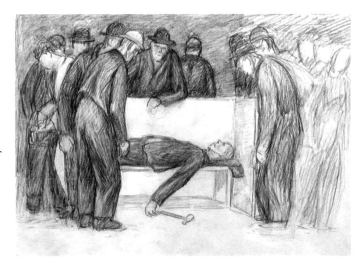

Arthur Runquist

The chatter of chipping guns hadn't started yet. The ship was quiet, and we were alone. I laid my tools down and motioned for him to do the same.

"When are you going in the Navy?" I asked.

"In six weeks," he replied.

"Then you've got just six weeks to practice what I'm going to tell you now," I said. "In the Navy, a ship is a ship. A boat is something that a ship carries. A kitchen is a galley. A toilet is a head. Forget this front-end and back-end stuff. Say forward or aft. If you're going to join the Navy, learn to talk like a Navy man." Beans stayed on as my helper for the short time I was kept on the steam crew. I coached him in pipe as best I could, and I tried also to give him some idea of what would be required of him as a serviceman. I liked the youngster and his million-dollar grin.

The tank landers were difficult ships to outfit—especially in the winter. The long expanse of weather deck between the control superstructure and the bow was always cluttered with small buildings and outfitting gear. Whenever it rained—and that was somewhat more often than occasionally—puddles of water stood inches deep all over the weather deck. An elevator large enough to lower vehicles from the weather deck to the tank deck was located forward. While the elevator wasn't completed until the ship reached berth six,[6] the hole in the weather deck was always open, waiting for the elevator. Broad ladders extended from the tank deck to the weather deck.

A dozen men could go up or down the elevator at the same time. All heavy, or long, material installed in the lower part of the ship had to be put in through this elevator shaft entrance. Some of the pipe crews became very expert at "walking a pipe down the ladder." The trick was to keep one's balance, to carry one's share of the weight of the pipe with one hand, and to hold onto a rung of the ladder with the other, until all fellow workers were ready for the next step down.

During construction of the LSTs, a worker was killed in a fall from the ladder. Several of us saw the man fall. Beans and I climbed through a maze of scaffolding to reach his body, but other workers reached him first. When they lifted him, his head rolled loosely on his shoulders. I knelt beside the man and put the beam of my flashlight on his face. The grey cast of death had settled on his lips. I motioned to the men to stop pumping his arms. "This man is dead," I told them. "Beans, go tell the ship supervisor to get the meat wagon," I added. The interns who came with the stretcher attributed the death to a broken neck. Later, the report came out that his fall had happened because of heart failure.

That report precipitated a raging argument in our pipe crew. Did the man have heart failure, fall, and break his neck; or did he fall, break his neck, and have heart failure? Like most arguments, it was never settled. The only facts we could agree upon was that the man's neck was broken and that he was dead.

Enough rain fell through the elevator shaft hole to keep the tank deck in much the same condition as the weather deck. The winds that haunt the Columbia River also used that entrance as a starting point as they made their way through the ship. Those winds got down to zero throughout January, and ice cakes of chicken-house size dotted the river's surface. It was not unusual, when working at water level below deck, to hear a series of scraping bumps. That would be an ice cake rubbing the ship's skin as the current took the cake downriver to the sea.

The very cool winds and the darkness of work sites brought forth an invention. The fact that it was never patented or made in commercial quantities does not detract from the crying need it met. First, a large number of workers became afflicted with poor eyesight. Also, since there was no heat of any kind on ships being outfitted, when a worker got cold, he stayed cold.

In an effort to produce more light and heat, an electrician hooked up light sockets that rested in dishpans. Only these dishpans with light would put out the amount of light and heat needed. The electrical department hooked up hundreds of dishpans, but the supply never equaled the demand. Those who somehow acquired one of these light units guarded it carefully so that it might not be "acquired" by someone else.

To generate heat, we managed to invert a section of large-sized pipe over a burner torch and get a stove-like effect that warmed a chilled hand or foot. In addition, there was a method of banking the flame of a blowtorch against a piece of scrap steel, which exuded heat in the fireplace tradition. But these methods were frowned upon by brass hats whose tours of inspection always ended in a warm office.

One of the most memorable characters of the first tank lander I worked on was a huge Negro leadman. His all-Negro crew worked as a bull gang,[7] taking heavy material out of the ship. Much of their work involved "toting" heavy steel scrap, unused pipe, or long planks taken down by the shipwrights. He and all of his crew lived at Hudson House. He was "leadman, twenty-foh hours a day," as one of his crew maintained.

There was never any question as to who was boss of that bull gang. Every activity of the man's crew was preceded by his roaring voice giving minute directions. Once, when he caught one of his crew basking in the warming light of a dishpan, his voice became a bellow: "Git up offen yo' big black butt an' git goin'. Ah tol' yo, that ol' po't wine you was lappin' up would put lead in yo' pants. Yo' didn' listen then, but yo' will now. This heah ain't no WPA[8] peace wo'k. Yo' Uncle Sammy is at wah. Git up an' git goin' befoh ah makes yo' a crown of tho'ns with these heah light bulbs in this ol' dishpan!"

His black crew loved him even though they griped and bitched about the way he rode them. "He's sho tough," one of his crew told me, "but he good to us, too. He wuz in de 92nd—de Buffaloes[9]—in de las' wah. Uncle Sammy sent him a Pu'ple Heart. He didn' git them scahs on his face—or de biggah ones on his body—playin' solo. No, sah, he didn'."

The shipways needed the big black leadman and his crew. It was not until they were transferred that we realized how much we had appreciated the

Crowded buses and trains awaited workers at the end of a long shift. "Rides-and-Rider Service" was an important part of each shipyard transportation department. Although ample parking areas provided space for private cars, employees were encouraged to increase the number of riders per car because of fuel and rubber shortages. Beginning in February 1943, the "Van-ship Limited," a ten-car train, ran from downtown Portland to the Vancouver yard.

Arthur Runquist

roaring voice of that black man who had fought and been wounded in the French Argonne forest during World War I.

The weather continued to be cold without snow. By accident, or error, one day the day-shift pipe crews left water pressure on the freshwater lines when they finished testing. The entire system was frozen solid by the time we came on shift. Every available pipe fitter on the outfitting dock was thrown into the job of freeing those lines of ice. Making the job more complicated was the fact that the ship was nearing completion on berth five. Many of the frozen pipes were behind furniture or ventilation ducts, where their removal meant ripping out other equipment.

Four days' work by all three shifts were required to clear the pipes. Blowtorches and burner torches were used wherever possible, but in the main the job was to replace the entire system piece by piece. Only a fraction of the original pipe was saved. Painters went to work as soon as the torches were put out. The "Buckler Boys," from the Buckler Company, waited until the pipe was replaced and the paint was dry. Then Buckler teams moved in and replaced furniture and torn-out partitions. The ship moved to berth six on schedule, and it even went to the Navy on time. Deliveries were what the Navy wanted—not alibis.

The schedule of deliveries became the unseen whip of every worker on the outfitting dock. In January it called for deliveries of completely outfitted ships every fourth and fifth day. If a ship stayed at berth five for five days, it was to leave berth six promptly four days after arrival. The only schedule break came when snow blanketed the Pacific Northwest and tied up all transportation for a couple of days.

The Northwest does not get a great deal of snow. As a consequence, most cities and counties have little equipment for snow removal. The Vancouver shipyard had *no* such equipment, but fortunately it did have a lot of men living within walking distance. The stags of Hudson House and the married papas of

McLoughlin Heights were issued shovels when they reported for work. Most of these men were from the East and Midwest, and they made a game of the job. Snow fights and impromptu wrestling matches enlivened the drudgery of the shovel labor. This unofficial "picnic" reflected the high morale of the workers employed. At the end of the second day, the yard was again ready for business.

The snow underscored some of the difficulties for commuters in more remote communities. For example, it caused me to be absent for four days. The snowfall started during swing shift, and it grew heavier during the two-hour bus ride back to Salem. The last ten miles of that trip taxed every horsepower of the overloaded bus. I shared rides with another worker who lived near my suburban home. From Salem, he succeeded in getting me to a crossroad within a mile of my house, and I hiked that last mile in time to get to bed at 5 a.m. The bus made it through to Vancouver three days later, but the drifts around my home were still too high to permit travel to Salem.

Arthur Runquist

33

2 DAYS
23 ½ Hrs.

Vancouver smashed records for building ships. LST Hull 179, Navy No. 475 was launched in just under three days after the keel was laid.

Louis S. Lee

When regular transportation resumed, the yard moved back on schedule. That schedule, incidentally, was stepped up in February to two and three-day ships. It did not seem possible, and *was* possible only because there were already a lot of ships on the outfitting dock. They were berthed two and three deep all along the dock. Unlimited quantities of labor power were concentrated on these partly finished ships.

Harry, Jimmy, and I "woiked de tanks" for six weeks. There were freshwater tanks to port, starboard, and amidships—the latter down under the deck where the vehicles were carried. Entrance to all was by manhole. The Navy designed these entrances to permit sailors to inspect the tank's water or its interior. However, the system's original designer failed to consider that the entrance hole should be large enough to permit entry of a couple of hoses for air and water, a burner hose, a welder lead, and a large flexible ventilation duct. The designer also apparently planned for a streamlined sailor. In other words, no provision was made for a pipe fitter who weighed 230 pounds, with about 40 pounds of that weight around his belt. In time, the three of us—Harry, Jimmy and I—developed effective teamwork. We discovered, for example, that it was possible to signal across the ship by hammering on pipe we had just installed. The simple code we started with became more intricate, and more valuable as a time-saver, each shift we worked. When testing pipelines, it became possible for us to tell each other when to turn water pressure on and off, when we needed a welder or burner, and when the line was ready for service. The signal for the latter—that everything was OK—was a direct copy of the "Indian beat" which every trap drummer knows: a strong rap followed by three lighter ones. That became the signature of Al's crew as those ships, and the ones that followed, went "down the crick" to Nimitz.

The stepped-up schedule—the continuous pressure for speed—required more manpower. Al was given more men, but they were put to work on feeder lines to the plumbing fixtures. Red, our foreman, was given more crews. Big Mike, an old-time plumber, took over the installation of all plumb-

This cartoon appeared in the *Oregonian* December 1, 1943: "My you ARE fast! You started building that ship the same day I started this sweater—and here you've beat me through."

ing fixtures. His crew, like Al's, received their "boot camp" training on the LSTs. Long before that contract was completed, they were veterans. So great was the pressure for speed that no individual letdowns were tolerated. If a man became dissatisfied, or lazy, Red traded him to some other foreman.

In peacetime, Red's merciless driving would have caused every member of his crew to hate him. But this was war. Every man capable of staying on Red's crews respected his ability, his knowledge of pipe, and the unlimited amount of information on the freshwater system that he carried under his old black hat.

While there were many times when the Safety Department made strenuous efforts to enforce the rule that production workers wear hard hats, Red never bothered much with it. While the heat was on, Red's greasy black felt hat would remain in his locker. Then, later, in some arc-splashed room of a tank lander or carrier, the pipe fitters would exchange winks and grins. If it happened to be Al's crew, the Indian beat would start slowly, speed up tempo, and finish in a chorus of Indian yells. Everything was OK. Red's old, black hat—the one that covered all the blueprints—was back on his head again.

3

"Please don't think I'm picking on you"

During those first weeks, I had tried to get Jess a job. In spite of the fact that hundreds were being hired, that proved difficult. She traveled to Vancouver several times and made the rounds of the union hiring halls. The fact that she was past fifty years in age became a barrier. The war was still too young to admit the aged, I guess. In justice to the unions, many of them had insurance programs for their members which would have been weakened by admission of those past insurance age. But it is to the credit of all the unions supplying the yard that they *did* make every effort to hire the best workers available, and that they *did* change their rules to fit the changing labor picture.

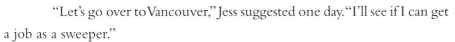

When America moved into the full war effort, her young men and women exchanged their denims for khakis and blues. Upon the shoulders of the gray-haired, the handicapped, the 4-Fs, and the What-Fors fell the burden of building ships. Quite capable shoulders they proved to be, too. The production record of the yard was highest after nearly all its young men had left the shipyards for service.

"Let's go over to Vancouver," Jess suggested one day. "I'll see if I can get a job as a sweeper."

"You have to have a doctor's certificate saying that you are capable of performing manual labor," I reminded her.

"I have it in my purse," she said calmly. "I want to be in production, wear a union button, and work on the ships just like you do."

Within an hour she had been accepted as a candidate for membership in the International Hod Carriers and Common Laborers Union! That same afternoon she went through the hiring mill. When swing-shift gates opened,

Drawings and articles in the *Bo's'n's Whistle* encouraged shipyard employees to practice safety first.

Douglas Lynch

we went in to the union offices together, with much the same feeling as when we set out to explore a new trail in our Oregon Cascades. Actually, we were beginning a new way of living that was to last for almost four years.

I guided Jess to shipway five, where she was issued a hard hat. No Parisian *chapeau* could have given her the perky, alert appearance that brown-

In the plate shop, this Runquist painting shows workers marking and cutting steel plate.

Arthur Runquist

rimmed creation of plastic and steel imparted. She took one look at herself in the tiny mirror on the wall. "Good heavens!" she exclaimed. "It looks like an iron bucket and feels like an iron bucket. Am I going to have to wear that?" She was to wear a hard hat, without further protest, for the duration.

With time to spare before the start of swing shift, we watched operations in one of the huge assembly bays which faced the ways. Here steel for the ships was being welded into each ship's sections. Throughout the length and breadth of the building, the blue lights of the welding arcs were making weird patterns of light and shadow.

As we watched, a group of welder-hooded men and women scrambled off of a massive section of an LST stern. An overhead crane lowered a huge hook to men who fastened cables to the big section. When the cables had been placed, the crane operator started his motors. With all the casualness of a woman turning a pancake, the crane operator turned the section upside down. Almost before the sound of the crash of that turning had died away, the welders were moving back onto the section. I explained to Jess that the welding, as much as possible, was done on a flat surface—that it was easier and faster to weld a

crack on the floor than it would be to do that same weld on a ceiling. That was the reason for turning the massive piece of steel. A ship section might be turned for flat welding a half dozen times before it was placed in reach of a whirly crane. Once the whirly[1] picked up the section, it was lifted high over the scaffolding of the shipway and lowered into place on the hull, where it became an integral part of the ship.

We had plenty of time for sightseeing after we left the assembly area. The huge plate shop was by then going full speed. Plates and beams were being shaped to the size and form required by the blueprints of the ship. The men who toiled here in the glare of the heating furnaces were part of the team, too. It was impossible to watch any group without that teamwork becoming apparent.

A workman rigs the big hook for a giant whirly crane.

C. Herald Campbell

Still on our way back to the dock, we peeked in on the activity at the electrical shop. It was a huge room crammed with workers, the vast majority of whom were women. Housewives and high-school girls stood elbow to elbow, assembling and wiring intricate-looking electrical gadgets. Everyone seemed to be busy, as if a boss were standing there, but nowhere in the big room was there anyone with the appearance of a boss. These people were busy, as was the rest of the yard, because America needed their efforts.

I showed Jess the way to the labor shack on the dock and left her there. I knew, and she knew, that she was tackling a mighty tough task. As a sweeper, she would be involved in cleanup on tank landers (LSTs), a difficult job. She had come dressed for the weather. It was still bitterly cold, and the wind off the Columbia River had a biting edge to it. In spite of her heavy shoes, overalls (a couple sizes too large for her), a heavy coat over her work jumper, and the painted newness of her hard hat, Jess still looked little. She *was* small. Bets were made among the women she worked with that she would not last a week as a sweeper. They knew how tough the job was, but they did not know her. I was proud of her then, and I am even prouder of her now as she takes over this narrative to tell of her first night's work on a tank lander.

Chat mentioned a labor shack, but what I entered was just a big tarpaulin-covered section of the dock. It was jammed with women. Some were seated on rough benches, some on bales of rags. There were piles of buckets and brooms in the corners. In the center of the room was a yard-made stove whose red-hot sides made the place comfortable.

There was only one man in the place, and I laid my hiring papers on the crate that served as his desk. Then I had my first look at my foreman. He had a big square face and the wrinkles that creased it seemed only to emphasize the kindness in his eyes. He looked over my papers and motioned to a young woman. "Here's some more help for you, Brownie," he said. "Suppose you two get acquainted. Brownie will be your leadlady."

Brownie hadn't much more than taken my name and badge number when the whistle blew to start the shift. The leadladies crowded around the foreman for their work assignments. Brownie emerged from the group looking a bit on the grim side. "An engine room again!" she exclaimed. "That's three shifts straight we've been hooked to clean up for the painters."

Under Brownie's directions, one of the bales of rags was broken open. Each of us carried a bucket stuffed with clean rags to the ship. It seemed unreal, and a little fantastic, to suddenly be one of fifteen women carrying buckets of rags aboard a ship. One of the girls also carried a coiled rope with a steel hook on one end of it.

Work was in full swing when we went aboard. We picked our way over the piled material that littered the deck, then down a steep flight of steel steps to the deck below. Every room was crowded with workers of all crafts and of both sexes. At each side of the ship were long, narrow passageways. With Brownie leading us, we threaded our way among the workers. Most of them were cable pullers, and they were installing an electrical conduit that, apparently, ran the length of the ship. It was as thick as my wrist, and I was to learn later that it was almost solid with copper wire, shielded with soft lead, and then wrapped with aluminum sheathing. The men were "shouting it in." Stationed about fifteen feet apart, they waited for the starting "heave-ho" before echoing the cry and beginning their pull. The big cable slid only a yard or less. Teamwork counted here, too.

We worked our way past the cable pullers, stopping when each pull was on, edging past the men while they waited for their next signal. Brownie stopped at a narrow door covered with many latches. When all those latches were closed, the door was watertight. In battle action, those watertight doors sealed the men at their battle stations.

Brownie moved among us "picking women" for the various jobs to be performed. Some of the women were too wide to get through the door or down the laddered shaft it guarded. These "broad-axles" were assigned as carriers to relay the removed material to the upper decks. Due to my half-pint size, I climbed down the shaft to the engine room with ten others. It wasn't as scary as it looked. The shaft was very narrow; but once I had my handhold, and my feet on the steel rungs, I felt secure, even though the shaft itself was quite dark.

The engine room I stepped into was about double the size of our living room at home. Two mounds of steel reaching almost to the ceiling filled one-third of the area. Those were the diesel engines that powered the ship. Lining the walls and filling all the remaining floor space were control boards, tanks, pumps of all kinds, huge valves, and pipes. Around the engines, and off the floor about four feet, were steel walkways leading to all major control equipment. The engines rested on massive steel bed frames. A couple of manholes about dishpan size permitted inspection and cleaning of the underengine area.

The engine room was full of men, women, and equipment. Scaffolds almost covered the engines and most of the sidewalls. Hoses and electrical

Prior to World War II, the shipyard had been a man's world. Bringing in women as union workers was a huge change in the nation's cultural patterns. The employment of women in shipyards was accurately recorded, reaching levels of 10 to more than 20 percent in most yards, with the highest on the West Coast. By 1944, over 20,000 women were on the job in the three Portland-Vancouver Kaiser shipyards.

Martina Gangle

wires spider-webbed the entire room. Streams of cold, fresh air were forced into the room by a half dozen stovepipe-size conduits. Each welder had a similar conduit sucking out fumes and oxides created by the heat of his 6000° Fahrenheit electric arc. In spite of the fresh air brought in and the exhaust conduits, the room was filled with the choking blue smoke of the welders.

All of our crew gathered around a fresh-air blower while we waited for Brownie. When she came down the shaft, she selected a young woman and myself. "Please don't think I'm picking on you because you're new," she said. "I need someone small enough to get under the engines. It's plenty tough. Come out and rest whenever you feel like it. We've got to get it clean so the graveyard painters can chromate[2] it."

When I crawled through the "dishpan hole" in the side of the engine bed, I could see that Brownie had understated the job. The electric bulb on my extension cord revealed a small lake composed of a mixture of diesel oil, water, and lubricating oil. Sticking through this gooey mess were tiny islands of discarded material—pipe, steel, and thrown-away tools. The plank upon which I knelt was the only dry object in the place, but it didn't stay dry for long. I called for a bucket and began scooping the mixture into it with, of all things, a dustpan.

When each bucket was filled, I pushed it into the reach of a helper, who lifted it through the hole and started it on its way to the upper decks. It took me a couple of hours to remove the lake, and another hour to get the discarded material moved out. Then armfuls of rags were passed into me. I filled bucket after bucket with dirty rags as I mopped the floor, the walls, and the ceiling. Then Brownie crawled through the hole and joined me. "You go on out. I'll finish this one," she said, and, looked at me curiously. "You haven't been out since we started. One of the girls will go with you to the restroom."

I didn't realize how tired I was until I got to the upper decks. My body felt as if it had been hammered, and my overalls were an oil-soaked mess. My guide, a woman half my age, had news for me: "Gee, you was under for three hours! That kid under the other engine passed out. She didn't come to until the riggers an' the interns got her to the meat wagon. She'll probably be down at first aid the rest of the shift."

The whistle closing the first half of the shift blew as we left the engine room. Warmed, rested, and fed, I felt pretty good. Brownie didn't ask me to get under the other engine; but when I crawled in and started to fill buckets, she joined me. She stayed with me, too, until the last bucket was passed out. She had what the job took; that's why she was a leadlady.

When we left the ship at the close of the shift, the white-overalled painters were waiting at the gangplank. They were going to paint under the engines. Brownie and I—and the girl who fainted—knew what it took to clean those places.

Every member of our crew must have been as dog-tired as I was. Two of them had cleaned the floor of the engine room away from the engine area. Two others had relayed every bucket I filled to the foot of the shaft. Two husky young women at the top of the shaft had lifted, via the hook-tipped rope, every bucket of material taken from the engine room. Nor had the job of the "broad axles" been an easy one. Every full bucket, every piece of pipe, and every piece of discarded steel had been carried through that crowded, narrow passageway, relayed up the steep steel steps, and dumped into a steel skip[3] for final removal from the ship. That was one type of housekeeping I learned on the tank landers.

When the whistle blew to close the shift, I joined the mob that surged off the ship. In just a few minutes, the dock was full of hurrying people. All of them were headed for the check stations, where I had been told to leave my work badge. Chat and I had agreed upon a meeting place outside the gates, and he had warned me to hurry so we could get seats on the bus. I succeeded in getting close to my check station, but the crowd carried me past the box in the window where I was required to put my badge.

I edged around the little building and joined the crowd again. On my first try, I had been shoved, elbowed, and had my toes stepped on. On my second try, only the fact that I had a lunch bucket under one arm kept me from using both elbows. Even then, I barely got close enough to throw my badge into the box. It fell, along with a shower of other badges, as I hurried to meet Chat.

We *did* get seats on the bus, which proved to be an old rattle box that had been salvaged from a junkyard for emergency duty. The looseness of each window made the bus a good ventilator and restricted the effectiveness of the heater for the driver and those fortunate enough to get front seats. Our seats were well to the rear of the bus. In spite of warm clothes, we were blue with cold when that seventy-mile ride ended. We hurried to the storage garage, got our car out, and drove the three miles to our suburban home. The car was cold, and the house was cold. When I finally snapped out the light to

METAL LUNCH KIT

THERMOS LUNCH KIT. Strong Black metal box with rounded corners has sanitary lithographed inside finish. Large size 10¼ x 4⅝ x 7¼ in. Ventilating slots. One-pint Thermos Vacuum Bottle with double walled silvered glass filler keeps liquids hot 24 hours, cold 72 hours. Bottle clamps in lid.
60 C 9360—Kit complete with bottle. Postpaid................$1.69
(4) 60 C 9359—Lunch Box only. Described fully above.
    Shipping weight 2 lbs. 12 oz......................................59c
(5) 60 C 9355—Genuine Thermos Bottle. Also sold as part of
    kit above. 1-pint size. Postpaid...............................$1.09
(6) VACUUM BOTTLE REFILLS. Double walled silvered glass.
    60 C 9361—½-Pint Size. 6½ inches long, 2¼-in. diam-
    eter, 1½-in. neck diameter. With cork. Ship. wt. 1 lb....63c
    60 C 9362—1-Pint Size. 8 in. long, 2¾-in. diameter, 1⅝-in.
    neck diameter. With cork. Ship. wt. 1 lb. 4 oz................66c
    60 C 9363—1-Quart Size. 11½ in. long, 3¼-in. diameter, 1¾-
    in. neck diameter. With cork. Ship. wt. 2 lbs. 4 oz........$1.05
(7) VACUUM BOTTLE CORKS. Ship. wt. for two, 2 oz.
    60 C 9365—Fits ½-Pint and 1-Pint size.............2 for 9c
    60 C 9366—Fits 1-Quart Size Bottle...............2 for 9c

More than 60,000 lunches were packed each day for the three Kaiser shipyards. The employee bi-weekly newsletter, the *Bo's'n's Whistle,* provided helpful hints for healthy food.

end the day's activities, it was 4 a.m. My first swing shift had been anything but pleasant. I wondered how many of them I could stand.

When Jess told me of her experiences on her first shift, I promised
that I would get her an easier job. But she was deaf to my suggestion that
she quit until I could get one for her. Since both of us knew that we could
not continue the long bus ride, we talked of federal housing and decided
to investigate Vanport.

Vanport, in its baby days, was anything but attractive. Contractors'
sheds, which housed offices, tools, supplies, and equipment, were scattered
about the muddy streets that marked the entrance. The sidewalks were
piled high with the debris of construction. After a considerable amount of

Workers arrive at the
shipyard to begin their
shift in the complex
process of shipbuilding at
speed.

Louis S. Lee

Portland General Electric (PGE) supplied inexpensive electricity (2¢ per kilowatt-hour) to Vanport, the world's largest war housing city. In 1943, the power company commissioned four paintings depicting life in Vanport and had thousands printed as gifts for its 40,000 resident shipbuilders. Douglas Lynch was art director for the project. He remembers that the purpose was to bring together wartime workers and soldiers. Shown here is "Sandlot Baseball in the Sunshine."

Sergeant Robert Jakobsen

wading and inquiry, I located the rental office. There was a line of people waiting as usual.

The girl in charge of apartment rentals had obviously been exposed to an education which did not include training in courtesy. It is possible that her manners had withered under exposure to the public. The reactions of those in the line ahead of me were interesting: Some would get rednecked in the face of her sarcasm; others would assume an air of resignation. To most people, she was just one more thing that had to be endured if they wanted to get a roof over their heads. My contact with this clerk was brief.

She took my name and address, the fact that I was married, and my place of employment. "We had hoped to get a two-room apartment, possibly next week," I began.

She made her pencil click as she laid it down. That was for emphasis. "You won't get a two-room apartment next week—or any other week," she snapped. "We will notify you when we have space. A guide will take you to the apartment we select for you. If there are but two of you, it will be *one* room—and you can take it or leave it."

"I'm leaving it right now, sister," I told her quietly. "Just tear up that application, and don't try holding your breath until you see me again."

With Vanport eliminated, I made inquiries about housing conditions in the Vancouver area. There was considerable—but probably necessary—red tape. For example, an order for housing from my department head was needed before my requirements could be "screened" by the federal housing officials at McLoughlin Heights. Getting the order was easy; getting screened was not. That meant, for us, an extra-early rising—so early, in fact, that we got only three hours of sleep. A bus took us to Portland, another took us from Portland to Vancouver, and a third to McLoughlin Heights for screening.

We arrived at the rental office about ten minutes before noon. There was a long line, as usual. At noon, the office force went to lunch; those in line did not. When the office force returned an hour later, not a single person had left the line. Housing was important. It was almost four o'clock when Jess and I cleared the office. We caught the last "on-time" bus to the shipyard. We had gone without lunch, and there would not be time for coffee at the cafeteria, but we had the necessary papers for an apartment at Ogden Meadows.[4] All we had to do was go through the same screening rigmarole again, this time at Ogden Meadows.

It was several days before we could attempt another twenty-hour day. But when the third bus finally unloaded us at Vancouver's Ogden Meadows, we could sense that our long daily bus rides were over. The store's center and the administration offices were yet to be built. The total lack of sidewalks, the muddy streets, and the contractor's shed gave the place a Vanport-like look, but the man in charge of the rental office was a square shooter.

There was, of course, a line of people waiting to see him, but at least he had organized his job so that the line moved. When it came my turn to talk to him, I asked for a two-room apartment.

"All I have at present are singles," he told me. "Tenants come and go here pretty fast, though. I'd advise you to take a single until I can give you what you want. It might take a month."

That sounded as sensible to Jess as it did to me. So we moved over to the lease clerk and signed up for the single. With our rent paid for a week in advance, we went to look at our new home away from home. It was definitely not attractive, in any sense of the word. As we looked over the bare floor, the daveno bed, the dinky chest of drawers, and the meager cooking equipment, we knew that we were going to be "camping out" insofar as our usual home comforts were concerned.

The walls were made of some sort of thin paperboard. Normal conversational tones could be heard two apartments away in either direction. All bodily noises had to be subdued if one did not want them broadcasted.

We rode our shipyard bus home that night and said good-bye to friends made on the long ride. With our car piled full of bedding, cooking utensils, and spare garments, we moved into Ogden Meadows the following day. In our innocence, we believed that our problem of rest between shifts had been solved.

When we arrived at the apartment at the close of the shift, we found that a party was in progress in the next apartment. Our neighbors, we discovered, were two attractive young women. The party was in its building-up stage when we arrived and, at that time, still a modest effort of clinking glasses, a blaring radio, and an occasional squeal of protest. However, by 3 a.m. other couples had arrived and the party had begun to boom. A rousing fistfight broke up the orgy at about 4 o'clock. Then a drunken argument raged between a man and a woman. There was the crash of breaking glass and a man's bitter cursing. In the silence that followed a slammed door, we heard one of the attractive ladies say to the other: "Listen, you little snub-nosed chippy, I don't give a damn how many of your boyfriends you bop with a bottle; but I don't want you boppin' my boyfriends with no bottle. You lay off bopping my boyfriends. If you don't, I'll give that permanent red hair of yourn an honest-to-Gawd finger wave."

The argument droned on, but finally sleep came to us. Then, about 6:30 a.m., the baby in the other apartment next to us started to cry. There was no other sound save the child's crying. It was not until nearly 9 o'clock that there were any other sounds, and by then the child's crying had stopped.

We stayed in bed until noon in an attempt to get back some of our lost rest. Breakfast was not a cheerful affair. We realized that there would continue

to be parties thrown by the attractive ladies next door, who were shipyard swing shifters. There could be no question of their youth and vitality. A new set of boyfriends had arrived with the dawn, the radio was knobbed wide open, and all the anguish of the soap operas once again throbbed through the eight-apartment wing. Only in the apartment where the child had cried was there silence.

Lack of sleep had us pretty much exhausted when we finished the next shift. There was a party in progress when we arrived at our apartment, but to our relief it was only a preparatory one. The group was planning to "do" some nightclubs in Portland. So we went to sleep with the hope of getting some real rest.

But with all the promptness of an alarm clock, the baby started his wailing again at 6:30. The wail rose to a thin screaming and continued for two hours. Then, again, we heard voices and the crying stopped. We were all set to go back to sleep when there was a commotion in the opposite apartment. The nightclubbers had returned, and maudlin conversation thundered through the thin walls.

After we dressed and had breakfast that day, we went to the rental manager with the problem. He had his officer's report, which stated that the baby next

U.S. Maritime Commission and public buses carried nearly half of all workers to the three Portland-Vancouver shipyards. Shown here is "Waiting for the 4:40 Bus," painted for the PGE "Life in Vanport" series.

Sergeant John W. Hatch

49

Homes in McLoughlin Heights rented for $36 to $45 per month. Each housing development had its own water, electrical, and sewer systems, its own streets and sidewalks, fuel yards, police and fire departments, schools, stores, and recreation and health centers. The Boulevard Shopping Center in the heights was designed by Pietro Belluschi, who later became an internationally-acclaimed architect. The center received recognition from the Museum of Modern Art in New York as a model for future retail shopping.

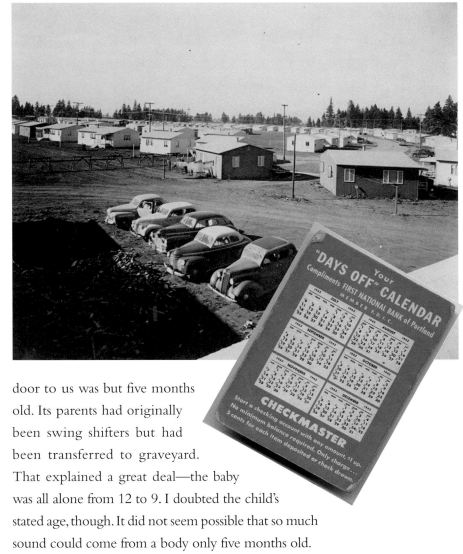

By staggering worker's days off, the "letter-day off" system helped relieve crowded conditions in establishments providing goods and services.

door to us was but five months old. Its parents had originally been swing shifters but had been transferred to graveyard. That explained a great deal—the baby was all alone from 12 to 9. I doubted the child's stated age, though. It did not seem possible that so much sound could come from a body only five months old.

"We've got to have rest when we finish the day's work," I told the manager.

He made a check of his rental files. "You are in luck," he told us after some minutes of searching. "There will be a two-room vacancy in a swing-shift area tomorrow." That sounded good to us.

We had most of our belongings loaded into our car when, for the first time, we saw the parents of the baby. They were not young. The man seemed to be well past middle age; the woman wore a scaler's hard hat and moved as if she were utterly weary. It was only by chance that I passed their window after they had entered their apartment. The woman was kneeling beside a tiny chest of drawers. The bottom drawer was open. Something moved in it. As she fumbled at a strap arrangement that partially covered the drawer, I saw that the baby was actually tied to its bed. No wonder the little fellow cried!

Our new apartment was a real improvement in living. It had a decent bedroom with a real bed. Its culinary and bath arrangements were the same as we were used to. The most appreciated difference was the fact that the two rooms ran to the full width of the wing, and there were windows on both ends to give us cross ventilation. We were to live there for six days a week for nearly three years. Neither of us would have believed that then.

Best of all was the fact that we had no noise problem. Neighbors on each side were swing shifters. We matched the courtesy of their silence with a silence of our own. It took a few nights of real rest to put us right on top of our jobs. Both of us had become toughened to the work. Both of us looked forward each week to our "letter-day off." On that day, we loaded our car with soiled laundry, extra bedding, and our street clothes. We did what shopping for food we needed, and, when the shift closed, we pulled out for our Salem home. Then, and only then, did we realize what a different world we lived in at Ogden Meadows.

The "letter-day off" system, used by all the Kaiser shipyards, was perhaps the greatest morale builder ever devised. No explanation (satisfactory to the workers) was ever given for its discontinuance, which happened late in the carrier contract.

Under the letter-day system, each worker was assigned a letter day. The letter was permanent; the day changed each week. If a worker had "A" day off and "A" came on Monday, that worker's off day would be Monday for that week. It would be Tuesday for the following week, and Wednesday for the week after that. When the "A" day reached Saturday that worker took Saturday and Sunday off. In the rush of the war effort, which ignored Sundays and all legal holidays, those double days off were counted as carefully as beads on a rosary.

The morale-building effect of the letter day was hidden, but it was potent. When a foreman's letter day came around, one of his leadmen became foreman for that day. The leadman received foreman's pay for that day. One of the

Published as a bi-weekly, the *Bo's'n's Whistle* was launched July 18, 1941 as an eight-page one color magazine for workers at Oregon Ship. By March 1942, additional color and a larger format were added to serve the employees of Kaiser Company Inc., Vancouver and Swan Island and Oregon Shipbuilding Corporation. Circulation grew with the increase in workers. More than 2 million copies were printed in 1943.

Photo, Louis S. Lee
Illustration (opposite page),
Douglas Lynch

journeymen of that leadman's crew became leadman and got leadman's pay for the day. After the withholding tax came into existence, the effect on the worker's paycheck was insignificant. Most of the extra two dollars received went as prepayment on the worker's income tax for the following year. But being stepped up, even for a single day, gave those leadmen and journeymen a definite notion of the problems faced in supervision. Stepping into the other fellow's shoes often stretched the wearer's hatband permanently. The letter day must have been an invaluable guide to supervisors who dealt with promotions.

On February 1, 1943, the shipyard set a delivery schedule calling for a ship every three days. We had accomplished that goal once in January, and there had been several four-day ships. But at the start of February, under the handicap of bad weather and its follow-up of illness, a three-day schedule seemed impossible. However, every worker of each craft realized and accepted the challenge the schedule imposed. Groups of workers talked it over in the crowded engine rooms; men huddled over blueprints in the ship supervisor shanties. In much the same spirit of a basketball team shaking hands before the ball is tossed, the yard prepared to meet the new challenge. As it turned out, with one exception—the second ship of the month—three-day ships were the rule. In February, eleven LSTs (landing ship tanks) were delivered, complete

SPECIAL EDITION ★ LAUNCHING OF THE S. S. GEORGE VANCOUVER, JULY 4, 1942

and ready for combat. Of the last five ships, four were two-day ships and the final delivery was a solo—a one-day ship.

On one of those last February ships, Jess and I had the luck to be assigned to the "hot ship"[5] on the night of her first relief lead. Part of my job was to replace a valve that had proved defective. With the valve removed and an expediter dispatched for a new one, I was free to examine the ship. Almost the first person I met was my wife. She had no broom, and she was peeking into rooms, as I had been doing. "Aren't the officers' quarters beautiful?" she asked breathlessly. "The beds are all made, and the soft light over the desks make it look homey. The blackout curtains on the windows and doors…"

"Do I see a lead book in your pocket?" I interrupted.

"You do," she admitted.

After she had been properly congratulated, we looked over "our" ship. The control cabin was empty and unlighted save for the glow of the red smoking lamp. Brass gleamed like gold in the semidarkness. The gleam of the megaphone for the voice-tube communication system matched the shine of the brass-hooded compass. Jess joined me at the forward portholes, and we looked at the serried banks of lights that rose tier upon tier to make daylight for a mile up the Columbia and for a half mile back of it. That was the yard that had

Miles of anchor chain were necessary supplies for the emergency shipbuilding program.

C. Herald Campbell

produced "our" ship. But every person who worked there—and thousands who did not—had both personal interest and pride in it.

In thinking of the men who would sail and fight in "our" ship, the idea came to us that they would always have reminders of their homes, no matter how far away they might travel. Those truly American names of things were part and parcel of the whole construction enterprise. Down in the galleys, there were names like Hot Point, Frigidaire, and General Electric. In the engine room, the roll would be long—Worthington, Chicago Pump, General Motors, Buda, American Steel, Republic Steel, and General Electric again.[6]

Throughout the ship, those familiar names from American life would reappear. The plumbing fixtures might bear the names of Crane, Kohler, or Standard. The hooded and constantly guarded guns often bore names of cities: Detroit, St. Paul, and Pontiac. The room that held the Sperry gyrocompass[7] was always locked or under guard (so were the rooms that housed the intricate radio and radar installations).

On some part of each piece of furniture would be found the tiny trademark of the Buckler Company. That one firm did nearly 10 percent of all the joiner work performed on ships built during the war effort. In Vancouver, the black and white hatters of the Buckler Company worked with us. We exchanged pleasantries—or invectives—with them as the occasion required. But those other thousands whom we knew only by the trademarks on their finished products—and the thousands who hauled that equipment across a continent—they were shipbuilders, too. This was "their" ship just as it was "our" ship.

Jess and I examined the LST with the thoroughness of a couple of school kids. The guns in the big steel gun tub in the bow were covered, and the ammunition racks that lined the sides of the tub had an ominous look. Looking over the side, at the bow, we could see the white Navy numerals that identified the ship. Jess was curious about the big pipes that rose out of the weather deck.

Workers use Beatty Machines to cut steel ship plate.

Arthur or Albert Runquist

"Those pipes puzzled me for a long time," I admitted. "When this ship heads for a beach, it will be loaded with tanks, trucks, and guns. Some of that equipment will be on the weather deck and will be lowered by the elevators. The tank deck at water level—the one we call the 'big street'—will be full of motorized equipment, too. All of the motor equipment below decks will have to be warmed up and running before the ramp goes down. Those big pipes are part of the ventilation system that keeps the 'big street' full of clean air."

Men were working on the big winch at the stern of the ship. This winch, with its inches-thick cable and heavy anchor, was another of the features of an LST that no one talked about. When the ship approached a hostile beach, the heavy anchor was dropped and the cable played out until the ship beached. After the beach was secured, it was possible for the grounded ship to free itself from the sands by exerting the power of the winch, rewinding the cable attached to the heavy anchor.

The outfitting dock personnel had a lot of fun watching some of the starts the ships made. One LST swung away from the dock and headed directly across the stream. It looked as if her commander intended to make a practice run on Jantzen Beach,[8] across the Columbia River. Just short of that objective, the ship's engines were put in reverse and a figure-eight movement placed the ship in a splendid position to go through the Interstate Bridge sidewise (the hard way). After the nose of the ship had sniffed a gravel loading

LST is shown in action in the South Pacific. Vancouver ships appeared on sea lanes throughout the world and were involved in major battles. Five escort carriers were sunk in the Pacific and at least eleven others were damaged. Other known losses are two tank landing ships and one Liberty ship.

plant, the ship backed out into the stream, gained headway, and passed through the open draw. Its whistle for the railroad bridge, two miles downstream, had a distinct sound of relief. Crews and commanders, like our workers, learned fast when they had a real job to do.

Months later, Jess and I sat in a newsreel theater in Portland. All our LSTs were things of memory. The newsreel sound explained that General Douglas MacArthur had begun moving up through the Pacific islands to keep his promised rendezvous in Manila with Japanese General Tomoyuki Yamashita,[9] the "Tiger of Malaya." Like all Americans, we saw or read of that journey. There were many battle stories, but the war was far away. Suddenly the screen pictured an ocean-girt beach. Palm trees were shedding branches as if they were being pruned by an invisible sickle. LSTs were rammed up on the beach, and the blink of cannon fire showed to seaward. The angle of the camera changed as another LST came charging in. The nose opened, and the ramp came down almost to the sand. Out of the LST's interior and down the ramp came a tank. It hit the water with a splash and churned away. A stubby little truck followed the tank; then came an ambulance and more tanks.

The gun in the big-gun tub on the bow of the LST was in action. We could see only the bottom rim of the gun tub, but from it a stream of something resembling tennis balls soared skyward. Splashes in the sea close to the ship indicated that it was under artillery fire, and a suddenly made row of splashes—the height of a picket fence—proved that an air attack was in progress. For a fleeting second, as the camera angle shifted to pick up a shot of an ambulance backing toward the ramp of another ship, we got a glimpse of the Navy number on the bow of the ship under attack. We gasped—and then hugged each other in the darkness. It was "our" ship. Ours— and the ship of thousands of others. The war was suddenly intimate. "Our" ship was fighting in "our" war.

About the time we saw the newsreel, the national hubbub over absenteeism was at its peak. The subject rated headlines in the news, and there had been several more or less profound debates concerning the subject in Congress. At Vancouver, an open house on a near-complete ship, for an hour or two twice a month, would have solved much of the absenteeism. There were thousands of workers—lacking brass-hat connections—who never were aboard a completed ship! The will to work sets production records; the will to win brings victory. The American worker—like the American serviceman—can be inspired to lead anywhere, but both worker and serviceman are difficult to drive.

According to the "sharp-pencil boys," absenteeism at Vancouver varied between 6 and 7 percent. Some overpaid statistician conceived the idea of

The *Bo's'n's Whistle* reminded workers of the importance of good attendance.

Douglas Lynch

Kaiser management attempted to improve the absentee rate at the three yards by reminding workers that the hours lost in three months were enough to "build" thirteen ships. "Way thirteen" appears (background on left) in this drawing of the assembly area by an unknown artist. "Way thirteen" did not exist except as a huge sign, built to represent "the little ship that wasn't there," the SS *Absentee*, "constructed" by workers who were off the job in Vancouver.

a "way thirteen," on which the lost man-hours of the yard "built" a ship for the Axis.[10] Surely, at the cost of thousands of dollars, huge billboards were erected at each entrance gate. Every day the lost man-hours that "built" some part of the ship on "way thirteen" were listed.

It did not take long for the workers to realize the utter unfairness of way thirteen. Thousands of clerks were employed in administration, personnel, and the various brass-hat offices, and their presence or absence was never connected with building ships. One old electrician summed it up: "I've got a girl that works in there." He nodded toward the administration building. "All she has done for the last six months is to answer questionnaires from Washington, D.C. She's only one of dozens of girls doing the same thing." He hesitated. "She's been off for a couple of days with those sick headaches women have every three weeks. According to this damn sign, she helped lay the keel on 'way thirteen.'"

On the production end, there was every reason to believe the Vancouver shipyard was in the process of doing a good job. The plate shop, boiler erection, deck erection, assembly, and the ways were a roaring chaos of sound and activity. The outfitting dock had ships berthed three deep along a half mile stretch of the Columbia River. Ships were being delivered, complete for combat, every two days.

On March 1, there were still nine LSTs to be outfitted. Our hurry-up contract for thirty of them was almost completed. Then the yard faced a tremendously bigger job. Trainloads of equipment were being shunted into the yard each day. There was steel—mountains of it. The piled spools of electrical cable were as high as a cherry picker (mobile crane) could stack them. Our modest lumberyard multiplied until it resembled a huge canyon of timber. By these signs, we knew that we were to build more, and bigger, combat ships. The escort carriers—baby flattops[11]—were to be our next task.

All of this material had been accumulated in ninety days. Actually, the keel for the first carrier had been laid in December 1942, but it had to wait for steel to be delivered and fabricated. Keels were laid for sister ships almost as fast as the ways were emptied of LSTs. On February 11, 1943, the keel of the twelfth carrier, the *White Plains,* marked the completion of the changeover. The ways were full of carriers; the outfitting dock was still swamped with

Procurement of materials and guiding the flow of supplies were critical functions of the emergency shipbuilding program. The capacity of the nation's steel production industry was stretched to meet an accelerated need. After the procurement department placed orders, expediters followed up to insure that urgently needed items were actually delivered on schedule. Kaiser's expediters were notorious for getting what was needed.

Louis S. Lee

A stern frame is portrayed upside down, turning the industrial form into an abstract, sculptural shape.

C. Herald Campbell

LSTs. As the yard had been originally designed to build Liberty ships (ten had been built before we were employed), this difference in models was actually the second major changeover. It had been accomplished so smoothly that many of those employed did not comprehend what was happening.

To those of us in production, the flattop was almost a legendary ship. It represented something of the new generation's way of fighting a war, and it was a part of the new use of air power on the sea. We had but little conception of the size of the ship we were to build: three times the size of the tank landers (LSTs) was the usual guess on a tonnage basis. A rumor raced through the yard that the carriers would be more than 500 feet long, that there would be two elevators, each as big as a tennis court, and that the hangar deck, floor to ceiling, would be two stories high. Another rumor seeped out of the blueprints of the pipe department: there would be sixty miles of pipe in each ship. In the smoky rooms of the tank landers, and over our lunch buckets during lunch breaks, we argued the merits of the things we had heard.

All of us understood that these were to be baby flattops—escort carriers to accompany a convoy and keep the submarines down. From press releases we gathered the fact that the Navy was not sold on the idea of small carriers—that it had been necessary for Henry Kaiser to sell the idea to President Franklin Roosevelt. The fact that there was a conference between the president and Kaiser was proven by a picture of the two men which appeared in the newspapers. Kaiser was shown holding a model of the ship we were to build. But Navy opposition to the program was pretty well proven by the fact that every other ship was to be British-named and was slated to go to England under the Lend-Lease Act.[12]

Speculation raged on all these factors as we hurried the outfitting of the last LSTs. The actual size of the carriers also was a subject seldom omitted in group discussions. A blueprint class I attended gave everyone present a graphic illustration of carrier size and detail, and our teacher was fairly staggering under an armload of blueprints. To each of the thirty or more class

Blueprints were run off twenty-four hours a day, stopping only a half hour for lunch and between shifts to clean the machine. The prints came off in a continuous run and then were cut, trimmed and folded to specifications. Girls on motor scooters carried folders full of blueprints to where they were needed.

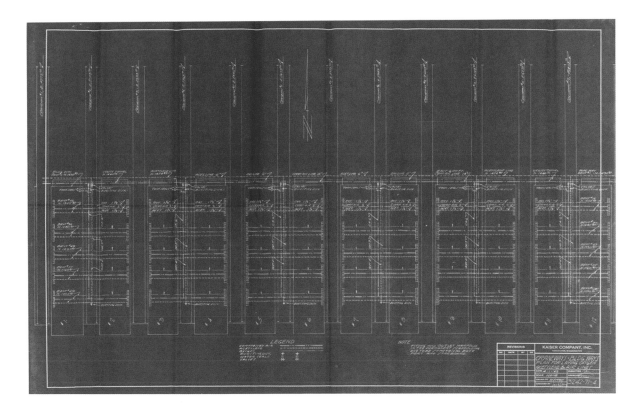

members, he gave a multifolded blueprint section. Unfolded and spread out on a table, each section covered a four-feet-by-six-feet area. As this was a pipe blueprint class, our lesson for the day was to list the various fittings and their sizes, as shown in the coded print. At the end of two hours—the time limit for our

This colorful view from the interior of the plate shop looks out toward the ways and the rising ship's hull cradled in its scaffolding. The Runquists used artistic license in their color choices. In reality, yard structures were gray or dirty white.

Arthur or Albert Runquist

test—many of us had not completed our listings. We were then told that all of these thirty-odd prints covered only one function of the carrier, the steam whistle.

Fast as the pace of the outfitting dock had been for the month of February, that pace was speeded up for March. The last nine LSTs of the contract were delivered in twenty days. The speed of those deliveries still seems impossible. If our pipe crew was assigned to install plumbing on berth four, we might take over a ship that was completely bare of anything resembling plumbing. Only the main water lines and the drainage lines would be complete. Due to space saving in the crowded quarters, most washbowls were located in the passageways. Through those passageways moved the workers. An electrician might be installing a light over the same bowl that the plumber was working on. Alongside them might be a sheet-metal crew putting finishing touches on a ventilation system. Through this crowd, every few minutes, would pass the "Buckler bull gang" carrying furniture.

Most of the plumber's work was done under the washbowl, and most of the time he was under the feet of all who worked nearby. It was no place for a man with a short temper. All of the plumbing fixtures would be installed in two days. The ship would then be moved to berth five for preliminary testing of all systems. After February 1, the pipe department's planning and manpower were so complete that a crew seldom worked on a ship for more than two shifts.

Our pipe crew had acquired several new men. A couple were youngsters slated to enlist in the Navy, Silent Robert and Big Paul. Silent Robert earned his nickname. He could do more work and say less than any man I ever knew. Big Paul owned a small piece of acreage a few miles from Vancouver. That made him an authority on all things local, including the weather. Being a large man—far more than two-hundred pounds—and possessing a genial disposition, a willingness to work, and an ability to fit pipe, his presence in our crew was a happy one. As a weather prophet, Big Paul had few equals. His daily prediction of rain was usually followed by rain.

But with these additions in February, we lost Harry. To the surprise of all of us, and certainly to Harry, the Brooklyn Navy Yard sent for him. Harry, who had arrived in Vancouver broke, was now in funds. The crap games during lunch hour were things of memory, but poker games for high stakes were the new rule at Hudson House. These, too, were suppressed later, but while Harry lived at Hudson House, they were regular and open. How much his total take from the yard and Hudson House amounted to remained his own business. There were many nights when he had a thousand dollars or more in his overalls. We guarded him then—never left him alone. Everybody liked this hardworking lad who could sing like Eddie Cantor, tap dance à la Bill Robinson, and who would cheerfully bet you one dollar—or a hundred—that the next worker to join us would have an odd or even number on his badge.

When Harry reported in for his last shift, he told us that he had lost a hundred dollars that day in a Hudson House poker game. He seemed so cheerful about it that we all suspected that he had lost the money deliberately. That was his way of saying good-bye to his friends. He worked with us as usual until lunchtime. Then, after lunch, neither Red nor Al could find him. Jimmy and I searched a couple of ships without success. We went back to work realizing that he had been telling us good-bye when we left the pipe shop after lunch. As we started back to the ship, Harry linked his arms in ours. "T'ree links—wit' de weak link in the middle," he said with a break in his voice. He had to "see a guy" and did not go aboard with us. His big, dark eyes looked us over as if they were photographing every detail so as not to forget. He gave us each a pat on the stern and disappeared into the crowd. We never saw him again.

The tank landers finished up fast in March. Eight ships were delivered between the second and the twenty-third. I went down with two coworkers, Al and Jimmy, to have a final look at the last LST. Since the ship had been commissioned, we knew better than to try to go aboard. The big sailor with the six-shooter strapped to him wasn't too friendly, either. After all, we were civilians. He was guarding the only gangplank leading aboard, and he seemed to resent our looking at the ship we had helped build. Still, we looked the ship over and ignored the dirty looks of the gangplank guard.

There were a lot of details in the LST's construction that were hush-hush. We didn't talk about them then or later. Those taboos were serious things then, especially since most of the workers had some link with the armed forces. A gray-haired shipfitter keynoted the feeling of the yard when he told a group of us: "I've got three boys in uniform. One of them is with MacArthur in that Red Arrow[13] outfit. One of the twins is with Patton's Third Army, and the other is with Nimitz. The less we say outside this yard, the more chance I've got of seeing them again."

Jimmy and I looked over our last LST—or "barge," as we sometimes called them—a little regretfully. She was painted a blue-gray, which would soon give way to camouflage. Big flat-bottomed landing craft hung in her davits. Canvas covered the big winch on the stern, and all the antiaircraft guns were hooded. Up on the yardarm on the single mast, Old Glory snapped in response to an upriver wind.

The previous year, Al had worked in a brickyard in Iowa, Jimmy was a Forest Service packer, and I had been teaching high-school students how to drive automobiles. Now we were part of a pipe team; now we were part of a host who had been trained on the first forty ships. And now we were ready for the bigger job that lay ahead.

4

"Eighteen or more by '44!"

My first glimpse of an escort carrier came late in February 1943. A shortage of fittings on the outfitting dock made it necessary for me to go to the shipways to get another supply. It wasn't possible to get anywhere near the ways without seeing the huge hulls. The ways emphasized the size of the ship they held. While each shipway held a hull that had been started there, on way seven the hull had actually taken form. I stared long and incredulously at what I saw.

Aft, the vessel was complete. Forward, the bow section was in place. Amidships, the steel of her sides swept upward with just enough gaps to reveal the tiers of decks inside the craft. My eyes sought out the place for the hangar deck. What I had heard was true: the hangar deck was two stories high. Atop this eggshell of steel were heavy plates running across the width of the ship—supports for the flight deck. Joined to the frames of the ship's sides (amidships),[1] they had the look of steel hands flung skyward by steel arms. Were they praying for steel to clothe them?

On way eight a sister ship was almost as complete as the one on way seven. I paced the length of the ship. It was more than 500 feet, I guessed. At the stern of the ship, another rumor was confirmed. There were twin propellers, and there were to be twin engine rooms. Going back for my fittings, I marveled at the sleekness of the welded sides.

Special printed programs were produced for ship launch ceremonies by the Kaiser Company.

Only the hull numbers—301 and 302—marked the ships. Mrs. Franklin D. Roosevelt would christen 301, the *Alazon Bay*. The workers, individually and collectively, held the opinion that the name was "lousy" for a fighting ship. Satisfaction was the rule when that name was changed to the *Casablanca*. Number 302 went into the Columbia River as HMS *Ameer* and was to go to England under the Lend-Lease Act.

I went back to the outfitting dock with my fittings, thrilled by what I had seen. The ships were huge, and the shipyard planned to deliver fifty of them within the year. That was so impossible it was a joke. No single shipyard could hope to complete such a schedule. To deliver half that number would equal a fantastic dream. Fifty flattops in a year—impossible!

Riggers stand ready to guide a bulkhead into place as it is lowered by a whirly crane.

C. Herald Campbell

There were many changes, especially in personnel, as the yard switched from the LSTs to the flattops. It was necessary that everyone possible in the outfitting organization be kept employed. At the same time, management wisely chose to carry out its first drastic weeding of the inept, the lazy, and the chronic absentee. No craft and no section of the yard was immune. Long lines of men and women formed in front of the "quit-slip" windows. Some of these people would be rehired later; some were hired by subcontractors; but for most of them, this was the end of their war service. The yard was clearing out for action such as few of us had ever known.

The movement of personnel from the outfitting dock to the ways affected all crews and crafts except the carpenters. Erection of new buildings began immediately. The dock was to have its own paint station, electrical shop, and headquarters. Restrooms for both sexes were spaced at regular intervals along the dock. Paint, electrical, sheet metal, marine machinist, trial crew, pipe maintenance, Navy ordnance, subcontractor space, and a Gold Room were part of the huge building known as west outfitting. The Gold Room, incidentally, got its name from the ap-

pearance of a shelf on one of the ships. Brass valves and brass plumbing fixtures glittered like gold, and the priority we gave them put them beyond
price.

All of the sweeper crews moved to the ways as the last of the LSTs
moved out. I didn't think Jess would like such work. The ships were noisy

beyond belief. There were
welders and burners everywhere, and no warmth. I
know now that I underesti-
mated her ability to adjust to
conditions. Jess described her
experience on the ways as
follows:

For several weeks
prior to our transfer to the
ways, crews were beset with
rumors of the purge that was
to come with the transfer.
But the actual layoff was less
than one for every hundred
employees, and those who
did draw quit slips were so

hopelessly inefficient that their leaving was never a cause for sorrow. Another,
and more scary, rumor stressed the dangers of working on the ways. Sweepers
would be required to climb the scaffolds and pick up steel scraps; there would
be no stairways, and it would be necessary to walk planks over high places.
Most of these rumors, I suspect, were put in circulation by crew members
who had worked on the ways.

It was easy to take these rumors with the traditional grain of salt.
Most of our work was done according to the "daisy-chain"[2] method of relaying steel. Every bit of discarded metal and unused wood had to be taken off
the ship. The job was to get what could be lifted and put it into steel skips.
Once filled, the skips were picked up by the whirly cranes and deposited on
the crane way. Trucks hauled the skips to salvage areas, where the iron was

This photo of crane hoist
drums shows Campbell's
interest in close-up views
of mechanical shapes.

C. Herald Campbell

67

Runquist's view of man and machine is reflected in this painting of a huge inner bottom section lifted by a crane weighing thirty-two tons.

Arthur Runquist

sorted for reuse. There were tons of small steel in the ships' double bottoms and in the tanks and cofferdams above the double bottoms.

It didn't take long to separate rumored fact from rumored fallacy. There was actually no more danger on the ways than on the dock. The lack of stairways, the necessity of walking planks and of working on the scaffolds, was fact. But the ladders that led from deck to deck were well built and were usually welded solidly in place. It was seldom that a two-by-twelve was the sole means of crossing an open well. Even then, the hazard was slight if one had decent balance. Many times, on our trips into our Oregon Cascades, Chat and I have walked logs over rushing streams where a misstep would mean an icy bath or worse. Walking a two-by-twelve or working on the ship scaffolds where two and three planks made solid footing was easy.

Nor did working high bother me as I believed it would. On one shift, after lunch hour, we were asked to report to way eight. It wasn't a pleasant night. A March wind whistled through scaffolds and rain fell with a steadiness peculiar to the Pacific Northwest. Our leadlady came to us with the gloomy news that we were to pick up loose steel on the scaffolds. The ship on way eight, soon to be named *Liscome Bay*, was nearly complete. High up on the bow, where the tow lines pass through the hawsehole, a welder worked. In spite of the rain, the wind made fireworks of the sparks thrown by his welding arc.

In fairness to the rest of the crew, all of them started the job. Everyone cleaned the lower levels, but halfway up only three of us remained on the job. There was not so much steel on the higher levels, and the job looked easy. Then one of my companions looked down and got sick. She had sense enough to get down on her hands and knees to vomit. The other girl helped her to the circular stairways and down to the crane way. Neither of them came back. I continued upward until I came to the welder. He seemed surprised to see me, more so when he saw the gray hair under my hat. He had a couple of boxes, and I accepted one as a seat while he dwelt, at some length, on how glad he would be to get back to Missouri.

The flare of the welding bow kept the wind and rain from us. It wasn't a bad place to work, even if the people below seemed like midgets whose tin hats shone like pearl buttons.

The longer I worked on the ways, the better I liked the job. By watching the shipfitters and asking questions, I soon learned what steel should be taken out and what should be left behind. My labor foreman found me sorting a pile of iron and nodded to a portion that I had set aside.

"Are you going to leave that?" he asked.

"The shipfitters will use most of it," I told him. He nodded approvingly. "You are saving your crew and the shipfitters a lot of work," he said. He then looked me over carefully and asked, "How did you learn what to leave?"

Gambling was a common activity at the shipyards, and big craps games occurred at the top of the cranes.

C. Herald Campbell

I said I thought it was silly for us to carry things out and then watch men carry them back. "When I asked questions, the men were glad to show me what material should be left," I told him.

He grinned at me. "I hope you stay on the ways," he said, as he started up the ladder.

Plate shop workers apply themselves to the task at hand, while a distant whirly looms in a surreal landscape.

Arthur Runquist

But the work on the ways had its drawbacks, too: the total lack of warmth, the never-ending thunder of the chipping guns, and the seeming chaos of material and activity. My biggest handicap was my lack of weight and strength to handle the heavier pieces of steel. That handicap swung my decision to go back to the dock as a sweeper, even though I knew swift promotion would be my reward for staying on the ways.

It was unfortunate for those who wanted me to stay on the ways that it rained hard the day I really had to decide. I got soaked walking "the long mile" from the west gate to way twelve. In the half hour that elapsed before the whistle blew to start the shift, I was able to get warm in a restroom but not dry off. Wet and cold, I finished the shift. Then I got resoaked during the long walk to the west gate. When I reached our Ogden Meadows bus, I must have looked as if I had just been fished out of the Columbia River. The bus was crowded, as usual, but no one wanted to stand close to me. (Why those buses were not permitted to pick up passengers inside the Kaiser gates, especially in stormy weather, remained a mystery to me.)

Teeth chattering, blue with cold, I got off the bus and found a warm haven in our Ogden Meadows apartment. For once, the apartment was really warm. Over steaming cups of coffee, Chat and I talked over our problem. We agreed that when the crews went back to the dock, we would go back to the dock together. His crew had no work to do; mine still had mountains of steel to move.

Those weeks on the ways taught me much. I wish I could put into words some of the thrill I felt when I saw two whirly cranes pick up one of

Giant whirly cranes dominate this shipyard night scene in winter. Workers in the foreground appear to be reviewing blueprints, while others carry materials in the assembly area.

Arthur Runquist

the big steam engines that would power one of our carriers. It was raised in one straight lift higher than the scaffolds on the ship. Then, with the same apparent effort that I would use to carry a jar of fruit, the whirlies moved with their load to the center of the ship. The huge engine was lowered into its place smoothly, gently, exactly. Americans—my kind of Americans—designed the ship, its engines, and the cranes. My kind of Americans operated the cranes, built the ships, and fought in them.

Workers gather around to read a set of blueprints before "hopping to the job."

Arthur Runquist

Chat continues: Our first intimate glimpse of the supply depot took much of the sweat off the job of marking time between the end of our LST activity and the start of work on the carriers. No one could look at those huge areas piled to the ceiling with electric motors, galley equipment, and plumbing fixtures, or those long rows of hundreds of antiaircraft guns, without getting a boost. Whatever was going to be done at Vancouver had a lot of America backing it up. We knew that.

Only a few days remained in March 1943 when the electricians and sheet-metal workers would get their first blueprints for the carriers. We watched, rather enviously, as their layout crews moved in and began burning holes in the bulkheads where the raceways and air ducts were to go. Before each burning, however, there were measurements and usually arguments. There was a sort of ritualism to the occasion. The crew foreman would appear, laden with a blueprint. With him would come the crew leadman carrying only a ruler and a steel tape. In close formation behind them would be a half dozen journeymen and a bored, indifferent burner. All the burner desired was a place to park his tail feathers until the location of the hole was decided upon.

The foreman would expose his blueprint, and all present, except the burner, would crowd around for a look at it. To most of those then present, the white lines on the blue paper might as well have been coding on an Egyptian tomb. The print was closely inspected for symbols showing port, starboard, and viewpoint. Arguments, with great gestures, would rage, and the print would move from one person to another until the arguments were solved. All hands present participated in and enjoyed the discussions, except the burner.

Steel plates are cut to the correct size and shape in the plate shop.

Arthur or Albert Runquist

Once the print had been oriented to the area, the search would start for centerline markings. These markings were placed by ship engineers on floors, bulkheads (walls), and ceilings. When newly placed on smooth steel, they were comparatively easy to find, but the markings got dimmer with each coat of paint applied. All shipbuilding, the location of bulkheads, doors, furniture and fixtures, were keyed to these centerline markings. While the ship rested on the ways, it was possible to use a level by placing it on a slope board, which would compensate for the angle of the way.

Once the all-important centerline markings had been found, the real job of measuring for the electrical raceway, air duct, or pipe location would begin. It was seldom possible to stretch a tape from centerline to the location desired. Bulkheads of varying widths might be located between the centerline

73

A crowd estimated at 75,000 turned out on April 5, 1943 to see Eleanor Roosevelt christen the first baby flattop, USS *Alazon Bay*.

Theodore Mentzer

and the skin of the ship. All present, except the burner, took part in this activity, too. All the burner wanted was a marked section of steel designated to be cut out. Once given the nod on the location, he would light his torch, snap on his dark glasses, and then, amid a shower of sparks that would shame a two-bit pinwheel, that section of the steel bulkhead would be cut out as easily as if it were so much butter.

We of the pipe crews learned a lot of what to do and what not to do by watching other crafts in those days before the launching. After a considerable delay, the crew on which I worked got our first blueprints—and our first order to draw tools. That was the best news we had received for a long time. We stormed the tool rooms in a group and drew tools by the armfuls. All of those tools had to be carried from the crane-way level to the level of the flight deck. Steep, spiral stairways were the only means of getting aboard. Once on the flight deck, the tools had to be toted down four levels to a combination toilet, shower, and washroom for the crew, in the forward end of the ship. This area was far forward. Between it and the bow of the ship was the anchor-chain locker. This level was to be our home for a long time.

We were to install welded pipe as well as the hot and cold supply mains. Leaving the welder to guard our pile of tools, the crew took off like a band of quail. Jimmy went for lights, Big Paul sought a burner, and my job was to get ventilation for our room. Silent Bob had the toughest detail. Some-

PANORAMIC VIEW WAY AREA
Launching
U.S.S. "ALAZON BAY"
Mrs. Franklin Delano Roosevelt
SPONSOR
KAISER COMPANY INC VANCOUVER
APRIL 5, 1943

where on the ship the riggers had parked a skip load of pipe for us. Finding that pipe in the half-dark ship did not promise to be easy.

When I got back to our work area, Jimmy and a maintenance electrician were stringing lights to the ceiling. The electrician was a brunette—very businesslike—who seemed to appreciate Jimmy's help much more than his interest in her off-duty life.

At last we "hopped to the job." By lunchtime, lines of pipe were in place in the berthing area. They extended around the jog in the bulkhead and into the toilet area. There was no letup in our pace after lunch. Each section of pipe was checked for elevation and for that all-important distance from centerline. At about 11 o'clock Red came back and motioned for us to gather around him. He had another blueprint, which he spread alongside the one we had been using. Everybody gathered around, except the burner. He remained seated.

Red was quite cheerful over the bad news he had for us. "Our pipe engineers have discovered that some revisions of our original print will be necessary," he told us. He pointed to the jog in the bulkhead: "That is an ammunition hoist. It has a door that opens into the berthing—don't ask me why. The sailors may use a clip of shells to comb their hair with for all I know. Our job is to build this ship the way the Navy thinks it wants it." His pencil moved over the new print. "We'll have to change here and here and here," he

75 ☆

said. "Don't install those last six pieces of prefab until we find out how big those tanks will be. Now let's hop right on that hoist-change job. Get it done before the whistle blows." Revisions became so frequent that a saying grew among us: "Odd days we install; even days we revise."

When we came on shift on April 3, we were amazed at the changes in appearance of 301 (the *Alazon Bay*, soon to be the *Casablanca*). The two shifts preceeding ours had painted the hull a dark gray-blue, and the shipwrights had erected a huge stand at the bow. Number 301 was to be launched the following day, and each of us received card passes for our families to attend the launching.

There was a lot of information on the card. Governors Arthur Langlie of Washington and Earl Snell of Oregon would speak. Mrs. Roosevelt would sponsor the event and spill wine. Edgar Kaiser, vice president and general manager of the Vancouver shipyard, was scheduled to be master of ceremonies. And best of all, his father, Henry Kaiser was scheduled to be there.

The yard buzzed with news of other happenings. Overnight the despised "way thirteen"—intended supposedly, to show the ill effects of absenteeism—disappeared. No official explanation was ever offered, but the half-built ship on "way thirteen" was "sunk" without a trace.

Activity on swing shift prior to the launching was intense. All usable pipe had to be piled and secured against shifting. Cleanup gangs of men and women removed hoses, planks, and scaffolding. When the shift closed, the ship was stripped and ready for launching. But long before the hour set for the launching, crowds began to gather at the gates. A spring day—warm and beautiful, in the manner of the Pacific Northwest—favored the occasion. The waiting throng was happy and good-natured. From the shipyard in front of them came the roar of day-shift activity. From overhead, we heard the drone of a Mitchell bomber on patrol. Behind the crowd, as the workers waited, a long freight train loaded with tanks, trucks, jeeps, and boxed equipment thundered by on Spokane, Portland & Seattle railway tracks on its way to embarkation depots.

Perhaps the crowd sensed the symbolism of the grim freight on the train, the plane overhead, and their own gray-blue ship. After all, this was America arming! Those who waited were but a tiny handful compared to the hosts who labored *in* the arsenal.

A crowd estimated at 75,000 streamed through the gates to witness the launching. Two great gray-blue ships soon became the center of attention. One of them was decked with bunting, and a band blared martial music under the ship's bow. This was 301, the first to be launched. The other ship (*Liscombe Bay*) served as a grandstand for workers who ate their lunch as they watched. Their ship was to write a bloody page in history. It had a rendezvous with a Japanese torpedo in the Gilbert Islands area of the Pacific Ocean; the ship was to be the tomb of more than 800 American seamen.

Launching ceremonies are simple rites. There was prayer. Edgar Kaiser introduced Governor Langlie, who made a short speech. Governor Earl Snell of Oregon was presented. The throng listened quietly to his message and the words of praise he had for the yard's accomplishments.

Then Edgar Kaiser presented his father, with a pride that was palpable. The public-address system could not hide the emotion that was in the younger man. Henry Kaiser stepped to the microphone. His first words were drowned in a murmur that swept out of the massed thousands and beat upon the launching stand like a breaker sweeping in from the Pacific. The murmur grew to a roar—a roar of disappointment. The crowd could not see Henry Kaiser. Only those on the packed platform could do so.

No finer tribute could have been paid—or paid more spontaneously—than Henry Kaiser's men and women paid him that day. They wanted to see the man who understood them because he had been one of them. Respect and admiration for those who create and achieve are deep-rooted in American thinking, especially so when the achievement blossoms out of a man's own efforts and his own brains.

The throng of employees did not stop its roaring until hasty rearrangements of the group on the platform permitted a view of Henry Kaiser. There were two highlights in Mr. Kaiser's speech. First, we of Vancouver were to build fifty escort carriers in one year. No one who heard and saw Henry Kaiser could doubt the assurance of the man who emphasized that statement. It was not possible to doubt him. And yet our crew had changed one system of pipe four times in six days. We had seen wire ways and ventilation lines changed with that same discouraging frequency. There was no way then of envisioning the smooth coordination that all crafts would adopt. The man talking to us knew how the coordination would come, and that it would be developed by us.

The second high point of Mr. Kaiser's speech brought a gasp from the assembled multitude. The Kaiser company of Vancouver had not yet put its full team on the field! Additional thousands were coming to work with us! A big part of our job would be to train those thousands who had never seen a ship. The crowd was too surprised to cheer when the venerable Mr. Kaiser stepped back from the microphone.

Mrs. Roosevelt told us of the president's appreciation for our work and emphasized the great need for ships. Then the public-address system blared the announcement that number 301 was held only by its tie plates. Mrs. Roosevelt took her place upon the sponsor's stand at the bow, the beribboned bottle of champagne in her hand. Now the burners were at work on the tie plate, one from each side of it. Each burned toward the middle. Long before those burning torches met, the weight of the ship would snap the steel plate. There was a slight quiver of movement in the mass of steel. Mrs. Roosevelt's voice rose clearly, "I christen thee *Alazon Bay!*" Champagne foamed over the bow—and over Mrs. Roosevelt's dress—as the hull slid gracefully down the greased way into the broad Columbia River.

Navy brass at first rejected Henry Kaiser's plan to build small escort carriers. After Kaiser wrote to President Roosevelt stating his case, top Navy officials reversed their initial decision. Kaiser Vancouver built fifty baby flattops, and they proved their worth in the Pacific theater.

Louis S. Lee

Once the ship was in the water, the crowd scrambled to see Mrs. Roosevelt and Henry Kaiser. Crowds lined the route the cars would take when the party left the launching stand. Once the cars had gone, the crowd surged toward the outfitting dock for a look at the ship. Kaiser guards and coastguardsmen turned them away by the hundreds, but thousands filtered past roped-off areas. Under the guidance of a couple of riverboats, the big hull was secured to the dock.

All the pennants, bunting, and flags had been removed when swing shift reported that night. Prior to the start of the shift, hundreds of those about to go on duty gathered near the ship. In the water it had a vastly different appearance from when it was cradled in the scaffolds of the shipways. Looking at it from the dock, the flare of the flight deck was more pronounced, and the trim lines of the bow seemed sharper. The big "blisters" that held the antiaircraft guns had not yet been installed, and much of the three-story-high control island was piled upon the dock. All of us who looked upon the scene realized still that it was going to take a long time and a lot of work to get that ship ready for action.

Shipwrights were busy building storehouses for outfitting materials and toolrooms on the spacious hangar deck. Riggers moved banks of welding machines aboard. A whirly crane was engaged in lifting lumber—a truckload at a time—from the dock to the flight deck.

The building of the flight decks was one of the outstanding jobs of the carrier program. The work was handled by the black-and-white-hatted men—and women—of the Buckler Company. The job involved not just the laying of timbers the length and width of the carrier deck. Each piece of that timber had to be fitted to the place where it belonged; each piece had to be drilled so that wooden pegs could be driven through the holes to fasten it to the adjoining timber. Once the pieces of timber were fastened, hot tar was poured in all cracks and crevices to seal the deck.

Eleanor Roosevelt took a two-handed swing with a beribboned champagne bottle to christen the *Alazon Bay,* later renamed the *Casablanca.*

Louis S. Lee

The job of fitting the timbers to the deck was made even more intricate by the number and character of other installations that were part of the ship. There were two elevators whose surfaces were so skillfully constructed and matched that it was difficult to determine where the elevator timbers ended and the deck timbers began.

The catapult was located forward on the port side. Deck timbers had to be fitted to this mechanism, which literally threw planes off the ship. The timber had to be fitted to the expansion joints designed to relieve strains on the steel when it was exposed to hot or cold temperatures.

Starting at the rear of the flight deck and extending at spaced intervals to the control island were a series of cables, mechanically operated, which could be raised to catch the hook of a landing plane. Fitting deck timbers to these cable troughs took time and skill. These intricately matched and fitted timbers, laid on the ground, would have made a solid highway eighty feet wide and eight miles long. That amount of lumber was expended on the flight decks of the fifty carriers.

The mechanism which raised and lowered the arresting cables was operated by compressed air. High pressures were necessary, but the actual operating pressure remained a secret in which the pipe crews had little interest. The pipe used was double extra heavy, and each fitting was massively oversized. When it was assembled, each piece of pipe interior was cleaned as thoroughly as the barrel of a fine firearm. Only about forty feet of pipe was required for each of the seven arresting gears, but each piece of pipe and each fitting were assembled with the utmost care. To pass Maritime Commission inspection, each assembly had to withstand a pressure of 15,000 pounds to the inch without leaking.

When the safety department heard of those high pressures, they insisted that the pipe be anchored to the flight deck in case of an explosion. Guards were placed throughout the area to keep stray workers away from the danger zone. About the only requirement the safety department overlooked was a sandbagged bunker for the test crews. Nonetheless, the tests went off without incident, and the crews continued to install and test high-pressure lines in the remaining carriers. And they did a good job. There were only five leaks in the entire contract of fifty carriers.

Just a few of the workers realized the magnitude of the task before us, or how complex the outfitting of one of these ships would be. Each ship was to be a fortified seagoing airfield, complete with gas stations, repair shops, and storage space for spare parts. The ship would be equipped with huge tanks for storing aviation gasoline, and with adequate space for bombs and ammunition. Far below the water line would be other tanks for fuel oil and freshwater.

Personnel required to operate the ship, fly its planes, and service and repair those planes totaled more than a thousand men. That number, in turn, required galley and baking equipment to serve 3,000 meals per day. Food storage for that potential force was thus designed for the ship. There were also to be toilet and bath facilities for the crew, a full-scale laundry, a barbershop, a tailor shop, and, of course, a jail. The latter was a two-cell, three-bunk arrangement not designed for comfort.

A dental office, complete with an X-ray machine and a darkroom, a hospital unit with a first-aid room, a dispensary, a surgery, a sterilization room, a sick bay, an isolation ward, and a galley—all these were part of each ship.

There was no hint of any of this equipment when we took over. The grim steel walls of the rooms were leopard-spotted from the heat of the torches. In some places, artistic (or obscene) pictures were drawn with chalk by the more or less talented. Some of the bulkheads carried involved mathematical calculations, and the floors and ceilings were not safe from the nut who wanted to practice his signature. Paint and equipment soon changed those rooms into comfortable, efficient units.

Painting crews painted water pipes on ships, white for ocean water and blue for fresh water.

There was a tremendous amount of conflict between the different craft installations in the outfitting of the first two escort carriers. So complex were the functions of this combat ship that space below decks had to be conserved in every possible way. Good planning and revisions by the thousands relieved most of the conflict as the program developed. Supervisory cooperation and good relations between various craft-installation teams reached an all-time high as the work went on.

Two minor installations made trouble for workers on the first study ships.[3] In the sterilization room a powerful electric light with a sixteen-inch shade was hung from the ceiling in the center of the room, and it was necessary for sheet-metal workers to change their air duct to avoid this light. On the blueprint our hot-and cold-water pipes were supposed to cross the room over the light shade and under the air duct. But once the air duct was moved, that was not practical. Therefore, a total revision of the pipe blueprint was necessary. All of the pipes which had been installed had to be torn out and refitted to match the revisions settled upon.

This welder is working on a pipe fitting.

C. Herald Campbell

The other minor installation change was not at all simple. The problem developed in the dentist's office, and had to do with the equipment stand adjoining the dentist's chair. The electric lines that served the motors in the equipment stand gave the least trouble in installation. It was easy to move these lines, but holes had to be bored in the beams and studs welded to the underside of the deck to hold the wires in place. Compressed air had to be piped from a supply main on the opposite side of the ship. That line passed through the beams of a half dozen rooms, crossed a couple of passageways, and went over or under wire ways and fire mains to its connection at the base of the equipment stand. Getting it there required many hands and many heads.

Difficulties multiplied when it was necessary to supply the stand with cold water and a drain. Although there was no cold-water main on the deck below the dentist's office, the dentist did have a wash-up lavatory stand as part of his office equipment. The cold-water pipe for the wash-up lavatory was extended through the floor of the office and then under the floor to the equipment stand. In all, ten feet of pipe traveled through the floor of the office, through two ceiling beams in the NCO (noncommissioned officers) room below, through the bulkhead of the NCO room out into the passageway, over a wire way, through the bulkhead of the adjoining room, and through two more ceiling beams to its connection with the base. Two pipe fitters, a burner, and a welder needed a half shift to install that ten feet of pipe.

The drain posed even greater problems. After many conferences and much blueprint searching, a deck drain line was chosen as the outlet for the equipment stand. Everybody in all the crafts breathed a sigh of relief when the base was "hooked up." But then some inquiring soul discovered that the base was in the way of the X-ray machine, which could not function unless the base was moved. Moving the base meant moving the chair as well, and the brass hats conferred plenty on that one.

When the conference ended, the decision had been made to move the stand and the chair. Therefore the pipes and wires were disconnected from the base of the stand. The stand and the chair were removed. Where the stand had been, there were now five holes through the deck—all inside a circle that was a foot in diameter—and a burner removed the section of deck that contained all five holes. A new section was carefully fitted, welded in place, and ground smooth. A chipper worked an entire shift removing the welded plate, which had fastened the chair to the floor. Now we were finally ready to start over.

The distance from centerline was checked and rechecked to ascertain the exact new location of the template for the base and chair. Five more holes were burned through the deck. The electricians changed their wire layout

The advertisement, published in the August 15, 1945 issue of *Modern Industry,* points out the safety importance of eye protection for war production workers. *Modern Industry* was published from 1941 to 1953. It was geared to "management men concerned with making and marketing better products at lower cost."

Ship's templates, measured from blueprints, were laid out in the mold loft. They served as patterns for shaping steel.

Arthur Runquist

beneath the deck to fit the new location. Air, water, and drain lines were also changed and fitted. The chair base was rewelded and the equipment stand connected. All hands in all crafts, including the various brass hats, felt pretty good when everything was in working order. The room was now ready for the Buckler boys who would install some furniture.

That furniture included a modern office desk and chair, which were installed in a corner next to the entrance door. There was also a cabinet for tools, such as forceps, pliers, gougers, etc., common to the dental trade. The only place the cabinet could go was alongside the dental chair. When in place, it was quite close. Too close, in fact. We proved it while we waited for the brass hats to inspect.

After the inspection, there was a bigger, better, and more profane conference. It was quite apparent that the "tool box" couldn't be moved forward. Equally apparent was the fact that if it were moved aft, the office door wouldn't be able to open. The lefthand side of the chair was cluttered with the equipment stand and the X-ray machine, and the righthand side was occupied by the tool box. We, of the pipe crews, listened—unhopefully—to a suggestion by one of the conferees that the bulkhead between the dental office and the sick bay be moved. But the sick-bay area was so precisely planned that the loss of a foot of its space would have caused congestion. There was a much more simple way to solve the problem: move the chair and the equipment stand aft.

Those were the conditions encountered in the outfitting of our first carrier. That final move of the cabinet, however, did establish the location of the dental equipment on the remaining forty-nine carriers. Much of this revising, to a greater or lesser degree, was happening all over the ship and to all crafts. We were establishing reality over theory.

The additional help that Henry Kaiser had promised on launching day was now arriving in force. They came in by the hundreds—long lines of men and women herded by Kaiser guards. There was little of military appearance in their ranks. There were no drums, no flags, no cheers—but they were part of America's industrial army, and they were prepared to do a job whose size could have been conceived only in America.

Those long lines of "new hires" certainly did put life in the shipyard. Most had been recruited from the Midwest and the Southeast of the United States. In sharp contrast to the later stages of the recruiting, there was only a sprinkling of blacks in this new wave. Only a few of these people had trade training considered valuable in the building of ships, but almost all of them had one definite American trait: they seldom had to be shown how to do anything twice.

Arthur Runquist's art grew in assurance during his years in the shipyard. He liked mechanical kinds of things, and his quick studies were able to define a particular movement or gesture in a graceful kind of calligraphic way. The worker is preparing plate for welding.

Arthur Runquist

Our pipe crews thrived on the influx of workers. Red's foremanship had been broadened by additional pipe crews, and the numbers of additional men in those crews were increased. Faced with the job of installing all the hot and cold water lines, plus the salt-water system and the plumbing on all decks in the forward half of each ship, Red really did need a lot of help.

Our own unit was shorthanded when we returned to the dock. The two youngsters we had acquired both enlisted in the Navy while we were stationed on the ways. From the flood of labor pouring into the yard, our crew was strengthened with Big George and Buttsy.

Big George, from West Virginia, was a hillbilly—and proud of it. Genial, likeable, tremendously strong, and with an all-consuming desire to work every minute, Big George was God's gift to the speedy production of aircraft carriers. Where he had learned to fit pipe remained a mystery. He could—and regularly did—cut pipe by the armload for showers. When Big George assembled that pipe, each piece fit, and there were no leaks when the showers were tested. Big George became one of us. Trustworthy, dependable, efficient—there were many times when his will to work shamed us into imitating him—Big George was an all-American.

"Just call me Buttsy," the other new worker had requested when Al introduced him to the crew. He had been ill before hiring, and his illness had sharpened his features and thinned his body to the point that it seemed a breath would blow him away. Set deep in his edged face were a pair of big, brown, spaniel-type eyes—eyes that could follow a pack of cigarettes until one was offered to him. He was hired as a journeyman pipe fitter, but he knew nothing whatsoever about ships and even less about fitting pipe. It didn't take us long to uncover those facts, but in less than a shift Buttsy proved to all of us that he was the world's champion helper. In spite of his failings—which included careless and inaccurate spitting of chewing tobacco—we took him to our collective bosoms.

It was amazing and inspiring to see that first ship change from the hull we had launched to a fighting unit of our Navy. We watched the control island go up, section by section, until it towered high over the flight deck. Topping that mass of steel was the "bedspring" of the radar equipment. Much like a huge double chin, the gun platforms for the antiaircraft weapons were fastened just below the flight deck. Overnight, it seemed, the guns were mounted. Electricians replaced the machinists, in order to install intricate fire-control and sighting apparatus. As soon as the electrical installations were complete, the testing of the equipment began.

Those tests were impressive. Each gun could be aimed and fired solo by its crew. Or an entire battery of guns could be aimed and fired by a man stationed at the gun director—the gun crew's job being merely to keep the guns loaded. There is small need for wonder as to why Japan's suicide pilots failed. The wonder should really be about how any of them ever succeeded in hitting our carriers.

Below decks the ship had taken on a new beauty. Paint, in soft matching colors, transformed the berthing and mess rooms. The huge galley on second deck amidships was agleam with stainless steel. Steam cooking kettles, each one large enough to hold three washtubs of potatoes, were banked in batteries in front of the ranges. Steam tables, 100-gallon coffee kettles, and utensil dispensaries—all in stainless steel—lined the passageways on each side of the galley. Across the starboard passage-way were a garbage-disposal room, a vegetable-preparation room, and a dishwashing room. The dishwashing machine in the washup room was as modern as the nation could produce. Unlimited quantities of live steam to the washer, and 180-degree water, assured the cleanliness of all dishes. When the Navy cleans something, it's clean.

Across the opposite passageway, to port, was the ship's bakery, with the finest equipment that could be produced. Giant electric ovens, lined with brick, did the actual baking.

Beneath this, the crew's galley was refrigerated, with separate refrigeration rooms for meat, eggs, and butter. The huge vegetable room was equipped with an air-control unit to maintain a constant temperature. We saw our first "mechanical cow" in the milk rooms of the carriers. This "critter" could be milked anytime by adding water to dehydrated milk, and by replacing a por-

In many Runquist paintings, man dominates with large forms on the field. His figural shapes are strong and solid, almost sculptural. Taken as a whole, they are simple, appealing, and memorable.

Arthur Runquist

tion of butter in the content. Tasting the product gave one the impression of milk, but it was a far cry from the real thing. Each carrier also had an ice-cream machine in its milk room.

There were many galleys in addition to the main crew galley. The officers had a galley, as did the noncommissioned officers. The captain had a tiny galley adjoining his stateroom. There was a galley in the hospital section, and the flight officers had a galley lounge where coffee and snacks could be obtained between flights.

Any commercial laundryman would have been happy to own the equipment installed on each carrier. I believe the equipment would have served a city of up to 10,000 people. There was a battery of steam pressers, there were mangles,[4] washers, and hot-air dryers, and there was all the special equipment needed for the care and cleaning of every sort of garment and fabric.

A tiny tailor shop and a full-size, two-chair barbershop that would have been the envy of any Main Street barbershop were located aft, also on the second deck. The floor was always painted a dark, bull-blood red, "so the bloodstains wouldn't show," and all the shop needed were a few pinups and a couple of dog-eared copies of the *Police Gazette* to make a sailor feel at home.

Far below decks were bomb rooms, each with an ammunition hoist operating in a sealed waterproof hatch. Even when they were empty, the grim bomb racks were a constant reminder that this was a combat ship.

Slightly aft of the forward bomb room were the big tanks designed to hold high-octane aviation gasoline. These tanks had been sprayed with a special preparation which gave them a silvery appearance, and every possible fire-prevention device was installed in the vicinity.

As the ships' outfitting developed, all the workers were impressed by the differentiation imposed by rank. We realized that its crew would not eat as a crew; nor would they sleep as a crew. Rather, the sharp breaks existing between the seamen, the noncommissioned officers, and the officers were readily apparent in the blueprints. The seamen might have been fighting for their country's idea of democracy, but there was little of it in evidence aboard the ship.

The day before the date of departure for the sea-run trials of the *Casablanca*, many supervisors were still uncertain about what crew would handle the ship. This should have been an easy matter to decide, as many of those employed had served in the Navy and in the Merchant Marines. But no attempt was made to ascertain what men had received such training. For the first trial run of this new type of ship, hit-or-miss methods were the rule in the selection of trial personnel.

Jess had a chance to go as a stewardess helper. The prospect of ten days or more at sea was an alluring one. But the sailing date of July 2 conflicted with many of our plans. The Fourth of July weekend happened to be our letter-days off. We had waited six weeks for those two days at home, and at our Salem home a bumper crop of cherries hung on our trees. We decided to save as much of that crop as possible. Jess waived her chance to go in favor of a comrade who had never seen the Pacific.

Time and destination were unknown to those selected. When the crews for the three shifts had been chosen, only six of the sixty had ever seen an ocean wave. But almost to a man, those men knew steam. Some of them had acquired knowledge of the old, reliable power by running threshing engines in the Midwest; some would have been at home on either side of a locomotive cab; and some of them could have taken a steam sawmill engine apart blindfolded. The crew evinced the liveliest curiosity about the performance of the engines and boilers, but there was little, if any, doubt about their ability to get top performance from those engines and boilers.

The folklore of that crew yielded the following illustration of how one of the men was selected and trained for this important trial run. This man (let's call him Steve) met his supervisor the day before the trial run, a warm July day. Now because a warm July day to men off duty means beer, Steve and his supervisor had a couple of beers. Over the first beer they talked of how HMS *Ameer* was coming along. Delivery date had been set for August 7, and bets were being made on the dock that the ship would not be ready on that date. When the second beer arrived, the supervisor casually informed Steve that he was to be the aft throttle man for swing shift on the *Casablanca* run.

With that, Steve admitted spilling some of his beer on the bar. No one knew better than he that the aft throttle man was the key to all cooperation between the two engine rooms.

"I've never had my hands on one of those throttles," he protested. "No one has ever shown me how to set them for lead, how to adjust cutoff, or how to get those engines in reverse!"

"You were chosen for throttle man because you are capable and dependable," the supervisor said confidently. "So far as the actual operation of the engines is concerned, look."

He arranged the empty beer bottles and the partially emptied glasses on the bar. "This stubby and this glass are your boilers and the aft engine, the other two are the boilers and engine on the port side forward. Being aft, your prop shaft will be shorter. The trick will be to synchronize the revolutions of the two shafts. When you get an order from the bridge, relay it to the forward throttle man, and then give him your revolutions per minute so he can match you."

"But what about throttle lead, cutoff, and reverse?" asked Steve. "How do I get going?" Steve was a practical person.

"You'll probably make some mistakes; but after you've run her for a week or so, it won't bother you," the supervisor said. "Throttle positions—let me see."

The supervisor pulled out a change purse and paid for the beers. He shook a half dozen tokens[5] out of the purse and arranged them in Steve's spilled beer. Using those tax tokens as throttle positions, and with his finger tracing movement on the wet bar, the supervisor explained the slight difference between the operation of a marine steam engine, a steam locomotive, and a steam threshing machine. From that vague, but aromatic, blueprint traced on a tavern bar, Steve gleaned enough information to take an $11 million carrier out on a sea trial run.

Our ship, the *Casablanca*, was taken for a sea trial run in early July. At Astoria, the *Casablanca* picked up a large contingent of Navy brass and Navy observers. Then, with a destroyer leading the way through the antisubmarine nets guarding the mouth of the Columbia River—and with Navy planes patrolling and a Navy blimp rechecking the plane patrol—the *Casablanca* steamed out over the bar and headed north en route to Bremerton on Puget Sound in Washington state. Just in case there might be Japanese subs in the area, the destroyer maintained a patrol to seaward throughout the run.

Distinguished visitors awaited the *Casablanca* at Bremerton: the secretary of the Navy, Henry Kaiser, and some real fighting admirals (one of whom had a carrier shot out from under his feet). Out into the Pacific from Bremerton the sea trials began. After the trials, the *Casablanca* returned to Astoria to become the training ship for the men who would man the fleet we were building.

When the run ended, the *Casablanca* had proved her right to a place in the greatest navy in the world. She had done something more than that. No Vancouver flattops were to go to Britain under lend-lease. The *Ameer* became the *Liscome Bay*; the *Atheling* became the *Corregidor;* and the third ship earmarked for the British became the *Guadalcanal.*

The Navy wanted a lot of baby flattops—quick. How quick? The original schedule—the impossible schedule—called for delivery of sixteen carriers in 1943. Our production chiefs at Vancouver held a conference on that urgent Navy request. Vancouver, they decided, could build eighteen carriers by January 1, 1944!

Eighteen or more by '44! That catchy slogan helped as the yard settled down to the job. But behind that task was an even greater one. If we took Henry Kaiser's word for it, we would have to build and outfit thirty-two other carriers in the first six months of 1944.

None of us doubted the need for these seemingly impossible schedules. Our daily papers told of German submarine wolf packs in the Atlantic Ocean. They told, too, of ship after ship being sunk within sight of our shores, and of lifeboats shelled and machine-gunned by the submarine crews. We

This drawing exhorts Vancouver shipyard workers to complete eighteen escort carriers by the end of 1943. Uncle Sam marches across a bridge of baby flattops towards a Nazi swastika and Japanese rising sun in the distance. Admiral Ernest J. King, Commander in Chief of the U.S. Fleet, requested sixteen. Edgar Kaiser urged his workers to beat that promise.

didn't know it then—perhaps even the Navy only guessed by then—but the real antidote for the vicious submarine assaults was escort carriers such as lined our dock at Vancouver.

The proof came as the little flattops began accompanying the convoys. No longer was a submarine able to surface, observe, and move in for the kill without fear of detection. Carrier planes, ranging far and wide in areas around the convoy, bombed and strafed submarines until they forced a complete change in former tactics. The dreaded wolf packs were blasted out of the Atlantic.

In the closing months of our war with Germany, one of our Vancouver-built escort carriers, the *Guadalcanal*, actually captured a German submarine and its entire crew undamaged. The story of that unusual feat, as published in one of our national magazines, made thrilling reading for Vancouver workers. The fact that we had built the *Guadalcanal* gave the reading an especially intimate touch.

There were convoys to be guarded in the Pacific, too. Vast amounts of munitions were moved to Hawaii and to Army and Navy bases in the South Pacific. The bloody page of history entitled Guadalcanal[6] had been written. There were bloodier pages to come as General Douglas MacArthur started back to Corregidor to keep a promise.[7]

Out in the Pacific, the Japanese had many island airfields. To strike them effectively required air power. In those vast reaches of water, such air power had to be carrier-based. The Navy speeded the building of carriers of all sizes to meet the needs of the war in the Pacific.

Part of the speed the yard picked up in its drive for deliveries came from understanding the need for ships, and much of this understanding came from letters received from those in service. In the early fall of 1943, a group of us were eating lunch on the flight deck of the *Midway*. It was dusk, and the last golden rays of sunlight were slanting over the forest-clad hills of the Coast Range.

There may have been twenty or more of us grouped on the ship's flight deck. The discussion which ensued involved the value of big carriers versus little carriers. None of us knew anything about naval tactics, but we all had our opinions. A Buckler Company worker from Kansas joined the argument. He pulled a letter from his pocket and showed it to us. "Remember my kid, Jerry?" he asked. "He's got almost as many bosses in the Navy as he had here at Kaiser. He says in this letter that he's serving on a carrier almost twice as big as ours.

"Now get this from Jerry's letter: 'When a plane goes up with a bomb in its belly, that bomb raises hell when it's dropped on something. It don't make any difference whether the plane flew off a big carrier or a little one. Just keep on batting them out, Dad. We need more ships and more planes.' "

The Buckler man paused and folded the letter carefully before putting it away in an inside pocket. "Jerry's a good kid," he said quietly. "His ma and me would like to have him back—all in one chunk—when Japan is licked. We've got a chance to get them eighteen boats they're hollering for." He waited for the chorus of disbelief to die down. "All right, I'll grant that it's a damn slim chance, but they're launching 314 (*Kalinin Bay*) day after tomorrow. That means all of the eighteen will be launched by the middle of November. We'll have a dozen of them delivered by that time." He snapped his lunch bucket shut and stood up. "This yard's in step now," he said. "We're still getting extra hands. The way I see it, if we don't get held up for materials, all hell can't stop us short of eighteen."

The Buckler man might well have been the spirit of the shipyard speaking. Throughout that summer, every incentive was used to bolster morale. Each department had pledged "18 or more by '44," and pennants, in departmental colors, adorned all buildings in the yard. As part of that drive for ships, some publicity man had a real idea, in the form of a simple poster: *This Is a Fighting Ship. Give It Your Best.* Simple, but the words probed deeply.

The posters were eye-catching, and their timing was excellent. It was interesting to watch workers' reactions to them. They would stop, read the poster, and then look at the ship. Often, their backs would straighten, their chins would come up, and their walk seemed to be timed to a drum beating inside of them. It did not seem to make any difference whether the worker was an ex-schoolteacher from North Dakota, an ex-grocery man from Pennsylvania, or an ex-prostitute from Galveston, Texas.

The lady from Galveston, in fact, was respected for her willingness to work. When originally hired, she labored as a sweeper on day shift, but later she transferred to swing shift. All she wanted was work—perhaps as a method of self-punishment. What tragedies of girlhood lay cloaked in her years can only be guessed. She never mentioned them. The first forty years of her life had sharpened—and hardened—her features, but even the rough denims could not hide the trimness of her figure. Those eye-catching contours made her a target for the "yard wolves," but those amorously inclined males soon discovered that the lady had a soft Texas vocabulary that could raise paint blisters on a newly painted deck.

Once, in the blazing-hot summer of 1943, the lady from Galveston passed out from heat prostration. Riggers carried her on a stretcher from the ovenlike engine room to the hangar deck. A whirly lifted the stretcher and its burden to a waiting ambulance on the dock. The gray-haired rigger who had "rode the lift" out of the ship watched the ambulance thread its way up the crowded dock toward a first aid station.

"Quite a gal—that one," he observed. "She's got a kid's picture in a locket. The intern opened it. Nice lookin' kid—a Navy flier. No wonder she works like hell!"

The lady from Galveston did not stay at first aid. She came back to the heat of the engine room within an hour. She did not mention the locket, nor did anyone else.

Morale was high as the shipyard moved into the carrier program. In fact, the departure of the *Liscome Bay* put morale at an all-time high, in spite of the fact that eighteen ships by January 1 seemed a fantastic objective. The *Liscome Bay* was complete and ready for a dry-dock inspection, which was to precede her river run (delivery) to Astoria. Late in the afternoon, a small cadre of the ship's crew was brought into the yard and put aboard. Our pipe crew was completing a crew washroom just under a flight deck of the *Coral Sea*, berthed next upriver from the *Liscome Bay*. Big Paul, who was working outside, called out: "Hey gang, look! Navy station wagons!"

All of us clambered out to a gun platform where we could see. The station wagons were jam-packed with sailors who were wolf whistling, yoo-hooing, and throwing kisses at every female in sight. Being Navy-minded, most of the girls were throwing kisses back.

By lunchtime the *Liscome Bay* was almost ready to pull away from the dock. After the whistle had blown, the riggers placed their cables on the last gangplank and the whirly lifted it away. Crowds of workers gathered at berth six to watch the departure. All of our crew watched from the *Coral Sea.*

Long before the lines had been released, thousands of workers had crowded the dock at berth six. Up on the flight deck of the *Coral Sea,* we had a lot of company, too. Out in the Columbia a couple of sternwheelers had taken up positions where they could assist in turning the *Liscome Bay* around when she was free of the dock. Then a flag went up, a dark blue banner with the insignia of the Maritime Commission emblazoned on it.

Hats began coming off as the flag started up. On the packed dock, the hats' removal looked like a silvery wave running along a beach. White faces and black watched that bright bundle go up. The Navy color guard was at attention, and an officer stationed high on the control island of the *Liscome Bay* was frozen into a stiff salute.

With all lines cast off, the bow of the ship inched out into the current. At first the movement was so little that it could scarcely be seen. Then the ship's twin propellers churned white water at her stern, and she gathered headway. The two sternwheelers stood by to help, but the skillfully handled ship did not need them. In just a few minutes after that first inching movement, we were looking at her stern, and her whistle had blown its signal for

Most women production workers were welders. Employer-provided training taught flat, vertical, horizontal and overhead welds. Women welders earned up to $1.20 an hour—when they could master two types of welds—the same rate as men. Approximately 40 percent of all welders were women. Note the background graffiti for yardwolf "Pete."

Martina Gangle

Male control and sexual harassment of women took place in the yards. Women did what they could to avoid or stop it.

Arthur Runquist

the opening of the Interstate Bridge. The *Liscome Bay* was on its way to a rendezvous in the far Pacific waters.

During the past weeks, Jess had continued busy on her sweeper crew. Here she describes the work: It was seldom that our crew was lucky enough to get ordinary deck-cleanup jobs. Instead, we drew tanks and engine rooms with a regularity that proved our work was satisfactory. Working in the tanks and cofferdams is never a pleasant job. No air circulates in them unless it is pumped in. And if the air temperature is ninety, the air is still ninety-odd degrees when it is delivered to the tank or cofferdam. Our crew had that fact demonstrated to it many times during the blazing hot summer of 1943.

Our cleaning in the tanks raised clouds of rust dust. At times we could scarcely see each other when we were only a few feet apart. We climbed, coughed, and squeezed through the manholes in the steel partitions, and we sweated and swore until the area was ready for paint. Then there would be another tank or an engine room waiting for our services.

When the job of testing the boilers and engines began, our work doubled. Almost every pipe in the engine room was protected (insulated) by some form of asbestos. The insulation work was done by a subcontractor, the Bartells Company, whose employees, dressed in white coveralls, were called "seagulls." Their job was a messy one requiring a considerable amount of skill. When two insulation halves were wired around a pipe, the pipe had a protective covering of asbestos an inch thick. Asbestos mixed with cement, which looked as if it were gray mud, was molded over each turn and union in the pipeline to make a continuous sheath. Over this sheath was wrapped a ribbon of cloth or fiberglass, which had been dipped in a gluelike paste. One or two coats of white paint completed the sealing of the insulation.

Our "seagulls" were not noted for their cleanliness. No craft employed on the ship could muss up an area as completely as the insulators. Asbestos was wasted by the ton. I have spent whole shifts picking up fragments and slightly broken pieces of the stuff, which were then put in a skip and hauled to the dump. Buckets of paste and the mud mixture were also thrown into the skips. Wherever a crew of seagulls had worked, there would be a mat of asbestos, inches thick, on the floor. When mixed with the glue paste scraped off in the wrapping process, plus the discarded paper wrappings of the asbestos halves and the scraps of the fiberglass rolls of ribbon, the resulting mat took almost as much labor to remove as was required to cover the pipes in the first place. Cleaning up behind the seagulls became one of our regular jobs.

Our first real summer weather was timed for the first trial of the boilers. None of us who worked in the engine rooms of the *Casablanca* during those boiler trials will ever forget our experience. Ship's ventilation to the engine rooms had not been completed. With the temperature on the dock in the nineties, all of us dreaded the oil-cleaning job we drew. Heat waves shimmered above the steel of the usually cool hangar deck. Climbing down the steel stairways into the engine room was like descending into an oven. We discarded all the garments that we dared to, and we envied the men who could work bare to the belt. Brownie watched us carefully for signs of heat exhaustion and kept sending us, by ones and twos, out to first aid or to the restrooms. That first day was probably the worst, for we gradually became inured to the heat and the toil.

Before the health hazards of asbestos were understood, the substance was widely used in industry because of its fire-resistant and sound-proofing properties.

Jess was getting a reward for her efforts. Her crew had picked her as their representative on a *Liscome Bay* river run to Astoria, to work as a steward's helper, passing out mattresses and bedding for the ship's berthing areas. The Kaiser helpers were bused to Oregon Ship, a huge Kaiser yard at Portland, then taken to the St. Johns dry dock on the Willamette River, where the *Liscome Bay* awaited.

Jess continues: On that short six-mile bus ride, I saw, for the first time, our great sister shipyard (Oregon Ship), then in full production of a Liberty ship every other day! What a perfectly wonderful production job was performed there! Imagine, if you can, what the delivery of a freight ship every forty-eight hours meant to our armed forces overseas. Ship production from that one shipyard was a definite guarantee that none of our fighting men overseas was going to be without food, equipment, or medicine for the duration of the war.

Then, at the St. Johns dry dock, we saw our own great gray-blue ship. She had a look of readiness. The hooded guns of her antiaircraft batteries circled the ship like a cartridge belt on a fighting man. There, on the Willamette, with the golden rays of sundown gilding her topmast, she represented America's anger—shaped in steel.

We were up early the next morning and ate breakfast while the ship was getting under way. It was thrilling to stand aft, on the fantail, and watch the wake wave formed by the twin propellers crash into the shoreline.

It was even more thrilling to go down into the engine room. There was no confusion now. The engine room in service and the engine room I had known at our dock were totally different things. I missed the jumbled piles of catwalk steel, the webs of hoses, welder leads, and the squashy feel of asbestos underfoot. Gone, too, was the gagging odor of raw fuel oil. Now all piping gleamed with white paint, and much of the metalwork had been painted with silvery-like aluminum. Best of all, there was no hint of heat. So thorough was the system of ventilation that the engine room was as cool as the spacious hangar deck.

Jess and the rest of her crew spent several days with the *Liscome Bay* during her river trials before returning to what she called "the heat, chaos, and toil" of the shipyard in Vancouver.

President Roosevelt's speech to Congress in January 1941 stated that settlements between nations made after World War II should be based on "four freedoms"—freedom of speech, freedom of worship, freedom from want, and freedom from fear. Douglas Lynch, designer of the *Bo's'n's Whistle*, made these drawings, inspired by the President's message. They appeared on the back cover of the Kaiser Company newsletter in May, June, and July 1943 and helped boost worker morale.

Douglas Lynch

Big Paul, Jimmy, and I went to the ways to size up future deliveries. We found the *Tripoli*, the *Wake Island*, and the *White Plains* well along in construction, and all of them were scheduled for launching in September. The other hulls, *The Solomons*, the *Kalinin Bay*, and the *Kasaan Bay*, were to be launched in October. All the remaining five hulls were slated for November launchings! We looked long at the ribbed outline of the *Tulagi*; that was the eighteenth ship. That hull had to be completed, launched, and then go through the routine of outfitting before January 1. On the outfitting dock at that time, we had the *Coral Sea* and the *Corregidor*, which were almost as far along in outfitting.

Teamwork and coordination of craft effort became necessary if the yard was to meet its commitments. Those factors can be planned by management, but the full harvest of their fruit come only when each worker has the will to work. That will to work was present throughout the escort-carrier contract. And that will to work came from that intangible thing called morale. Throughout the carrier contract, Vancouver workers had plenty of morale, and the workers' haste stemmed from a knowledge of the *need* of their labor.

My crew hurried. We were a highball[1] crew, but there were many other pipe crews who produced as much as we did. When we were first detailed to install hot and cold water lines in the hospital area, it was a two-shift job. We did not install the twenty-odd fixtures. Our job was to get the pipes to the proper places for the fixture crews. We cut, threaded, and bent every foot of pipe we installed. After the fifth carrier was delivered, we completed that same job in one shift. Such determination took crew cooperation of the highest order. When we did get done ahead of time, Red usually had another job for us to "hop to" immediately.

Red and Al were too wise to try to drive us. They assigned the jobs and let us drive ourselves. Al worked among us and with us—much the same as Buttsy, who flitted about like a jet-propelled scarecrow. The end of each shift found us tired, sweat-caked, and unbelievably dirty. Still, we walked out of the yard's guarded gates at the close of each shift with the comforting knowledge that none of us owed Henry Kaiser or the Maritime Commission—or the people of the United States—a dime of the pay we got for our hard night's work. It is that feeling which gives labor its dignity.

Suppliers of vitally important equipment and materials placed full-page advertisements in trade magazines such as *Modern Industry*.

We did more than work at speed. Whenever we got a chance to buy tools that would accelerate the job, we bought enough for the crew. Rulers, tapes, center punches, dividers—there were not enough of them in the yard to go around. We planned and schemed ways to cut corners on the job, and out of those impromptu huddles came a host of timesaving methods. For example, burners were scarce. We drew out burning torches and kept them ready to go in our work area. Consequently, when we needed a hole in a bulkhead, we made it. The basic idea was to get the job done.

Working at speed gave us little tolerance for defective tools or fittings. If a pipe fitting showed a defect, we threw it in the river. If we had merely discarded it, such a fitting would be collected, taken to salvage, polished, and then returned for use—probably still in defective condition. Our crew or some other crew would install it and then have to remove it. Defective pipe and worn-out, un-trustworthy tools met the same fate. We could not af-ford to slow down. Time was a-wasting.

Just prior to the C4 contract—long after the carri-ers were gone—it was decided to deepen the river alongside the dock. The dredger crews got an eyeful. Everything that could fall or be thrown into the Columbia was resting on the river's muddy bottom.

There was waste in that frenzy of construction. But certainly no one who had ever seen the huge salvage depots in operation in the yard could have failed to be impressed with the efforts to reclaim and reuse every bit of usable material. Most of the criticism stemmed from the rumors of "surplus manpower" in the Kaiser yards. Throughout the building program and after, there was the oft-repeated story of the "shipyard workers who got big pay for doing nothing." Even if such jobs had been available, I doubt if 1 percent of the workers employed would have signed up for them. True, there were many times when whole crews did little for several hours, but those usually were occasions in which the waiting was brought on by a lack of materials, or by the failure of some other craft to maintain speed in production. Welders and burners frequently had hour-long waits between jobs; but if such craftsmen were not available when needed, several crews might be held up for half-shift periods.

All through 1942 and 1943 the draft for the armed forces made heavy inroads into Vancouver's manpower reserve. The draft continued right up to V-J (Victory over Japan) Day,[2] and those taken during those years were usually young craftsmen whose skill was difficult to replace. Jimmy was one of them. After entering the Army, Jimmy wrote many letters to his old pipe crew members. One of them, to me, was written after the Normandy invasion.[3] I got Jimmy's old crew together and read them the letter. Big Paul choked up suddenly when I read the heading "Somewhere in France." In the long-gone years, Big Paul, also then in the Engineers, had written letters with similar headings. Jimmy's outfit had landed on Omaha Beach. The 347th Engineers[4] built the needed roads in spite of German guns by day and German planes by night.

Patriotism, good wages, and the belief that everyone was working together for a common cause—Allied victory—kept war production workers on the job. Shipyard welder and artist Martina Gangle is the second figure on the right.

On October 5 we delivered our seventh carrier, the *Manila Bay*. Co-ordination of craft installations was still far from perfect, but it was definitely improved. But our goal of a ship per week was still out of reach. In spite of every effort by labor and management, it took nine days each for the next two ships, the *Notoma Bay* and our *Midway*. Then, it took a lot of extra effort on the part of all outfitting crafts to get delivery on the *Tripoli* on the last day of

October. But we had delivered four ships in one month! In an effort to speed progress on the dock still more, additional crews were created on the shipways to install dock jobs. Speed was the need.

Working with our Vancouver team was an unforgettable experience. To say that the workforce was a cross section of America would be an understatement. It was a cross section of all humanity and of all races. Out in the parking lots and throughout the shipyard, the handicapped picked up loose paper. Tucked away in little shanties were aged men and women, doing small but necessary services well. The one and only good phase of war work was the opportunity it opened to the aged to earn decent wages for the last time in their lives. The skilled worked with the unskilled, the educated often labored with the illiterate, the blacks worked with the whites.

And there were many outstanding characters—too many for memory. Some were outstanding because of their learning; others were equally outstanding in their lack of learning. Some stood out from the crowd because of their appearance; some attained distinction by way of simple personality. As I think back on all of the group, my memory centers on a woman of outstanding appearance.

She was tall. The artist Petty could have used her for a model without needing to fake a single line. She was cream blonde with a wealth of golden tresses. Her spotless white coveralls fitted with glovelike precision, and somehow they seemed to add to the unstudied grace of her every movement. She carried paint, and toiled but little. It was easy to imagine her presiding over teacups in a candlelit sanctuary dedicated to gossip and small talk. Or she might have easily qualified, I thought, as the type of girl who would welcome a rushee to a Greek sorority. Every bit of her makeup, physical and otherwise, spoke of refinement, of inbred culture, of chastity, and of thought. And yet, on the most curvilinear rear section of her white coveralls was stenciled, in two-inch block letters, the words *Bomb Room*.

There was another character, a man whose liquor-wrecked life's story was etched on his face. When he looked up from the cacophony of his air chisel, one could see flames dancing in his eyes. He never spoke of his past, but he could quote page after page of Homer's *Odyssey* verbatim. Once, for me, he pointed out and named a hundred stars. And once, for a group of us at lunchtime, he mentally totaled the number of hours in the year. Nor did he forget that 1944 was a leap year. He was past sixty years of age. What had he done in the first thirty years to give his brain such a tremendous capacity for memory? What had happened to him in the second thirty years to smash his willpower so completely? He simply couldn't put a cork back in a bottle. When the war was over, he would be walking the roads again—a gray man with the classics in his heart, the names of the stars embedded in his brain, and lights flickering in his eyes like fires.

There was one worker who stood out because of his temper. He could get flaming mad in a second and stay mad for hours. This man had suffered a leg injury, and its healing had left it shorter than its mate. His temper quickly earned him the nickname Grouchy, which, strangely enough, he did not resent. Coming from Texas, Grouchy disliked the fact that his helper was colored. He tolerated the Negro but prided himself on the fact that "he kept him in his place."

Grouchy and his helper drew the job of testing steam lines for leaks—and there were many leaks (which put an edge on Grouchy's temper as the shift got underway). Grouchy's helper found a leak in one room, turned off the main steam valve for the area, and proceeded to repair the leak. Grouchy discovered a leak in an adjoining room but was uncertain as of its source. He looked in on his helper's activity and saw that the repair was almost completed. Grouchy then opened the valve his helper had closed and went to work on the leak he had found. He was busy on a pipe under a steam table when the helper entered. The black helper squatted alongside the steam table and his eyes searched the pipes. He reached for a pipe wrench and adjusted it for size. "Leak in de union right ovah yo' haid," he confided. "Ah'll take it apa't."

"Steam in that line? Wait!" Grouchy shouted. He began to squirm out from under the table.

"Ah shuts off ol' steam long time ago," the helper explained as he continued to loosen the union.

"Wait! I turned it—" Grouchy said.

But Grouchy never got to finish. There was a fizz of steam and a splash of hot water as the union parted. Mixed with that was a bellow of rage as Grouchy's clothes absorbed hot water. The helper didn't need the second

Annual Red Cross drives for funds to support its huge wartime service and relief programs occurred in the three Kaiser shipyards. Employees contributed through payroll deduction.

Douglas Lynch

bellow for a signal to flee. Out of the steam-filled room he went, with a wrench-waving Grouchy in hot pursuit. The colored helper lost time going up a couple of stairways; but when he reached the broad level of the uncluttered hangar deck, he really picked up speed. It was then that Grouchy threw the wrench. When it flicked past the speeding helper's heels in a clean miss, Grouchy gave up the chase. He retrieved his wrench and went back to work. He was working—seemingly quiet—when his supervisor entered the galley.

"Your helper tells me you threatened him," the supervisor said. He wanted to be just a little severe.

"I did not threaten him. I never threaten anybody," said Grouchy. His voice was rising with every word. "I promised that black bastard I'd kill him. I promised that no-good son of a bitch I'd flatten his goddam head down level with his long ears."

"He says you threw a wrench at him," said the supervisor. He still wanted to be severe.

"I was tryin' to cripple him so's I could keep my promise," Grouchy explained. He snatched up a pipe wrench and declared, "An' now I'm promisin' you somethin'. You give me anymore of your lip an' I'll bat your shiny hat flat on top with this plumber's plaything. Get the hell out of here an' leave me alone. I got work to do." With all the wisdom that made the supervisor a supervisor, Grouchy was left alone.

Grouchy was mad. But on the following shift, a slightly crippled white man from Texas and a very fleet-footed black man from Alabama worked together as if nothing had ever broken the peace between them.

Thousands worked with us, and their personalities, too, pried their way into our memories. The personality of one was especially indelible. She was a

journeyman electrician. Her job
on the carriers, the attack transports, and the C4 troopships was
to hook up the power panels
which controlled lights and power
installations. I doubt if she had ever
done that type of work before, but
her swift, deft fingers did the work
of two electricians. In all of the
time she worked on the dock, I
never saw those fingers idle.

Nor did this woman
electrician tolerate idleness in
those around her. If a pipe crew
spilled water on the floor of the

area in which she was working, she told them about it. The plainspoken, matter-
of-fact way she handled such subjects took much of the sting away. Still, she made
it very plain when she didn't like something. If an insulator crew or a vent crew
stalled on the job, she had a habit of reminding them: if they wanted to practice
WPA habits, they would probably get another chance after the war was over. She
shed dirty looks and hot retorts with an urbanity that was as disconcerting as her
sharp tongue. Her hair turned gray while she worked with us on the dock. She
had not heard from her son since the fall of Bataan.[5]

A Navy escort carrier
task group on the USS
Guadalcanal, the first
Vancouver-built baby
flattop, captured a
German U-Boat on June
4, 1944.

At the start of November, the drive for the last eight ships picked
up speed. No longer was berth six the sole "crazy corner." Every berth on
the dock was a madhouse of effort. Speed in production was by no means
confined to the dock. The *Kitkun Bay*, the seventeenth carrier, was launched
eight days ahead of schedule. The *Tulagi*, the eighteenth, was put in the
water ten days prior to her original launching date. It was easy to get
betting odds that the yard would not deliver four ships in November, and
even easier to get better odds that there would not be eighteen ships delivered by January 1.

But the *Wake Island* went out on November 7—on schedule as a
seven-day ship. The *White Plains* took eight days. While there just wasn't room

enough on the ships for additional work crews, the disappointment was short-lived when word circulated that the next two ships would be only six days apiece on berth six. "Get your job done or get yourself a blue suit and go with the ship"[6] was a saying of that time. *The Solomons* went out on the 21st, and the *Kalinin Bay* headed for Astoria on the 27th. Both were six-day ships.

The yard was still catching its breath from that effort when the news came of the loss of the *Liscome Bay*. Those first Navy releases didn't tell too much, but mention was made of heavy loss of personnel. Heavy loss, we learned much later, meant that 644 of the *Liscome Bay's* crew went down with her. Grim groups of men and women read the first news releases. The yard workers mourned their lost ship and its crew. That mourning was then reflected in the work—an extra mile of cable pulled, another six feet of welding, another forty feet of pipe installed, a few more squares of paint applied. "Eighteen by '44" was a certainty when the *Kasaan Bay* went "down the creek" on December 4. Could we make it nineteen? Could we give the Navy an extra ship for a Christmas present? The chips were down now. Could we make it?

How does it feel to win a race against time, especially when crews were shorthanded because of a flu epidemic? The Kaiser company shut down operations for Christmas, but the *Gambier Bay*, the nineteenth ship, was still delivered December 28. This was the bonus ship—our Christmas present to the Navy. At Astoria, the Navy was getting ships faster than they could train the men to man them. "18 or more by '44": Vancouver workers met—and exceeded—that impossible schedule!

Changes in outfitting methods came fast as the year closed. The system of letter-days off was abolished, presumably by order from Washington.

USS *Liscome Bay* was launched April 19, 1943. A torpedo from a Japanese submarine sank the ship the following November.

Louis S. Lee

Perhaps it had served its purpose as a morale builder, but its discontinuance could hardly be called a blessing. Under the letter-day system, the job of entertainment and feeding of the war workers had been, to a large extent, spread over all the days of the week. With the weekend fixed (on Sunday), by Washington fiat, all of the load was thrown on the already over-crowded transportation system, theaters, churches, and restaurants. Restaurants were often out of food by noon, and lines of people extending blocks formed outside the movie palaces. Regardless of the disruption caused by the order to abolish the letter-day off, it remained in force.

In our pipe department, an effort was made on the outfitting dock to switch as many pipe crews as possible from swing shift to day shift. All of Red's crews, for example, were affected by the order. Some of the men—like myself—could not make the changeover for personal reasons. A few were transferred to other crews still working swing. Big George and Buttsy took quit slips. Buttsy, who had saved every penny of his earnings, became part owner of a Texas chicken ranch. Big George had a dual reason for quitting: "I've et so much salmon an' turkey at Hoodlum House[7] I feel like gobblin' when I see white meat, an' that red fish makes me want to lay a million eggs somewheres. I could stand that easy, but I'm danged if I'm goin' to work for 10 percent less an' do the same work. I'm hikin' for Hico." And quit he did, in spite of our pleading. When he walked out of the guarded gates, the production equivalent of three men went with him.

In the meantime, Jess had gotten a promotion—to leadlady of a newly formed, sixteen-member sweeper crew consisting of white women, mostly middle-aged, and seven young blacks, all working on cleanup. As Jessie put it:

The blacks all looked alike to me. Now I find myself ashamed of my ignorance and lack of perception. Being western born and raised, I have never

In 1943, when women began to be hired in substantial numbers, President Roosevelt wrote the Chairman of the Maritime Commission, Admiral Emory S. Land, urging the need for more cafeterias, child care facilities, toilets, and locker facilities. Contractors like Henry Kaiser made adjustments in the workplace to accommodate female war workers.

109

had close contact with the Negro race. To find that these strange (to me) black people had the same hopes, likes, and dislikes that I had was like discovering another world. Their constant, undefeatable cheerfulness impressed me.

Once, in a cofferdam deep in the bowels of a carrier, I worked with blacks. Their task was the nadir of drudgery. Ventilation had failed and the heat was stifling. Our clothes were sweat-soaked. We stumbled as we passed the laden buckets out. Then one of my black gals began singing, and the others joined her. Maybe it was the sight of the empty bucket swinging down a rope from the oval hole above us that inspired the music; but with the song going, the loaded buckets were lighter, the air was fresher, and we did not stumble. Soon, it seemed, the job was done, and we were climbing out. How can I ever hear "Swing Low, Sweet Chariot" again without thinking of my black co-workers?

On my first day as a supervisor, I ate my lunch with rather mixed feelings. Pride of promotion was uppermost. There were almost 9,000 women working in the yard; less than one hundred were leadladies. Mixed with all of my worries of that first night of responsibilities was a restroom incident that brightened the shift. I had guided three of my colored gals to that feminine sanctuary. While I waited to guide them back to our ship, another young colored gal came hurrying in. She had hardly disappeared into the more cloistered section of the restroom when a commotion arose. An excited medley of colored voices rose higher and higher.

One of my gals then stuck her head around the partition between the entrance and the rear room and said, "Miss Jessie, can you he'p us? Annie cain't git her pants down." Annie was in the center of a group of colored gals. All of them were trying to help her unfasten the patented catch of one of her shoulder straps. Annie was doing a little jig. She really needed that catch unfastened. "Fust time ah evah wore ovahalls," she explained as I tugged at the fastening. "Mah husband he'ps me git 'em on. Nevah thought ah would have to git a leadlady to git 'em off. Leadladies have to know heaps o' things."

Suddenly, I managed to tip the button back and throw the strap clear of her shoulder. There was a clatter of feet and a shout of laughter from all of the colored gals. Annie had her pants down.

6

"Another one in the creek"

Four ships, the *Nehenta Bay*, the *Hoggatt Bay*, the *Kadashan Bay*, and the *Marcus Island*, were delivered in January 1944. The yard had its full team on the field, but the coordination needed to produce a ship every six days had not yet been reached, even though there were signs that such coordination was on the way.

In January the marine electric crews on the dock teamed up to set world records in the installation of cable. Each carrier required 227,000 feet—nearly fifty-three miles—of various sizes of cable. The quality of the cable's construction was an eloquent tribute to the near-perfection attained by American industry. The current-carrying wires were enclosed in a rubberized, waterproof material. A continuous wrap of cloth, resembling linen, covered the rubberized material. A sheath of heavy-gauge lead, which was encased in a tightly woven lacing of aluminum wires, completed the cable assembly. It was flexible, waterproof, and as completely free of shorts as man could devise.

Ship launch ceremonies were special occasions with printed programs, a sponsor, and a maid or matron of honor. Flower girls were a component of each program. Wives of prominent people and naval personnel were invited to be sponsors to send the ship on its way.

Louis S. Lee

Whenever possible, marine cable was installed in unbroken lengths. For example, many of the power and signal lines extended unbroken from the control island to the engine rooms, and to the steering flat over the rudders at the stern of the ship. For these runs of cable, lengths of 300 to 500 feet were not unusual. Threading them through the wire ways took skill, ingenuity, and plenty of hard labor.

Competition between shifts was keen. In order that each shift might have equal labor, the "pull for the record" was spread among four hulls. Day shift finished with the highest amount of cable pulled per man. Swing shift pulled the most cable, and graveyard—according to graveyard—did the hardest work. But a total of 188,710 feet of cable passed through the wire ways in twenty-four hours. That was a record for any shipyard in the world to shoot at.

T2 Tanker propeller

C. Herald Campbell

The short month of February was marked by four more ships delivered: the *Savo Island*, the *Ommaney Bay*, the *Petrof Bay*, and the *Rudyerd Bay*. The last two were seven-day ships. The yard was acquiring speed.

On February 19 the yard launched the *Sitkoh Bay*. By this time, most of the workers had become rather bored with launchings. Oftentimes, on swing shift, the launchings would be held at lunchtime, and the flurry of whistles announcing the event would go almost unnoticed, or would be accompanied by the bored comment "another one in the creek." But the *Sitkoh Bay* launching was an event. Every old-timer in the yard wanted to be present when Mrs. Henry Mullinix was picked as sponsor. The deluge of applications for passes which swamped the management proved that the workers had not forgotten the *Liscome Bay*. Nor had they forgotten that Rear Admiral Henry Mullinix went down with his flagship.

It rained steadily throughout the ceremonies, and we were all soaked to the skin; but none of us would have missed that launching for a day's pay. From the management, Mrs. Mullinix got the usual banquet and presents that go to a ship's sponsor. From the workers—and unknown to her—came the honor of being voted their All-American Navy wife.

Teamwork had been developed in all crafts, as proven by the fact that March had five deliveries: the *Saginaw Bay* on the 2nd, the *Sargent Bay* on the 9th, the *Shamrock Bay* on the 15th, the *Shipley Bay* on the 21st, and the *Sitkoh Bay* on the 28th. Only thirty-eight outfitting days were needed from launching to delivery.

A dynamic triangular pattern created by the booms of whirly cranes defines a cluster of workers gathered to celebrate the completion of another ship.

Arthur Runquist

Work never stopped on the ships. Early in the morning or late at night it was possible to hear the roar of construction at Ogden Meadows, five miles from the shipyard. It was a steady sound, as continuous as the mutter of artillery on the Camp Adair[1] range in Oregon. The activity of the gunners of the 104th Division—more than twenty miles away—could be heard quite plainly from our Salem home.

We had new neighbors many times at Ogden Meadows. The two original families who had been present when we moved in were long gone. Sickness, injuries, death, and the attrition of the task at hand, along with all the personal problems of those employed, gave us different neighbors often. The job was tough on people.

In March we acquired a bachelor on one side and a family from somewhere in the Midwest on the other. The paper-thin walls between the apartments gave us drama. It was like having TV without the picture tube.

The bachelor didn't appear to be the type who would become a nuisance as a neighbor. He was middle-aged, homely of face, and not too clean in personal appearance. It took but a few days to discover that he was the world's champion sneezer. These outbursts came at any hour of the day or night. They were short, sharp snorts, popping with the rapidity of a fast-triggered pistol; they were loaded in him, apparently, in clips of six. We nicknamed him Sneezer. We tried to overlook his handicap, even though he woke us at times when we considered being awakened was almost a crime.

For safety reasons, women working in industrial jobs were required to wear their hair tied up and covered by a scarf.

Arthur Runquist

Sneezer had other shortcomings, too. He was seldom sober. Worse than that, he accumulated wives—a sort of lend-lease variety—about every other week. Where he found all the frowsy women willing to live with him for short periods is a real mystery. But he developed a set formula for terminating a "lease": "I'm not givin' you nothin' from now on, an' you ain' got nothin' I want! So get out an' stay out."

There was one memorable occasion when Sneezer's brother visited him to point out the error of his ways. Sneezer had an ample liquor supply on hand, and the visit wound up in a drunken brawl, with violence that knocked the pictures off our apartment wall. The project policeman moved in, subdued both men, and hauled both off to jail for a cooling-off period. But we didn't lose Sneezer. When he got out of jail he came back.

The family on the other side of us—two boys in their late teens, a mother, and a teenage daughter—was from somewhere in the Midwest. One of the boys, unfortunately, was musically inclined. He had just bought a trumpet, and that was only one of the many problems that developed. Upon the shoulders of that young widow fell the job of keeping the kids in line. We know that she tried, and we know that she failed.

Both of the boys were of draft age. We have often wondered if the move to Vancouver was that mother's last-chance gamble to keep her sons out of the Army. In less than three weeks, one of the boys (unfortunately, not the would-be musician) was engaged to marry a girl he had met at the shipyard. From all we could see of her, his judgment was good, but his mother opposed the match actively, until it was an accomplished fact. Then she accepted the bride with resignation. We counted ourselves lucky when we saw the bride carried over the threshold of an apartment a half block away.

But the lad with the cornet was still very much at home. Regardless of the fact that he worked swing shift, he had a habit of rising early, about 7 a.m. With breakfast over at 8:30, he was ready for his morning's practice. Practice is a weak, inadequate word for what he did to that cornet. There were times when he could string together a half dozen bars of some popular song before he soured the next half dozen notes. Then his foot would stop its stomp, and silence would fall while he reread the sheet. All we could do was to wait for him to begin again.

Henry Kaiser strongly believed in providing medical care for his workers and their families. When Kaiser came to the Portland-Vancouver area, he brought with him the medical team that had provided health services to his workers on the Grand Coulee Dam. Shipyard workers had the option of participating in the prepaid medical and hospital plan. Members contributed through payroll deduction at the rate of 60 cents per week. The coverage included physician's service, hospital care, ambulance service, laboratory, X-rays, and drugs.

Three families came and went in the other apartment next to the musician. At last, in desperation, I found a cure for his practicing. In the window of a Portland music store, I spied a tin fife. I paid 50 cents for it, and I rejected as unnecessary the clerk's offer of an address where I could take lessons. I wanted to approach my adoption of that instrument in the lowest

Northern Permanente Foundation Hospital opened with seventy beds in September 1942 to serve the Vancouver war workers. The hospital was located on a fifteen-acre site one mile east of the shipyard on a bluff overlooking the Columbia River. The innovative design by Portland architects George Wolff and Truman Phillips enabled efficient patient care incorporating the latest technology and medical practices. Kaiser Permanente sold the property in 1959 when they opened Bess Kaiser Medical Center in Portland.

Arthur Runquist

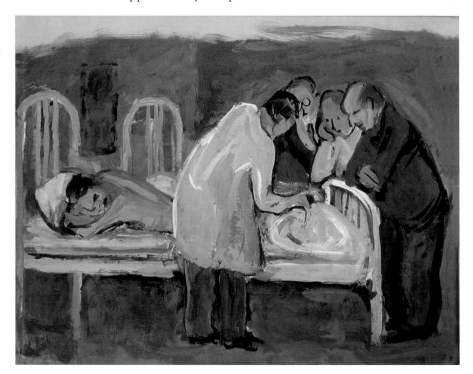

possible musical bracket. My fondest hope, at the time, was to be able to play "Mairzy Doats" worse than the lad with the cornet.

According to the rules of the housing project, no musical instrument could be played between the hours of 10 p.m. and 10 a.m. But Leroy (we'll just call him that) was as liable to strike up his band at 3 a.m. as he was at 8:30 a.m. Whenever I caught him out of those time bounds, I played on the fife, and that fife, as I played it, was potent. I suspect that I broke his musical heart— but I also broke him of getting out of the designated time bounds. His playing improved, however, as if the discovery that there was someone worse had cheered and inspired him.

Less than a month had passed when the bridegroom (the fellow who had moved from the apartment next to us) was taken ill. There came a morning when we heard the erstwhile bride sobbing her heart out to the groom's sister: "Jeanie, I've just got to do something for him. He's sick—awful sick. The doctors I've had just shake their heads."

"Are you going to take him to Permanente hospital?"[2] the sister asked.

"Yes, I am. This afternoon," the bride said. "I don't care whether your mother likes it or not. I can't help what some ignorant fool at the yard told her. The hospital is clean—spotless. I looked plenty. He'll get good care from people who know what care means. I'm afraid he's going to die. But he's not going to die out in this doghouse if I can help it."

A door slammed, and there was silence. That afternoon an ambulance backed to the door of the apartment. A stretcher was carried in, and a form was carried out and placed in the ambulance. The honeymoon was over.

We saw the bride occasionally during the next two weeks. She kept her job at the yard, and she kept her apartment. Almost daily, Leroy, Jeanie, and the bride would climb into the battered coupe, which had been the groom's pride, and go for a bedside call on the sick man. The little car would start off gaily, its fenders swinging as it bounced over the chuckholes; but when it was parked, after the call, it seemed to droop dejectedly, as if it were adding its tears to those of the passengers.

When we returned from one of our weekend trips to Salem, the bride was in black. She told us that her husband had died of inflammatory rheumatism. She talked to us freely—hungrily, in fact—as if having someone outside the family for a listener was a boon. His mother was against local burial and had insisted that he be buried in the family plot in the Midwest. But there were no funds for such an expensive trip.

"You'll have his union insurance," I assured her. (She had never heard of it.) "Does anyone at the yard know of your loss?" I asked.

In 1944, the Vancouver Kaiser hospital was the first non-military medical center to use the new miracle drug, penicillin. The Kaiser newspaper, *Flat Top Flash*, February 11, 1944, reported that penicillin saved the life of seven-year-old Betty Hall, daughter of a swing shift chipper on the outfitting docks. The Army-developed drug was not yet available for commercial use and had to be flown to Vancouver from a special supply in Boston, Massachusetts. Since Betty was a member of the family medical plan, all hospital expenses were taken care of during her three-month confinement at Kaiser Permanente.

COMPLETE *medical and hospital care for less than 10¢ a day*

FOR EMPLOYEES OF KAISER COMPANY, INC., VANCOUVER, WASHINGTON

BY NORTHERN PERMANENTE FOUNDATION

117 ★

She shook her head and said, "Nobody knows we're broke. I told my leadman my husband was dying day before yesterday. You see, I work on the dock, and John worked on the ways. His foreman, Roxie, knows he's gone. I met him at Permanente yesterday. I'm going to check out today—I guess I'll have to—to get some money I've earned."

"I wish you'd let me advise you," I told her. "Don't quit unless you really want to quit. Take a leave of absence. You can get that, under the circumstances. I'm sure the union will pay the insurance promptly, and I know the gang well enough to believe you won't have financial troubles long."

We saw her packing the next day and went over to see if we could help. She was almost cheerful. "His union steward told me they would have a check for me tomorrow," she said. "I won't have to quit, and I won't even have to use his union money. That gang on the dock—and his bunch on the ways—were wonderful." She dabbed at her eyes with a damp handkerchief. "Those wonderful people didn't know me. All they needed to know was that I needed help. I'm coming back here to work. Maybe I can prove that I appreciate what they've done for me."

Leroy took over the battered coupe when the widow went east. He didn't get to drive it far. The arrival of the mail girl one morning started a hubbub in their apartment next to us. As the thin boards recorded the event, the mother took it tough, the sister thought it was a dirty trick, and Leroy had his "greetings letter."

Leroy had his own ideas: "What's the use of squawking 'cause I'm drafted? So what? I'm no better than anybody else, an' I never have liked the idea of somebody else doin' my fighting for me. All I hope is that they'll let me pick my outfit. Infantry—that's what I'm goin' to ask for— they're the guys that know what the score is."

Leroy came home on a furlough after his boot-camp training. He was a different-looking Leroy—straighter, grimmer, but also with a confidence in his bearing that he had never shown before. Once, during his visit, he gave the cornet a workout. Nothing in his training had contributed to his musical ability. He was still the world's worst musician. But when I told him good-bye, the crossed rifles on his lapels shouted that he knew how to be a soldier.

The weeks following Leroy's return to camp were marked with steadily increasing quarrels between mother and daughter. We paid little attention to them. They were much like a soap opera which could not be turned off. It was usually possible to hear a much better argument from the Sneezer side if we needed entertainment. Whenever Sneezer was in his cups, or when he was firing his wife-of-the-week, he reached heights of vocabulary far above the ordinary. One "lend-lease" wife, incidentally, refused to get out on Sneezer's order. She told him to go to hell, among other and more lurid things, and stayed in the Sneezer apartment for a week devoted to defamatory debate.

But the final argument between mother and daughter could not be ignored. It started about 7 a.m. when Jeanie came in from a swing-shift dance. Our apartment wing was fairly quiet at the time. Sneezer had celebrated the end of a wifeless week by getting on a one-quart drunk before going to bed.

The first tenants moved into Vanport in December 1942, three months after ground was broken on the 650-acre site in north Portland. It was the nation's largest single war-housing project. Six nursery schools were completed, including the day nursery shown here.

Charles Voorhies

119 ⭐

His snoring partially cloaked the muted anger in the voices of the quarreling women in the nearby apartment. But the tempo and pitch of the voices rose higher and higher:

"I'm not going to give him up," Jeanie shouted. "They were planning a divorce before he ever saw me."

"Did his wife tell you that?" the mother asked. "She's had three kids by him. Can't you see that she believed him and trusted him? He lied to her so that he could take you out last night. How do you know he won't lie to you later? How do you know he's not lying about the divorce now? Jeanie, can't you see he's just a chippy chaser like the rest of them?"

"You talk that way about everybody you don't like," Jeanie said. "I'm getting out!"

"Let me tell you something before you go," the mother responded. "All of us came out here to make money. We were going to get rich, quick. We were going to make $200 a week and buy the Simmons place when we went back home. Remember that? We had $500 when we came here. We made $200 a week for three weeks. Then John married. I'm glad he did now. Since Leroy is gone, we're still making a $100 a week; but we haven't saved anything but our payroll bonds. All our bank money is gone."

"I suppose that's my fault, too?" the girl asked sarcastically.

"Not all of it," the older woman answered. "Listen, when I came out here, I had two fine boys and a good girl. I was proud of all of you; you were my family. Now John is gone, and I'm prouder of Leroy than I ever have been in my life. Why in hell don't you get in the WACs, instead of chippying around with a married man old enough to be your father?"

"If you think I'm going to learn to march, deliver messages, and wear a funny hat for fifty bucks a month, you're crazy," Jeanie said.

"Your brother's hat don't look funny," the mother said. "But if you keep on cabin dating that foreman, you will look funny, wearing an oversized girdle and a phony wedding ring."

There was a stamp of angry feet in the next room, "I'm getting out," muttered Jeanie.

"So am I," declared the mother. "I'm going back home tomorrow. Go ahead and learn your lesson the hard way. Do whatever you damn well please. Jeanie, honey, listen. You have to pay for that kind of fun. You have to pay and pay."

A door slammed. The thin, broken sound of a woman's grief seeped through the sounding boards and merged with the ripsaw pulse of Sneezer's snoring. Jess and I motored to Salem at the close of the shift. When we returned from our weekend, the "heartbreak" apartment was empty. We never saw any of its occupants again.

In quick succession, a parade of tenants used the vacated apartment. The first two couples were newlyweds full of the joy in each other. The male of one couple I remember chiefly because his morning salutation to his bride was, "Where in hell will I find a clean pair of drawers ?" When the Army took him after two weeks of residence, the bride went home to Mama. We have often wondered if his comrades helped him search for his underclothes.

The other groom lived beside us for a month. The imprint of a Kansas farm was still on him, and to that farm he and his bride eventually departed. "Not gonna live in any damn country where you have to wear rubber suits," he declared. "Not gonna work for any son of a bitch that tells me how to drive nails." They raise them to be independent in Kansas, I guess. We liked him and his shy little bride. Part of the groom's farmer complex was an amusing imitation of a rooster's crow—just before he retired for the night. It was, apparently, a signal to the bride.

The rather aged couple that moved in when Kansas left were from Nebraska and way points. "We had a farm," the man told us, "and we managed to keep it even through the early part of the Depression. Then the dust hit us. When the dirt got as high as the kitchen window, Ma just insisted we move. There was no market for farm machinery, and what furniture we had was pretty well shot. So we just left everything to set there. Took our clothes and beat it."

"Did you have any children to go to, Dad?" I asked.

"Nope. We had a son, but he's buried in France," the old man answered. "Served under Gen. John J. Pershing," he said. "Nope, we didn't have anywheres to go. I got a job in Lincoln, Nebraska for a couple of weeks. Too many gray hairs got me fired from a street construction job. They hired two younger men to take my place. I got another job washing dishes in Omaha.

After two weeks, I got fired. Me and Ma had it kinda tough for a long time. I kept getting fired. Jobs is hard to get and easy to lose when your hair gets white.

"Me and Ma missed meals sometimes, but we didn't owe anybody and we didn't holler for help," he continued. "Since '37, I've had scores of jobs in a dozen or more states, but I've never took a dime from WPA or any of the rest of them crackpot schemes to make phony good times. The thing that gave me the biggest pain in the pants was to see a lot of husky young bucks leaning on government shovels because they didn't have brains enough or guts enough to get out and get themselves a real job."

"What do you do down in the yard, Dad?" I questioned.

"I'm a chisel sharpener," he said. "Don't ask me how come. It took me about two hours to get the knack of it. Mister, I get 'em sharp. Maybe it ain't so important as some of the jobs in the yard, but it *is* my part of the war effort. Ma and me figures that the more bonds we buy—and the sharper I get the chisels—the fewer crosses there will be over boys like our Sammy."

Pa and Ma lived beside us for several months. Each night when he came in, Ma's voice invariably asked the question, "Did you get fired today, Pa?" "Nope," he would say. That cheerful reply took on a singing quality as the weeks passed. Each payday they bought a bond to "help finish the job their Sammy had started to do." They moved to McLoughlin Heights[3] so that Ma could have "one of them newfangled iceboxes and a real electric stove."

We saw their few possessions loaded on a pickup for the move to their new home. No installment payments were due on anything. Pa's light, striped coat almost matched his pants. Ma's coat had a sheen from many pressings. If one looked closely, it was easy to see that the sleeves were frayed on the bottoms and the buttonholes drooped like tired eyes. But there was a glory to that aged coat.

Living in Ogden Meadows when it was crowded to capacity was an educational experience. The Ogden Meadows shopping center consisted of a large grocery store, a meat market, a barbershop, a beauty shop, and a drugstore. There was also an ice-storage house and a laundry. The stores—grocery, meat, and drugs—were jam-packed twelve hours a day. The barbershop was definitely catch-as-catch-can in the matter of haircuts; the beauty parlor dated appointments two weeks ahead. The laundry operated on the theory that when and if you got your washing back, you paid for it. All the tenants learned patience; in fact, they majored in it.

There were other lessons taught at Ogden Meadows that were definitely not in the book. One of my pipe-fitter friends and his wife learned to recognize a certain Ogden Meadows odor, for example. This is what he told a group of us when we joshed him about being absent on one particularly warm day.

"You fellows can laugh all you want to," the pipe fitter said, "but I was damn sick yesterday. So was the wife; she didn't work, either. We moved to another apartment to get away from the odor. The management permitted it; they encouraged it, in fact.

"Any of you guys remember the 300-pounder who used to run a tool room on the barges? Well, anyhow, we had him for a neighbor. He bunked right next door to us. Been hitting the wine heavy for a month, too, Tubby has. He's got a porch full of empties. Last Saturday he got on a roaring solo drunk."

The fellow went on: "We pulled out for Fort Lewis[4] to see my kid Sunday morning and didn't get back until almost shift time Monday. Everything was quiet next door—first time it had been really quiet for a long time. It was so damn still next door for the next couple of days that we thought Tubby had moved out. Thursday we could smell wine, so we knew he was back. When we came in off shift the wine smell was stronger—and sweeter, if you could call it that. Yesterday morning that sickly, sweet smell got to the wife. She had to vomit while we were eating breakfast. I then knocked on Tubby's door and told him to mop up the grape, but he didn't answer."

"I was tempted to kick the door in," he said. "There's lots of busted doors at the Meadows; but the wife wanted everything legal, so I goes for the clown (the project policeman). I'll bet that guy was a sergeant in the First World War. Of all the lazy, buck-passing coppers I've ever known, he takes the cake. I have to argue with him. 'How do I know there's been a crime committed?' he asked. 'Have you any facts you can prove? If your neighbor is quiet you should be satisfied.' He gives me that kind of stuff. I finally get sore and tell him off. All I wanted is a door kicked in. He could do it legal, or I would do it illegal. Finally, he went with me."

"He pried a window open with a pinch bar and took one sniff. 'I haven't smelled one as strong as that since 1918,' the cop says. 'What do you mean?' I ask. 'Your neighbor is dead—plenty dead,' he says. 'I'll betcha he's turned green.'

"The copper climbed into the room, and I followed him. Tubby was lying there naked on the bed. He had turned green, and he was swelled twice as big as he was. His feet were as big as paint buckets, and his hands were the size of hams. Then that sickly, sweet smell got to me and I vomited. I got out pronto, and we moved pronto. But the wife and me—we know what death smells like."

Many of the tenants learned, too, what to do in response to the numerous fires. Because of the flimsy construction, a fire in one apartment usually meant the loss of an entire wing of eight. It took only thirty minutes or so to reduce a wing to a pile of smoking ashes. The crowd helped save personal belongings while the firemen fought the fire. But unless the saved material was constantly guarded, onlookers looted the salvage. "Guard what you save" became good advice at Ogden Meadows.

7

"Hay-fork high and pick-handle broad"

In April 1944, the Vancouver yard still had seventeen ships to complete prior to July 8. That meant it would be necessary to deliver them faster than four ships per month—an impossible rate in itself. But now there could be no doubters. Everybody in the yard, from themessenger girls on scooters to the brassiest of brass hats, realized that the crews had to be in step. The coordination of effort we achieved made the impossible possible.

Five ships were delivered in April. The carrier-training depot at Astoria, where Navy personnel majored in carrier operation, was swamped with ships. The *Steamer Bay* was sent to Astoria on April 4, and the *Cape Esperance* followed five days later. The *Takanis Bay*, the *Thetis Bay*, and the *Makasser Strait* were all six-day ships. Vancouver's team was making touchdowns.

Many of the workers missed a significant event in those first days of April. When the *Steamer Bay* cleared on the 4th, the *Makin Island* was launched on April 5th. The shipway was still smoking when a whirly crane deposited a slab of steel on it. It was a keel for a new type of ship, designed for a specific task. All America can be thankful those ships were never used for the task planned; but all America can be thankful those ships were built. They were attack transports, built to carry "expendable" men one way. When the American armada moved into Tokyo Bay[1] to accept the surrender of the Japanese, the Marines in the attack transports went along, just in case. After the surrender those ships became part of the "magic carpet"[2] that ferried war-weary men home.

Only a few workers knew of the keel laying of the *Oconto*; but as fast as the remaining eleven ways were emptied, other keels were put down. There was a shortage of steel and trained draftsmen to plan the craft in detail, but the yard was hurrying to complete the contract on the carriers.

Vancouver received many U.S. Maritime Commission awards for distinguished service in the production of ships for war. In conferring the "M" Flag (merit award), Admiral Howard L. Vickery, vice-chairman of the Maritime Commission, stated, "I don't know of a single yard in the country that rates the 'M' Flag more than Vancouver."

This photo, taken from high up on a whirly, shows tiny workers on the outfitting dock. The yards were so big that bicycles were used to get around efficiently. The November 5, 1942, *Bo's'n's Whistle* explained that "over 238 bicycles are used . . . it was a common sight to see an executive slip on his trouser guards and take off for some distant point across the yard."

C. Herald Campbell

With all of this activity already in place, Vancouver accepted the job of completing the outfitting of some C4 troopships built at Kaiser's yard in Richmond, California.[3] In April, one of these big ships steamed up the Columbia River and was moored alongside a carrier. Due to wartime secrecy, there was no name emblazoned on the bow. We learned later that the ship was called the *General Taylor*.

The C4 was big. It was 522 feet long, with a molded breadth of 72 feet. Vancouver's workers came to the dock by the thousands to stare at it. Some came during lunch hour, some in the preshift hour, some probably sneaked down for a peek on company time. Many of those who came for the look attempted to go aboard. But to get aboard, a worker had to have a special C4 badge. Without such a badge, the would-be visitor was out of luck. Many a leadman, foreman, and supervisor had his ego punctured when he failed to convince the guards of his importance.

It took a couple of days to decommission the ship and to unload the outfitting material stored in her holds. During those two days, the Navy officers gave the management a list of necessary alterations, which were many and major. For example, an entire galley had to be moved down one deck, and a cafeteria-style serving room soon replaced it. A refrigeration room had to be moved. Bulkheads had to be installed around all stairways. The ship's firefighting system had to be changed and improved, more gun platforms installed, and the outfitting completed. All of that was to be done in twenty-one days!

For this job, I was selected as leadman of a pipe-fitting crew, totaling fourteen, of whom only four were real pipe fitters. A boss told me: "Your crew works twelve hours beginning tomorrow. Take a look at the big boy talking to Natalie. Do you want a smoked Irishman[4] on your crew?"

Henry Kaiser helped keep workers motivated with his inspiring messages. In a speech to Vancouver employees on July 6, 1943, he said, "We will finish this job. We will win this war. That is not a problem. The problem is for what is in the future!"

Arthur Runquist

The Negro was big: "Hay-fork high and pick-handle broad" would describe him. Once later I measured his left arm at the biceps; that arm, hanging loose and unflexed, halfway between the elbow and the shoulder, took seventeen inches of my steel tape to encircle.

I did some fast thinking on Earl's question. About half of my all-white crew were from below the Mason-Dixon Line. Would they object to working with a colored man? I looked the big fellow over again. He didn't look as if he was a sorehead or a troublemaker. Part of the job ahead of me was the installation of fire mains, and heavy pipe and heavy valves had to be moved and lifted for that. As I thought of the strength it would require to install that stuff, I made my decision. "I'd like to have that big fellow," I told Earl. "If any of my crew refuse to work with him, I'll send them in for transfer."

A few minutes later, the big fellow and I walked out of the pipe shop and headed for the ship. John Willie was officially a member of my crew. As soon as we were outside the noisy shop, I stopped and told him: "Listen to me carefully, big boy; I want to get things straight at the start. You're going to be the only colored man on my crew for a while, at least. I'm a western man and I have no color prejudices whatsoever, but some of my men may have. If they bother you, I'm asking you to let me handle the matter. I'll do it quick and definitely. If *you* get out of line, I'll trade you fast. While you work under me, I won't ask you to do any job I wouldn't tackle myself. I'm promising you no discrimination and no favors."

"Sounds good to me," the big black man replied. "Ah nevah had any trouble with white folks in Arkansas. Shouldn't have any heah. Ol' Army takes three of mah brothahs, but tu'ned me down foh high blood pressah. If'n Ah stays home an runs mah garage, mah brothahs would be 'shamed of me foh not gittin' in wah work. So Ah sells mah garage an' comes way out heah to he'p Mistah Kaisah build ships."

Three crew members griped about Big John being a member of the crew. I ignored the comments briefly, but after lunch on that shift I sent those three men—and Big John Willie—to get a twenty-foot section of eight-inch fire main. It lay out on the dock, and it had to be conveyed through a carrier and to the superstructure deck of the C4. I knew that the original weight of the pipe would seem to increase about every five steps it was carried, and that its length would make it awkward to maneuver from ship to ship and then up two decks. If the whirly for our berth had not been swamped with work for two other ships, I would have had the big pipe relayed to its place on the C4. After the men had gone to get the pipe, I regretted that I had not sent another man or two along to help.

About an hour later one of the three men I had sent for the fire main found me in the generator room. He was sweating freely, and that was unusual. His grin testified that he was happy about something, and that was also very unusual. "I got somethin' to tell you," he began. He produced a slab of "eating tobacco" and bit off a Southern-sized chunk. He chewed reflectively for a moment, worked the cud into talking position, and bull's-eyed a deck drain with excess liquid.

"When you brought that big Negro into the crew before lunch," he said, "I figgered it was time for me to have you write her out. The Cajun kid from Florida and that guy from Waco felt the same way about it. None of us ever worked shoulder to shoulder with a Negro before." He looked at me, as if for encouragement to go on, and to be believed. I nodded. He was telling the truth. He spat at the deck drain again, missed, and sighed a little.

"Lemme tell you somethin,' " he confessed. "That big Negro is all man! That danged pipe was heavier than it looked. Cajun, Waco, an' me gits a piece of board under the front end of it an' we picks her up, just to see if we could carry her. That big Negro had walked back to the hind end. Do you know what he did? When he seen us pick up the front end, he just reaches down with one hand—one hand, I'm sayin'—bats his eyes a couple of times, raises his end, and is ready to foller us. What in hell else could we do but tote our end then? We gits up onto the hangar deck of the carrier in good shape, but we has to wiggle her around them banks of welding machines. That made the fried potatoes slide in all of us. Whenever we got stuck, that big boy'd wrap them black hands around the pipe an' move it.

"We finally gits her out onto the C4 gangplank. We showed our badges to the Kaiser clown an' rested a bit. None of us liked the idea of gittin' her up them next two decks. The big boy disappears while Cajun, Waco, and me is coolin' our motors. When he come back he's luggin' a block an' tackle. That

This photo shows a bridge crane hoist drum for a sub-assembly structure.

C. Herald Campbell

Trains ran between Portland and Vancouver to accommodate the growing number of shipyard workers who lived south of the Columbia River. Two ferries shuttled workers across the Willamette River from downtown Portland to Oregon Ship and Swan Island shipyards. The ferries were brought out of retirement in the Bay Area. The *Bo's'n's Whistle* announced their arrival with the following lyric from the shipyards' Singing Sentinels: *The ferries comin' 'round the bend—Will soon be filled with shipyard men.*

Douglas Lynch

don't look like the answer to us, 'cause the only place it could be hung is up on a gun platform on top of the house deck. But the big boy has her figgered: If'n we pulls her way up, we kin unhook de ropes an' slide her down dem steps easiah den we kin tote her up. Brains, that's what he's got. Cajun, Waco, and me is pooped when we gits her where she goes, but that big Negro ain't even sweatin'. He's all man, an' he kin work with us anytime, anywhere. I just wanted you to savvy why."

John Willie had clearly made good in his first shift. It didn't take long for stories of his strength to get around on the outfitting dock. Later, on the same ship, he picked up and held overhead a huge fire main valve. He held it—a feat requiring tremendous strength—until his teammates bolted it in place. The foreman of another pipe crew who witnessed that performance exclaimed, "MiGawd, the man's a chain hoist!" John Willie earned his nickname, Chain Hoist Johnnie.

Our series of long-hour shifts took a heavy toll on the physical reserves of every man who worked them. But being a leadman also gave me a chance to see some human drama, which pictured how close some of the workers were to the conflict. Two of my men were riding a bus to work when a traffic accident disabled the bus. In their haste to transfer, they left their lunch buckets in the disabled carrier. I let them have my lunch and made arrangements to eat at the yard cafeteria. When I showed my out pass to the gate guard, he called my attention to a woman standing in the rain a short distance from the guard's booth.

"She's all hopped up about something," the guard said. "Won't stay in under the shelter. She's waiting for her husband—been waiting an hour or more now. I'm betting she's Jewish, and I'm wondering what in hell she's got in her hands."

She was middle-aged and undoubtedly Jewish. Every line of her face and body spelled mother. Her hands were tightly cupped one over the other, and she kept them that way. Her lips were moving as if she were repeating something over and over. Her face had much the same light in it as that which comes from the stained-glass windows of a church when only the candles are lit. The yellow trim on her round Kaiser badge showed her to be a day-shift worker. I wondered about her as I hurried to the cafeteria. When I checked back in with the guard after I had eaten, the Jewish lady was still waiting in the rain.

On the next shift, the guard drew duty on the gangplank of berth six. "What happened to our Jewish lady last night?" I asked.

He stared at me a moment. "That's right; you did see her," he said. "Take a few minutes; I'd like to tell you about her. In spite of all her watching, she didn't see her husband until he was almost to my gate. She made a run for him, and they clinched right in front of my booth. She's almost hysterical, and she kept screaming: 'The telegram lied, Papa! It lied! Maxie is alive! Maxie is alive!' When they embraced, her arms went around him, and her hands spilled a stream of two-bit pieces down his back. Yeah, that's what she had in her hands—two-bit pieces, a lot of them.

"Papa does his best to quiet her. He holds her tight for a while and keeps patting her here and there, where it will do the most good. He's a shipwright on the ways, and he's *some* Jew and *some* German.

" 'Are you sure he's 'live?' Papa asks when she has calmed down some.

" 'Our little Rebecca phones this afternoon from New York,' she said. 'The French underground gets him to a ship. He will be in our synagogue tonight; we can phone him if I got enough quarters.'

" 'In my pocket I got enough money to buy a lunch bucket full of quarters,' the Jewish man said, 'but I got no way to give you change; and I got no pass to get out.'

"I butts in then, and said, 'Look, you've got a kid in service?'

" 'Ja, he shoots the tail guns on a bomber,' Papa says quickly. 'Pick up your two-bit pieces and go over to the cafeteria and phone him,' I said. 'They'll have more change if you need it. Don't worry about a pass. I've got a kid in the South Pacific I'd like to talk to for three minutes for any kind of money.'

"They both got down on their knees to pick up the two-bit pieces. Then, at about a half-run, they lit out for the cafeteria. They was gone a long time. I seen the couple come out, and Mama gets on a bus. Papa heads right back to my booth. He's cryin', and he don't give a damn who knows it. 'My son is 'live—I talks to him,' he said happily. 'God seen Mama and me on our knees. He heard the prayers we whispered and the things Mama told her pillow. Ja, my son lives!'

"How long before he gets home?" I ask.

"His back straightened and his chin came up: 'He ain't coming home now. To England he sails tomorrow. His chob ain't done yet.' "

When the carrier contract closed, Papa and Mama were laid off along with thousands of others. They became part of the First Exodus, which was a vast migration of work-weary people back to the homes they had left.

This migration was caused by many factors—not by any single act of management, and certainly not by any planned, concerted action on the part of the workers. It was much to management's interest to keep these trained workers on the job. The cost of recruiting and training a journeyman in any craft averaged $225. That sum, which the books showed, was really but a fraction of the real cost. Add to it the cost of the mistakes every beginner made, the spoilage of material, and the inevitable slowdown in the crew's production. The book cost would have had to be trebled to be even close to the real total. And yet workers were laid off by the thousands. True, they were sup-

5

"I did not threaten him"

In the middle of July 1943, the water level of the Columbia River began dropping sharply. Rumors swept through the shipyard that it would be necessary to lengthen the shipways. The cost of such a job was estimated at a quarter million dollars, but the cost was a minor part of the problem. Work on the carriers would be slowed, if not stopped entirely, and any hope of getting eighteen deliveries by January would be gone. It was then that one of Vancouver's naval architects came up with the idea of *Little Audrey.*

When completed, *Little Audrey* was a steel pontoon which weighed ninety tons and had cost $15,000. She was built in Vancouver's plate shop in eleven days. Christening ceremonies were held, after which a couple of whirly cranes picked up *Little Audrey* and placed her gently in the Columbia River. *Little Audrey* received her first test when she buoyed up the stern of Vancouver's *Midway.* The effect of this maneuver was to raise the river level about three feet. After the launching, the pontoon was partially submerged and towed out from under the stern of the ship. With the launching problem solved by *Little Audrey,* the yard still had its chance for "18 or more by '44."

The workers really turned out for the launching of the *Midway,* but most of them wanted to see the newfangled *Audrey* in action. Many of them also went because it was the ninth ship—half of our objective for the year. Most of us who were interested in the lifting action of the pontoon watched from berth one on the dock. We all agreed that the stern did lift when the ship slid into the Columbia. *Little Audrey* was a success.

This story appeared in the *Bo's'n's Whistle,* September 2, 1943, describing the pontoon, dubbed *Little Audrey.* It was named after the design engineer's secretary, Audrey Palm, and built to keep escort carriers' sterns buoyant in periods of low water. Otherwise, the carriers could teeter on the end of the ways during launchings, causing buckled plates in the ships' centers.

posed to be the unskilled. But in the vast majority of cases, the layoff of the unskilled automatically caused the skilled to leave also.

Suppose a welder and his wife were working in the yard. The wife, a tool picker, got laid off. With a fixed rental of $1.25 per day at any housing project, the wife's layoff slip meant there would be no more savings. The welder's earnings would support the family in Vancouver. His earnings, also in war work, would support them in Mason City, Iowa or St. Paul, Minnesota, too. So, when the welder's wife came home with her layoff slip, the welder asked for his quit slip, too. Then, back in St. Paul or Mason City, a Kaiser recruiter hired another welder and another tool picker, effectively taking their places in Vancouver.

The biggest factors in the first shipyard exodus, as well as those which followed, had nothing to do with management or working conditions. Management could be blamed only for its failure to recognize or stop other factors, if it did know what was happening. Speaking as a worker and for the workers, I am thinking of the gyp practices which were permitted to flourish.

With the full knowledge that wartime prices had to be higher than peacetime prices, I cite the following: the price of $1.25 per day for any housing available in the various Vancouver housing projects was a mild form of robbery. I quote from a housing project booklet: "The Housing Authority collects over $5,300,000 a year in rents, on the basis of 90 percent occupancy, and spends $2,800,000 a year for fuel, water, electricity, garbage collection, taxes, street upkeep, maintenance and office overhead, returning $2,500,000 to the federal treasury." That profit sum of $2.5 million was nothing less than an additional direct tax upon those engaged in war work in Vancouver. Those war-working tenants should have had housing at cost. The total investment of $50 million in Vancouver housing should have been a debt shared by all people of the United States. It was their war. It would have been just as logical for the Army to have charged its soldiers rent for the barracks which sheltered them.

Bus fares from Ogden Meadows and Bagley Downs[5] to the yard were 15 cents one way, 25 cents a round trip. But, the total distance from the yard was only slightly more than three miles! Most of the buses used were the famous "Kaiser Kattle Kars,"[6] supplied by the Maritime Commission and op-

Kaiser buses were referred to as "Kattle Kars," because people were jammed in like cattle. Some workers traveled as far as fifty miles or more from home to job. The *Bo's'n's Whistle* for January 14, 1944, noted that learning how to sleep sitting up was an important art to master.

Arthur Runquist

erated by local transportation companies. These buses had a rated capacity of 100 persons, a normal load of 150 people, and an abnormal load which usually brought a protest: "For Chrisake! How many more are you goin' to jam in this gut shaker?" A sign just inside the doors read, "Don't Spit on the Floor." Whenever one of those buses pulled away from the yard, it was not possible to spit on the floor unless the spitee had a crowbar on his person. During the time they were in service—until V-J Day—the bus haul from the yard must have averaged well over 20,000 round-trip fares per day. The total was probably much higher. The tremendously excessive fares charged for the service rendered were never satisfactorily explained to the working groups. That service to and from the yard should have been free, or at least provided at cost.

Two of the greatest causes of dissatisfaction among workers were the high prices and the minute portions of meals served at Hudson House and the shipyard cafeteria. At the start of the shipbuilding program, Hudson House meals were adequate and fairly low priced. Later, a contractor took over the feeding of the 12,000 tenants at Hudson House; some idea of the new pricing can be had by a single illustration. Bread (two slices) was furnished with the meal. If a worker wanted additional bread, the price was 10 cents for the two extra slices. As there are twenty-two slices to a loaf of bread, the gross income for one loaf was $1.10. All prices charged were listed as having Office of Price Administration[7] approval, but OPA took no interest in the size of the portions.

In all the time of my employment, I never heard a worker complain about Hudson House room service. There were gripes about the "room searches" by Kaiser guards, but the sleeping conditions, cleanliness, and so on must have been excellent, for they were never criticized. The meals were a different story. When men quit on account of inadequate meals, the department heads knew the reason, the yard's counselors knew the reason, the clerks who handled the quit slips had the reason in writing—and yet nothing was ever done about it. A welder who worked with our crew voiced the thought of the hundreds who quit on that account alone: "Whenever I eat a meal that costs me $1.35 and I'm still hungry, I know I've been gypped. I can do war work at home, and that's where I'm going." Thus somewhere in the East, a Kaiser recruiter hired another welder-trainee, and it did cost $225 to recruit and train a journeyman. The taxpayers were losers, too.

Throughout the war's duration, the Machinists Local of the American Federation of Labor[8] fought a losing battle with the syndicate which controlled gambling in Vancouver. The history of that battle is a matter of public record. The machinists' union could not win without some measure of public support and police enforcement. As a public service, the machinists fought—and lost. No excuse is offered here for those who participated, but the open, flagrant gambling wrecked lives and homes, and it was a prime cause of absenteeism and quitting. The fact that it raged unchecked for the duration and beyond is a dirty page in Vancouver's local history.

These were some of the major causes of the First Exodus. There were other gyps, too—some of them with ramifications whose roots could only be guessed. When the workers found they had no recourse, they took the only action available—a quit slip.

When the carrier contract closed, long lines of workers formed outside the quit-slip windows. Only a small percentage were in that line willingly. For every person who had quit, there were scores who had been laid off. They were not blessing the Maritime Commission, which they suspected of being the agency requesting the reduction in force; the workers had been discarded, and they were going home. The war was still on, so that made the leaving a tough thing to do. For a couple of weeks, the highways leading east were filled with cars, trucks, and cars towing trailers. Their going was a setback to the war effort.

8

"Let's stake this kid to enough dough"

The unofficial celebration on the dock which marked the departure of the C4 was tempered only by the fact that another troopship of the same type was being decommissioned. This was the *General Sturgis*. It had taken all of the twenty-one days to complete the alterations and finish the outfitting of the first ship. We expected to take the second ship in stride. There was also the matter of carriers. Five of them, the *Windham Bay*, the *Makin Island*, the *Lunga Point*, the *Bismarck Sea*, and the *Salamaua*, were slated for delivery in May. That would leave us eight to go by July 8.

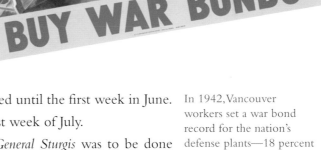

Even at the speed the yard was moving, that plan had an impossible look to it. To keep to the schedule, six ships would have to be delivered in June. Ships every five or six days would have to be the rule for the entire month. The *Roi* and the *Munda*, the last two of the fifty-ship contract, were not even to be launched until the first week in June. Then they were to be delivered during the first week of July.

In 1942, Vancouver workers set a war bond record for the nation's defense plants—18 percent of the yard's payroll.

The work we were to start on the *General Sturgis* was to be done without overtime. True, we had made big paychecks on the twelve-hour shifts, but the treadmillish routine of working, sleeping, eating, working, sleeping, eating, made one wonder if the extra pay was in any way comparable to the sacrifice made. With much of the ease which comes from good coordination, the work on the ship was completed, and the ship was delivered about three days ahead of schedule.

Workers are assembling a whirly crane. These cranes could lift a couple hundred tons. The cab was seventy feet up and the boom extended 120 feet.

C. Herald Campbell

The outfitting of the *General Sturgis* cost, in addition to other treasure expended, the life of one of our pipe fitters. In our group of workers we called him Chuckles, because his laugh was unusual. Nature had endowed him with a laugh that would have made him famous if it could have been broadcast to a laugh-hungry world. Once, when he worked with us on swing shift, he won four of our check pools in a month. It was worth the losing to hear his laughter when he won.

Check pools, incidentally, were a yard habit. Each paycheck bore serial numbers running into five or six figures, and all sorts of pools based on these numbers were organized among the crews of the various crafts. Some, costing 25 to 50 cents to enter, were for fun; others, at a dollar and up, were for blood. A common arrangement made the naughts (zeros) wild and the winner determined by the best poker hand serial numbers.

Chuckles was electrocuted while installing a pipe in a fan room, where all of the big ventilating fans were operating. The motor of one was not grounded, and in some way the pipe he was carrying short-circuited the current through him. Chuckles was knocked down, probably unconscious, his face just inches from the spinning electrical machinery.

He was still alive when he was found, just before shift change. His lips and nose were almost burned away, and the gold had melted from some dental crowns in his mouth. Interns worked over him, and a pulmotor[1] was used; but after a couple of hours, Chuckles passed on.

A statistical survey by the Vancouver Housing Authority of African American workers living in VHA housing projects at the close of the war indicated that 57 percent were planning on remaining in the area. Seventy-eight percent of African American public housing tenants were from the South. They were realistic about jobs after the war and would follow employment opportunities "in any direction except the deep South" according to the survey.

Martina Gangle

Accidental deaths were not uncommon at Vancouver, but they were held to a low level in comparison to man-hours of labor expended. How many accidental deaths actually happened is cloaked in records of the Safety Department, but up to V-J Day Vancouver used 212 million man-hours of labor. The yard lost men and women with the same regret, and for the same purpose, no different than a fighting combat division in the front line.

After the second C4 departed, my crew was assigned to test plumbing and deck drains on the carriers. Final inspection was done by Maritime. To most of the pipe crew the Maritime inspection was a routine: something that had to be done to clear the bookkeeping. The actual objective of sound, watertight, dependable pipe lines was a matter of crew pride. Often, very often, lines which had been passed by Maritime were torn down and re-worked until they met the standards of our pipe department. They had to be right. Our Navy was going to use them.

But, we did get another C4 at Vancouver—the *General Hase*. In my rounds early on the new job, I went down to check the progress of work being done in the hold. The flickering blue glare of a welder's arc flamed on the aft bulkhead. Somewhere in that arc-splashed gloom a man was singing.

It was the welder, a Negro. His voice was a full, rich baritone, and he had all the soaring resonance which is the heritage of the colored. The melody was almost a chant, but as he sang it slowly, it seemed almost a prayer. Hooded, and working steadily, he did not see me. I pulled out my lead book, propped my flashlight so that it would shine on a page of my booklet, and wrote down the words:

> *Big ship gwine to go places.*
> *Big ship gwine to do things.*
> *Big ship takes de boys to wah.*
> *Big ship brings de men home.*

I stared at the words for a moment. In that differentiation between the boys who went to war and the *men* who came home, there was truth. I wanted to talk to the black man. Cautiously I picked my way over the piled chaos of material to him. I waited until he snapped his hood up to change rods.

"Where did you hear that song?" I asked.

He stared at me; then his face showed a line of white teeth as he smiled. "Ah nevah did heah it 'til Ah sings it," he replied.

"Did you write it?" I questioned.

Again came that dazzling smile. "Lookee, Mistah Leadman. Ah cain't read, cain't write, but Ah can sing music. Ah got it in me nateral; it comes out of me nateral."

"How did you know I was a leadman?" I asked.

"Big John Willie wo'ks foh you," came the prompt reply. "He say Mistah Kaisah pays him, but he wo'ks foh leadman Frenchie. Most evah collud boy on de dock knows how you tried to git his wife an' them othah boys' wives jobs in de ya'd. Hit sho is fine to know they is white folks wo'kin' with us who practices some of de things de ministers preaches."

It was possible for me to get employment, as buffers, for two of the wives of Negro pipe fitters. John Willie's wife was finally employed at Oregon Ship as a sweeper. The labor personnel boss of Vancouver's dock refused my suggestion that he send her name in to the union for employment. He stated that such employment would be, of all things, favoritism.

"Are you going to stay in the West when the war ends?" I asked the welder.

"Yassuh. De spinnin' mills down South don' pay no wages. Befoh de wah, hit took de wages of mah wife an' me an' mah son to make rent and eats foh us. De house we lived in was built foh cullud folks only. De mill owned de house, an' if we move somewheahs else, we don' work at de mill.

"When de wah comes on, mah boy enlists when it's decla'hed. He asks foh de infantry, but he gits put in a labor regiment 'cause he big an' strong—an' black. Mah wife an' me stays on at de mill, but we has to use what little we saved to keep even. We heahs 'bout de Kaisah hirin' man, an' we goes to see him. We been heah six months, an' we likes evahthing but de rain. Mah wife gits a dollah five a hour, an' Ah gits a dollah thirty-two. 'Course, hit's Roosevelt money,[2] an' hit don' buy so much; but we is puttin' evah cent we gits into dem bonds. We is puttin' some of dem bonds in de boy's name. When he gits back, we'll have bonds to buy a farm. Wo'k some an' play some, an' go to chu'ch on Sunday." His smile lit up the gloom again. "That's why Ah was singin' when you comes down heah."

I watched him work for a few minutes. The progress he was making made certain that the pump platform would be ready when the shift ended. The glare of his welding arc lighted my way to the long ladder that led to the upper decks. When I paused at the top of the ladder in the bright sunlight, I could hear him down in the gloomy hold, singing.

There was more than sunlight at the top of the ladder. There was a sticky heat which the steel of the ship seemed to absorb. The humidity below decks was relieved by the ship's ventilation, except in those areas where ventilation was being changed. Three of my pipe fitters drew one of those areas—the officers' lounge on the super deck. It was a large room, and in it were

"Here comes Mom with her home work!"

"Here comes Mom with her home work!" Few women were promoted to be leadmen or supervisors except on the sweepers.

141

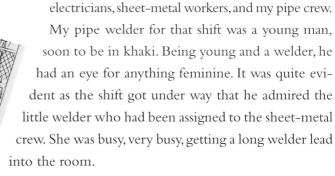

1942

1943

Promotional campaigns encouraged women to enter defense work, when their labor was desperately needed. Subsequent campaigns after the war helped guide women back to the kitchen. The glorification of domesticity in the media shaped cultural values. Most women responding to a *Bo's'n's Whistle* survey said "they intend to make a full time job of keeping house." When there was a rumor the shipyard would reopen, some women wanted to continue in industrial jobs. However, the Vancouver *Columbian* reported on October 2, 1952, that women would only be hired for clerical work.

electricians, sheet-metal workers, and my pipe crew. My pipe welder for that shift was a young man, soon to be in khaki. Being young and a welder, he had an eye for anything feminine. It was quite evident as the shift got under way that he admired the little welder who had been assigned to the sheet-metal crew. She was busy, very busy, getting a long welder lead into the room.

One of my older pipe fitters nudged my young welder. "If you had something like that around the house, you wouldn't need to whistle at anything else," he suggested.

"She is cute," my welder admitted. "Pony type. Lots of Shetland, and no Clydesdale at all. She must have transferred from the ways. Got a nice voice, too. I offered to help her pull lead, and she dogged me off."

All of us watched the young lady as she fastened her stinger to the lead and put a welding rod in it. She touched it to the deck to test it. There was no spark. Pausing only to wipe a bead of sweat from her nose, the lady departed.

"Maybe somebody turned off her machine," my welder observed sympathetically. "It makes me sore when somebody does that to me. I had to climb out of the hold three times yesterday to reset it. Never did catch the guy who did it."

"You don't think you can date her, huh?" my older pipe fitter asked. "Can't you just see her leading a couple of your kids to Sunday school along about 1950?"

"She dogged me off," the young man said. "'No, thank you,' she says. She kinda coos when she talks. Here she comes. Migawd, look at the way her shape pushes her leathers around."

It was evident the young lady was angry. Her face was flushed, and her lips were a thin line. Some bond of the craft,[3] perhaps, caused her to stop in front of my welder. "Look, Curly Locks," she said harshly, "wouldn't that give you a pain in the OPA? My welding bank is clear up on the bow of this GI tub. I pull lead until my tits ache. When I'm already to go, there's more fire

in your eye than there is in my stinger. So I trace lead an' find that one of them black-and-white-hatted Buckler bastards has swiped a chunk of my lead. And did I tell that son of a bitch off! He tried to play innocent. He offers to smack me down. Hell's fire! He can't scare me. I been smacked down in more beer parlors than he ever saw. I don't get his goat until I call him a sheepherder. Then his gang begins razzin' him. He puts my chunk of lead back an tries to 'pologize. Then he wants to know how in hell did I know he'd been a sheepherder? I couldn't tell him that anybody that acted like a son of a bitch looked like a sheepherder. It wouldn't have been ladylike."

From a pocket in her leathers, the little welderette produced a bandanna handkerchief and a compact. She mopped her face vigorously, powdered her nose, and replaced some streaked lipstick. She surveyed the result in the compact mirror and seemed satisfied. Back into her leathers went the hanky and compact. "Look me over, Good Looking," she commanded. "I'm a late model." She spun around for my welder's inspection. "New paint job,

Workers are dwarfed by the giant whirly and tons of steel plate in this night view of the plate storage area.

Arthur Runquist

143

body by Fisher, form-fitting cushions, full-floating rear axle, knee action, easy steering! Where do we go and what do we do when we get out of Kaiser's Koncentration Kamp tonight?"

My welder's mouth was as frankly open as a bird's nest. "I—ugh—my Mother is sick," he stammered.

The welderette eyed him unbelievingly. "You're young enough to have a mother, and you're old enough to be a corporal by Christmas," she observed acidly. "If your mother gets better before the whistle blows, let me know." She walked over and picked up her lead. Just before she snapped down her hood, she gave him a long, searching look. "Sheepherder!" she said explosively.

My older pipe fitter also looked over my young welder disapprovingly. "If I was you, I'd get my mama well, but quick," he said. "When you get to be a corporal, and you've got a six-month's growth, you'll think about what a damn fool you was tonight. Get your hood on, and let's get going. Here comes our Yiddisher[4] with the fittings."

My welder put on his hood. "You know, gang, that little gal has something on the ball besides naughty words," he said. "For the last two summers, in central Oregon, I *did* herd sheep."

Late in the shift the moon came up to make the broad Columbia River a gorgeous thing of silver and blue shadows. The little homey lights of the river's south bank were but the outposts of the broad files of streets which marked Portland's residential districts. Shadowy, but plain in the moonlight, the white cone of Mount Hood haunted the eastern skyline. Up in the bow of the C4, where the moon shadows played hide-and-seek among the banked welding machines, there were a man and a maid. They were seated, side by side and quite close together, when I saw them. Perhaps they were discussing the river or the glowing city, or maybe the moon and the ghostly mountain. When my ex-sheepherder-welder became a corporal, he would be expendable. Perhaps the little welderette sensed that she, too, was expendable. When my pipe welder came back, just before the shift closed, all of my pipe crew noticed the tiny smear of lipstick on his chin. From that we judged that his mother was better.

Our forty-third carrier, the *Hollandia*, was delivered to the Navy on June 1, 1944. That was a day ahead of schedule, and each day was a precious thing as the dock raced to deliver six ships in June. The *Kwajalein* went out on the 7th—two days ahead of schedule. Two five-day ships and two six-day ships would fill out the month. When the *Attu* was launched on May 27, the big, bare, unpainted hull defied anyone's imagination that it could be made into a fighting unit in thirty-three days. Miracles in outfitting were being accomplished on the dock.

Outfitting and repairs were slightly out of the ordinary on the C4. Shipfitters broke records as they installed bulkheads around all the hatches. New gun platforms and larger antiaircraft guns were installed and tested in record-breaking time.

When the pump had been installed and the tanks were in place, my crew tackled the job of the fuel lines. Part of the work entailed the cutting in of a siren up high on the ship's smokestack. I had the services, temporarily, of a tall, colored pipe fitter from Florida. I guided him up the maze of catwalks to a point high in the engine room. From that spot on up a narrow iron ladder rose vertically to the ceiling. Ventilation doors were open, and through them a brisk Columbia River breeze whistled monotonously. With a huge pipe wrench in his hip pocket, Florida began to climb the ladder. He went up and came right back, quickly. There was little steeplejack blood in him.

"Did you do anything up there?" I asked.

"Nosuh, ah didn,' " he replied. He rolled his eyes until the whites showed and shivered a little. "When Ah gits up theah, Ah cain't do a damn thing with mah feet an' Ah has to hol' on wif bofe hands."

There were so many workers in the yard who had had the same experience when they were first required to work high. I thought the humor of it worth sharing with all the workers and tried to get the incident relayed to the originator of Stubby Bilgebottom.

Stubby appeared regularly in a cartoon strip in our shipyard paper, the *Bo's'n's Whistle*. His troubles were our troubles. Once he carried a heavy plate—to the top of the wrong ship. He had his new-shined hard hat spray-painted by a seagull. He lost everything but his shorts in a shipyard-bus craps game. The cute welderette he tried to date turned out to be his own wife. He became a stretcher-borne case for the bughouse when his car-sharing companion unloaded the story of a day's work—in shipyard jargon—as Stubby drove in traffic. Stubby brought laughter to three great shipyards in the Vancouver-Portland area, and at a time when humor was a thing above price. He, too, helped win a war.

The *Munda*, the last of fifty flattops, was launched on June 8. On that date the *Admiralty Island* moved down to berth six to become the "hot" ship.

Cartoonists helped morale and patriotism with their view of shipyard life. Stubby Bilgebottom was created by Ernie Hager, an engineer's aide on the graveyard shift at Swan Island. Stubby was a composite of all shipyard workers. He appeared regularly in the *Bo's'n's Whistle*.

The *Bouganville* was next in line and due out on June 18. The *Matanikau* and the *Attu* were also slated for delivery in June. This was the big ninth inning for Vancouver. Could we make those seemingly impossible deliveries in June, and then deliver the *Roi* and the *Munda* by July 8? Bets were made on the outfitting dock that it could not be done.

It was routine procedure for me to check the "hot" ship at the close of each shift. I had completed my check of the *Admiralty Island* and was talking to the gangplank guard and a group of leadmen of other crafts. It was almost time for the whistle to blow marking the close of the shift when we heard the moan of a siren. It was our first-aid "meat wagon" being driven at speed down the dock's main street. All traffic and the workers of the graveyard shift dove for the sidelines to let the ambulance through. It stopped in front of the *Bouganville*, and a white-clad intern hurried up the gangplank.

"That's damn funny; no stretcher went aboard," a rigger commented. "It looked like the ship supervisor, the sawbones, and a colored gal. What would a colored gal be excited about at this time of night?"

"I'll find out and let you guys know tomorrow night," the guard offered.

The ambulance was still waiting in front of the *Bouganville* when swing-

STUBBY BILGEBOTTOM   by Ernie Hager

shift workers left the yard. Much the same group gathered on the gangplank of the *Admiralty Island* the following shift. There was a chorus of assent. "That colored gal had a right to be excited; her partner had a baby in a cofferdam!" the guard said.

The guard could see that he wasn't believed. "I got it straight from the guards on the *Bouganville*," he assured us. "There was a lot of colored women scraping and buffing in the cofferdams. When they knocked off work to check in their tools, this one gal missed her partner. She went back down into the cofferdam, and the other gal is having birth pains. The gal we saw come up told the ship supervisor, and he phoned for the meat wagon. You fellows saw that part of it. But they couldn't find the expectant mother. The little colored gal was new, and she couldn't remember just what cofferdam she had been working in."

"When the whistle blew, the supervisor had to go. The intern figured that the mother-to-be had got over her pains and had climbed out. So he went back to first aid. But that little gal borrowed a flashlight and kept on searching. When she did find her partner—an hour later—the baby had been born. It was the kid's cry in the dark that located them. The mother had fainted."

After the war, Kaiser Permanente offered membership to the general public. The nonprofit health-care organization prospered and became a national leader in prepaid medical care. It was the model for health maintenance organizations in the United States. On his eighty-fifth birthday, Henry Kaiser remarked to reporters, "Of all the things I've done, I expect only to be remembered for my hospitals. They're filling the people's greatest need—good health."

"It was a boy—premature, of course, and not in too good a shape. The guard on the *Bouganville* guessed that his weight was less than six pounds. The mother was OK. They got her out by loading her into one of those wire-basket stretchers."

"Anybody get her name? We ought to throw a shower for the first kid born in the yard," someone suggested.

"Let's let the women take care of the shower stuff while we do something for the kid," an aged painter-leadman suggested.

"What have you got in mind, Dad—a super shower?" a rigger questioned.

"I worked down South long enough to know that any Negro kid has a tough time getting any kind of education," the painter said. "Only a few get to go to a good high school, and not one in 10,000 gets to go to college. They just don't earn money enough to get an education. Let's stake this kid to enough dough to get him a full medical education. It'll cost ten grand or so to do it right."

"Got any plan for raising that much money?" an electrical leadman asked.

"Nope," the old man admitted. "But it will be easy to do with the gang that's working here. We've got seven big craft unions, and they are not broke. We'll tap them for a grand apiece. Uncle Henry ought to be good for a grand, and so should Edgar.[5] We'll get us a working committee, and we'll canvass this yard, ship by ship, way by way, and into every office until we go over the top. Hell's fire! That's the way we put over the last Red Cross drive, wasn't it? French, can you get us publicity in the *Bo's'n's Whistle?*"

"I can get all the publicity we need whenever we start our collection—'A Buck for the Doc,'" I assured the group. "I believe my Steamfitters Union will contribute a thousand dollars, and I think our pipe department is capable of raising another thousand for Doctor Bouganville."

"You've got an idea there, pipe fitter," a Buckler leadman agreed. "The kid was born on the *Bouganville;* let's insist that one of his names be Bouganville. Doctor Vancouver Bouganville Jones—or Brown or Smith or whatever it is. Migawd, with a name like that he'd be in the chips as soon as he hung out his sign."

"Are you going to be in on this?" I asked the Buckler leadman.

"I hope to tell you we are. We'll match your Steamfitters thousand, and I'll bet you my week's pay the Buckler Company will match whatever cash the Kaiser Company puts in."

"You're too certain to get a bet from me," I replied. "Let's all meet in the men's locker room tomorrow and get organized."

When the meeting was held the following day, there were a dozen or more interested workers present. It was entirely informal, but the old painter leadman served as master of ceremonies. A cash goal of $12,000 was agreed upon, the money to be put in trust.

A great deal of argument ensued regarding this trust. It was finally settled that all the original cash would be converted to war bonds. Two thousand dollars of these bonds would be made available to young Doc Bouganville, when he reached the age of six years. These small initial funds were to be used for clothes, books, and, if necessary, board. The funds were to be released in increasing amounts as the student moved up into the higher fields of learning. If, at any time during the trust, the student died, or refused to continue his education, the remaining funds were to go, as revolving loans, to two Negro colleges in the South.

We were all happy about that settlement. We agreed, too, on the requirement that our doctor should have Bouganville somewhere in his name. We were busy choosing committees when the safety man came in with the news that the little Negro baby had died that day. Our little Doc Bouganville, for whom we had planned so much—and whom none of us had ever seen—was gone.

My crew had been divided and was working on a half dozen ships along the dock. Then, after the C4 *General Hase* had departed, the crew was broken up, and the men went back to their old jobs. Having no men to lead, I was "busted back to a pipe fitter" and reassigned to my old job of inspection and pickup on berth six. Jess was now the only "boss" in the house.

Jess described her part of the carrier program in the following terms: The heat of summer came early in 1944. Perhaps we noticed it more by having to work the two hot berths. The twin boilers were usually steamed up on those berths, and it was not unusual for the pipe crews to test the functioning of the steam heating system, even though the temperature might be well above eighty degrees in the shade.

The warm weather brought its usual problems on and off the job. On the job we took salt tablets and tried to limit the amount of water we drank. Ventilation was a must if we were working below decks. The sight of a stretcher being lowered into a hold to pick up some woman who had fainted from heat exhaustion was not uncommon. I made it a habit to stay close to my crew and to send anyone topside if he showed signs of distress.

Off the job, ice storage was a must if one wanted food to keep. With milk, butter, and meat so closely rationed, ice was a necessity. At Ogden Meadows the windows were screened, but the doors were not. Flies hung in clouds about the garbage cans. Tightly shut doors were the rule in the housing projects. Those who failed to use every precaution often paid unusual penalties. It was entirely by accident that I got to see a couple make such a penalty payment.

While helping my crew break up empty packing cases, I sprained my wrist. After lunch during that shift, I reported at first aid for treatment. The nurse who attended my injury advised me to wait until I could get the use of a heat lamp. I had been waiting only a few minutes when a man and woman hurried in. It was easy to see that both were "brass hats." They were highly agitated, and the man called loudly for a nurse. The ordinarily hard-boiled receptionist was impressed enough by their appearance to get him a nurse at once.

The woman explained: "It was dark where we ate lunch. I ate all of my sandwich; thought it had a damn funny flavor, too."

"Just what was the matter?" the nurse interrupted.

"Show her what's left of your sandwich—just show her!" the man barked excitedly.

The woman handed a wax paper-wrapped sandwich to the nurse. There was some sort of dark meat between the halves of a bun. Being made with a bun automatically let our yard cafeteria and Hudson House off the hook. Buns were too expensive. Only about half the sandwich remained. The nurse lifted a topping of lettuce off the meat, and I could see that the meat was crawling with maggots! "See that? See? That's what we've got in us! Thousands of 'em! And by God we want 'em out of us—but quick!"

The nurse attempted to reason with the couple. In a low voice she explained that many foods frequently had living organisms in them. She was just nicely started on her explanation of the difference between microbes and maggots: microbes were tiny things; maggots were merely elephant-sized microbes. Neither, taken internally and in the raw, were harmful to the human system. The nurse sounded reassuring and was warming to her subject when the man interrupted.

"Hell's bells, sister! Lay off the lecture," the man said. "Both of us have got elephant-sized microbes in us, and we don't want 'em in us. Not by a damn sight! Both of us tried ramming our fingers past our tonsils, but neither of us could puke a drop. Now get on the balls of your feet and do something. Try a stomach pump. Try an emetic, or a physic—or both! An' don' give us any more of that old bull about worms not being harmful to the human system. It'll be six months before my guts gets through turning handsprings."

The nurse was leading them away as my nurse called for me. I have often wondered just what method was used to get "thousands" of active maggots out of two very distressed persons.

As the end of the carrier contract neared, there were all sorts of rumors of huge layoffs, of crews being transferred to the shipways, and of the terrible dangers that lurked at the ways. But, now experienced and job-tested, I secretly hoped we would be fortunate enough to be sent to the ways.

Comfortable shoes with steel caps in the toes for safety were important necessities for performing the job. They needed to be large enough to accommodate heavy wool socks during the cold winter months.

151

My crew and I had good reasons for remembering June 1944. There were six aircraft carriers delivered in that month. We cleaned tanks ahead of the painters. We mucked out asbestos in the engine rooms and cleaned the bilges under them. There was no place in the ship that was strange to us. The last two days before the departure of the ship almost invariably found us working behind the black-and-white hats of the Buckler crews—and just ahead of the painters. There is no single day in that month of June which I remember without thinking of hard work.

But it was a wonderful and inspiring experience to see the ships completed. Whole rooms were agleam with stainless steel. Above the hangar deck forwards were the hush-hush rooms, catapult control, the gyro room, radar, and communications. The contents of these hush-hush rooms were so secret and so well guarded that, of the thousands employed at Vancouver, only a few hundred ever knew what they contained.

Being swing shifters, it was quite often necessary for Chat and I to do our shopping in our work clothes. At first it was a bother to be stared at—and my hard hat, overalls, and heavy shoes certainly brought out the stares. Most of the offenders were women younger than myself. Their faces usually registered curiosity, envy, and sometimes pity. I learned to ignore the stares. Their curiosity I could understand, for it was unusual for a woman of my age to be in heavy war work. It was easy to understand their envy, too. I had the feeling that I was doing something about Pearl Harbor in addition to remembering that it had happened. To tell the truth, I really pitied *them*. They had never gazed into the glass-domed beauty of a Sperry gyrocompass. None of them had ever seen a half-dozen cannon move in unison with a man's body. Nor had they ever viewed the intricate maze of piping whose hidden power could throw an airplane faster than a young man could throw a baseball.

There was something else that we, of Vancouver, share among ourselves. Somehow our yard was casually doing the impossible, making deliveries on a schedule which the entire shipbuilding world had deemed fantastic. The Navy needed those ships then, not later, and the Navy got those ships on time.

9

"This is a fighting ship—give it your best"

The building of the AP5 attack transports was a speed program timed with stopwatch accuracy. The Vancouver shipyard had maintained high speed in the delivery of fifty aircraft carriers. In accepting this contract for the AP5s, the yard moved out of high gear into overdrive. Along with the plans for obtaining material—steel, equipment, and accessories—came some of the best morale and promotional programs the yard workers had ever seen. Best of all, it came at a time when the surging might of America's armed forces was being felt all over the world. We who labored in the arsenal knew that our work was good. Our Navy was no longer the bomb-battered remnants salvaged from Pearl Harbor. It was well on its way to becoming the mightiest fleet the world had ever known.

There were carriers lining the dock when Admiral Howard Leroy Vickery,[1] vice chairman of the Maritime Commission, came to Vancouver to outline the details of the building program. Swing shifters heard him during their lunchtime. It was dusk of a summer evening, and the dock and ships adjacent to the speaker's stand were thronged with workers.

The admiral told of the need for the ships we were to build, which were to play an important part in the attack on Japan. Events were moving fast in the South Pacific, he told us, and we would have to move fast to keep in step. This old-time Navy man told us that we were to build thirty-one ships, and he wanted fourteen before November 1.

Kaiser yards on the West Coast—Cal Ship, Richmond, and Oregon Ship[2]—were to be the teams competing with us. There would be an honor pennant awarded monthly to the leading yard.

The Kaiser Shipyards credo was "It Can Be Done." Illustrations in the *Bo's'n's Whistle* by Douglas Lynch helped motivate workers to labor more efficiently.

Douglas Lynch

153

Oregon Ship had already delivered a score or more Victory-type ships, after producing Liberty ships. Because the Victory-type hull and its turbine power plant were identical to the attack transport, the prospects for Vancouver's winning a race with Oregon Ship looked dim. All phases of the job were new to Vancouver, and we had to go through the sweating-it-out routine with our "study" ships. That job proved to be just as tough with the transports as it had

The secret to fast shipbuilding was prefabrication. Here, two whirly cranes lifted into place a whole deckhouse section weighing seventy and one-half tons.

Louis S. Lee

been with the carriers and the LSTs. It took a couple of months to get through the original revisions, and the revisions of the revisions. But once the construction details were cleared, ship deliveries picked up speed.

Late in July, 1944 I was notified by my pipe supervisor that I would be a leadman again, and I organized a new crew. We tested water lines and drain lines for leaks; we moved pipes and fixtures when their location conflicted with the installations of other crafts. Decontamination of the freshwater system was our biggest regular job, and decontamination of the tanks and freshwater piping of an AP5 was a big job. Three huge tanks aboard ship held a total of 130,000 gallons of water. When those tanks received their first filling, a large amount of chlorine was added to the water. The tanks were then sealed for twelve hours. To make certain that the pipes and fixtures aboard ship were free from bacteria, the chlorinated water was pumped through the entire pipe system. All faucets and valves to the sinks, lavatories, steam kettles, coffee urns, and drinking fountains had to be kept open while the pumps emptied the tanks. Extreme care had to be used to be certain that all chlorinated water had been pumped out of the tanks.

This powerful illustration appeared in the October 22, 1942 *Bo's'n's Whistle*. A full page editorial, "Time is our only weapon," urged shipbuilders to work more effectively and warning that "men and women who deliberately loaf…are slackers not worthy to bear the name of Americans."

Douglas Lynch

IT'S A TRADE SHIPBUILDERS…

…you waste 1 minute, I'll take 8 more lives!

Deliveries of completed ships began in September. The entire yard moved into overdrive when management announced the establishment of a seven-day workweek. Workdays of ten and twelve hours were the rule for many crafts. Only the sweepers remained on an eight-hour day. Under that surge of manpower, our first two ships, the *Oconto* and the *Olmstead,* were sent down the river on September 2 and September 5, respectively. The *Oxford* followed six days later.

The goal of fourteen ships by November didn't look so sure when the *Pickens*, which had taken a week, was delivered on September 18. When the *Pondera* moved down to berth six, it was probably the roughest-looking craft ever to get to that finishing berth. On berth five was the *Rutland*, in even worse condition. Both ships were scheduled to be delivered in

September. On the dock, five dollars got you ten that they would not be delivered on schedule.

As I think back to the work aboard the *Pondera* and the *Rutland*, my memories are those of a chaos indescribable and a confusion unbelievable. The workers were a mob that filled every room. Electricians and pipe fitters worked in the paint clouds of the spray-paint guns; the engine room was a madhouse. The gangplanks were a never-ending parade of men and women going on or off the ship. With all of the crowding, chaos, and confusion, construction went on. Perhaps what was accomplished was not a miracle, but the *Pondera* was delivered on September 24—two days ahead of that impossible schedule. The *Rutland* also beat the deadline and went out September 29— one day ahead of schedule and a week ahead of any date believed possible.

With six ships delivered, the "get 14" program didn't look so impossible. Vancouver had only to deliver two ships each week throughout October. The schedule stated the program quite simply: "Ships will be delivered on Tuesday and Friday of each week." To the everlasting credit of the hundreds who led us, and to the thousands who worked with us, that impossible task was accomplished—and exceeded! Nine ships were delivered in October, for a total of fifteen before November 1.

Those ship deliveries won for Vancouver the AP5 championship pennant for October. Oregon Ship had beat us rather easily in September. That had been expected. Motivated by the same inspiration, they were already in fast production of the same hull, and much the same deck-unloading mechanisms. The fact that we had caught and passed them when they were at speed made our October triumph all the sweeter.

The two California shipyards never really got into the race. In fairness to them, there were labor situations which handicapped the yards' doing new construction. Wages for ship repair were considerably higher than those paid for new construction. That circumstance tended to denude the new construction yards of the skilled labor needed for all-out production. The tremendous attrition of war on all types of ships jammed the repair yards of the Pacific Coast. Late in 1944, the repair needs became so great that it was necessary to tow unfinished ships to Vancouver for final outfitting.

As we moved into our October production, we had one definite indication that we were going to move at top speed. The flood of man- and woman-power began to push the outfitting up river. More and more equipment was installed on the first berths. That power was paying dividends on the ways, too,

One of the first buildings to be completed in Vancouver was the pipe shop.

Louis S. Lee

as nearly all of the heavy equipment and much of the piping was on the ship when it went into the water. By the end of the first week of October, the ships arriving at berth six were almost completely equipped. The testing remained to be done, but the big jobs had been taken in stride on the ways and on the first five berths.

No word picture can convey an adequate idea of the size of the task performed. The ships were not small. Imagine the building of two hotels a week, each hotel to be completely furnished and equipped to care for 2,000 men. Each hotel must have its own water, fuel, and food storage of sufficient capacity to meet the needs of its patrons for six weeks. But these hotels must also float, steer, and be able to drive themselves through the water. The roof of the hotel would be dotted with antiaircraft guns, and every available bit of roof space would have to be utilized to provide space for the hotel patrons' landing boats. On that roof, too, must be located the mechanisms for lowering the patrons' boats three stories below roof level—and to do that job very quickly. Only by such a comparison can anyone conceive the magnitude of the task.

In the rush of outfitting, records were made and broken almost weekly. Many of them are not available. There is one, however, that I can mention with pride. The workers, including myself, did not know we were breaking records. In seven days, October 15 to 21, the marine pipe department installed 132,694 feet of pipe of all sizes. From October 22 to 28, 144,647 additional feet were installed in the ships. My pride comes from the fact that I worked with the men who did that tremendous job and under executives capable of directing and planning it.

Just prior to the national election, there was a naval battle off Leyte.[3] Being shipbuilders, most of Vancouver's workers were Navy-minded. The disappearance of the *Houston* was a prime subject for lunchtime discussion. The loss of four cruisers off Guadalcanal when they were caught "like sitting ducks" by the Tokyo Express was also reviewed many times. We wondered what the Navy would do to the officer responsible for that debacle. The carrier battles of the Coral Sea and Midway were refought many times. But the Leyte scrap held tremendous interest for Vancouver's workers. Facing a power-packed task force of the Japanese Navy was a handful of destroyers, destroyer-escorts, and baby flattops.

The stakes the Japanese gambled for were high. Once the flattops had been brushed aside, the unarmed shipping on the Leyte beachhead would be easy prey. With that supply armada sunk, another Bataan was possible. To win such stakes, the Japanese high command sent the best ships they had at hand. Confronted with this force, Rear Admiral Thomas L. Sprague[4] faced and expected a quick bath and a long swim. In full justice to him and his men, they played the hand well that was dealt to them.

When the Navy released its first dispatches on the Leyte battle, Vancouver's daily newspapers were sold out within minutes after the papers were unloaded. Anyone lucky enough to get a copy was besieged with pleas for resale. Men and women lined the fences and begged for copies—or for word-of-mouth news of the Navy releases. After all, they were "our" ships.

The accounts were read with pride, sorrow, and satisfaction. There was plenty of scope for pride. The carrier planes bombed while they had bombs, and they strafed with machine guns as long as they had ammunition. Then they teamed up with comrades who did have bombs and made diversionary dry runs to let the bomb attacks smash home. There was "smoke on the water" that day. Heroes flew over it, and heroes died in it.

Admiral Sprague stalled for time. He moved away from the beach-head and pounded hard with what he had; his planes and the "peashooters" of carriers. Early in the action the American destroyers and destroyer escorts made a torpedo attack on the Japanese armada. Battered and with their torpedoes expended, they all returned. When the need for relieving fire pressure on the carriers grew great, they attacked again, and did not return. All honor to them.

The *Gambier Bay* was hit hard. The first shell from the Japanese fleet tore through her superstructure. Twenty-five more shells plowed through her in the next hour and one half. Even as the heavy shells riddled her unarmored hull, the *Gambier Bay* continued to make headway. Fire- and damage-control parties worked desperately to save the ship. Her five-inch gun blazed away as fast as it could be aimed and fired until the ship's list made it inoperative. One engine became damaged and useless. The ship kept its place in the line on the other engine. Then, with the list exposing the underbody, a shell tore through both engine rooms. What a hell of white-hot steam and blazing oil those engine rooms must have been!

That hit doomed the *Gambier Bay*. Many of her crew "just waded off the flight deck into the water and began swimming," to quote one survivor. Many of those in the water clung to rafts which had been cut loose from the gun platforms. Some of those rescued were in the water for four days before being picked up.

But many of the American sailors in the water were to see high drama. Past them, as they clung to their rafts, swept the mighty task force of the Japanese Navy. It was on its way to Leyte. There was nothing between it and that objective except the remaining badly battered carriers, and the planes of those carriers.

Time was running out for the Japanese. Ahead of them the damaged carriers were still full of fight. Their five-inch guns could not sink the Japanese heavy units, but they were getting in damaging blows. Overhead the swarm of bombers increased as the battle continued. Under the whip of gunfire from the carriers and a scourge of bombs from planes, the Japanese fleet wavered. Did the airwaves whisper of an eagle screaming in the north? Vice Admiral

Riggers guide a cross-ventilation tunnel into place while welders prepare to do their part.

Arthur Runquist

William Halsey[5]—free to choose ships from the world's greatest naval force—had dispatched his fastest units racing south. These ships were not zigzagging. They were headed for battle at all-out flank speed—in excess of battleships, cruisers, and aircraft carriers—hoping to arrive in time for the kill. Did the enemy get word of the coming of this force? Or did they get all the battle they wanted from the unarmored carriers and their planes?

Far short of the Leyte beachhead, the Japanese fleet turned back. Up above the bridge on Rear Admiral Sprague's flagship, an observer stared unbelievingly through his binoculars. "Goddamnit, sir, they're getting away from us!" he reported disgustedly. That meant victory.

Beyond the survivors of the lost American ships steamed what was left of the Japanese fleet. Many of its ships were unseaworthy. Some went dead in the water and were sunk later by air attack. Those air attacks never ceased until the Imperial Japanese Navy was a broken and useless force, hiding and waiting for its final destruction in the waters of its homeland.

As we read of that sea battle, we shared, too, the sorrow of the American nation. The price of victory had not been cheap; casualties in men and ships had been high. In addition to the loss of the destroyers and the *Gambier Bay*, the *St. Lo* was lost late in the action to an enemy dive bomber. (When launched at Vancouver, the *St. Lo* was christened the *Midway*.) Although tremendous battle damage had been inflicted on many of the remaining carriers, the Vancouver yard's sorrow was mixed with satisfaction for the way the ships had fought. We, who had seen the Stars and Stripes go up on the *Gambier Bay* and the *Midway* for the first time, knew exactly where those flags were when the ships went down for the last time. Our old gangplank slogan, "This is a fighting ship—give it your best," was still in effect. Those who fought on those ships certainly gave their best.

After the battle, many of the damaged ships were brought back to the United States for repairs, but none were brought back to the home of its construction. That was a mistake. There were hundreds of us—old-timers in the yard—who would have considered it a high privilege to repair battle damage. We would have worked our vacation time and donated our pay to Navy relief funds if we could have patched the scars on the ships we loved.

The sea victory, the awarding of the AP5 championship pennant in October, and the election boosted morale in the shipyard to an all-out peak. With the competitive race narrowed to Oregon Ship and Vancouver, the start for November honors was even. Vancouver delivered its sixteenth ship, the *Menifee*, on the day of the election.

The relentless drive for ship deliveries must have caused an endless chain of headaches for those entrusted with procuring supplies. One measure

At night, lights and torches blazed, and the shipyards operated around-the-clock, three shifts a day, seven days a week.

Louis S. Lee

of urgency was that many badly needed items were flown from manufacturing centers in the Midwest. Many items sent by plane were quite heavy and included equipment for turbines, electrical motors, and crates of prefabricated refrigeration control panels. Rumor had it that one bomber load consisted of dishwashing machines!

At one point in the building program, Oregon Ship ran out of steam whistles for the ships under construction. Would Vancouver "loan" Oregon Ship a half dozen whistles? Vancouver responded, but said all its whistles except one were already installed. That last whistle, incidentally, had been sent to the engineering department for detailed blueprinting. Whistles were available on order as soon as Vancouver's machine shop got a chance to work on the blueprints. There were more real journeymen to the square foot in Vancouver's machine shop than in any other department in the shipyard. There were many times when those capable men had no blueprints at all—only a few measurements, perhaps, and a description of the piece needed. "Describe it, and we'll make it"—that was the attitude. The plane deliveries and the yard's own craftsmen kept the needed supplies on hand.

With such heroic efforts to get us the urgently needed supplies, it was easy to push for production. Every crew of every craft highballed. For the first time in the history of the yard, it was possible for foremen and leadmen to take hard-boiled attitudes toward any slackening of production. Close, critical supervision—usually by the leadmen—speeded ship production.

All crafts had speed problems. Perhaps the most affected of all were the painters, since their work could not start until other crafts had finished. Some areas required several coats of paint, and drying periods were required between applications. Painting floors was another headache, because such an area had to be locked or guarded if it was to remain unspoiled until the paint dried.

Oregon Ship and Vancouver staged a hot race for November. Oregon Ship set a quota of eleven ship deliveries for the month. In due respect to our great sister yard, Oregon Ship made its quota. But Vancouver stubbed its toe on its twenty-second ship. There was a defect in the steam turbines that powered the ship.

The turbines themselves were massive pieces of machinery. They were supplied to the yard by Westinghouse, Allis-Chalmers, and Hendy, and each was a marvel of close machine work. For example, gear tolerance was in thousandths of an inch. The space between the meshed gears was "closer than the meat portion of a Hudson House sandwich," to use a well-known yard definition. But on the *Crockett*, those gears were just not right. During the dock trials of the vessel, the gears made a whining noise that spelled trouble.

Men worked around the clock, snatched a few hours of sleep, and worked around the clock again; but the *Crockett* had to be moved out of the line and double-berthed while her gears were honed to tolerance. Yard morale dropped every day the ship lay double-berthed. To make matters worse, another ship, the *Saint Croix*, also developed gear trouble. It was not so serious as that of the *Crockett*, but it delayed the ship's river run for several days. On the big scoreboards over the entrance gates, Oregon Ship moved ahead. In spite of every effort Vancouver could turn out, Oregon Ship kept that lead of two deliveries and was awarded the championship flag for November.

With the Maritime Commission begging for "anything that would steam, steer, and float," three ships were delivered in record time. The *San Saba* was delivered November 30, the *Sevier* on December 4, and the *Bollinger* on December 7. Dock trials on the *Bottineau* were held on December 9, but the jinx was still riding the gears at Vancouver. In the *Bottineau* they were noisy, and the ship's delivery was delayed until December 22.

How fast the pace had been is shown in the following record:

Hull Number	Name	Days from keel laying to delivery	Days from launching to delivery
401	Oconto	150	74
402	Olmstead	147	63
403	Oxford	147	61
404	Pickens	149	59
405	Pondera	149	59
406	Rutland	148	50
407	Sanborn	146	45
408	Sandoval	143	34
409	Lenawee	141	29
410	Logan	139	24
411	Lubbock	137	22
412	McCracken	134	21
413	Magoffin	126	20
414	Marathon	115	20
415	Menard	111	20
416	Menifee	106	20
417	Meriwether	103	20
418	Rawlins	92	20
419	Renville	88	21
420	Rockbridge	77	21
421	Rockingham	71	20
422	Rockwall	72	25
423	Saint Croix	66	21
424	San Saba	62	18
425	Sevier	61	18
426	Bollinger	61	18
427	Bottineau	72	30
428	Cottle	60	19
429	Crockett	91	50
430	Audubon	59	16
431	Bergen	58	17

The end of the attack transport contract was in sight when December began. Only seven ships remained to be outfitted. However, on December 9 the first two of five ships launched at California Ship arrived at Vancouver for outfitting. The remaining ships followed during the next five days. Six ships were delivered in December. Only the much-delayed *Crockett* remained.

Although the AP5 contract record itself is eloquent, the full story cannot be told without mentioning the heavy percentage of absentees as the contract neared its close. The seven-day weeks, long hours of overtime, and broken sequences of meals and sleep left workers physically run down. With the coming of the first cold days of winter, an epidemic of colds and flu riddled yard crews. Those affected most were the older people. There were already few, if any, young men left in the yard. Long gone were the young men who had worked with us on the LSTs and carriers. The AP5 job was done by the 54s, the 64s, the 4-Fs—and the What 4s.

And playing no little part in the grand job were the Negroes. There were full crews of Negro pipe fitters supervised by Negro leadmen, and crews of Negro cable pullers. Negroes installed electrical fixtures, and there were Negro buffers, chippers, shipfitters, welders of both sexes, and painters. Many of these people were full–fledged journeymen before they ever saw a shipyard; many of them achieved that status through study, hard work, and merit after they were employed.

In my memory of topflight journeymen, there were two colored men whose daily work made them especially outstanding characters. I'll call them Jerry and Allen. They were spray painters, and they worked as a team. One of them was tall and broad shouldered. The other was halfpint size. "Ah gits the up-highs an' he gits the down-lows," the taller one said. So well did they do their work that no touch-up was ever needed where they had sprayed. Their average consumption, per shift, was more than sixty gallons of paint. No ribbons are given to shipyard workers, but Jerry and Allen gave their country distinguished service.

On December 20 the *Bergen*, the last ship of the AP5 contract, was delivered. True, the *Crockett* was still with us, waiting for a new set of turbines, but the delivery of the *Bergen* marked the completion of the AP5 job. All of the outfitting crews were busy on the five Cal Ship AP5s, and on another C4, the *General Muir*, which had been brought up from Kaiser's Richmond yard to Vancouver for outfitting. Another C4, the *General Freeman*, was slated to arrive about mid-January. The outfitting dock had plenty of work to do.

The shipways were busy, too. Those of us who had helped outfit the first C4s got a real thrill when the announcement was made that Vancouver had received a contract to build twenty of those huge transports. Within a few weeks, that contract was increased to twenty-five, and on November 15 the first keel was laid for the largest ship ever built in the Portland-Vancouver area. Keels were laid on all twelve ways by December 12. Vancouver—the "Short-Order Shipyard"[6]—was certainly living up to its nickname.

The ways also had a side job on hand. A temporary, special way (number thirteen), had been built to hold the first of two 14,000-ton dry docks the yard had contracted. The middle section was well along in its construction during December, and the launching was scheduled for the middle of January. The Navy wanted that dry dock almost as badly as it wanted AP5s, and work went on around the clock on it. Just for the record, that dry dock was launched on time and delivered on time—Vancouver fashion.

10

"War is waste"

Many people left the shipyard when the AP5 contract closed, but there was no general exodus such as had marked the close of the carrier contract. Most of those who left had definite reasons. Some of them doubted whether the job would last another full school term and merely wanted to get their children started again in their home school. Some who quit wanted to secure a steady job in their home job market. In many of the skilled trades, too, the wages outside were considerably higher than those paid in the shipyards. Still, for every hundred who quit, there were thousands who intended to "hoe on out to the end of the row."

Although many of the workers were familiar with the C4 troopship, only a few realized how much larger they were than the attack transport. In comparison, the welding footage on the C4 was double that of the smaller transport. Pipe footage totaled 150,000 feet per C4. There were fifty-one miles of electric cable in each ship! Each ship had a net steel tonnage of 8,000, a length of 523 feet, and a beam width of seventy-one and a half feet. Steam turbines that generated 9,000 horsepower drove the ship. The C4 was big, and we were scheduled to deliver a ship a week!

To speed the building of C4s, a branch construction plant was built at The Dalles, ninety miles upriver from the Vancouver yard. The C4 required an unusual number of erection sections—wall and room divisions. In an ordinary Liberty freighter, only 400 such sections were required; but in a C4 there were 1,665.

Much of this work was welding, and local people were encouraged to train for the task. With pay at $1.20 an hour, Indian tribesmen from the

The Singing Sentinels quartet provided music at launchings and other shipyard activities such as state picnics. These popular annual summertime events would gather together people from different states at local parks or Jantzen Beach amusement park. Scheduled sports events included adult men's races such as: "Life Begins at 50," and "Fat Men's Sack Race," and for women, the "Egg and Spoon Race."

nearby reservation took to training for welding in a big way. Indians of all ages attended the welding schools and then moved into production. And many of the shipyard's regular welders moved to The Dalles to get better living conditions. When the new plant began production, the completed sections were loaded onto barges and floated downriver to the assembly yard at Vancouver.

Time-saving machines such as the "travagraph" simultaneously performed cutting operations on one steel plate.

C. Herald Campbell

But the welders at The Dalles were a unique group. It was not possible to tell, until they raised their welding hood, whether the welders were male or female, red or white or black.

The transition between contracts was handled better than any previous changeover. There was considerable slack time in some crafts, but it was not the enforced idleness we had known while waiting for the carriers.

There was enough slack time, however, to encourage another cycle of jewelry making. The manufacturing of shipyard jewelry—more or less sub rosa—had flourished in the latter stages of the carrier contract. It burst into full bloom again as we waited for the first of our own C4s. Only a few of the thousands who attempted to manufacture were genuine artists; but when one of the artists did turn out an especially well-designed bracelet or ring, he would be swamped with requests for duplicates from his immediate superiors in the shipyard. Quite frequently, those superiors relayed further orders for more jewelry from their superiors. One welder was kept busy for six weeks on requests from Kaiser brass hats for a ring he designed.

The most austere of the bracelets was made simply by twisting a couple of stainless steel welding rods tightly in a small-diameter pipe. The ends were then welded solidly, and the bracelet-to-be was flattened by lining up a whirly to flatten it. It was then cut to size and shaped to fit a lady's wrist. This preliminary work usually used up a couple of shifts. Polishing and buffing might require several additional shifts before the *objet d'art* acquired the gleam its designer intended.

Some of the more intricately designed bracelets were made from bits of stainless steel salvaged from galley-trim scrap. These were frequently en-closed in patterns of woven stainless-steel rods and beautifully engraved. Some of them would have brought twenty dollars in the better stores—and many of them cost the taxpayers five or six times that amount. So general was the

Huge monolithic cranes in the assembly area are colored yellow and act as a counterpoint to the yellow ship hull in the distant ways. The painting's style, with its sketchy line work, suggests that Albert Runquist is the artist.

Albert Runquist

jewelry making that neatly stenciled signs appeared in all the welding booths: No Rings Welded Here.

There were many other "home projects" conducted on a major scale. Lamps and lamp stands were made of bits of bronze and copper. Knives of all kinds—butcher knives, hunting knives, and knives for attack—were made from discarded files, and from heavy-gauge saw blades. Some inquiring soul reasoned that armor plate should make a good frying pan. Most of the stuff in the yard was a half-inch thick and capable of taking a high polish. Frying pans and hotcake griddles were made by the ton. Every bit of armor-steel scrap was diverted to home-project artisans.

Curiously, much of the yen to make something of scrap came from the worker's hatred of waste. If the armor-plate scrap had been saved and guarded until the last ship was built, it would have been a rusty pile of steel which some junkman would have bought for a few dollars a ton. Many of the knives made of old files and heavy-gauge hacksaw blades found their way into the hands of fighting sons in the South Pacific.

Time and human effort were wasted by the workers at Vancouver who made useful articles out of the waste scrap. Time and human effort also were wasted by the miners who dug the ore for making armor plate. The same can be said about steelmakers who fashioned the scrap's hardness. Every shell, plane, gun, tank, and ship was waste. Millions of crosses standing over remembered—and unremembered—mounds speak mutely of the waste in human lives. War is waste.

At the height of the changeover, when the ways were swamped with production needs, outfitting dockworkers were encouraged to take vacations if they had been earned. The sweeper crew headed by Jess had been active on both the outfitting dock and ways during this time. She worried about safety on the docks because of pickups, fast-moving Hysters, and other vehicles, and whirly crane loads that "moved overhead continually."

Jess commented about the ways: It was just as noisy there as ever—but I loved it. When the shipfitters "wedged in" a steel plate, the clang of their sledgehammers had all the majesty of the hammers in the Anvil Chorus.[1] The roar of a score of chipping guns was deafening at times, but their thundering sound crept into one's blood and stayed there.

When our temporary transfer to the ways ended, we were asked to take a week's vacation. I welcomed that, too, and I used that week to do some long-delayed housecleaning at our home in Salem. That week at home was heavenly. All my yard flowers were in bloom, and my wildflower bed was a riot of color. Being home with all the comforts of refrigeration, radio, and a real stove only served to place in sharp contrast our method of living at Ogden Meadows.

The two-burner electric plate at Ogden Meadows, for example, was a definite handicap in the preparation of adequate meals. We used it only for breakfasts and our midnight lunches. To get meat, and a variety of other food, we usually ate at the yard cafeteria just before going on shift.

Early in February 1945, Chat continues, Vancouver's workers read of the loss of the *Ommaney Bay*. The ship was a victim of a Japanese suicide plane on January 4. The plane crashed into the bridge and then onto the flight deck. One of its bombs exploded on the flight deck; the other exploded four decks below. The second bomb must have ignited the aviation gasoline in the huge tanks. Fires raged uncontrolled below decks, and fires exploded gasoline tanks and ammunition in the parked planes on the flight deck. Racked by explosions and swept by fire from bow to stern, the ship had to be abandoned. It was finally sunk by our own forces. How many of her men perished with their ship was not stated in the Navy release, but the additional loss of two of our Vancouver-built LSTs was confirmed.

The platform for the launching of the *Casablanca* gets spruced up before the ceremony.

Louis S. Lee

Late in February we received news of the loss of the *Bismarck Sea* off Iwo Jima.[2] Two suicide planes got the ship. One crashed into her starboard side just above hangar deck; the other plane crashed through the flight deck just forward of the aft elevator. Fires started among the planes parked there and explosions raged throughout the ship. The *Bismarck Sea* capsized and floated bottom side up for almost a half hour. Many—too many—of those fine boys I had seen at Astoria went to the bottom with her.

Early in the carrier contract, it had been easy for griping Navy personnel to call our flattops Kaiser Koffins,[3] but after the Leyte push the attitude changed in the Navy. There was no more talk of "wavering plates" when it became known that the *Kalinin Bay* took twelve eight-inch shells and remained afloat. Within three hours after that hammering, two suicide planes crashed the ship. The *Kalinin Bay* was one of the ships brought back to the United States for repair.

Following the Leyte battle, the baby flattops continued to give air cover to the invasion forces. Each ship was a preferred target for Japan's air forces. In the battles which raged around the Philippine Islands, many of the carriers were damaged by suicide planes. Among them were the *Marcus Island*, the *Savo Island*, the *Kadashan Bay*, the *Kitkun Bay,* and the *Salamaua*. The *Fanshaw Bay* had been heavily damaged off Saipan,[4] the *Lunga Point* was damaged off Iwo Jima, and the *Wake Island* had a huge hole blown in her bow plating off Okinawa. The ships were part of the "Fleet That Came To Stay," and stay they did, in spite of every method the Japanese could devise to get rid of them.

Although there was still grim news of losses of men and ships in the South Pacific, it was clear to all that Japan was taking a beating. In Europe, too, the Battle of the Bulge[5] was a thing of history; Allied armies were across the Rhine River, and the end of Hitlerism was in sight. In March 1945, at Vancouver, we were building transports "to bring the boys home in." On March 23, Vancouver launched its first C4 trooper, the *Marine Tiger*, and on that day our last Richmond conversion job, the *General Freeman*, went on her river trial run.

But the names selected for our C4s were somebody's brainstorm. Vancouver's workers nursed a deep suspicion that some ex-high school girl had been entrusted with the duty of selecting them, and had achieved her inspiration after a visit to an aquarium. All the ship names, except one, were preceded by the word *Marine*. In the order of their launching, they were: *Tiger, Shark, Cardinal, Falcon, Flasher, Jumper, Serpent, Ernie Pyle, Carp, Marlin,* and *Phoenix*.

Throughout the yard, the feeling was that the naming of a troopship for Ernie Pyle was a nice tribute to the man who had endeared himself to millions of his fellow Americans. But the ridiculous names selected for the other ships left a sour feeling. There must have been enough names of servicemen who won the Medal of Honor—posthumously—to have graced the other ships.

One of the events most vividly remembered by yard workers occurred shortly before V-E Day.[6] Jess describes that happening: There came a day in April when we entered the cafeteria to find it hushed and quiet. We selected a table and prepared to line up for food selection. We were still wondering why everyone was so solemn when one of Chat's *Bo's'n's Whistle* friends entered. He was hatless and somewhat breathless. He stopped in the middle of the room and held up his hand for attention. "Ladies and gentlemen, we have just had confirmation from Washington," he said. "The President passed away twenty minutes ago." He pointed toward the Administration Building. "Look," he said.

The proud flag that flew there was coming down—slowly. At half-mast it stopped, and we knew then that all the world had lost a friend. We, of the little people, had lost a true one.

The flag was still at half-mast when V-E Day arrived, and that fact tempered any celebration that might have developed. Throughout the yard the most common regret expressed was, "If only FDR could have lived to see it through."

Conditions for the fast construction of ships about this time were not good. In spite of new hires—and rehires—the total employed personnel kept dropping month by month. The unrest among the workers stemmed from many sources. There had been an all-out attempt in Congress to draft labor, and there had been loose talk in Washington, D.C., of ship cancellations following V-E Day. Many of the thousands who remained until V-E Day had

Launching of the
S. S. ERNIE PYLE

JUNE 25, 1945
SPONSORED BY
MISS BABETTE JOHNSON

Named for the noted war correspondent and Pulitzer Prize winner, Ernie Pyle (1900-1945), this ship launch was a well-publicized event.

Three riggers maneuver material on a hoist while the huge wheel of a steel-plate cutting machine dominates the background. Workers stayed on the job and finished the job to win the war on the home front.

Arthur Runquist

farms in the Midwest or in nearby states, and with the coming of another crop season they wanted to go home and get in their crops before it was too late. So after V-E Day, the employment curve plunged downward: between October 1944 and August 1945 the net loss was 11,400 workers.

V-E Day was quiet at Vancouver. All hands were glad the war in Europe was over, but there was no celebration to speak of when the end did come. There was a great deal more patriotic enthusiasm over the battle off Leyte. So far as the West Coast was concerned, the real war had been in the Pacific. That was the grudge fight. Pearl Harbor had not been forgotten.

After V-E Day, we knew the ships we were building would go to the South Pacific. We had guessed that to be their area of service because of many signs. Seaweed was reported to be heavy in those waters; there were seaweed strainers on all the firefighting nozzles aboard ship. Ventilation and refrigeration were more than adequate, and great care was taken in their installation.

With the reduced labor force available, it took until June 15 to get delivery on the first of the troopships. Shortly before its delivery date, an accident nearly caused the sinking of a vessel. The ship, the *Marine Tiger*, was on berth six when a workman received orders to fill the deep ballast tanks on the starboard side. The workman protested the order, claiming that filling the tanks on that side would only cause the ship to list.

In the bays of the plate shop, workers cut, bend, drill, and punch steel plate, an average of 1,900 tons a day according to the *Bo's'n's Whistle*.

Arthur Runquist

Under protest, the workman began the filling. Before the tanks were half full, the ship suddenly lurched to starboard, and all shore connections for lights and water were broken. The gangplank connecting the ship to the dock fell into the Columbia, trapping those aboard. Only the steel cables which held the ship to the dock kept it from capsizing. So great was the strain that one huge section of the dock and its piling were torn loose. But the remaining cables managed to hold the ship.

There was confusion aboard for a short time. Scaffolding blocked doors and other exits. Darkness made any movement difficult. But the whirlies removed workers to safer quarters on the dock, until the list was overcome and the ship was on an even keel. In the height of the confusion, a group of Negroes gathered on the aft end of the ship to pray. One Negro kept interrupting a very sincere prayer with the moan, "Why in hell didn't

175

Ah stay in Memphis?" Another colored man earned the nickname V–1 (German rocket bomb) by his rocket-like ascension from the depths of the engine room to the superstructure deck. There were many others who would have liked to have had his speed.

The *Marine Tiger* had the dubious honor of being the first ship Vancouver had ever delivered behind schedule. It was fifteen days late. The *Shark* was delivered twenty-five days late and the *Cardinal* was thirty-three days off the pace.

The ships were supposed to be urgently needed, and the yard received a telegram from Vice Admiral Vickery stressing the need for the ships. Henry Kaiser, in his V-E Day message to the yard on May 8, 1945, had restated that need, and asked all workers to stay on the job. From every bit of information the workers could get, the need for their services was great. Production of ships was a vital thing, and yet on June 18 all leadmen at Vancouver were downgraded. About one of every fifty was promoted to foreman. The order did not apply to sweepers, or in some cases, to painters. But in almost all other crafts the leadmen were out.

Shipfitters and electrical personnel, sheet-metal employees and pipe workers, were hard hit. Hundreds of leadmen took their quit slips and left the yard. Those men were key personnel and almost to a man were irreplaceable. At one stroke, all the teamwork built through three years of trial and error was destroyed. Real supervision was never present in the yard after that. Each ship, as it lagged behind its delivery date, helped prove the fact.

Most of the men who left the yard did so with regret. It was not the loss of a job that concerned them. Jobs were for the asking. One young man, an old-timer in the yard, summed up the feeling of all of them: "If our government really needs the ships, no act of sabotage by a foreign agent could have slowed down production so effectively."

The "busting" of the leadmen was preceded by about two weeks of rumors of what was to happen. Rumors traveled fast at Vancouver. One reportedly traveled the length of the 3,000-foot dock in eight minutes flat.

No one knew better than I that the promotions would go to the leadmen of the installation crews. My crew was essentially turned into a repair and inspection outfit.

As part of the yard changes, I had to take a setback to a pipefitting job. It wasn't the easiest thing for me to do, but it did prove to be the wisest. Jess and I talked over the various angles and mutually agreed to "hoe on to the end of the row." We had planned some home improvements on our Salem home and were saving to meet their cost. Overnight the crew I formerly led was scattered among other crews on the dock.

Despite my loss of status, my work on the C4 troopships proved to be as interesting as it had been on the carriers. I learned much from the association with my co-workers. When one got to know them intimately, all their hopes, ambitions, and despairs came to light in their conversations.

The sweeper leadlady whose captain son helped take St. Lô[7] in France never wore the Gold Star she was entitled to wear. Our sharp-tongued electrician lady who had a son on Bataan learned that her son would be on Bataan forever.

There was one young lady who worked sheet metal who had personality plus. She worked hard, regularly, and with considerable skill. Jess and I knew her first on the carriers, and we shared a table at the cafeteria with her. Part of her personality showed in the decorations on her lunch bucket. It was neatly stenciled—*fore* and *aft, port* and *starboard*. There had been a considerable number of thefts of dinner pails, and to prevent a "mistake" her bucket also read: *The hell it's yours, put it back.*

Late in the AP5 contract, the young lady told us that she had signed up to join the WAC (Women's Army Corps).[8] Within just a few days, we missed her and her "unstealable" lunch bucket. Months later, though, she visited the yard again. She was in uniform, and her figure did as much to the uniform as the uniform did to her figure. She was as neat and trim as anyone

This brightly colored scene shows female workers taking a break. The faceless males seem to appear as a menacing force in the background.

Arthur Runquist

could hope to picture an American girl. I offered congratulations and told her I thought she was smart to join the WAC. She shook her head. "I wasn't too smart," she said. "I should have joined up two years ago. So should have all the rest of the young women in this yard. We've all missed the best part of the show." We were very proud of that young lady. She was one of us.

This oil sketch study was commissioned by the *Oregonian* for a public relations campaign on Oregon's contribution to the war that appeared in *Time* magazine.

Douglas Lynch

After V-E Day, there was a pronounced letdown in the yard workers' morale. There was a feeling that victory was a foregone conclusion, and many of those who quit did so because of that feeling. The leadmen's supervision was missed, too—far more than those who planned the quit slips had imagined. There were "sitting ducks" all over the ship; whole crews hid out for hours at a time.

One hard-driving ship supervisor summed up the situation as he pointed to the men and women lining the shady side of a ship one hot day: "This is the first damned job I've ever had where a hundred so-called workers can just stand and look at me, and I can't do a damned thing about it." He was right. The job had become a glorified WPA. Nobody seemed to give a damn.

The fast-moving events in the Pacific stood in sharp contrast to the letdown in the yard. It was no longer easy to read of the war in the Pacific. Before Okinawa was taken, one newspaper release was callous enough to state that "only six of our bombers failed to return." That was probably a slipup in the handling of the news; and, with hundreds of bombers taking part in the mission, it *was* probably a small loss. But liberated prisoners of the Japanese had talked to us in the yard—men of Bataan and Corrigedor—and told us what kind of an enemy we were facing. It was easy to guess what happened to the crews of those six bombers, even if the bailouts had been successful. But the B-29s continued to trace America's anger, in fire, on the cities of Japan.

During a lunch period in the early fall, we were called to attention by the yard's public-address system. We heard our new president, Harry Truman, tell of an event—the elimination of an entire city by one atomic bomb! It was a strange word in a strange message. We looked at one another in the dusk, on August 6, 1945. What was atomic power?

Many of the yard's workers had been employed on a gigantic secret project called Hanford,[9] near Yakima. They told us of huge buildings whose floors, walls, and ceilings were made of twelve-foot-thick concrete. Their guesses were that some sort of explosive was to be manufactured at Hanford, but so well was the secret guarded that none of them knew any more than we did.

After the president's message that night, I found a colored woman crying as she prayed on a ship. She was hidden in the shadows of the five-inch gun on the stern of the ship, and I tried to move away without her seeing me. But she spotted me and got to her feet. "Ah got to tell somebody besides God," she said huskily. "Mah boy is out yondah wid de fleet. He jest a boy—but he 'listed lak a man. He say nobody gwine to do his fightin' foh him. Mistah French, Ah been so worried 'bout dat boy 'cause he on one of dem little hellships.[10] Dey jest one-beach boats. You hear'd de Presumdent tonight? Dat new bomb thing means dis ol' wah's 'bout ovah, an' mah boy is still 'live. Ah'll see mah boy ag'in—bless de lawd—ah'll see mah boy ag'in!"

She was standing in the shadow of a five-inch cannon. It was now another gun that would never be fired to kill—a gun, like all guns, that had been made completely obsolete by a new power God had given to man to use.

We read of Hiroshima and, a little later, of Nagasaki. The end of the war was near. It was even nearer after Vice Admiral Halsey's power-packed fleet currycombed the edges of the Japanese homeland with screaming steel. The Russians were on the move in Manchuria, and peace was near.

Jess and I had a vacation due. Throughout that long, hot summer we had consoled ourselves with the thought that the Newberry Crater in central Oregon would be quiet, peaceful, and cool. We argued the merits of the fishing in the twin lakes (East and Paulina) of the crater. We flipped a coin, and East Lake won the toss. We departed on our vacation.

A doe watched us put up our tent in the Forest Service campground. It was that peaceful. We could hear the rustle of the doe's dainty feet in the pumice of the shoreline as we made our bough mattress. It was that quiet. We dined that first evening on one trout, a three-pound rainbow whose three sections filled our big frying pan. Two other fish of equal size hung in sacks from a pine limb in front of the tent.

We had camped four or five days, and with three or four other boat parties we fished on the north side of the lake. It was late in the afternoon when another boat joined us and dropped anchor. The lone fisherman, a man, got out his tackle, baited up, and began fishing. "You folks heard the latest war news?" he asked casually. "The Japs throwed in the towel about an hour ago. I got the flash on my car radio while I was coming up the mountain." That was the way the news of the end of World War II came to us. Nobody cheered. Everybody went right on fishing.

Nobody doubted him, but actual confirmation that World War II was really over came from another source. One of the first parties to arrive at the campground shortly afterward told us that gas stations in Bend no longer required OPA gas coupons. The war really was over.

When we returned to the job, we found that many things had happened. The atomic bombs had not only blown Hiroshima and Nagasaki off the map, they had also blown the aircraft contract (CVEs)[11] right off the yard's drafting boards. Five of the C4s had been cancelled; the first twelve troopships were to be completed. The remaining eight hulls were to be converted into modern freighters.

There was other interesting news. No more guns were to be installed on the ships. If the guns were already aboard, they were to be left. The first ship affected by that order was the *Ernie Pyle.*

"Streamlining" became part of shipbuilding. Whenever a man or woman or crew could be spared, they were streamlined (laid off). In the efforts to reduce the working force, some strange activity resulted. For example, half the available force of firefighters was terminated in a body. While the guards were supposed to take over fireman duties—checking fire cans to see if they had water in them and filling the cans when they had been used—they griped about the work.

On November 8, there was more streamlining. For many of the paint crews that was *the day.* With an hour and a half left in the shift, foremen went through the ship giving out layoff slips. Painters and paint carriers took off like so many flushed quail to their locker room, where they retrieved liquor from its hiding place. A half hour later, the "painters' parade" started up the dock. Men and women, arm in arm, sang *Auld Lang Syne* in the rain. They had their honorable discharge papers and were going to collect their "rocking chair money" (unemployment pay) and live the life of Riley.[12] On the *Marine Phoenix*, the half-painted floors, the paint brushes, and the partially filled buckets marked the exact spot where each painter got his layoff slip. The graveyard crews took over the unfinished job, completed it, and then got their layoff slips.

The *Marine Phoenix* sailed at dawn on November 9, 1945. It was the last troopship built at Vancouver, and I believe it was the last troopship built in the United States. The broad, gun-less gun decks flattened the ship's outline and enhanced the beauty of her contour. It was a beautiful ship. But it was a troopship built to carry American boys to and from distant battlefields, and there were installations aboard it that were not beautiful. There was a hospital aboard, complete with surgery, dispensary, and sick bays. There were two complete dental offices and a sickbay galley. There was a modern sterilization room where chrome plating gleamed under soft lights. There was a room for the treatment of venereal diseases acquired by our fighting men in foreign lands, and three observation wards for mentally injured or diseased GIs. One section of six small rooms was set aside for those who knew not what they did; the peepholed doors of the rooms locked automatically, and they contained no furniture or heat.

The *Marine Phoenix* did not carry guns because the atom bomb had made them obsolete, at least for a time. Our nation was at peace and wanted only peace. If cannons were obsolete, then armies, as such, were also obsolete. We hoped that most of the paraphernalia of war had been outmoded by science. The science that had conceived and developed atomic power doomed the kind of war our histories recorded. No history will be written of an all-out atomic war. There will be no one to write it and no one to read it. If the *Marine Phoenix* was *not* to be the last troopship, and if the wars should continue, may God have mercy on the world we knew.

11

"All that we wanted was peace"

Eight freighters to go. That was the job on November 10, 1945. We had heard glowing reports of progress in reconversion of the *Louis McHenry Howe*. The ship was to come to the outfitting dock 90 percent complete. The *Mt. Whitney*, the second freighter, was supposed to be almost as far along as *Louis McHenry Howe*. But when we first went aboard the ships, it was quite evident that somebody's pencil had slipped. If anything, they were 90 percent incomplete. So were all the rest of the ships the ways were launching as soon as they were floatable.

Plans called for ship deliveries ten days apart after the *Louis McHenry Howe* had been completed. Again, someone was doing some mighty wishful thinking. The driving, job-tested leadmen were long gone. The old, wartime, full "power pack" of men and women on the upper berths of the outfitting dock were gone, too.

One by one, the big input plants went down—the plate shop, deck erection, assembly, and boiler erection. After each launching, the way shut down and most of the workers on it were laid off. The activity of each of the big whirly cranes ceased when a ship was launched from its way. One of the strange contrasts of the busy yard we had known was the sight of all twelve of those cranes in perfect motionless alignment.

The scaffolds came down from the ways to be piled as "standby timber for World War III." The yard's trucks and the Maritime Commission buses

Launching of the last ship, SS Scott E. Land, a C4 cargo carrier took place at 6 p.m. Saturday, November 24, 1945, on way eleven. The C4 cargo carrier was named for the father of Admiral Land, chairman of the U.S. Maritime Commission.

The Vancouver shipyard closed down in May 1946. It was "mothballed" as a reserve yard and kept on standby basis in case of another national emergency. The yard was considered for other uses during the 1950s, but by 1957 the twelve shipways, craneways, and eleven service buildings were demolished and removed from the long-dormant yard. In 1960, the government sold the property. Of the more than seventy-five U. S. Maritime Commission shipyards active during the war, only four installations were held in reserve.

Arthur Runquist

became backup material. Parked in neat rows, and with their tires removed and in storage, they were mute reminders of the days when thousands depended upon them for transportation, and hundreds fought for the privilege of being overcharged to ride in them. The "golden stairs" of the shipways were burned on the dump. So were the sawhorses and ship-scaffold timber. Good dimension timbers of all sizes and grades and plywood in broken lots and sizes were burned in carload lot amounts daily at Vancouver as the close of the contract neared. Right at the time when civilian housing needs were the greatest ever known in the Portland-Vancouver area, lumber was considered expendable.

It took a long, long time to get the *Louis McHenry Howe* ready for delivery. It was a month late in the ship's launching, which was held up until the ship's two upper decks had been removed. Actual launching took place on September 22. Its presence on berth one was signaled by the roar of chipping guns, which for months were removed as bulkheads to make freighter holds. The ship followed the outgoing troopers down through the berths, but each move only emphasized the vast amount of revisions that were yet to be made.

The long delays on the *Louis McHenry Howe* did make possible the transfer of some surplus labor to other ships on berth six. The pipe crews, of course, were far ahead of most of the other crafts and were working on all the ships. The shipfitters, sheet-metal people, electricians, and painters were all far behind schedule. Two sections of the Buckler Company group—

the furniture installers and the crews that put wallboard on bulkheads and ceilings—were also tardy.

After the *Louis McHenry Howe* was delivered early in February and the *Mt. Whitney* on the twenty-first of that month, a new schedule was arranged. It showed the *Scott E. Land*, the last ship to be delivered, on April 10. Many of the crews of welders, burners, and shipfitters that had been transferred from the ways to the dock were laid off as their jobs were completed. On many calendars throughout the dock offices, the date April 10 had a red circle around it. April 10, 1946, was *the day*.

Just the fact that there was a date for the job to end caused a resurgence of the old Vancouver spirit. There were no bunting and slogans this time, but the desire to finish with the task was planted in those people. Instead of complaining when they were laid off, they celebrated. Some work might have been done by those laid off in the first part of the shift, but the second half was devoted to saying "good-byes" and to sampling the various brands of liquid refreshment carried by those who were "caught in the draft."

Many of these people were packed, ready to pull out for their Eastern or Midwestern homes within a few hours after their layoff. But there were thousands who planned to settle in Oregon or Washington permanently. Many had already bought farms or homes.

With the exception of painters, all crafts were cut to a standby force when the *Mt. Davis* departed. All major installations on the last ship were to be done by day-shift workers. The dock had a deserted look during swing-shift hours. Labor crews on day shift were busy tearing down the dock's tool and supply rooms. Some of the better-built supervisor shanties were saved for Navy use. The Navy, incidentally, had arranged for use of the dock for small-craft moorage. Some of the ships were to be packed in grease—inactivated— just in case the much-publicized organization of the United Nations turned out to be the "Frisco fiasco."

The cafeteria closed in mid-April. Its staring, empty-eyed windows in the yard's west end matched similar windows in Hudson House on the east end. A couple of aged men prowling through the debris of the salvage dump for bronze, brass, and lead were the only signs of life in the east-end area. No skiptrucks roared past the giant assembly building on their way to salvage or the dump. The big Hysters, whose automatic horns once added to the din of the yard, were parked and silent. The twin homes of the "twenty-four-hour-a-day roar"—boiler erection and deck erection—were very quiet. In the yard's Tin Pan Alley—the sheet-metal building—a low whistle echoed. All assembly ways were in use for storage of surplus equipment. Some worker had linked two of the big hooks of the overhead cranes together; they looked as if they were a pair of folded hands. The plate shop, where men labored with flame to shape steel, was as quiet as a white-crossed mound on Biak Island[1], a wartime battle area. Kaiser-Vancouver was at standby, waiting to see if the United Nations would stay united.

The buildings that had housed the thunder were quiet because the little people who created that thunder were little people again. The shipfitter was again a service-station operator. The rigger was back in the timber again. John Willie, the black chain-hoist man, was repairing automobiles. John Willie, like other thousands, had never seen a ship until he worked on one, but he *did* put a lot of pipe in a lot of ships. The bold-eyed lady from Galveston had gone back to Texas. Perhaps she made her tin hat into a flowerpot. It is also possible that, among her trinkets, she had a membership button of the International Hod Carriers and Laborers Union. If she resumed her former activity, the oldest profession, she would not need a tin hat *or* a union button. At Vancouver, she swept the decks of many a ship. If there was fuel oil to be mopped up, she was there, on her hands and knees in the reeking filth, with the rest of the sweeper crew. On Bataan and on Corregidor in 1942, MacArthur's men prayed for ships. The lady from Galveston, and those other thousands, built the ships that made it back to Bataan and Corregidor.

The huge, equipment-stored buildings of the yard, the big whirly cranes, the locomotives and those miles of track, the fleets of trucks and buses, the mountains of typewriters and filing cases—those things were also on standby. So were the Mabels, the Bills, the Old Black Joes, and the lady from Galveston. Let any nation mark the fact that the strength of America lies in the ability of her people to work intelligently in the creation of things America needs.

Let any other nation, too, note and remember that America's little people will always be well directed in any emergency. America has many Henry Kaisers.

Her system of free enterprise produces leaders who develop executive ability and organizations capable of accomplishing any task America conceives.

In the closing weeks of the job, we missed the people we had known so well. We missed the lady in the rigging loft whose skill made magic in canvas. Gone, too, were most of the expediters and the old, gray men who issued tools in the little shacks along the dock. Scant weeks earlier, the dock had been thronged with thousands of workers like ourselves; then there were only hundreds. As the ships were sent out, the hundreds dropped to scores of people we knew. All of our joy of completing a task was marred by remembering those no longer with us. They were not dead, but the effect was much the same. We hoped to see them again someday, but that day was a vague thing. Our friends had just gone on, a little ahead of us.

When Mrs. O'Leary's famous cow kicked over a lantern, the fire that resulted set Chicago back on its heels. Much the same thing happened to the *Scott E. Land.* Two welders, working on the deck above tank top in the refrigeration hold, set the ship afire. It happened on day shift, and by tremendous effort was confined to the refrigeration hold. When the yard's fire department and equipment, called from the city of Vancouver, brought the blaze under control, all of the third-deck refrigeration had been gutted. The

Laborers with very different backgrounds all worked together in a common cause to win the war for the Allies.

C. Herald Campbell

refrigeration area on the tank top was completely flooded, and smoke damage had been extensive on the decks above. The fire's cost was estimated at more than $50,000.

The fire moved *the day* forward. The day of the fire became *the day* for a couple of thousand day shifters. On swing shift, the standby crews were cut in half. Reductions in force continued as the first week after the fire ended. Riggers, shipfitters, sheet-metal workers, electricians, and many of the buffers made up the hundreds laid off on swing shift. With full knowledge that they were to go by the weekend, most of those workers came prepared to celebrate.

And celebrate they did. The rigger's room on berth six became a place of song and story throughout the shift. The singing was not particularly good, the stories were "aged in the woods," but the imbibing was of topflight quality. There was so much earnest imbibing, in fact, that some of the celebrators used one of the idle whirlies to take parties aloft for sightseeing in a skip. It took considerable persuasion on the part of a very sober ship supervisor to get the fun stopped.

With only standby installation crews on day shift, and with the standby crews on swing shift reduced in half, the final work on the *Scott E. Land* progressed slowly. The Buckler and refrigeration crews worked feverishly tearing out the damaged equipment. It was estimated that six weeks would be required to complete the replacement. There was no need of hurry. There was no need of swing shift. Thursday, April 25, would be *the day* for swing shift.

The day was mellow. In the early part of the shift, the paint foremen "pushed" desperately in the forlorn hope of getting some painting done before the celebration got out of hand. Long before the lunch period, those same foremen were sending the paint carriers back. The crews were no longer in condition to apply paint. Lunchtime for the painters had all the ingredients of a riot, and several of the feminine carriers took turns kissing all of the painters good-bye.

The lunch period really started about an hour ahead of time—at least it did for the pipe fitters who were left in the yard. Their supply of liquor had been modest, and most of the effects had worn off when we gathered for the last time. Just the fact that it was the last time took much of the edge off the celebration. Being without a job didn't bother us, but all of us realized that we were going to miss our friendly contacts with one another. It was natural, too, that our talk would swing to the men and the crews we had known. We talked of Old Grouchy, Big George, the all-American from Hico, highballing Red and his greasy black hat. We also talked of Chuckles and Jonesy—both killed on the job. All of us knew that some of the things it takes to build ships are not on the blueprints; we had cared for our injured, and we had looked upon our dead.

As soon as the lunch period closed, pickup trucks began arriving at berth six to collect painters, shipfitters, riggers, and others who could not walk to the tool-clearance office. Most of the prettier paint carriers were kissed again and again before the loaded pickups headed up the dock. The painters, at least, rated taxi service to speed their departure from the yard.

That day, Jess met me at berth six—little Jess, ex-leadlady to the yard but my leadlady for keeps. Her hard hat gave her that same perky appearance as when she first put it on three years earlier. She was smiling and happy. "My foreman said you wanted to go for a walk with me," she said. "He called me away from the rest of the crew, wished me luck, and told me to beat it."

She tugged at my arm. "Isn't it wonderful?" she said. "We are going to live like human beings again!"

We stopped at the dock office for her checkout slip. Here she had to surrender her work badge. She did it happily and without remorse. I think she has always retained an inner conviction that her photo was not a good likeness. Her checkout slip read "Laid off, reduction of force." She had not quit, and she had not been fired. Of the thousands who had worked at the same tough job, she was one of the last to go. I was deeply proud of her, and I always will be. At the pipe office I got my checkout slip. It read the same as that of Jess. When we did reach the tool-clearance office, the last of the painters was just being poured back into the pickup.

Three objectives were slated for the following day. First, we loaded our personal belongings into our car. When it was loaded, we notified the Ogden Meadows management that we were ready for a furniture checkout. When that formality was over, our Ogden Meadows existence closed.

However, just living there, anyone could acquire a master's degree in the study of humanity.

The second objective was a final visit to the yard to get our last paychecks and to close out payment on our bonds. Berth six on the dock looked deserted. The only signs of life were seagulls swinging overhead as if they were suspended on strings. Our checks were waiting at the pay windows. The job was done. There were only a few other workers present, and one of them, a pretty paint carrier, suddenly pointed to the quiet shipyard. "Look! The Navy!"

Entering the yard was a long line of station wagons loaded with sailors. The Navy was taking custody of the arsenal. The sailors waved and threw kisses at the pretty paint carrier, just as the boys who went down with the *Liscome Bay* had done when they entered the yard years before. The pretty paint carrier didn't throw kisses. She just held out her arms to all of them. They couldn't see the tears that came, and they did not know that her bridegroom husband would always be in the South Pacific.

The third item for us that day was the most satisfactory of all: the drive home. Back to normal life, to normal hours of eating and sleeping, back to all the comforts, contacts, and duties of home. Like those other thousands who had worked with us, we had helped win a war; like other thousands, we were praying that our leaders would not lose the peace.

There was too much traffic on the Interstate Bridge across the Columbia River for an upriver look at the shipyard. Besides, that was something that now was behind us. We, along with those other thousands who worked with us, wanted to look forward. Once across the bridge, the Oregon side looked greener. The Willamette Valley was green as we drove along its highway. The rolling summits of the Coast Range bounded the horizon to our right; the snowy peaks of the Cascade Mountains thrust themselves up into the fleecy clouds of the eastern skyline to our left.

As I drove into the yard of our Salem home, I thought of the words of the colored welder of the "Big Ship"—"work some an' play some, an' go to chu'ch on Sunday." His program—and those of other thousands who wore Kaiser badges—was our program. All that we wanted was peace.

Appendix

The following charts are selected from a document produced by the Kaiser Company entitled "Ship Construction 1941–1945."

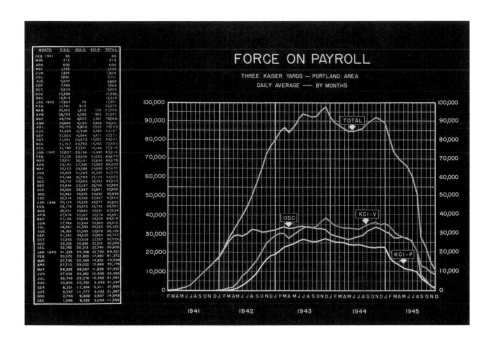

VESSELS SPECIFICATIONS
General Characteristics

	EC2 Liberty	AP3 Victory Cargo	AP5 Attack Transport	BB3 Escort Carrier
Length, Overall	441'-6"	455'-3"	455'-3"	512'-3"
Length, Between Perpendiculars	416'-0"	436'-6"	436'-6"	490'-0"
Breadth, Molded	56'-10 3/4"	62'-0"	62'-0"	65'-0"
Depth, Molded to Upper Deck	37'-4"	38'-0"	38'-0"	36'-4"
Draft Loaded, Summer Freeboard	25'-3 1/4"	28'-6 3/4"	24'-0"	20'-8"
Draft Light	8'-4 1/2"	9'-8 9/16"	13'-8 13/16"	14'-9 1/2"
Light Weight	3,830	4,479	6,614	6,625
Deadweight	10,439	10,720	5,836	3,575
Displacement	14,269	15,199	12,450	10,200
Block Coefficient	0.765	0.675	0.654	0.590
Number of Screws	Single	Single	Single	Twin
Type of Main Propulsion Motors	3 Cylinder Steam reciprocating triple expansion	1 high & 1 low pressure pressure turbine reduced to single drive	1 high & 1 low pressure pressure turbine reduced to single drive	Skinners uniflow steam reciprocating triple expansion
Number of Main Propulsion Motors	1	1	1	2
Rated H. P. of Main Propulsion Motors (Each)	2,500	8,500	8,500	4,500
Maximum H. P. of Main Propulsion Motors (Each)	—	9,350	9,350	5,600
R. P. M. Normal	76	85	85	162
R. P. M. Maximum	—	88	88	—
Number of Main Boilers	2	2	2	4
Propeller Diameter	18'-6"	20'-6"	20'-6"	(2) 12'-6"
Number Propeller Blades	4	4	4	
Shaft Length	180'-3 1/4"	166'-6 3/8"	166'-6 3/8"	(2) 200'-10"
Fuel Capacity in Barrels	16,396	19,113.5	7,577.2	—
Speed Knots	11.5	17.7	17.7	20
Cargo Capacity	501,092 cu. ft.	453,210 cu. ft.	150,180 cu. ft.	—
Complement	Military 26 Other 44 Total 70	Military 28 Other 54 Total 82	Total 2,085	Total 764

ATL Landing Ship Tank	C1-M-AV1 Coastal Cargo	T2-SE-A1 Tanker	AO Fleet Oiler	C4-S-A3 Transport
327'-9"	338'-6½"	523'-6"	523'-6"	522'-10½"
316'-0"	320'-0"	503'-6"	503'-0"	496'-0"
50'-0"	50'-0"	68'-0"	68'-0"	71'-6"
28'-0"	29'-0"	39'-3"	39'-3"	43'-6"
6'-8" Bow 13'-0" Stern	18'-0"	30'-2"	30'-2"	26'-6"
—	—	8'-6¾"	—	17'-0"
1,490	2,400	5,320	—	10,461
3,590	3,846	16,560	—	6,829
5,080	6,246	21,880	21,880	17,290
0.790	0.759	0.750	0.750	0.644
Twin	Single	Single	Single	Single
GMC Diesel	6 Cycle Diesel (Nordberg)	Single turbo-electric generator powering a synchronous induction motor	Single turbo-electric generator powering a synchronous induction motor	1 high & 1 low pressure pressure turbine reduced to single drive
2	1	1	1	1
950	1,750	6,000	9,000	9,000
—	—	6,600	9,900	9,900
300	180	90	103	88
—	—	93	106	—
—	—	2	2	2
(2) 5'-10"	11'-0"	19'-6"	19'-6"	21'-8"
	3	4	4	
(2) 40'-0"	36'-9"	55'-5¾"	55'-5¾"	—
—	2,762 3,520	5,500	4,920	13,609
10.5	11	14.5	16.5	16.75
—	232,000 cu. ft. 10,000 Rfr.	141,158 Barrels	4,920 Barrels	13,609 Barrels
Total 480	Military 25 Other 39 Total 64	Military 28 Other 54 Total 82	Total 255	Total 4,209

193 ☆

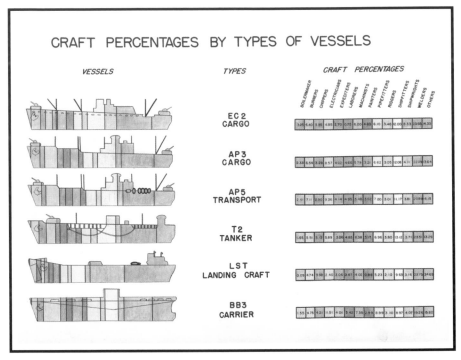

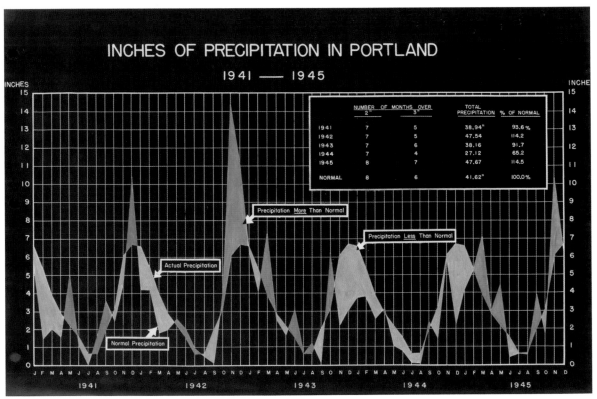

Notes

Ships by the Thousands

1. Henry J. Kaiser (1882-1967) was an industrialist with little formal education. He began his career running photography studios in upstate New York. Later, moving west to Spokane, Washington, he entered the hardware business. Successively, Kaiser managed operations in road construction and dams, as well as cement, steel, and aluminum plants, before building ships in World War II.
2. In his illustrious career, Edgar Kaiser delivered the same business skills and held the same humanitarian values exemplified by his father, Henry J. Kaiser. In 1979, as he began stepping down from his active direction, Edgar stated, "We must make our investment of heart and soul, as surely as we make our investment of money."
3. Vancouver Housing Authority (VHA), was the local authority providing public housing. The VHA was responsible for the construction and administration of the housing projects with funding provided by the federal government. Portland had a similar authority for its huge housing project, Vanport.

Preface

1. The island of Malta, a British colony during World War II, controlled the vital sea lanes between Italy and Africa. Murmansk is Russia's chief port on the Arctic Ocean. It lies about 620 miles north of St. Petersburg and was used as a port for Allied convoys in World War II carrying lend-lease material to the Soviet Union. But the route was especially dangerous because of German submarines.
2. Douglas MacArthur (1880-1964) was one of the leading U.S. commanders of World War II. He defended the Philippine Islands at the beginning of the war, and later led the Allied forces to victory in the South Pacific.
3. Chester W. Nimitz (1885-1966) served as commander-in-chief of the United States Pacific fleet and Pacific Ocean area during World War II. He was promoted to fleet admiral in 1944.

1. "He hired every danged one of us"

1. Trains served as a vital method of transportation during World War II for companies bringing in workers for West Coast shipyards and for the Hanford Atomic Works in Washington state.
2. A burner cuts metal plate.
3. A chipper finishes and smoothes metal surfaces.
4. Charles (Chic) Sale (1885-1936) was an actor and comedian who wrote a book called *The Specialist*, featuring a carpenter who was active in constructing outhouses, known as "privies." The volume became widely popular with readers, and Chic Sale soon became a common name for "privies" in the United States, even some built by U.S. troops overseas.
5. The Hudson House dormitory housed single men, with 5,018 beds. Operated by the Vancouver Housing Authority, seven units were built in 1942 close to the Kaiser shipyard. Roomers paid $3.50 a week for double occupancy and $5.00 a week for single rooms.
6. Columbia House provided an additional 7,000 units of dormitory housing for single men and women and was located just off Grand Avenue.

7. Americans were encouraged to grow "Victory gardens" at home during World War II in a time when much of the populace was involved in war-related activity and less labor was available for farms and orchards.

8. The service flag displayed by families indicated members serving in the armed forces. A gold star represented a loss of life. Many women became eligible for the title of gold star mother.

9. The federal government ordered the rationing of foodstuffs and consumer goods during World War II. Ration books were issued for some items that were in short supply or needed for the military and other purposes.

10. "Contours Percheron" refers to the worker's size, indicating the measurements of a draft horse.

11. Overall pockets may have bulged with tools or other items, adding to an ungainly appearance.

12. "Daveno" was a contemporary designation for couches, also known as davenports and sofas.

13. The "screws" were propellers.

2. "Put him to work"

1. Tanks, trucks, and other vehicles could roll out of an LST when a front section was lowered during a beach landing.

2. A "welder lead" is the electrical cable between the arc welding machine and the work location.

3. "Shipways" or "ways" refer to the supporting structure and track on which the ship is built and from which it is launched.

4. "Gob" is slang for a sailor.

5. "Brass hats" are high-ranking officials.

6. After a ship was launched, it moved to the outfitting dock where there were six berths. The ship's prow was pointed into the current, and the port or leftside was adjacent to the dock. When the ship was ready for sea trials, it was turned over to the Navy.

7. A "bull gang" is a crew of unskilled laborers.

8. The Works Projects Administration (WPA) was an agency of the New Deal during Franklin D. Roosevelt's tenure as U. S. President.

9. In 1918, the Ninety-second Infantry Division fought on the western front in Europe. A buffalo was featured on the unit's insignia.

3. "Please don't think I'm picking on you"

1. The word "whirly" indicates a rotary or whirling motion.

2. "Chromate" is a salt or ester of chromic acid.

3. "Skips" are small open boxes about 8 feet square by 30 inches high and made of metal and wood. They are used to move equipment, materials, scrap, or workers around the yard, often hoisted by the whirly cranes moving materials between the ship and dock.

4. The Ogden Meadows housing project had been constructed in a field off Fourth Plain Road, at the site of what is now Fort Vancouver High School. The project was named for Peter Skene Ogden of the Hudson's Bay Company.

5. The "hot ship" was the next to be launched.

6. Hot Point, Frigidaire, Worthington, Chicago Pump, General Motors, Buda, American Steel, Republic Steel, and General Electric were companies active during the war years.

7. A compass used on ships that locates true north—the direction of the earth's rotation as opposed to magnetic north. An American inventor, Elmer Ambrose Sperry, patented the gyrocompass in the U.S. in 1908.

8. Jantzen Beach opened in 1928 as a popular amusement park on Hayden Island in the Columbia River. The park closed in 1970 and was displaced by a shopping mall.

9. Yamashita led the Japanese troops who conquered Malaya and Singapore in World War II. In 1944-45, he defended the Philippines against U.S. forces led by Gen. Douglas MacArthur.

10. "Axis" refers to Germany, Italy, and Japan, the three countries aligned against the Allies during World War II. Hungary, Bulgaria, and Rumania were among the Axis partners.

11. Carriers were ships designed as a floating base for military aircraft. One type of this vessel was the escort carrier, such as those built at Vancouver, based on merchant ship designs. These ships provided air protection for convoys and amphibious landings. They also were used in anti-submarine work.

12. The 1941 Lend-Lease Act allowed the United States to aid countries which were then fighting the Axis powers. Billions of dollars of American supplies were transferred to Great Britain, the Soviet Union, and China.

13. The Army's Thirty-second Division, known as the Red Arrow unit, won fame during World War I for its fierce combat exploits on the front lines.

4. "Eighteen or more by '44!"

1. Amidships is toward the middle of a ship or half way between the bow and stern.

2. "Daisy chain" refers to moving the metal and wood from one worker to another en route to the skips.

3. The *Casablanca* was the study ship or model for all the later escort carriers constructed at Vancouver. The Vancouver-built carriers became known as the Casablanca type.

4. A "mangle" is a machine used to iron and wring out laundry.

5. Beginning in the 1930s, Washington state issued aluminum sales tax tokens, denominated in fractions of a cent, to help calculate the final price of items. The federal government issued red and blue dime-sized fiber tokens during the war to make change for ration coupons.

6. American troops landed on the Pacific island of Guadalcanal in August 1942 and fierce fighting ensued. The last organized Japanese resistance ended in early 1943.

7. In 1942, a PT boat evacuated Douglas MacArthur from Corregidor in the Philippine Islands shortly before it was captured by Japanese troops. MacArthur's pledge that he would return finally became a reality late in World War II.

5. "I did not threaten him"

1. "Highball" refers to a crew working at full speed; this slang term is also used in the logging industry.

2. September 2, 1945 was designated as V-J (Victory over Japan) Day, following Japan's acceptance of Allied surrender terms on August 14, 1945.

3. Allied troops invaded France on June 6, 1944.

4. Army Corps of Engineers.

5. Japanese troops completed the occupation of the Bataan peninsula in April 1942. This was followed by the "death march" of U.S. and Filipino troops to a prison camp in the Philippines.

6. "Get yourself a blue suit" meant that laggardly workers should join the Navy.

7. Some of the less desirable characters at the Hudson House may have inspired the designation Hoodlum House for the housing project.

6. "Another one in the creek"

1. The U. S. Army operated Camp Adair north of Corvallis, Oregon, from 1943 to 1946. The 104th Infantry Division was organized at Camp Adair, Oregon, in 1942 and trained in Colorado and California before shipment to the European war front in 1944.

2. Henry Kaiser offered medical and hospital care to shipyard employees and their families. The Northern Permanente Foundation Hospital opened in September 1942. The hospital was built by the charitable organization founded by Henry and Edgar Kaiser and their associates. The building, long vacant, is slated for demolition.

3. Before World War II, McLoughlin Heights was a largely undeveloped area east of Vancouver. The Vancouver Housing Authority constructed the largest of its World War II residential projects on the Heights starting in 1942. Occupancy there declined after the war, practically all the temporary housing was removed, and a new residential area was developed, along with commercial facilities and schools.

4. Fort Lewis is an army base near Tacoma, Washington.

7. "Hay-fork high and pick-handle broad"

1. The formal surrender of Japan took place September 2, 1945 on board the battleship USS *Missouri*, anchored with other U. S. and British ships in Tokyo Bay.

2. "Magic carpet" refers to the fleet of ships called into service to return the troops home from the European and Pacific theaters.

3. In addition to three shipyards in the Portland-Vancouver area, Kaiser operated four yards at Richmond in the Bay Area and Calship at San Pedro near Los Angeles.

4. "Smoked Irishman" is a slang term applied to an African American. The term may have originated in the docks of Liverpool, England.

5. Bagley Downs, one of six housing projects built and operated by the Vancouver Housing Authority, was once the site of a horse race track. Some 8,000 people lived there in 2,100 row houses.

6. Crowded conditions on buses traveling to and from the shipyard earned them the name "Kattle Kars."

7. To curb inflation, the U. S. and Canada imposed price controls during World War II. The Office of Price Administration (OPA) determined and supervised the U.S. price control program during the war.

8. American Federation of Labor (AFL) was a membership group of labor unions formed in 1886. Its objective was to organize laborers by crafts and skills.

8. "Let's stake this kid to enough dough"

1. "Pulmotor" is machinery used in applying artificial respiration by forcing oxygen into the lungs.

2. "Roosevelt money" refers to the inflated cost of goods during the war.

3. "Bond of the craft" refers to the connections between workers doing the same task.

4. "Our Yiddisher" is an affectionate yet biting reference to a Jewish member of the crew.

5. Refers to Henry J. Kaiser and his son, Edgar F. Kaiser

9. *"This is a fighting ship—give it your best"*

1. Admiral Howard Vickery (1892-1946) was vice-chairman of the U.S. Maritime Commission from 1942 to 1945 and deputy administrator of the War Shipping Administration starting in 1942. He was a 1915 graduate of the U.S. Naval Academy.

2. Kaiser's competitive contests among his shipyards for speed production were great morale boosters. As a managerial group, Kaiser built 1,552 ships with a total tonnage of 6,327,000 for the Maritime Commission, 1941-1945.

3. The Battle of Leyte Gulf, October 23-26, 1944, resulted in a decisive victory for the mostly United States forces near the Philippine Islands. The Japanese fleet suffered heavy losses in men and ships.

4. Rear Admiral Thomas Sprague was in charge of the Escort Carrier Group during the Battle for Leyte Gulf.

5. William F. ("Bull") Halsey led U.S. naval forces in battle against the Japanese in World War II, including the famous Battle of Leyte Gulf. His final promotion was to fleet admiral in 1945.

6. The "short order shipyard" refers to the shipyard's speed in constructing ships, serving them up like diner food at a lunch counter.

10. *"War is waste"*

1. The rousing chorus from Giuseppe Verdi's opera, *The Troubador*, 1853.

2. The Battle for Iwo Jima, an eight-square-mile-island in the northwestern Pacific Ocean, took place during February and March, 1945. Control of the island's strategic airstrips were important to Allied victory.

3. Initially, Navy brass did not support the escort carrier program. Kaiser had to first persuade Roosevelt.

4. Saipan, an island in the western Pacific Ocean, was the location of heavy fighting in June 1944. Saipan became an important air base for attacks on Japan.

5. German troops surprised Allied forces with an attack through the Ardennes forest of Belgium in December 1944. Eventually they were stopped and finally pushed back after heavy fighting.

6. Hostilities ended officially in Europe on May 8, 1945, which became known as V-E (Victory in Europe) Day. Adolf Hitler was dead and Germany surrendered.

7. St. Lô, a town in Normandy, had been heavily damaged during fighting in June and July 1944, and was captured by American forces shortly before the Allied breakout from their beachhead.

8. In World War II, women played a significant role in the military. Part of this activity was in the Women's Army Corps (WAC).

9. The U.S. Army opened the Hanford Atomic Works on the Columbia River north of Richland in 1943 to produce plutonium for atomic bombs, but kept the activity secret until August 1945.

10. The more notorious "Hellships" were manned by Japanese, carrying prisoners of war.

11. Between 1940 and 1945 the U.S. Navy received 111 escort carriers (called CVEs by the Navy) for its use.

12. The expression, "life of Riley," dates from the 1890s and refers to a prosperous, enjoyable life. A television program, "The Life of Riley" was broadcast shortly after World War II.

11. *"All that we wanted was peace"*

1. Biak Island in New Guinea, a Japanese base in World War II, was regained for the Allies in July 1944 by American troops.

Illustration Credits

Ships by the Thousands

Louis S. Lee: xiv; Douglas Magedanz: xv; Oregon State Library: xvi; Editor's Collection: xvi

The Artistic Environment

Mary Barrier: xxi; Barbara and Jack McLarty: xxii; Douglas Lynch: xxiii; Louis S. Lee: xxiv; C. Herald Campbell: xxv

Preface

Editor's Collection: xxviii, Douglas Magedanz: xxix

1. "He hired every danged one of us"

John Wilson Room, Multnomah County Library, Portland, Oregon: 1; Editor's Collection: 2, 14, 16; C. Herald Campbell: 3; Oregon Historical Society #OrHi 104416: 4, #OrHi 64477, 12; Sue and Phil Augustyn: 5; Louis S. Lee: 7; Editor's Collection: 8; Vancouver Housing Authority: 9; Peter Belluschi: 10; ArtSpace Gallery: 11; Ron Ennis: 13; Pat Koehler: 17

2. "Put him to work"

Clark County Museum: 19; Jimmy Onstott: 20, 28; Tonkon Torp LLP: 22; Editor's Collection: 23, 24; Private Collection: 26; ArtSpace Gallery: 29; Ron Ennis: 32; ArtSpace Gallery: 33; Louis S. Lee: 34; 35

3. "Please don't think I'm picking on you"

Kaiser Permanente Northwest Region Historical Files: 37; Tonkon Torp LLP: 38; Oregon Historical Society #OrHi 104418, 39; C. Herald Campbell: 54, 60; Michael Parsons and Marte Lamb: 42; Editor's Collection: 44; John Wilson Room, Multnomah County Library, Portland, Oregon: 45; Douglas Lynch: 46, 49, 52, 53, 57; Clark County Museum: 50, 61; Sue and Phil Augustyn: 55; Louis S. Lee: 56, 59; Douglas Magedanz: 58; Jimmy Onstott: 62

4. "Eighteen or more by '44"

Louis S. Lee: 65, 79; C. Herald Campbell: 66, 67, 69; Jimmy Onstott: 68, 70, 73; David Horowitz and Gloria Myers: 71; Randy Gragg: 72; Bonnie Mentzer: 74-75; John Wilson Room, Multnomah County Library, Portland, Oregon: 78; Editor's Collection: 81, 83, 91, 97; Oregon Historical Society #OrHi 104417, 82; Sue and Phil Augustyn: 84; Private Collection: 85, 87; ArtSpace Gallery: 95; Portland Art Museum, Portland, Oregon, Helen Thurston Ayer Fund Purchase: 96

5. "I did not threaten him"

C. Herald Campbell: 99; Douglas Lynch: 100, 101; Editor's Collection: 102, 108, 109; Oregon Historical Society #OrHi 61308, 103; Kaiser Permanente Northwest Region Historical Files: 106; Louis S. Lee: 107

Additional Reading

Bailey, Ronald H., ed. *The Home Front: U.S.A.* Alexandria, Virginia: Time-Life Books, 1977.

Bona, Milton, ed. *A Survey of Negro Tenants*, Housing Authority of Vancouver, Washington. 1945.

Bo's'n's Whistle. 1941-1945. Bi-weekly employee magazine for the Oregon Shipbuilding Corporation of Portland and Kaiser Companies, Inc. Vancouver and Swan Island.

Burke, Kathleen. "Together WE win! Get a War Job! Save Waste Fats!" *Smithsonian* 24 (March 1994): 66-69.

Canon, Belle. "The Kaiser Shipyard Experiment of WW II: A Forgotten Revolution in Child Care." *Oregon Times Magazine* (February-March 1976): 21-24.

Child Service Centers. Portland, Ore.: Kaiser Company, Inc. 1943.

Clawson, Augusta H. *Shipyard Diary of a Woman Welder*. New York: Penguin Books, 1944.

Coleman, Penny. *Rosie the Riveter: Women Working on the Home Front in World War II*. New York: Crown Publishers, 1995.

Colton, Barrows F. "Winning the War of Supply." *National Geographic Magazine* (December 1945): 705-36.

Columbian (Vancouver, Wash.). 1942-1946.

Fabry, Joseph. *Swing Shift: Building the Liberty Ships*. San Francisco: Strawberry Hill Press, 1982.

Foster, Mark S. *Henry J. Kaiser: Builder in the Modern American West*. American Studies Series. Austin: University of Texas Press, 1989.

Fry, Ken. "Vancouver's Boom Town War Years." *Clark County History* 28 (1987): 45-54.

"Good Work, Sister!" Women Shipyard Workers of World War II: An Oral History. Portland, Ore.: Northwest Women's History Project, 1982.

Harding, G. L. *A Survey of Shipyard Operations in the Portland Oregon Metropolitan Area,* Prepared for the War Manpower Commission, L.C. Stoll, Area Director, December 1943.

Hendricks, Richey. *A Model for National Health Care: The History of Kaiser Permanente*. New Brunswick, New Jersey: Rutgers University Press, 1993.

Hymes, James L. *Living History Interviews, Early Childhood Education*. Vol. 2. *Care of the Children of Working Mothers*. Carmel, California: Hacienda Press, 1978.

Kaiser Company, Inc. *How'dy Stranger*. n.p.: 1942.

———. *Ships for Victory*. Portland, Ore.: Glass-Keystone Press, 1944.

———. *The Ships We Build*. n.p., n.d.

———. *Telephone Directory, Vancouver Yard*, n.d.

Kaiser Industries Corporation, *The Kaiser Story*. Oakland, Calif. 1968.

Kaiser Permanente Northwest Region. Historical Files. Portland, Ore.

Kesselman, Amy. *Fleeting Opportunities: Women Shipyard Workers in Portland and Vancouver During World War II and Reconversion*. Albany: State University of New York Press, 1990.

Lane, Frederic C. *Ships for Victory: A History of Shipbuilding under the U.S. Maritime Commission in World War II*. Baltimore: The Johns Hopkins University Press, 1952, 2001.

Maben, Manly. *Vanport*. Portland: Oregon Historical Society Press, 1987.

Mack, Lois. *One Place across Time: Vancouver National Historic Reserve*. Vancouver, Wash.: Vancouver National Historic Reserve Trust, 2001.

Van Arsdol, Ted. "World War II in Vancouver." *Clark County History* 19 (1978): 5-32.

———. "The Shipyard Era." *Columbian* (Vancouver, Wash.). June 7-11, 1971.

Vancouver Housing Authority. *50 Years of Progress Dedicated to People.* Vancouver Housing Authority, 1993.

———. *A Tale of Six Cities and How They Became a Permanent Part of Vancouver, Washington*, n.d.

"War Housing." *Architectural Forum* 76 (May 1942).

Winters, J. C. *Marine Pipefitting.* Portland: Oregon Shipbuilding Corporation, Kaiser Company, Inc. and the U. S. Maritime Commission, 1942

Wollner, Craig and W. Tracy Dillon, eds. *A Richer Harvest: The Literature of Work in the Pacific Northwest.* Corvallis: Oregon State University Press, 1999.

Zinsser, Caroline. "The Best Day Care There Ever Was." *Working Mother* (October 1984): 76-80.

The Artistic Environment

Bullock, Margaret. *Back to Work: Oregon and the New Deal Art Projects*, permanent collection brochure. Portland, Ore.: Portland Art Museum, 2001.

Bustard, Bruce I. *A New Deal for the Arts.* Washington, D.C.: National Archives and Records Administration, in association with the University of Washington Press, 1997.

Cleaver, J. D. "Introduction to Oregon Art History" in *Oregon Painters: The First Hundred Years (1859-1959).* Ginny Allen and Jody Klevit, eds. Portland: Oregon Historical Society Press, 1999.

Gragg, Randy. "The Workers and the War Effort," *Oregonian* (Portland, Ore.). September 26, 1999.

Griffin, Rachael. "Portland and Its Environs" in *Art of the Pacific Northwest: From the 1930s to the Present.* Washington, D.C.: Smithsonian Institution Press, 1974.

Harris, Jonathan. *Federal Art and National Culture: The Politics of Identity in New Deal America.* Cambridge, England: Cambridge University Press, 1995.

Hull, Roger. "The Lure of Pacific Northwest Art," *American Art Review*, (vol. XI, no. 1, 1999): 168-77.

———. "Region, Expression and 'Oregon Art'—1930-1970," *Oregon Humanities* (Spring 2000): 46-52.

Kimbrell, Leonard B. "Artist Brothers Armed with a Strong Social Conscience," *Northwest Magazine*, November 22, 1981.

Kingsbury, Martha. *Art of the Thirties: The Pacific Northwest.* Seattle: University of Washington Press, 1972.

O'Connor, Francis V. *Federal Support for the Visual Arts: The New Deal and Now.* Greenwich, Conn.: New York Graphic Society, Ltd., 1969.

———, ed., *Art for the Millions.* Boston, Mass.: New York Graphic Society, 1973.

Wheeler, Susan. "Oregon Exhibit Features WPA-era Art of Martina Gangle Curl," *People's Weekly World,* March 22, 1997, 20.

Index

Page numbers in italics refer to images of the person or thing.

10,000 SHIPYARD WORKERS WANTED

Shipyard Workers Are Happy and Are Doing a Grand Job!

at SWAN ISLAND · VANCOUVER · OREGON SHIP

★ Here it is—in plain words that every patriotic American can understand:

To win the War, we must build more ships. To build more ships WE MUST GET MORE MEN. These men, whoever they are and wherever they may be—*perhaps you are one*—are entitled to the shipyard employment picture.

PREVIOUS EXPERIENCE NOT NECESSARY

Practically all of the 55,000 employees of the three Kaiser yards never saw a shipyard before. Yet they are the men who have broken record after record in shipbuilding.

Previous experience is not necessary. Training will be given on the job. Willingness to work and a desire to do that work where it will do the maximum good—those are the things that count.

WAGES

Along with the patriotic viewpoint look at the practical side—wages. Here is the pay scale at Oregon Shipbuilding Corporation, Portland; Kaiser Co., Inc., Swan Island, and Kaiser Co., Inc., Vancouver, as contained in the Master Agreement between the Pacific Coast Shipbuilders and the Metal Trades Department, A. F. of L.

LABORERS	**88¢**	per hour
HELPERS	**95¢**	per hour
JOURNEYMEN	**$1.20**	per hour
LEADMEN	**1.43**	per hour
FOREMEN	**1.58**	per hour

IMPORTANT

This message is directed particularly to men in Portland and vicinity who are not working in an essential war industry.

We Will Not Consider for Employment—

1. Any present worker in an essential war industry.

2. Any worker who has been employed since September 1, 1942, in the non - ferrous metal mining, milling and smelting industry, or in the lumber and logging industry in the states of California, Oregon, Washington, New Mexico, Nevada, Arizona, Colorado, Texas, Montana, Idaho, Wyoming and Utah.

Time and a half pay for all time above 40 hours in any calendar week, or above 8 hours in any one day. Day Shift—8 A. M. to 4:30 P. M. with 30 minutes for lunch.

Plus 10% Extra Pay for Swing Shift

Swing Shift 7½ hours work with pay for 8 hours. Hours—4:30 P. M. to 12:30 A. M. with 30 minutes for lunch.

Plus 15% Extra Pay for Graveyard Shift

Graveyard Shift 7 hours work with pay for 8 hours. Hours—12:30 A. M. to 8 A. M. with 30 minutes for lunch.

NOTICE—All shipyard employees must become members of the A. F. of L. having jurisdiction over their particular craft.

WORK DAYS—AND VACATION

Yard employees work 6 days in a calendar week. Every 7th week they have both Saturday and Sunday off.

The vacation agreement provides for one week's vacation (with 40 hours' pay) in a year's period and is given after 1200 working hours.

ENLARGED TRANSPORTATION FACILITIES

BUSSES—150 additional busses are on order; 45 have been received and the balance should be in operation within two weeks.

FERRIES—2 former San Francisco Bay ferries will be in operation shortly, carrying workers from downtown Portland to the yards. Each ferry can accommodate 3500 men.

TRAINS—Direct train service will be started soon from downtown Portland to the Vancouver yards.

All of these transportation services are in addition to present facilities.

10,000 WORKERS NEEDED IMMEDIATELY

The sooner you can come to work, the better. *There is a definite shortage of 10,000 men in the Kaiser shipyards right now.* Time is vital in the job that all of us have to do to win the war. *We need you!* The instructions below on what to do are for your convenience.

UNION EMPLOYMENT OFFICES OPEN EVERY WEEK DAY

LABORERS—Apply for immediate employment at the Labor Temple, 4th and Jefferson.

GENERAL HELPERS—Apply at the International Brotherhood of Boilermakers, Iron Ship Builders and Helpers of America at 1313 S. W. Third, for immediate employment.

JOURNEYMEN—Apply direct to your respective locals at the Labor Temple for immediate employment.

IF YOU CAN COME TO WORK WITHIN 5 DAYS

Telephone WE 2201 or fill out coupon and mail:

—5

Within 5 days from now I can come to work

....
Name   Street and Number   City, State   Phone

....
Age   Trade or Business   Single or Married   No. Children

Do you have living quarters in Portland or vicinity?.......
(Yes or No)

Mail to Oregon Shipbuilding Corp., Portland, or Kaiser Co., Inc., Portland, or Kaiser Co., Inc., Vancouver.

DO THIS

If You Can Come to Work Right Now

Telephone WE 2201 7 A.M. to 10 P.M.

(Starting Sunday, September 20)

for information or apply in person to the proper union headquarters given above.

IF YOU CAN COME TO WORK AFTER 5 DAYS

Telephone WE 2201 or fill out coupon and mail:

+5

On ...., 1942, I can come to work.

....
Name   Street and Number   City, State   Phone

....
Age   Trade or Business   Single or Married   No. Children

Do you have living quarters in Portland or vicinity?.......
(Yes or No)

Mail to Oregon Shipbuilding Corp., Portland, or Kaiser Co., Inc., Portland, or Kaiser Co., Inc., Vancouver.

THE CARD

Arnold Bennett was born in Hanley, Staffordshire, in 1867. After a secondary school education, he worked first for his father, a self-taught solicitor, and then moved to London as a shorthand clerk with a firm of solicitors. He began to write to make extra money and in 1893 became assistant editor and subsequently editor of the weekly magazine, *Woman*, reviewing books and writing articles on general subjects, something he continued to do all his life. His first novel, *A Man From the North*, appeared in 1898 and in 1900 he finished *The Grand Babylon Hotel*, published in 1902, and began *Anna of the Five Towns* (1902) in which he first started to use the Potteries of his boyhood as a setting for his novels. In these contrasting works, he also reveals his lifelong fascination for, on the one hand, the worlds of beauty and opulence, and on the other, puritanism and people who can endure hard work.

In 1903 Arnold Bennett moved to Paris, where he met people such as Turgenev and the composer, Ravel. In 1907 he married a Frenchwoman (from whom he separated in 1921) and in the following year they returned to England. *The Old Wives' Tale* (1908) was written in France and shows Bennett's main influences, the first being that of his own background and the second that of the French realists such as Flaubert, Maupassant and Balzac. In it, Bennett also reveals his own preoccupations with the effects of time and history on the lives of ordinary people.

This was followed by the Clayhanger trilogy: *Clayhanger* (1910), *Hilda Lessways* (1911) and *These Twain* (1916). His works also include several plays, two volumes of short stories and several other novels. He died in 1931.

ARNOLD BENNETT

THE CARD

*A Story of Adventure in
the Five Towns*

PENGUIN BOOKS

PENGUIN BOOKS

Published by the Penguin Group
Penguin Books Ltd, 27 Wrights Lane, London w8 5tz, England
Viking Penguin, a division of Penguin Books USA Inc.
375 Hudson Street, New York, New York 10014, USA
Penguin Books Australia Ltd, Ringwood, Victoria, Australia
Penguin Books Canada Ltd, 2801 John Street, Markham, Ontario, Canada l3r 1b4
Penguin Books (NZ) Ltd, 182–190 Wairau Road, Auckland 10, New Zealand

Penguin Books Ltd, Registered Offices: Harmondsworth, Middlesex, England

First published by Methuen 1911
Published in Penguin Books 1975
7 9 10 8 6

All rights reserved

Printed in England by Clays Ltd, St Ives plc
Set in Linotype Granjon

CONTENTS

CHAPTER I

The Dance

I

EDWARD HENRY MACHIN first saw the smoke on the 27th
May 1867, in Brougham Street, Bursley, the most ancient of the
Five Towns. Brougham Street runs down from St Luke's
Square straight into the Shropshire Union Canal, and consists
partly of buildings known as 'potbanks' (until they come to
be sold by auction, when auctioneers describe them as 'extensive earthenware manufactories') and partly of cottages whose
highest rent is four-and-six a week. In such surroundings was
an extraordinary man born. He was the only anxiety of a
widowed mother, who gained her livelihood and his by making
up 'ladies' own materials' in ladies' own houses. Mrs Machin,
however, had a speciality apart from her vocation: she could
wash flannel with less shrinking than any other woman in the
district, and she could wash fine lace without ruining it; thus
often she came to sew and remained to wash. A somewhat
gloomy woman; thin, with a tongue! But I liked her. She saved
a certain amount of time every day by addressing her son as
Denry, instead of Edward Henry.

Not intellectual, not industrious, Denry would have maintained the average dignity of labour on a potbank had he not at
the age of twelve won a scholarship from the Board School to the
Endowed School. He owed his triumph to audacity rather than
learning, and to chance rather than design. On the second day of
examination he happened to arrive in the examination-
room ten minutes too soon for the afternoon sitting. He wandered about the place exercising his curiosity, and reached the
master's desk. On the desk was a tabulated form with names of
candidates and the number of marks achieved by each in each
subject of the previous day. He had done badly in geography,
and saw seven marks against his name in the geographical column, out of a possible thirty. The figures had been written in

7

pencil. The very pencil lay on the desk. He picked it up, glanced at the door and at the rows of empty desks, and wrote a neat '2' in front of the 7; then he strolled innocently forth and came back late. His trick ought to have been found out – the odds were against him – but it was not found out. Of course it was dishonest. Yes, but I will not agree that Denry was uncommonly vicious. Every schoolboy is dishonest, by the adult standard. If I knew an honest schoolboy I would begin to count my silver spoons as he grew up. All is fair between schoolboys and schoolmasters.

This dazzling feat seemed to influence not only Denry's career but also his character. He gradually came to believe that he had won the scholarship by genuine merit, and that he was a remarkable boy and destined to great ends. His new companions, whose mothers employed Denry's mother, also believed that he was a remarkable boy; but they did not forget, in their gentlemanly way, to call him 'washer-woman'. Happily Denry did not mind.

He had a thick skin, and fair hair and bright eyes and broad shoulders, and the jolly gaiety of his disposition developed daily. He did not shine at the school; he failed to fulfil the rosy promise of the scholarship; but he was not stupider than the majority; and his opinion of himself, having once risen, remained at 'set fair'. It was inconceivable that he should work in clay with his hands.

II

When he was sixteen his mother, by operations on a yard and a half of Brussels point lace, put Mrs Emery under an obligation. Mrs Emery was the sister of Mr Duncalf. Mr Duncalf was the Town Clerk of Bursley, and a solicitor. It is well known that all bureaucracies are honeycombed with intrigue. Denry Machin left school to be clerk to Mr Duncalf, on the condition that within a year he should be able to write shorthand at the rate of a hundred and fifty words a minute. In those days mediocre and incorrect shorthand was not a drug on the market. He complied (more or less, and decidedly less than more) with the condition.

And for several years he really thought that he had nothing further to hope for. Then he met the Countess.

The Countess of Chell was born of poor but picturesque parents, and she could put her finger on her great-grandfather's grandfather. Her mother gained her livelihood and her daughter's by allowing herself to be seen a great deal with humbler but richer people's daughters. The Countess was brought up to matrimony. She was aimed and timed to hit a given mark at a given moment. She succeeded. She married the Earl of Chell. She also married about twenty thousand acres in England, about a fifth of Scotland, a house in Piccadilly, seven country seats (including Sneyd), a steam yacht, and five hundred thousand pounds' worth of shares in the Midland Railway. She was young and pretty. She had travelled in China and written a book about China. She sang at charity concerts and acted in private theatricals. She sketched from nature. She was one of the great hostesses of London. And she had not the slightest tendency to stoutness. All this did not satisfy her. She was ambitious! She wanted to be taken seriously. She wanted to enter into the life of the people. She saw in the quarter of a million souls that constitute the Five Towns a unique means to her end, an unrivalled toy. And she determined to be identified with all that was most serious in the social progress of the Five Towns. Hence some fifteen thousand pounds were spent in refurbishing Sneyd Hall, which lies on the edge of the Five Towns, and the Earl and Countess passed four months of the year there. Hence the Earl, a mild, retiring man, when invited by the Town Council to be the ornamental Mayor of Bursley, accepted the invitation. Hence the Mayor and Mayoress gave an immense afternoon reception to practically the entire roll of burgesses. And hence, a little later, the Mayoress let it be known that she meant to give a municipal ball. The news of the ball thrilled Bursley more than anything had thrilled Bursley since the signing of Magna Charta. Nevertheless, balls had been offered by previous mayoresses. One can only suppose that in Bursley there remains a peculiar respect for land, railway stock, steam yachts, and great-grandfathers' grandfathers.

Now, everybody of account had been asked to the reception.

But everybody could not be asked to the ball, because not more than two hundred people could dance in the Town Hall. There were nearly thirty-five thousand inhabitants in Bursley, of whom quite two thousand 'counted', even though they did not dance.

III

Three weeks and three days before the ball Denry Machin was seated one Monday alone in Mr Duncalf's private offices in Duck Square (where he carried on his practice as a solicitor), when in stepped a tall and pretty young woman, dressed very smartly but soberly in dark green. On the desk in front of Denry were several wide sheets of 'abstract' paper, concealed by a copy of that morning's *Athletic News*. Before Denry could even think of reversing the positions of the abstract paper and the *Athletic News* the young woman said 'Good morning!' in a very friendly style. She had a shrill voice and an efficient smile.

'Good morning, madam,' said Denry.

'Mr Duncalf in?' asked the young woman brightly.

(Why should Denry have slipped off his stool? It is utterly against etiquette for solicitors' clerks to slip off their stools while answering inquiries.)

'No, madam; he's across at the Town Hall,' said Denry.

The young lady shook her head playfully, with a faint smile. 'I've just been there,' she said. 'They said he was here.'

'I daresay I could find him, madam – if you would –'

She now smiled broadly. 'Conservative Club, I suppose?' she said, with an air deliciously confidential.

He, too, smiled.

'Oh, no,' she said, after a little pause; 'just tell him I've called.'

'Certainly, madam. Nothing I can do?'

She was already turning away, but she turned back and scrutinized his face, as Denry thought, roguishly.

'You might just give him this list,' she said, taking a paper from her satchel and spreading it. She had come to the desk; their elbows touched. 'He isn't to take any notice of the crossings-out in red ink – you understand? Of course, I'm

10

relying on him for the other lists, and I expect all the invitations to be out on Wednesday. Good morning.'

She was gone. He sprang to the grimy window. Outside, in the snow, were a brougham, twin horses, twin men in yellow, and a little crowd of youngsters and oldsters. She flashed across the footpath, and vanished; the door of the carriage banged, one of the twins in yellow leaped up to his brother, and the whole affair dashed dangerously away. The face of the leaping twin was familiar to Denry. The man had, indeed, once inhabited Brougham Street, being known to the street as Jock, and his mother had for long years been a friend of Mrs Machin's.

It was the first time Denry had seen the Countess, save at a distance. Assuredly she was finer even than her photographs. Entirely different from what one would have expected! So easy to talk to! (Yet what had he said to her? Nothing – and everything.)

He nodded his head and murmured, 'No mistake about that lot!' Meaning, presumably, that all that one had read about the brilliance of the aristocracy was true, and more than true.

'She's the finest woman that ever came into this town,' he murmured.

The truth was that she surpassed his dreams of womanhood. At two o'clock she had been a name to him. At five minutes past two he was in love with her. He felt profoundly thankful that, for a church tea-meeting that evening, he happened to be wearing his best clothes.

It was while looking at her list of invitations to the ball that he first conceived the fantastic scheme of attending the ball himself. Mr Duncalf was, fussily and deferentially, managing the machinery of the ball for the Countess. He had prepared a little list of his own of people who ought to be invited. Several aldermen had been requested to do the same. There were thus about half-a-dozen lists to be combined into one. Denry did the combining. Nothing was easier than to insert the name of E. H. Machin inconspicuously towards the centre of the list! Nothing was easier than to lose the original lists, inadvertently, so that if a question arose as to any particular name, the responsibility for it could not be ascertained without inquiries too delicate to be made. On Wednesday Denry received a lovely Bristol board, stating in copper-plate that the Countess desired the pleasure of his company at the ball; and on Thursday his name was ticked off as one who had accepted.

IV

He had never been to a dance. He had no dress-suit, and no notion of dancing.

He was a strange, inconsequent mixture of courage and timidity. You and I are consistent in character; we are either one thing or the other but Denry Machin had no consistency.

For three days he hesitated, and then, secretly trembling, he slipped into Shillitoe's, the young tailor who had recently set up, and who was gathering together the *jeunesse dorée* of the town.

'I want a dress-suit,' he said.

Shillitoe, who knew that Denry only earned eighteen shillings a week, replied with only superficial politeness that a dress-suit was out of the question; he had already taken more orders than he could execute without killing himself. The whole town had uprisen as one man and demanded a dress-suit.

'So you're going to the ball, are you?' said Shillitoe, trying to condescend, but, in fact, slightly impressed.

'Yes,' said Denry; 'are you?'

Shillitoe started and then shook his head. 'No time for balls,' said he.

'I can get you an invitation, if you like,' said Denry, glancing at the door precisely as he had glanced at the door before adding 2 to 7.

'Oh!' Shillitoe cocked his ears. He was not a native of the town, and had no alderman to protect his legitimate interests.

To cut a shameful story short, in a week Denry was being tried on. Shillitoe allowed him two years' credit.

The prospect of the ball gave an immense impetus to the study of the art of dancing in Bursley, and so put quite a nice sum of money into the pocket of Miss Earp, a young mistress in that art. She was the daughter of a furniture dealer with a passion for the Bankruptcy Court. Miss Earp's evening classes were attended by Denry, but none of his money went into her

12

pocket. She was compensated by an expression of the Countess's desire for the pleasure of her company at the ball.

The Countess had aroused Denry's interest in women as a sex; Ruth Earp quickened the interest. She was plain, but she was only twenty-four, and very graceful on her feet. Denry had one or two strictly private lessons from her in reversing. She said to him one evening, when he was practising reversing and they were entwined in the attitude prescribed by the latest fashion: 'Never mind me! Think about yourself. It's the same in dancing as it is in life – the woman's duty is to adapt herself to the man.' He did think about himself. He was thinking about himself in the middle of the night, and about her too. There had been something in her tone ... her eye ... At the final lesson he inquired if she would give him the first waltz at the ball. She paused, then said yes.

v

On the evening of the ball, Denry spent at least two hours in the operation which was necessary before he could give the Countess the pleasure of his company. This operation took place in his minute bedroom at the back of the cottage in Brougham Street, and it was of a complex nature. Three weeks ago he had innocently thought that you had only to order a dress-suit and there you were! He now knew that a dress-suit is merely the beginning of anxiety. Shirt! Collar! Tie! Studs! Cuff-links! Gloves! Handkerchief! (He was very glad to learn authoritatively from Shillitoe that handkerchiefs were no longer worn in the waistcoat opening, and that men who so wore them were barbarians and the truth was not in them. Thus, an everyday handkerchief would do.) Boots! ... Boots were the rock on which he had struck. Shillitoe, in addition to being a tailor was a hosier, but by some flaw in the scheme of the universe hosiers do not sell boots. Except boots, Denry could get all he needed on credit; boots he could not get on credit, and he could not pay cash for them. Eventually he decided that his church boots must be dazzled up to the level for this great secular occasion. The pity was that he forgot – not that he was of a forgetful disposition in great matters; he was simply over-excited – he forgot to dazzle them up until after he had fairly put his collar on and his necktie in a bow. It is imprudent to touch blacking in a dress-shirt, so Denry had to undo the past and begin again. This hurried him. He was not afraid of being late for the first waltz with Miss Ruth Earp, but he was afraid of not being out of the house before his mother returned. Mrs Machin had been making up a lady's own materials all day, naturally – the day being what it was! If she had had twelve hands instead of two, she might have made up the own materials of half-a-dozen ladies instead of one, and earned twenty-four shillings instead of four. Denry did not want his mother to see him ere he departed. He had lavished an enormous amount of brains and energy to the end of displaying himself in this refined and novel attire to the gaze of two hundred persons, and yet his secret wish was to deprive his mother of the beautiful spectacle.

However, she slipped in, with her bag and her seamy fingers and her rather sardonic expression, at the very moment when Denry was putting on his overcoat in the kitchen (there being insufficient room in the passage). He did what he could to hide his shirt-front (though she knew all about it), and failed.

'Bless us!' she exclaimed briefly, going to the fire to warm her hands.

A harmless remark. But her tone seemed to strip bare the vanity of human greatness.

'I'm in a hurry,' said Denry, importantly, as if he was going forth to sign a treaty involving the welfare of the nations.

'Well,' said she, 'happen ye are, Denry. But th' kitchen table's no place for boot-brushes.'

He had one piece of luck. It froze. Therefore no anxiety about the condition of boots.

VI

The Countess was late; some trouble with a horse. Happily the Earl had been in Bursley all day, and had dressed at the Conservative Club; and his lordship had ordered that the programme of dances should be begun. Denry learned this as soon as he emerged, effulgent, from the gentlemen's cloak-room into

14

the broad red-carpeted corridor which runs from end to end of the ground-floor of the Town Hall. Many important townspeople were chatting in the corridor – the innumerable Swetnam family, the Stanways, the great Etches, the Fearnses, Mrs Clayton Vernon, the Suttons, including Beatrice Sutton. Of course everybody knew him for Duncalf's shorthand clerk and the son of the flannel-washer; but universal white kid gloves constitute a democracy, and Shillitoe could put more style into a suit than any other tailor in the Five Towns.

'How do?' the eldest of the Swetnam boys nodded carelessly.

'How do, Swetnam?' said Denry, with equal carelessness.

The thing was accomplished! That greeting was like a Masonic initiation, and henceforward he was the peer of no matter whom. At first he had thought that four hundred eyes would be fastened on him, their glance saying, 'This youth is wearing a dress-suit for the first time, and it is not paid for, either!' But it was not so. And the reason was that the entire population of the Town Hall was heartily engaged in pretending that never in its life had it been seen after seven o'clock of a night apart from a dress-suit. Denry observed with joy that, while numerous middle-aged and awkward men wore red or white silk handkerchiefs in their waistcoats, such people as Charles Fearns, the Swetnams, and Harold Etches did not. He was, then, in the shyness of his handkerchief, on the side of the angels.

He passed up the double staircase (decorated with white or pale frocks of unparalleled richness), and so into the grand hall. A scarlet orchestra was on the platform, and many people strolled about the floor in attitudes of expectation. The walls were festooned with flowers. The thrill of being magnificent seized him, and he was drenched in a vast desire to be truly magnificent himself. He dreamt of magnificence and bootbrushes kept sticking out of this dream like black mud out of snow. In his reverie he looked about for Ruth Earp, but she was invisible. Then he went downstairs again, idly; gorgeously feigning that he spent six evenings a week in ascending and descending monumental staircases, appropriately clad. He was determined to be as sublime as anyone.

There was a stir in the corridor, and the sublimest consented to be excited.

The Countess was announced to be imminent. Everybody was grouped round the main portal, careless of temperatures. Six times was the Countess announced to be imminent before she actually appeared, expanding from the narrow gloom of her black carriage like a magic vision. Aldermen received her – and they did not do it with any excess of gracefulness. They seemed afraid of her, as though she was recovering from influenza and they feared to catch it. She had precisely the same high voice, and precisely the same efficient smile, as she had employed to Denry, and these instruments worked marvels on aldermen; they were as melting as salt on snow. The Countess disappeared upstairs in a cloud of shrill apologies and trailing aldermen. She seemed to have greeted everybody except Denry. Somehow he was relieved that she had not drawn attention to him. He lingered, hesitating, and then he saw a being in a long yellow overcoat, with a bit of peacock's feather at the summit of a shiny high hat. This being held a lady's fur mantle. Their eyes met. Denry had to decide instantly. He decided.

'Hello, Jock!' he said.

'Hello, Denry!' said the other, pleased.

'What's been happening?' Denry inquired, friendly.

Then Jock told him about the antics of one of the Countess's horses.

He went upstairs again, and met Ruth Earp coming down. She was glorious in white. Except that nothing glittered in her hair, she looked the very equal of the Countess, at a little distance, plain though her features were.

'What about that waltz?' Denry began informally.

'That waltz is nearly over,' said Ruth Earp, with chilliness. 'I suppose you've been staring at her ladyship with all the other men.'

'I'm awfully sorry', he said. 'I didn't know the waltz was –'

'Well, why didn't you look at your programme?'

'Haven't got one,' he said naïvely.

He had omitted to take a programme. Ninny! Barbarian!

16

'Better get one,' she said cuttingly, somewhat in her role of dancing mistress.

'Can't we finish the waltz?' he suggested, crestfallen.

'No!' she said, and continued her solitary way downwards.

She was hurt. He tried to think of something to say that was equal to the situation, and equal to the style of his suit. But he could not. In a moment he heard her, below him, greeting some male acquaintance in the most effusive way.

Yet, if Denry had not committed a wicked crime for her, she could never have come to the dance at all!

He got a programme, and with terror gripping his heart he asked sundry young and middle-aged women whom he knew by sight and by name for a dance. (Ruth had taught him how to ask.) Not one of them had a dance left. Several looked at him as much as to say: 'You must be a goose to suppose that my programme is not filled up in the twinkling of my eye!'

Then he joined a group of despisers of dancing near the main door. Harold Etches was there, the wealthiest manufacturer of his years (barely twenty-four) in the Five Towns. Also Shillitoe, cause of another of Denry's wicked crimes. The group was taciturn, critical, and very doggish.

The group observed that the Countess was not dancing. The Earl was dancing (need it be said with Mrs Jos Curtenty, second wife of the Deputy Mayor?), but the Countess stood resolutely smiling, surrounded by aldermen. Possibly she was getting her breath; possibly nobody had had the pluck to ask her. Anyhow, she seemed to be stranded there, on a beach of aldermen. Very wisely she had brought with her no members of a house-party from Sneyd Hall. Members of a house-party, at a municipal ball, invariably operate as a bar between greatness and democracy; and the Countess desired to participate in the life of the people.

'Why don't some of those johnnies ask her?' Denry burst out. He had hitherto said nothing in the group, and he felt that he must be a man with the rest of them.

'Well, *you* go and do it. It's a free country,' said Shillitoe.

'So I would, for two pins!' said Denry.

Harold Etches glanced at him, apparently resentful of his

presence there. Harold Etches was determined to put the extinguisher on *him*.

'I'll bet you a fiver you don't,' said Etches scornfully.

'I'll take you,' said Denry, very quickly, and very quickly walked off.

VII

'She can't eat me. She can't eat me!'

This was what he said to himself as he crossed the floor. People seemed to make a lane for him, divining his incredible intention. If he had not started at once, if his legs had not started of themselves, he would never have started; and, not being in command of a fiver, he would afterwards have cut a preposterous figure in the group. But started he was, like a piece of clockwork that could not be stopped! In the grand crises of his life something not himself, something more powerful than himself, jumped up in him and forced him to do things. Now for the first time he seemed to understand what had occurred within him in previous crises.

In a second – so it appeared – he had reached the Countess. Just behind her was his employer, Mr Duncalf, whom Denry had not previously noticed there. Denry regretted this, for he had never mentioned to Mr Duncalf that he was coming to the ball, and he feared Mr Duncalf.

'Could I have this dance with you?' he demanded bluntly, but smiling and showing his teeth.

No ceremonial title! No mention of 'pleasure' or 'honour'. Not a trace of the formula in which Ruth Earp had instructed him! He forgot all such trivialities.

'I've won that fiver, Mr Harold Etches,' he said to himself.

The mouths of aldermen inadvertently opened. Mr Duncalf blenched.

'It's nearly over, isn't it?' said the Countess, still efficiently smiling. She did not recognize Denry. In that suit he might have been a Foreign Office attaché.

'Oh! that doesn't matter, I'm sure,' said Denry.

She yielded, and he took the paradisiacal creature in his arms. It was her business that evening to be universally and inclusively

18

polite. She could not have begun with a refusal. A refusal might have dried up all other invitations whatsoever. Besides, she saw that the aldermen wanted a lead. Besides, she was young, though a countess, and adored dancing.

Thus they waltzed together, while the flower of Bursley's chivalry gazed in enchantment. The Countess's fan, depending from her arm, dangled against Denry's suit in a rather confusing fashion, which withdrew his attention from his feet. He laid hold of it gingerly between two unemployed fingers. After that he managed fairly well. Once they came perilously near the Earl and his partner; nothing else. And then the dance ended, exactly when Denry had begun to savour the astounding spectacle of himself enclasping the Countess.

The Countess had soon perceived that he was the merest boy.

'You waltz quite nicely!' she said, like an aunt, but with more than an aunt's smile.

'Do I?' he beamed. Then something compelled him to say: 'Do you know, it's the first time I've ever waltzed in my life, except in a lesson, you know?'

'Really!' she murmured. 'You pick things up easily, I suppose?'

'Yes,' he said. 'Do you?'

Either the question or the tone sent the Countess off into carillons of amusement. Everybody could see that Denry had made the Countess laugh tremendously. It was on this note that the waltz finished. She was still laughing when he bowed to her (as taught by Ruth Earp). He could not comprehend why she had so laughed, save on the supposition that he was more humorous than he had suspected. Anyhow, he laughed too, and they parted laughing. He remembered that he had made a marked effect (though not one of laughter) on the tailor by quickly returning the question, 'Are you?' And his unpremeditated stroke with the Countess was similar. When he had got ten yards on his way towards Harold Etches and a fiver he felt something in his hand. The Countess's fan was sticking between his fingers. It had unhooked itself from her chain. He furtively pocketed it.

'Just the same as dancing with any other woman!' He told this untruth in reply to a question from Shillitoe. It was the least he could do. And any other young man in his place would have said as much or as little.

'What was she laughing at?' somebody asked.

'Ah!' said Denry, judiciously, 'wouldn't you like to know?'

'Here you are!' said Etches, with an inattentive, plutocratic gesture handing over a five-pound note. He was one of those men who never venture out of sight of a bank without a bank-note in their pockets – 'Because you never know what may turn up.'

Denry accepted the note with a silent nod. In some directions he was gifted with astounding insight, and he could read in the faces of the haughty males surrounding him that in the space of a few minutes he had risen from nonentity into renown. He had become a great man. He did not at once realize how great, how renowned. But he saw enough in those eyes to cause his heart to glow, and to rouse in his brain those ambitious dreams which stirred him upon occasion. He left the group; he had need of motion, and also of that mental privacy which one may enjoy while strolling about on a crowded floor in the midst of a considerable noise. He noticed that the Countess was now dancing with an alderman, and that the alderman, by an oversight inexcusable in an alderman, was not wearing gloves. It was he, Denry, who had broken the ice, so that the alderman might plunge into the water. He first had danced with the Countess, and had rendered her up to the alderman with delicious gaiety upon her countenance. By instinct he knew Bursley, and he knew that he would be talked of. He knew that, for a time at any rate, he would displace even Jos Curtenty, that almost professional 'card' and amuser of burgesses, in the popular imagination. It would not be: 'Have ye heard Jos's latest?' It would be: 'Have ye heard about young Machin, Duncalf's clerk?'

Then he met Ruth Earp, strolling in the opposite direction with a young girl, one of her pupils, of whom all he knew was that her name was Nellie, and that this was her first ball: a childish little thing with a wistful face. He could not decide whether to look at Ruth or to avoid her glance. She settled the point by smiling at him in a manner that could not be ignored.

'Are you going to make it up to me for that waltz you missed?' said Ruth Earp. She pretended to be vexed and stern, but he knew that she was not. 'Or is your programme full?' she added.

'I should like to,' he said simply.

'But perhaps you don't care to dance with us poor, ordinary people, now you've danced with the *Countess*!' she said, with a certain lofty and bitter pride.

He perceived that his tone had lacked eagerness.

'Don't talk like that,' he said, as if hurt.

'Well,' she said, 'you can have the supper dance.'

He took her programme to write on it.

'Why,' he said, 'there's a name down here for the supper dance. "Herbert", it looks like.'

'Oh!' she replied carelessly, 'that's nothing. Cross it out.'

So he crossed Herbert out.

'Why don't you ask Nellie here for a dance?' said Ruth Earp.

And Nellie blushed. He gathered that the possible honour of dancing with the supremely great man had surpassed Nellie's modest expectations.

'Can I have the next one?' he said.

'Oh, yes!' Nellie timidly whispered.

'It's a polka, and you aren't very good at polking, you know,' Ruth warned him. 'Still, Nellie will pull you through.'

Nellie laughed, in silver. The naïve child thought that Ruth was trying to joke at Denry's expense. Her very manifest joy and pride in being seen with the unique Mr Machin, in being the next after the Countess to dance with him, made another mirror in which Denry could discern the reflection of his vast importance.

At the supper, which was worthy of the hospitable traditions of the Chell family (though served standing-up in the police-court), he learnt all the gossip of the dance from Ruth Earp;

amongst other things that more than one young man had asked the Countess for a dance, and had been refused, though Ruth Earp for her part declined to believe that aldermen and councillors had utterly absorbed the Countess's programme. Ruth hinted that the Countess was keeping a second dance open for him, Denry. When she asked him squarely if he meant to request another from the Countess, he said no, positively. He knew when to let well alone, a knowledge which is more precious than a knowledge of geography. The supper was the summit of Denry's triumph. The best people spoke to him without being introduced. And lovely creatures mysteriously and intoxicatingly discovered that programmes which had been crammed two hours before were not, after all, quite full.

'Do tell us what the Countess was laughing at?' This question was shot at him at least thirty times. He always said he would not tell. And one girl who had danced with Mr Stanway, who had danced with the Countess, said that Mr Stanway had said that the Countess would not tell either. Proof, here, that he was being extensively talked about!

Towards the end of the festivity the rumour floated abroad that the Countess had lost her fan. The rumour reached Denry, who maintained a culpable silence. But when all was over, and the Countess was departing, he rushed down after her, and, in a dramatic fashion which demonstrated his genius for the effective, he caught her exactly as she was getting into her carriage.

'I've just picked it up,' he said, pushing through the crowd of worshippers.

'Oh! thank you so much!' she said. And the Earl also thanked Denry. And then the Countess, leaning from the carriage, said, with archness in her efficient smile: 'You do pick things up easily, don't you?'

And both Denry and the Countess laughed without restraint, and the pillars of Bursley society were mystified.

Denry winked at Jock as the horses pawed away. And Jock winked back.

The envied of all, Denry walked home, thinking violently. At a stroke he had become possessed of more than he could earn from Duncalf in a month. The faces of the Countess, of Ruth Earp, and of the timid Nellie mingled in exquisite hallucinations before his tired eyes. He was inexpressibly happy. Trouble, however, awaited him.

CHAPTER 2

The Widow Hullins's House

I

THE simple fact that he first, of all the citizens of Bursley, had asked a countess for a dance (and not been refused) made a new man of Denry Machin. He was not only regarded by the whole town as a fellow wonderful and dazzling, but he so regarded himself. He could not get over it. He had always been cheerful, even to optimism. He was now in a permanent state of calm, assured jollity. He would get up in the morning with song and dance. Bursley and the general world were no longer Bursley and the general world; they had been mysteriously transformed into an oyster; and Denry felt strangely that the oyster-knife was lying about somewhere handy, but just out of sight, and that presently he should spy it and seize it. He waited for something to happen. And not in vain.

A few days after the historic revelry, Mrs Codleyn called to see Denry's employer. Mr Duncalf was her solicitor. A stout, breathless, and yet muscular woman of near sixty, the widow of a chemist and druggist who had made money before limited companies had taken the liberty of being pharmaceutical. The money had been largely invested in mortgage on cottage property; the interest on it had not been paid, and latterly Mrs Codleyn had been obliged to foreclose, thus becoming the owner of some seventy cottages. Mrs Codleyn, though they brought her in about twelve pounds a week gross, esteemed these cottages an infliction, a bugbear, an affront, and a positive source of loss. Invariably she talked as though she would willingly present them to anybody who cared to accept – 'and glad to be rid of 'em!' Most owners of property talk thus. She particularly hated paying the rates on them.

Now there had recently occurred, under the direction of the Borough Surveyor, a revaluation of the whole town. This may not sound exciting; yet a revaluation is the most exciting event (save a municipal ball given by a titled mayor) that can happen in any town. If your house is rated at forty pounds a year, and rates are seven shillings in the pound, and the revaluation lifts you up to forty-five pounds, it means thirty-five shillings a year right out of your pocket, which is the interest on thirty-five pounds. And if the revaluation drops you to thirty-five pounds, it means thirty-five shillings *in* your pocket, which is a box of Havanas or a fancy waistcoat. Is not this exciting? And there are seven thousand houses in Bursley. Mrs Codleyn hoped that her rateable value would be reduced. She based the hope chiefly on the fact that she was a client of Mr Duncalf, the Town Clerk. The Town Clerk was not the Borough Surveyor and had nothing to do with the revaluation. Moreover, Mrs Codleyn presumably entrusted him with her affairs because she considered him an honest man, and an honest man could not honestly have sought to tickle the Borough Surveyor out of the narrow path of rectitude in order to oblige a client. Nevertheless, Mrs Codleyn thought that because she patronized the Town Clerk her rates ought to be reduced! Such is human nature in the provinces! So different from human nature in London, where nobody ever dreams of offering even a match to a municipal official, lest the act might be construed into an insult.

It was on a Saturday morning that Mrs Codleyn called to impart to Mr Duncalf the dissatisfaction with which she had learned the news (printed on a bit of bluish paper) that her rateable value, far from being reduced, had been slightly augmented. The interview, as judged by the clerks through a lath-and-plaster wall and by means of a speaking tube, atoned by its vivacity for its lack of ceremony. When the stairs had finished creaking under the descent of Mrs Codleyn's righteous fury, Mr Duncalf whistled sharply twice. Two whistles meant Denry. Denry picked up his shorthand note-book and obeyed the summons.

'Take this down!' said his master, rudely and angrily.

Just as though Denry had abetted Mrs Codleyn! Just as though Denry was not a personage of high importance in the

town, the friend of countesses, and a shorthand clerk only on
the surface.

'Do you hear?'

'Yes, sir.'

'MADAM' – hitherto it had always been 'Dear Madam', or
'Dear Mrs Codleyn' – 'MADAM, – Of course I need hardly say
that if, after our interview this morning, and your extraordinary
remarks, you wish to place your interests in other hands, I shall
be most happy to hand over all the papers, on payment of my
costs. Yours truly . . . To Mrs Codleyn.'

Denry reflected: 'Ass! Why doesn't he let her cool down?'
Also: 'He's got "hands" and "hand" in the same sentence.
Very ugly. Shows what a temper he's in!' Shorthand clerks are
always like that – hypercritical. Also: 'Well, I jolly well hope
she does chuck him! Then I shan't have those rents to collect.'
Every Monday, and often on Tuesday, too, Denry collected the
rents of Mrs Codleyn's cottages – an odious task for Denry. Mr
Duncalf, though not affected by its odiousness, deducted 7½
per cent for the job from the rents.

'That'll do,' said Mr Duncalf.

But as Denry was leaving the room Mr Duncalf called with
formidable brusqueness –

'Machin!'

'Yes, sir?'

In a flash Denry knew what was coming. He felt sickly that a
crisis had supervened with the suddenness of a tidal wave. And
for one little second it seemed to him that to have danced with a
countess while the flower of Bursley's chivalry watched in en-
vious wonder was not, after all, the key to the door of success
throughout life.

Undoubtedly he had practised fraud in sending to himself an
invitation to the ball. Undoubtedly he had practised fraud in
sending invitations to his tailor and his dancing-mistress. On the
day after the ball, beneath his great glory, he had trembled to
meet Mr Duncalf's eye, lest Mr Duncalf should ask him:
'Machin, what were *you* doing at the Town Hall last night,
behaving as if you were the Shah of Persia, the Prince of Wales,

and Henry Irving?' But Mr Duncalf had said nothing, and Mr Duncalf's eye had said nothing, and Denry thought that the danger was past.

Now it surged up.

'Who invited you to the Mayor's ball?' demanded Mr Duncalf like thunder.

Yes, there it was! And a very difficult question.

'I did, sir,' he blundered out. Transparent veracity. He simply could not think of a lie.

'Why?'

'I thought you'd perhaps forgotten to put my name down on the list of invitations, sir.'

'Oh!' This grimly. 'And I suppose you thought I'd also forgotten to put down that tailor chap, Shillitoe?'

So it was all out! Shillitoe must have been chattering. Denry remembered that the classic established tailor of the town, Hatterton, whose trade Shillitoe was getting, was a particular friend of Mr Duncalf's. He saw the whole thing.

'Well?' persisted Mr Duncalf, after a judicious silence from Denry.

Denry, sheltered in the castle of his silence, was not to be tempted out.

'I suppose you rather fancy yourself dancing with your betters?' growled Mr Duncalf, menacingly.

'Yes,' said Denry. 'Do *you*?'

He had not meant to say it. The question slipped out of his mouth. He had recently formed the habit of retorting swiftly upon people who put queries to him: 'Yes, are *you*?' or 'No, do *you*?' The trick of speech had been enormously effective with Shillitoe, for instance, and with the Countess. He was in process of acquiring renown for it. Certainly it was effective now. Mr Duncalf's dance with the Countess had come to an ignominious conclusion in the middle, Mr Duncalf preferring to dance on skirts rather than on the floor, and the fact was notorious.

'You can take a week's notice,' said Mr Duncalf, pompously.

It was no argument. But employers are so unscrupulous in an altercation.

'Oh, very well,' said Denry; and to himself he said: 'Something *must* turn up, now.'

He felt dizzy at being thus thrown upon the world – he who had been meditating the propriety of getting himself elected to the stylish and newly-established Sports Club at Hillport! He felt enraged, for Mr Duncalf had only been venting on Denry the annoyance induced in him by Mrs Codleyn. But it is remarkable that he was not depressed at all. No! he went about with songs and whistling, though he had no prospects except starvation or living on his mother. He traversed the streets in his grand, new manner, and his thoughts ran: 'What on earth can I do to live up to my reputation?' However, he possessed intact the five-pound note won from Harold Etches in the matter of the dance.

II

Every life is a series of coincidences. Nothing happens that is not rooted in coincidence. All great changes find their cause in coincidence. Therefore I shall not mince the fact that the next change in Denry's career was due to an enormous and complicated coincidence. On the following morning both Mrs Codleyn and Denry were late for service at St Luke's Church – Mrs Codleyn by accident and obesity, Denry by design. Denry was later than Mrs Codleyn, whom he discovered waiting in the porch. That Mrs Codleyn was waiting is an essential part of the coincidence. Now Mrs Codleyn would not have been waiting, if her pew had not been right at the front of the church, near the choir. Nor would she have been waiting if she had been a thin woman and not given to breathing loudly after a hurried walk. She waited partly to get her breath, and partly so that she might take advantage of a hymn or a psalm to gain her seat without attracting attention. If she had not been late, if she had not been stout, if she had not had a seat under the pulpit, if she had not had an objection to making herself conspicuous, she would have been already in the church and Denry would not have had a private colloquy with her.

'Well, you're nice people, I must say!' she observed, as he raised his hat.

She meant Duncalf and all Duncalf's myrmidons. She was still full of her grievance. The letter which she had received that morning had startled her. And even the shadow of the sacred edifice did not prevent her from referring to an affair that was more suited to Monday than to Sunday morning. A little more, and she would have snorted.

'Nothing to do with me, you know!' Denry defended himself.

'Oh!' she said, 'you're all alike, and I'll tell you this, Mr Machin, I'd take him at his word if it wasn't that I don't know who else I could trust to collect my rents. I've heard such tales about rent-collectors . . . I reckon I shall have to make my peace with him.'

'Why,' said Denry, 'I'll keep on collecting your rents for you if you like.'

'You?'

'I've given him notice to leave,' said Denry. 'The fact is, Mr Duncalf and I don't hit it off together.'

Another procrastinator arrived in the porch, and, by a singular simultaneous impulse, Mrs Codleyn and Denry fell into the silence of the overheard and wandered forth together among the graves.

There, among the graves, she eyed him. He was a clerk at eighteen shillings a week, and he looked it. His mother was a sempstress, and he looked it. The idea of neat but shabby Denry and the mighty Duncalf not hitting it off together seemed excessively comic. If only Denry could have worn his dress-suit at church! It vexed him exceedingly that he had only worn that expensive dress-suit once, and saw no faintest hope of ever being able to wear it again.

'And what's more,' Denry pursued, 'I'll collect 'em for five per cent instead of seven-and-a-half. Give me a free hand and see if I don't get better results than *he* did. And I'll settle accounts every month, or week if you like, instead of once a quarter, like he does.'

The bright and beautiful idea had smitten Denry like some heavenly arrow. It went through him and pierced Mrs Codleyn with equal success. It was an idea that appealed to the reason, to

29

the pocket, and to the instinct of revenge. Having revengefully settled the hash of Mr Duncalf, they went into church.

No need to continue this part of the narrative. Even the text of the rector's sermon has no bearing on the issue.

In a week there was a painted board affixed to the door of Denry's mother:

E. H. MACHIN
Rent Collector and Estate Agent

There was also an advertisement in the *Signal,* announcing that Denry managed estates large or small.

III

The next crucial event in Denry's career happened one Monday morning, in a cottage that was very much smaller even than his mother's. This cottage, part of Mrs Codleyn's multitudinous property, stood by itself in Chapel Alley, behind the Wesleyan chapel; the majority of the tenements were in Carpenter's Square, near to. The neighbourhood was not distinguished for its social splendour, but existence in it was picturesque, varied, exciting, full of accidents, as existence is apt to be in residences that cost their occupiers an average of three shillings a week. Some persons referred to the quarter as a slum, and ironically insisted on its adjacency to the Wesleyan chapel, as though that was the Wesleyan chapel's fault. Such people did not understand life and the joy thereof.

The solitary cottage had a front yard, about as large as a blanket, surrounded by an insecure brick wall and paved with mud. You went up two steps, pushed at a door, and instantly found yourself in the principal reception-room, which no earthly blanket could possibly have covered. Behind this chamber could be seen obscurely an apartment so tiny that an auctioneer would have been justified in terming it 'bijou', furnished simply but practically with a slopstone; also the beginnings of a stairway. The furniture of the reception-room comprised two chairs and a table, one or two saucepans, and some antique crockery. What lay at the upper end of the stairway no living person knew, save the old woman who slept there. The old woman sat at the fireplace, 'all bunched up', as they say in the Five Towns. The only fire in the room, however, was in the short clay pipe which she smoked; Mrs Hullins was one of the last old women in Bursley to smoke a cutty; and even then the pipe was considered coarse, and cigarettes were coming into fashion – though not in Chapel Alley. Mrs Hullins smoked her pipe, and thought about nothing in particular. Occasionally some vision of the past floated through her drowsy brain. She had lived in that residence for over forty years. She had brought up eleven children and two husbands there. She had coddled thirty-five grandchildren there, and given instruction to some half-dozen daughters-in-law. She had known midnights when she could scarcely move in that residence without disturbing somebody asleep. Now she was alone in it. She never left it, except to fetch water from the pump in the square. She had seen a lot of life, and she was tired.

Denry came unceremoniously in, smiling gaily and benevolently, with his bright, optimistic face under his fair brown hair. He had large and good teeth. He was getting – not stout, but plump.

'Well, mother!' he greeted Mrs Hullins, and sat down on the other chair.

A young fellow obviously at peace with the world, a young fellow content with himself for the moment. No longer a clerk; one of the employed; saying 'sir' to persons with no more fingers and toes than he had himself; bound by servile agreement to be in a fixed place at fixed hours! An independent unit, master of his own time and his own movements! In brief, a man! The truth was that he earned now in two days a week slightly more than Mr Duncalf paid him for the labour of five and a half days. His income, as collector of rents and manager of estates large or small, totalled about a pound a week. But, he walked forth in the town, smiled, joked, spoke vaguely, and said, 'Do *you*?' to such a tune that his income might have been guessed to be anything from ten pounds a week to ten thousand a year. And he had four days a week in which to excogitate new methods of creating a fortune.

'I've nowt for ye,' said the old woman, not moving.

'Come, come, now! That won't do,' said Denry. 'Have a pinch of my tobacco.'

She accepted a pinch of his tobacco, and refilled her pipe, and he gave her a match.

'I'm not going out of this house without half-a-crown at any rate!' said Denry, blithely.

And he rolled himself a cigarette, possibly to keep warm. It was very chilly in the stuffy residence, but the old woman never shivered. She was one of those old women who seem to wear all the skirts of all their lives, one over the other.

'Ye're here for th' better part o' some time, then,' observed Mrs Hullins, looking facts in the face. 'I've told you about my son Jack. He's been playing [out of work] six weeks. He starts today, and he'll gi' me summat Saturday.'

'That won't do,' said Denry, curtly and kindly.

He then, with his bluff benevolence, explained to Mother Hullins that Mrs Codleyn would stand no further increase of arrears from anybody, that she could not afford to stand any further increase of arrears, that her tenants were ruining her, and that he himself, with all his cheery good-will for the rent-paying classes, would be involved in her fall.

'Six-and-forty years have I been i' this 'ere house!' said Mrs Hullins.

'Yes, I know,' said Denry. 'And look at what you owe, mother!'

It was with immense good-humoured kindliness that he invited her attention to what she owed. She tacitly declined to look at it.

'Your children ought to keep you,' said Denry, upon her silence.

'Them as is dead, can't,' said Mrs Hullins, 'and them as is alive has their own to keep, except Jack.'

'Well, then, it's bailiffs,' said Denry, but still cheerfully.

'Nay, nay! Ye'll none turn me out.'

Denry threw up his hands, as if to exclaim: 'I've done all I can, and I've given you a pinch of tobacco. Besides, you oughtn't to be here alone. You ought to be with one of your children.'

There was more conversation, which ended in Denry's repeating, with sympathetic resignation:

'No, you'll have to get out. It's bailiffs.'

Immediately afterwards he left the residence with a bright filial smile. And then, in two minutes, he popped his cheerful head in at the door again.

'Look here, mother,' he said, 'I'll lend you half-a-crown if you like.'

Charity beamed on his face, and genuinely warmed his heart.

'But you must pay me something for the accommodation,' he added. 'I can't do it for nothing. You must pay me back next week and give me threepence. That's fair. I couldn't bear to see you turned out of your house. Now get your rent-book.'

And he marked half-a-crown as paid in her greasy, dirty rent-book, and the same in his large book.

'Eh, you're a queer 'un, Mester Machin!' murmured the old woman as he left. He never knew precisely what she meant. Fifteen – twenty – years later in his career her intonation of that phrase would recur to him and puzzle him.

On the following Monday everybody in Chapel Alley and Carpenter's Square seemed to know that the inconvenience of bailiffs and eviction could be avoided by arrangement with Denry the philanthropist. He did quite a business. And having regard to the fantastic nature of the security, he could not well charge less than threepence a week for half-a-crown. That was about 40 per cent a month and 500 per cent per annum. The security was merely fantastic, but nevertheless he had his remedy against evil-doers. He would take what they paid him for rent and refuse to mark it as rent, appropriating it to his loans, so that the fear of bailiffs was upon them again. Thus, as the good genius of Chapel Alley and Carpenter's Square, saving the distressed from the rigours of the open street, rescuing the needy from their tightest corners, keeping many a home together when but for him it would have fallen to pieces – always smiling, jolly, sympathetic, and picturesque – Denry at length employed the five-pound note won from Harold Etches. A five-pound note – especially a new and crisp one, as this was – is a miraculous fragment of matter, wonderful in the pleasure which the sight of it gives, even to millionaires; but perhaps no five-pound note was ever so miraculous as Denry's. Ten per cent per week, compound interest, mounts up; it ascends, and it lifts. Denry never talked precisely. But the town soon began to comprehend that he was a rising man, a man to watch. The town admitted that, so far, he had lived up to his reputation as a dancer with countesses. The town felt that there was something indefinable about Denry.

Denry himself felt this. He did not consider himself clever or brilliant. But he considered himself peculiarly gifted. He considered himself different from other men. His thoughts would run:

'Anybody but me would have knuckled down to Duncalf and remained a shorthand clerk for ever.'

'Who but me would have had the idea of going to the ball and asking the Countess to dance? ... And then that business with the fan!'

'Who but me would have had the idea of taking his rent-collecting off Duncalf?'

'Who but me would have had the idea of combining these loans with the rent-collecting? It's simple enough! It's just what they want! And yet nobody ever thought of it till I thought of it!'

And he knew of a surety that he was that most admired type in the bustling, industrial provinces – a card.

IV

The desire to become a member of the Sports Club revived in his breast. And yet, celebrity though he was, rising though he was, he secretly regarded the Sports Club at Hillport as being really a bit above him. The Sports Club was the latest and greatest phenomenon of social life in Bursley, and it was emphatically the club to which it behoved the golden youth of the town to belong. To Denry's generation the Conservative Club and the

34

Liberal Club did not seem like real clubs; they were machinery for politics, and membership carried nearly no distinction with it. But the Sports Club had been founded by the most dashing young men of Hillport, which is the most aristocratic suburb of Bursley and set on a lofty eminence. The sons of the wealthiest earthenware manufacturers made a point of belonging to it, and, after a period of disdain, their fathers also made a point of belonging to it. It was housed in an old mansion, with extensive grounds and a pond and tennis courts; it had a working agreement with the Golf Club and with the Hillport Cricket Club. But chiefly it was a social affair. The correctest thing was to be seen there at nights, rather late than early; and an exact knowledge of card games and billiards was worth more in it than prowess on the field.

It was a club in the Pall Mall sense of the word.

And Denry still lived in insignificant Brougham Street, and his mother was still a sempstress! These were apparently insurmountable truths. All the men whom he knew to be members were somehow more dashing than Denry – and it was a question of dash; few things are more mysterious than dash. Denry was unique, knew himself to be unique; he had danced with a countess, and yet ... these other fellows! ... Yes, there are puzzles, baffling puzzles, in the social career.

In going over on Tuesdays to Hanbridge, where he had a few trifling rents to collect, Denry often encountered Harold Etches in the tramcar. At that time Etches lived at Hillport, and the principal Etches manufactory was at Hanbridge. Etches partook of the riches of his family, and, though a bachelor, was reputed to have the spending of at least a thousand a year. He was famous, on summer Sundays, on the pier at Llandudno, in white flannels. He had been one of the originators of the Sports Club. He spent far more on clothes alone than Denry spent in the entire enterprise of keeping his soul in his body. At their first meeting little was said. They were not equals, and nothing but dress-suits could make them equals. However, even a king could not refuse speech with a scullion whom he had allowed to win money from him. And Etches and Denry chatted feebly. Bit by bit they chatted less feebly. And once, when they were almost

35

alone on the car, they chatted with vehemence during the complete journey of twenty minutes.

'He isn't so bad,' said Denry to himself, of the dashing Harold Etches.

And he took a private oath that at his very next encounter with Etches he would mention the Sports Club – just to see', This oath disturbed his sleep for several nights. But with Denry an oath was sacred. Having sworn that he would mention the club to Etches, he was bound to mention it. When Tuesday came, he hoped that Etches would not be on the tram, and the coward in him would have walked to Hanbridge instead of taking the tram. But he was brave. And he boarded the tram, and Etches was already in it. Now that he looked at it close, the enterprise of suggesting to Harold Etches that he, Denry, would be a suitable member of the Sports Club at Hillport, seemed in the highest degree preposterous. Why! He could not play any games at all! He was a figure only in the streets! Nevertheless – the oath!

He sat awkwardly silent for a few moments, wondering how to begin. And then Harold Etches leaned across the tram to him and said:

'I say, Machin, I've several times meant to ask you. Why don't you put up for the Sports Club? It's really very good, you know.'

Denry blushed, quite probably for the last time in his life. And he saw with fresh clearness how great he was, and how large he must loom in the life of the town. He perceived that he had been too modest.

v

You could not be elected to the Sports Club all in a minute. There were formalities; and that these formalities were complicated and took time is simply a proof that the club was correctly exclusive and worth belonging to. When at length Denry received notice from the 'Secretary and Steward' that he was elected to the most sparkling fellowship in the Five Towns, he was positively afraid to go and visit the club. He wanted some old and experienced member to lead him gently into the club and explain its usages and introduce him to the chief *habitués*. Or else he wanted to slip in unobserved while the heads of clubmen were turned. And then he had a distressing shock. Mrs Codleyn took it into her head that she must sell her cottage property. Now, Mrs Codleyn's cottage property was the backbone of Denry's livelihood, and he could by no means be sure that a new owner would employ him as rent-collector. A new owner might have the absurd notion of collecting rents in person. Vainly did Denry exhibit to Mrs Codleyn rows of figures, showing that her income from the property had increased under his control. Vainly did he assert that from no other form of investment would she derive such a handsome interest. She went so far as to consult an auctioneer. The auctioneer's idea of what could constitute a fair reserve price shook, but did not quite overthrow her. At this crisis it was that Denry happened to say to her, in his new large manner: 'Why! If I could afford, I'd buy the property off you myself, just to show you ...!' (He did not explain, and he did not perhaps know himself, what had to be shown.) She answered that she wished to goodness he would! Then he said wildly that he *would*, in instalments! And he actually did buy the Widow Hullins's half-a-crown a week cottage for forty-five pounds, of which he paid thirty pounds in cash and arranged that the balance should be deducted gradually from his weekly commission. He chose the Widow Hullins's because it stood by itself — an odd piece, as it were, chipped off from the block of Mrs Codleyn's realty. The transaction quietened Mrs Codleyn. And Denry felt secure because she could not now dispense with his services without losing her security for fifteen pounds. (He still thought in these small sums instead of thinking in thousands.)

He was now a property owner.

Encouraged by this great and solemn fact, he went up one afternoon to the club at Hillport. His entry was magnificent, superficially. No one suspected that he was nervous under the ordeal. The truth is that no one suspected because the place was empty. The emptiness of the hall gave him pause. He saw a large framed copy of the 'Rules' hanging under a deer's head, and he read them as carefully as though he had not got a copy in

37

his pocket. Then he read the notices, as though they had been latest telegrams from some dire seat of war. Then, perceiving a massive open door of oak (the club-house had once been a pretty stately mansion), he passed through it, and saw a bar (with bottles) and a number of small tables and wicker chairs, and on one of the tables an example of the *Staffordshire Signal* displaying in vast letters the fearful question: 'Is your skin troublesome?' Denry's skin was troublesome; it crept. He crossed the hall and went into another room which was placarded 'Silence'. And silence was. And on a table with copies of *The Potter's World*, *The British Australasian*, *The Iron Trades Review*, and the *Golfer's Annual*, was a second copy of the *Signal*, again demanding of Denry in vast letters whether his skin was troublesome. Evidently the reading-room.

He ascended the stairs and discovered a deserted billiard-room with two tables. Though he had never played at billiards, he seized a cue, but when he touched them the balls gave such a resounding click in the hush of the chamber that he put the cue away instantly. He noticed another door, curiously opened it, and started back at the sight of a small room, and eight middle-aged men, mostly hatted, playing cards in two groups. They had the air of conspirators, but they were merely some of the finest solo-whist players in Bursley. (This was before bridge had quitted Pall Mall.) Among them was Mr Duncalf. Denry shut the door quickly. He felt like a wanderer in an enchanted castle who had suddenly come across something that ought not to be come across. He returned to earth, and in the hall met a man in shirt-sleeves – the Secretary and Steward, a nice, homely man, who said, in the accents of ancient friendship, though he had never spoken to Denry before: 'Is it Mr Machin? Glad to see you, Mr Machin! Come and have a drink with me, will you? Give it a name.' Saying which, the Secretary and Steward went behind the bar, and Denry imbibed a little whisky and much information.

'Anyhow, I've *been*!' he said to himself, going home.

The next night he made another visit to the club, about ten o'clock. The reading-room, that haunt of learning, was as empty as ever; but the bar was full of men, smoke, and glasses. It was so full that Denry's arrival was scarcely observed. However, the Secretary and Steward observed him, and soon he was chatting with a group at the bar, presided over by the Secretary and Steward's shirt-sleeves. He glanced around, and was satisfied. It was a scene of dashing gaiety and worldliness that did not belie the club's reputation. Some of the most important men in Bursley were there. Charles Fearns, the solicitor, who practised at Hanbridge, was arguing vivaciously in a corner. Fearns lived at Bleakridge and belonged to the Bleakridge Club, and his presence at Hillport (two miles from Bleakridge) was a dramatic tribute to the prestige of Hillport's Club.

Fearns was apparently in one of his anarchistic moods. Though a successful business man who voted right, he was pleased occasionally to uproot the fabric of society and rebuild it on a new plan of his own. Tonight he was inveighing against landlords – he who by 'conveyancing' kept a wife and family, and a French governess for the family, in rather more than comfort. The Fearns's French governess was one of the seven wonders of the Five Towns. Men enjoyed him in these moods; and as he raised his voice, so he enlarged the circle of his audience.

'If the by-laws of this town were worth a bilberry,' he was saying, 'about a thousand so-called houses would have to come down tomorrow. Now there's that old woman I was talking about just now – Hullins. She's a Catholic – and my governess is always slumming about among Catholics – that's how I know. She's paid half-a-crown a week for pretty near half a century for a hovel that isn't worth eighteen-pence, and now she's going to be pitched into the street because she can't pay any more. And she's seventy if she's a day! And that's the basis of society. Nice refined society, eh?'

'Who's the grasping owner?' some one asked.

'Old Mrs Codleyn,' said Fearns.

'Here, Mr Machin, they're talking about you,' said the Secretary and Steward, genially. He knew that Denry collected Mrs Codleyn's rents.

'Mrs Codleyn isn't the owner,' Denry called out across the room, almost before he was aware what he was doing. There was a smile on his face and a glass in his hand.

'Oh!' said Fearns. 'I thought she was. Who is?'

Everybody looked inquisitively at the renowned Machin, the new member.

'I am,' said Denry.

He had concealed the change of ownership from the Widow Hullins. In his quality of owner he could not have lent her money in order that she might pay it instantly back to himself.

'I beg your pardon,' said Fearns, with polite sincerity. 'I'd no idea . . . !' He saw that unwittingly he had come near to committing a gross outrage on club etiquette.

'Not at all!' said Denry. 'But supposing the cottage was *yours*, what would *you* do, Mr Fearns? Before I bought the property I used to lend her money myself to pay her rent.'

'I know,' Fearns answered, with a certain dryness of tone.

It occurred to Denry that the lawyer knew too much.

'Well, what should you do?' he repeated obstinately.

'She's an old woman,' said Fearns. 'And honest enough, you must admit. She came up to see my governess, and I happened to see her.'

'But what should you do in my place?' Denry insisted.

'Since you ask, I should lower the rent and let her off the arrears,' said Fearns.

'And supposing she didn't pay then? Let her have it rent-free because she's seventy? Or pitch her into the street?'

'Oh – well –'

'Fearns would make her a present of the blooming house and give her a conveyance free!' a voice said humorously, and everybody laughed.

'Well, that's what I'll do,' said Denry. 'If Mr Fearns will do the conveyance free, I'll make her a present of the blooming house. That's the sort of grasping owner I am.'

There was a startled pause. 'I mean it,' said Denry firmly,

even fiercely, and raised his glass. 'Here's to the Widow Hullins!'

There was a sensation, because, incredible though the thing was, it had to be believed. Denry himself was not the least astounded person in the crowded, smoky room. To him, it had been like somebody else talking, not himself. But, as always when he did something crucial, spectacular, and effective, the deed had seemed to be done by a mysterious power within him, over which he had no control.

This particular deed was quixotic, enormously unusual; a deed assuredly without precedent in the annals of the Five Towns. And he, Denry, had done it. The cost was prodigious, ridiculously and dangerously beyond his means. He could find no rational excuse for the deed. But he had done it. And men again wondered. Men had wondered when he led the Countess out to waltz. That was nothing to this. What! A smooth-chinned youth giving houses away – out of mere, mad, impulsive generosity.

And men said, on reflection, 'Of course, that's just the sort of thing Machin *would* do!' They appeared to find a logical connection between dancing with a Countess and tossing a house or so to a poor widow. And the next morning every man who had been in the Sports Club that night was remarking eagerly to his friends: 'I say, have you heard young Machin's latest?'

And Denry, inwardly aghast at his own rashness, was saying to himself: 'Well, no one but me would ever have done that!'

He was now not simply a card; he was *the* card.

CHAPTER 3

The Pantechnicon

I

'How do you do, Miss Earp?' said Denry, in a worldly manner, which he had acquired for himself by taking the most effective features of the manners of several prominent citizens, and piecing them together so that, as a whole, they formed Denry's manner.

'Oh! How do you do, Mr Machin?' said Ruth Earp, who had opened her door to him at the corner of Tudor Passage and St Luke's Square.

It was an afternoon in July. Denry wore a new summer suit, whose pattern indicated not only present prosperity but the firm belief that prosperity would continue. As for Ruth, that plain but piquant girl was in one of her simpler costumes; blue linen; no jewellery. Her hair was in its usual calculated disorder; its outer fleeces held the light. She was now at least twenty-five, and her gaze disconcertingly combined extreme maturity with extreme candour. At one moment a man would be saying to himself: 'This woman knows more of the secrets of human nature than I can ever know.' And the next he would be saying to himself: 'What a simple little thing she is!' The career of nearly every man is marked at the sharp corners with such women. Speaking generally, Ruth Earp's demeanour was hard and challenging. It was evident that she could not be subject to the common weaknesses of her sex. Denry was glad. A youth of quick intelligence, he had perceived all the dangers of the mission upon which he was engaged, and had planned his precautions.

'May I come in a minute?' he asked in a purely business tone. There was no hint in that tone of the fact that once she had accorded him a supper-dance.

'Please do,' said Ruth.

An agreeable flouncing swish of linen skirts as she turned to precede him down the passage! But he ignored it. That is to say, he easily steeled himself against it.

She led him to the large room which served as her dancing academy — the bare-boarded place in which, a year and a half before, she had taught his clumsy limbs the principles of grace and rhythm. She occupied the back part of a building of which the front part was an empty shop. The shop had been tenanted by her father, one of whose frequent bankruptcies had happened there; after which his stock of the latest novelties in inexpensive furniture had been seized by rapacious creditors, and Mr Earp had migrated to Birmingham, where he was courting the Official Receiver anew. Ruth had remained solitary and unprotected, with a considerable amount of household goods which had been her mother's. (Like all professional bankrupts, Mr Earp had invariably had belongings which, as he could prove to his creditors, did not belong to him.) Public opinion had justified Ruth in her enterprise of staying in Bursley on her own responsibility and renting part of the building, in order not to lose her 'connection' as a dancing-mistress. Public opinion said that 'there would have been no sense in her going dangling after her wastrel of a father'.

'Quite a long time since we saw anything of each other,' observed Ruth in rather a pleasant style, as she sat down and as he sat down.

It was. The intimate ecstasy of the supper-dance had never been repeated. Denry's exceeding industry in carving out his career, and his desire to graduate as an accomplished clubman, had prevented him from giving to his heart that attention which it deserved, having regard to his tender years.

'Yes, it is, isn't it?' said Denry.

Then there was a pause, and they both glanced vaguely about the inhospitable and very wooden room. Now was the moment for Denry to carry out his pre-arranged plan in all its savage simplicity. He did so.

'I've called about the rent, Miss Earp,' he said, and by an effort looked her in the eyes.

'The rent?' exclaimed Ruth, as though she had never in all her life heard of such a thing as rent; as though June 24 (recently past) was an ordinary day like any other day.

'Yes,' said Denry.

'What rent?' asked Ruth, as though for aught she guessed it might have been the rent of Buckingham Palace that he had called about.

'Yours,' said Denry.

'Mine!' she murmured. 'But what has my rent got to do with you?' she demanded. And it was just as if she had said, 'But what has my rent got to do with you, little boy?'

'Well,' he said, 'I suppose you know I'm a rent-collector?'

'No, I didn't,' she said.

He thought she was fibbing out of sheer naughtiness. But she was not. She did not know that he collected rents. She knew that he was a card, a figure, a celebrity; and that was all. It is strange how the knowledge of even the cleverest woman will confine itself to certain fields.

'Yes,' he said, always in a cold, commercial tone, 'I collect rents.'

'I should have thought you'd have preferred postage-stamps,' she said, gazing out of the window at a kiln that was blackening all the sky.

If he could have invented something clever and cutting in response to this sally he might have made the mistake of quitting his role of hard, unsentimental man of business. But he could think of nothing. So he proceeded sternly:

'Mr Herbert Calvert has put all his property into my hands, and he has given me strict instructions that no rent is to be allowed to remain in arrear.'

No answer from Ruth. Mr Calvert was a little fellow of fifty who had made money in the mysterious calling of a 'commission agent'. By reputation he was really very much harder than Denry could even pretend to be, and indeed Denry had been considerably startled by the advent of such a client. Surely if any man in Bursley were capable of unmercifully collecting rents on his own account, Herbert Calvert must be that man!

'Let me see,' said Denry further, pulling a book from his

pocket and peering into it, 'you owe five quarters rent – thirty pounds.'

He knew without the book precisely what Ruth owed, but the book kept him in countenance, supplied him with needed moral support.

Ruth Earp, without the least warning, exploded into a long peal of gay laughter. Her laugh was far prettier than her face. She laughed well. She might, with advantage to Bursley, have given lessons in laughing as well as in dancing, for Bursley laughs without grace. Her laughter was a proof that she had not a care in the world, and that the world for her was naught but a source of light amusement.

Denry smiled guardedly.

'Of course, with me it's purely a matter of business,' said he.

'So that's what Mr Herbert Calvert has done!' she exclaimed, amid the embers of her mirth. 'I wondered what he would do! I presume you know all about Mr Herbert Calvert,' she added.

'No,' said Denry, 'I don't know anything about him, except that he owns some property and I'm in charge of it. Stay,' he corrected himself, 'I think I do remember crossing his name off your programme once.'

And he said to himself: 'That's one for her. If she likes to be so desperately funny about postage-stamps, I don't see why I shouldn't have my turn.' The recollection that it was precisely Herbert Calvert whom he had supplanted in the supper-dance at the Countess of Chell's historic ball somehow increased his confidence in his ability to manage the interview with brilliance.

Ruth's voice grew severe and chilly. It seemed incredible that she had just been laughing.

'I will tell you about Mr Herbert Calvert'; she enunciated her words with slow, stern clearness. 'Mr Herbert Calvert took advantage of his visits here for his rent to pay his attentions to me. At one time he was so far – well – gone, that he would scarcely take his rent.'

'Really!' murmured Denry, genuinely staggered by this

45

symptom of the distance to which Mr Herbert Calvert was once 'gone'.

'Yes,' said Ruth, still sternly and inimically. 'Naturally a woman can't make up her mind about these things all of a sudden,' she continued. 'Naturally!' she repeated.

'Of course,' Denry agreed, perceiving that his experience of life and deep knowledge of human nature were being appealed to.

'And when I did decide definitely, Mr Herbert Calvert did not behave like a gentleman. He forgot what was due to himself and to me. I won't describe to you the scene he made. I'm simply telling you this, so that you may know. To cut a long story short, he behaved in a very vulgar way. And a woman doesn't forget these things, Mr Machin.' Her eyes threatened him. 'I decided to punish Mr Herbert Calvert. I thought if he wouldn't take his rent before – well, let him wait for it now! I might have given him notice to leave. But I didn't. I didn't see why I should let myself be upset because Mr Herbert Calvert had forgotten that he was a gentleman. I said, "Let him wait for his rent," and I promised myself I would just see what he would dare to do.'

'I don't quite follow your argument,' Denry put in.

'Perhaps you don't,' she silenced him. 'I didn't expect you would. You and Mr Herbert Calvert . . . ! So he didn't dare to do anything himself, and he's paying you to do his dirty work for him! Very well! Very well! . . .' She lifted her head defiantly. 'What will happen if I don't pay the rent?'

'I shall have to let things take their course,' said Denry with a genial smile.

'All right, then,' Ruth Earp responded. 'If you choose to mix yourself up with people like Mr Herbert Calvert, you must take the consequences! It's all the same to me, after all.'

'Then it isn't convenient for you to pay anything on account?' said Denry, more and more affable.

'Convenient!' she cried. 'It's perfectly convenient, only I don't care to. I won't pay a penny until I'm forced. Let Mr Herbert Calvert do his worst, and then I'll pay. And not before! And the whole town shall hear all about Mr Herbert Calvert!'

46

'I see,' he laughed easily.

'Convenient!' she reiterated, contemptuously. 'I think everybody in Bursley knows how my *clientèle* gets larger and larger every year! . . . Convenient!'

'So that's final, Miss Earp?'

'Perfectly!' said Miss Earp.

He rose. 'Then the simplest thing will be for me to send round a bailiff tomorrow morning, early.' He might have been saying: 'The simplest thing will be for me to send round a bunch of orchids.'

Another man would have felt emotion, and probably expressed it. But not Denry, the rent-collector and manager of estates large and small. There were several different men in Denry, but he had the great gift of not mixing up two different Denrys when he found himself in a complicated situation.

Ruth Earp rose also. She dropped her eyelids and looked at him from under them. And then she gradually smiled.

'I thought I'd just see what you'd do,' she said, in a low, confidential voice from which all trace of hostility had suddenly departed. 'You're a strange creature,' she went on curiously, as though fascinated by the problems presented by his individuality. 'Of course, I shan't let it go as far as that. I only thought I'd see what you'd say. I'll write you tonight.'

'With a cheque?' Denry demanded, with suave, jolly courtesy. 'I don't collect postage-stamps.'

(And to himself: 'She's got her stamps back.')

She hesitated. 'Stay!' she said. 'I'll tell you what will be better. Can you call tomorrow afternoon? The bank will be closed now.'

'Yes,' he said, 'I can call. What time?'

'Oh!' she answered, 'any time. If you come in about four, I'll give you a cup of tea into the bargain. Though you don't deserve it!' After an instant, she added reassuringly: 'Of course I know business is business with you. But I'm glad I've told you the real truth about your precious Mr Herbert Calvert, all the same.'

And as he walked slowly home Denry pondered upon the

singular, erratic, incalculable strangeness of woman, and of the possibly magic effect of his own personality on women.

II

It was the next afternoon, in July. Denry wore his new summer suit, but with a necktie of higher rank than the previous day's. As for Ruth, that plain but piquant girl was in one of her more elaborate and foamier costumes. The wonder was that such a costume could survive even for an hour the smuts that lend continual interest and excitement to the atmosphere of Bursley. It was a white muslin, spotted with spots of opaque white, and founded on something pink. Denry imagined that he had seen parts of it before – at the ball – and he had; but it was now a tea-gown, with long, languishing sleeves; the waves of it broke at her shoulders, sending lacy surf high up the precipices of Ruth's neck. Denry did not know it was a tea-gown. But he knew that it had a most peculiar and agreeable effect on himself, and that she had promised him tea. He was glad that he had paid her the homage of his best necktie.

Although the month was July, Ruth wore a kind of shawl over the tea-gown. It was not a shawl, Denry noted; it was merely about two yards of very thin muslin. He puzzled himself as to its purpose. It could not be for warmth, for it would not have helped to melt an icicle. Could it be meant to fulfil the same function as muslin in a confectioner's shop? She was pale. Her voice was weak and had an imploring quality.

She led him, not into the inhospitable wooden academy, but into a very small room which, like herself, was dressed in muslin and bows of ribbon. Photographs of amiable men and women decorated the pinkish-green walls. The mantelpiece was concealed in drapery as though it had been a sin. A writing-desk as green as a leaf stood carelessly in one corner; on the desk a vase containing some Cape gooseberries. In the middle of the room a small table, on the table a spirit-lamp in full blast, and on the lamp a kettle practising scales; a tray occupied the remainder of the table. There were two easy chairs; Ruth sank delicately into one, and Denry took the other with precautions.

He was nervous. Nothing equals muslin for imparting nervousness to the naïve. But he felt pleased.

'Not much of the Widow Hullins touch about this!' he reflected privately.

And he wished that all rent-collecting might be done with such ease, and amid such surroundings, as this particular piece of rent-collecting. He saw what a fine thing it was to be a free man, under orders from nobody; not many men in Bursley were in a position to accept invitations to four o'clock tea at a day's notice. Further 5 per cent on thirty pounds was thirty shillings, so that if he stayed an hour – and he meant to stay an hour – he would, while enjoying himself, be earning money steadily at the rate of sixpence a minute.

It was the ideal of a business career.

When the kettle, having finished its scales, burst into song with an accompaniment of castanets and vapour, and Ruth's sleeves rose and fell as she made the tea, Denry acknowledged frankly to himself that it was this sort of thing, and not the Brougham Street sort of thing, that he was really born for. He acknowledged to himself humbly that this sort of thing was 'life', and that hitherto he had had no adequate idea of what 'life' was. For, with all his ability as a card and a rising man, with all his assiduous frequenting of the Sports Club, he had not penetrated into the upper domestic strata of Bursley society. He had never been invited to any house where, as he put it, he would have had to mind his p's and q's. He still remained the kind of man whom you familiarly chat with in the street and club, and no more. His mother's fame as a flannel-washer was against him; Brougham Street was against him; and, chiefly, his poverty was against him. True, he had gorgeously given a house away to an aged widow! True, he succeeded in transmitting to his acquaintances a vague idea that he was doing well and waxing financially from strength to strength! But the idea was too vague, too much in the air. And save by a suit of clothes, he never gave ocular proof that he had money to waste. He could not. It was impossible for him to compete with even the more modest of the bloods and the blades. To keep a satisfactory straight crease down the middle of each leg of his trousers was all he could accomplish with the money regularly at his disposal. The town was waiting for him to do something decisive in the matter of what it called 'the stuff'.

Thus Ruth Earp was the first to introduce him to the higher intimate civilizations, the refinements lurking behind the foul walls of Bursley.

'Sugar?' she questioned, her head on one side, her arm uplifted, her sleeve drooping, and a bit of sugar caught like a white mouse between the claws of the tongs.

Nobody before had ever said 'Sugar?' to him like that. His mother never said 'Sugar?' to him. His mother was aware that he liked three pieces, but she would not give him more than two. 'Sugar?' in that slightly weak, imploring voice seemed to be charged with a significance at once tremendous and elusive.

'Yes, please.'

'Another?'

And the 'Another?' was even more delicious. He said to himself: 'I suppose this is what they call flirting.'

When a chronicler tells the exact truth, there is always a danger that he will not be believed. Yet, in spite of the risk, it must be said plainly that at this point Denry actually thought of marriage. An absurd and childish thought, preposterously rash; but it came into his mind, and – what is more – it stuck there! He pictured marriage as a perpetual afternoon tea alone with an elegant woman, amid an environment of ribboned muslin. And the picture appealed to him very strongly. And Ruth appeared to him in a new light. It was perhaps the change in her voice that did it. She appeared to him at once as a creature very feminine and enchanting, and as a creature who could earn her own living in a manner that was both original and ladylike. A woman such as Ruth would be a delight without being a drag. And, truly, was she not a remarkable woman, as remarkable as he was a man? Here she was living amid the refinements of luxury. Not an expensive luxury (he had an excellent notion of the monetary value of things), but still luxury. And the whole affair was so stylish. His heart went out to the stylish.

The slices of bread-and-butter were rolled up. There, now, was a pleasing device! It cost nothing to roll up a slice of bread-

and-butter – her fingers had doubtless done the rolling – and yet it gave quite a different taste to the food.

'What made you give that house to Mrs Hullins?' she asked him suddenly, with a candour that seemed to demand candour.

'Oh,' he said, 'just a lark! I thought I would. It came to me all in a second, and I did.'

She shook her head. 'Strange boy!' she observed.

There was a pause.

'It was something Charlie Fearns said, wasn't it?' she inquired.

She uttered the name 'Charlie Fearns' with a certain faint hint of disdain, as if indicating to Denry that of course she and Denry were quite able to put Fearns into his proper place in the scheme of things.

'Oh!' he said. 'So you know all about it?'

'Well, said she, 'naturally it was all over the town. Mrs Fearns's girl, Annunciata – what a name, eh? – is one of my pupils – the youngest, in fact.'

'Well,' said he, after another pause, 'I wasn't going to have Fearns coming the duke over me!'

She smiled sympathetically. He felt that they understood each other deeply.

'You'll find some cigarettes in that box,' she said, when he had been there thirty minutes, and pointed to the mantelpiece.

'Sure you don't mind?' he murmured.

She raised her eyebrows.

There was also a silver match-box in the larger box. No detail lacked. It seemed to him that he stood on a mountain and had only to walk down a winding path in order to enter the promised land. He was decidedly pleased with the worldly way in which he had said: 'Sure you don't mind?'

He puffed out smoke delicately. And, the cigarette between his lips, as with his left hand he waved the match into extinction, he demanded:

'You smoke?'

'Yes,' she said, 'but not in public. I know what you men are.'

This was in the early, timid days of feminine smoking.

51

'I assure you!' he protested, and pushed the box towards her. But she would not smoke.

'It isn't that I mind *you*,' she said, 'not at all. But I'm not well. I've got a frightful headache.'

He put on a concerned expression.

'I *thought* you looked rather pale,' he said awkwardly.

'Pale!' she repeated the word. 'You should have seen me this morning: I have fits of dizziness, you know, too. The doctor says it's nothing but dyspepsia. However, don't let's talk about poor little me and my silly complaints. Perhaps the tea will do me good.'

He protested again, but his experience of intimate civilization was too brief to allow him to protest with effectiveness. The truth was, he could not say these things naturally. He had to compose them, and then pronounce them, and the result failed in the necessary air of spontaneity. He could not help thinking what marvellous self-control women had. Now, when he had a headache – which happily was seldom – he could think of nothing else and talk of nothing else; the entire universe consisted solely of his headache. And here she was overcome with a headache, and during more than half-an-hour had not even mentioned it!

She began talking gossip about the Fearnses and the Swetnams, and she mentioned rumours concerning Henry Mynors (who had scruples against dancing) and Anna Tellwright, the daughter of that rich old skinflint Ephraim Tellwright. No mistake; she was on the inside of things in Bursley society! It was just as if she had removed the front walls of every house and examined every room at her leisure, with minute particularity. But of course a teacher of dancing had opportunities ... Denry had to pretend to be nearly as omniscient as she was.

Then she broke off, without warning, and lay back in her chair.

'I wonder if you'd mind going into the barn for me?' she murmured.

She generally referred to her academy as the barn. It had once been a warehouse.

He jumped up. 'Certainly,' he said, very eager.

'I think you'll see a small bottle of eau-de-Cologne on the top of the piano,' she said, and shut her eyes.

He hastened away, full of his mission, and feeling himself to be a terrific cavalier and guardian of weak women. He felt keenly that he must be equal to the situation. Yes, the small bottle of eau-de-Cologne was on top of the piano. He seized it and bore it to her on the wings of chivalry. He had not been aware that eau-de-Cologne was a remedy for, or a palliative of, headaches.

She opened her eyes, and with a great effort tried to be bright and better. But it was a failure. She took the stopper out of the bottle and sniffed first at the stopper and then at the bottle; then she spilled a few drops of the liquid on her handkerchief and applied the handkerchief to her temples.

'It's easier,' she said.

'Sure?' he asked. He did not know what to do with himself – whether to sit down and feign that she was well, or to remain standing in an attitude of respectful and grave anxiety. He thought he ought to depart; yet would it not be ungallant to desert her under the circumstances? She was alone. She had no servant, only an occasional charwoman.

She nodded with brave, false gaiety. And then she had a relapse.

'Don't you think you'd better lie down?' he suggested in more masterful accents. And added: 'And I'll go ...?' You ought to lie down. It's the only thing.' He was now speaking to her like a wise uncle.

'Oh no!' she said, without conviction. 'Besides, you can't go till I've paid you.'

It was on the tip of his tongue to say, 'Oh! don't bother about that now!' But he restrained himself. There was a notable core of common-sense in Denry. He had been puzzling how he might neatly mention the rent while departing in a hurry so that she might lie down. And now she had solved the difficulty for him.

She stretched out her arm, and picked up a bunch of keys from a basket on a little table.

'You might just unlock that desk for me, will you?' she said.

And, further, as she went through the keys one by one to select the right key: 'Each quarter I've put your precious Mr Herbert Calvert's rent in a drawer in that desk ... Here's the key.' She held up the whole ring by the chosen key, and he accepted it. And she lay back once more in her chair, exhausted by her exertions.

'You must turn the key sharply in the lock,' she said weakly, as he fumbled at the locked part of the desk.

So he turned the key sharply.

'You'll see a bag in the little drawer on the right,' she murmured.

The key turned round and round. It had begun by resisting, but now it yielded too easily.

'It doesn't seem to open,' he said, feeling clumsy.

The key clicked and slid, and the other keys rattled together.

'Oh yes,' she replied. 'I opened it quite easily this morning. It *is* a bit catchy.'

The key kept going round and round.

'Here! I'll do it,' she said wearily.

'Oh no!' he urged.

But she rose courageously, and tottered to the desk, and took the bunch from him.

'I'm afraid you've broken something in the lock,' she announced, with gentle resignation, after she had tried to open the desk and failed.

'Have I?' he mumbled. He knew that he was not shining.

'Would you mind calling in at Allman's,' she said, resuming her chair, 'and tell them to send a man down at once to pick the lock? There's nothing else for it. Or perhaps you'd better say first thing tomorrow morning. And then as soon as he's done it I'll call and pay you the money myself. And you might tell your precious Mr Herbert Calvert that next quarter I shall give notice to leave.'

'Don't you trouble to call, please,' said he. 'I can easily pop in here.'

She sped him away in an enigmatic tone. He could not be sure whether he had succeeded or failed, in her estimation, as a man of the world and a partaker of delicate teas.

'Don't *forget* Allman's!' she enjoined him as he left the room. He was to let himself out.

He was coming home late that night from the Sports Club, from a delectable evening which had lasted till one o'clock in the morning, when just as he put the large door-key into his mother's cottage he grew aware of peculiar phenomena at the top end of Brougham Street, where it runs into St Luke's Square. And then in the gas-lit gloom of the warm summer night he perceived a vast and vague rectangular form in slow movement towards the slope of Brougham Street.

It was a pantechnicon van.

But the extraordinary thing was, not that it should be a pantechnicon van, but that it should be moving of its own accord and power. For there were no horses in front of it, and Denry saw that the double shafts had been pushed up perpendicularly, after the manner of carmen when they outspan. The pantechnicon was running away. It had perceived the wrath to come and was fleeing. Its guardians had evidently left it imperfectly scotched or braked, and it had got loose.

It proceeded down the first bit of Brougham Street with a dignity worthy of its dimensions, and at the same time with apparently a certain sense of the humour of the situation. Then it seemed to be saying to itself: 'Pantechnicons will be pantechnicons.' Then it took on the absurd gravity of a man who is perfectly sure that he is not drunk. Nevertheless it kept fairly well to the middle of the road, but as though the road were a tight-rope.

The rumble of it increased as it approached Denry. He withdrew the key from his mother's cottage and put it in his pocket. He was always at his finest in a crisis. And the onrush of the pantechnicon constituted a clear crisis. Lower down the gradient of Brougham Street was more dangerous, and it was within the possibilities that people inhabiting the depths of the street might find themselves pitched out of bed by the sharp corner of a pantechnicon that was determined to be a pantechnicon. A pantechnicon whose ardour is fairly aroused may be capable of surpassing deeds. Whole thoroughfares might crumble before it.

As the pantechnicon passed Denry, at the rate of about three and a half miles an hour, he leaped, or rather he scrambled, on to it, losing nothing in the process except his straw hat, which remained a witness at his mother's door that her boy had been that way and departed under unusual circumstances. Denry had the bright idea of dropping the shafts down to act as a brake. But, unaccustomed to the manipulation of shafts, he was rather slow in accomplishing the deed, and ere the first pair of shafts had fallen the pantechnicon was doing quite eight miles an hour and the steepest declivity was yet to come. Further, the dropping of the left-hand shafts jerked the van to the left, and Denry dropped the other pair only just in time to avoid the sudden uprooting of a lamp-post. The four points of the shaft digging and prodding into the surface of the road gave the pantechnicon something to think about for a few seconds. But unfortunately the precipitousness of the street encouraged its head-strong caprices, and a few seconds later all four shafts were broken, and the pantechnicon seemed to scent the open prairie. (What it really did scent was the canal.) Then Denry discovered the brake, and furiously struggled with the iron handle. He turned it and turned it, some forty revolutions. It seemed to have no effect. The miracle was that the pantechnicon maintained its course in the middle of the street. Presently Denry could vaguely distinguish the wall and double wooden gates of the canal wharf. He could not jump off; the pantechnicon was now an express, and I doubt whether he would have jumped off, even if jumping off had not been madness. His was the kind of perseverance that, for the fun of it, will perish in an attempt. The final fifty or sixty yards of Brougham Street were level, and the pantechnicon slightly abated its haste. Denry could now plainly see, in the radiance of a gas-lamp, the gates of the wharf, and on them the painted letters:

SHROPSHIRE UNION CANAL COY., LTD.

GENERAL CARRIERS

No Admittance except on Business

He was heading straight for those gates, and the pantechnicon evidently had business within. It jolted over the iron guard of the weighing-machine, and this jolt deflected it, so that instead of aiming at the gates it aimed for part of a gate and part of a brick pillar. Denry ground his teeth together and clung to his seat. The gate might have been paper, and the brick pillar a cardboard pillar. The pantechnicon went through them as a sword will go through a ghost, and Denry was still alive. The remainder of the journey was brief and violent, owing partly to a number of bags of cement, and partly to the propinquity of the canal basin. The pantechnicon jumped into the canal like a mastodon, and drank.

Denry, clinging to the woodwork, was submerged for a moment, but, by standing on the narrow platform from which sprouted the splintered ends of the shafts, he could get his waist clear of the water. He was not a swimmer.

All was still and dark, save for the faint stream of starlight on the broad bosom of the canal basin. The pantechnicon had encountered nobody whatever *en route*. Of its strange escapade Denry had been the sole witness.

'Well, I'm dashed!' he murmured aloud.

And a voice replied from the belly of the pantechnicon:

'Who is there?'

All Denry's body shook.

'It's me!' said he.

'Not Mr Machin?' said the voice.

'Yes,' said he. 'I jumped on as it came down the street – and here we are!'

'Oh!' cried the voice. 'I do wish you could get round to me.'

Ruth Earp's voice.

He saw the truth in a moment of piercing insight. Ruth had been playing with him! She had performed a comedy for him in two acts. She had meant to do what is called in the Five Towns 'a moonlight flit'. The pantechnicon (doubtless from Birmingham, where her father was) had been brought to her door late in the evening, and was to have been filled and taken away during the night. The horses had been stabled, probably in Ruth's own

57

yard, and while the carmen were reposing the pantechnicon had got off, Ruth in it. She had no money locked in her unlockable desk. Her reason for not having paid the precious Mr Herbert Calvert was not the reason which she had advanced.

His first staggered thought was:

'She's got a nerve! No mistake!'

Her duplicity, her wickedness, did not shock him. He admired her tremendous and audacious enterprise: it appealed strongly to every cell in his brain. He felt that she and he were kindred spirits.

He tried to clamber round the side of the van so as to get to the doors at the back, but a pantechnicon has a wheel-base which forbids leaping from wheel to wheel, especially when the wheels are under water. Hence he was obliged to climb on to the roof, and so slide down on to the top of one of the doors, which was swinging loose. The feat was not simple. At last he felt the floor of the van under half a yard of water.

'Where are you?'

'I'm here,' said Ruth, very plaintively. 'I'm on a table. It was the only thing they had put into the van before they went off to have their supper or something. Furniture removers are always like that. Haven't you got a match?'

'I've got scores of matches,' said Denry. 'But what good do you suppose they'll be now, all soaked through?'

A short silence. He noticed that she had offered no explanation of her conduct towards himself. She seemed to take it for granted that he would understand.

'I'm frightfully bumped, and I believe my nose is bleeding,' said Ruth, still more plaintively. 'It's a good thing there was a lot of straw and sacks here.'

Then, after much groping, his hand touched her wet dress.

'You know you're a very naughty girl,' he said.

He heard a sob, a wild sob. The proud, independent creature had broken down under the stress of events. He climbed out of the water on to the part of the table which she was not occupying. And the van was as black as Erebus.

Gradually, out of the welter of sobs, came faint articulations, and little by little he learnt the entire story of her difficulties, her misfortunes, her struggles, and her defeats. He listened to a frank confession of guilt. But what could she do? She had meant well. But what could she do? She had been driven into a corner. And she had her father to think of! Honestly, on the previous day, she had intended to pay the rent, or part of it. But there had been a disappointment! And she had been so unwell. In short . . .

The van gave a lurch. She clutched at him and he at her. The van was settling down for a comfortable night in the mud.

(Queer that it had not occurred to him before, but at the first visit she had postponed paying him on the plea that the bank was closed, while at the second visit she had stated that the actual cash had been slowly accumulating in her desk! And the discrepancy had not struck him. Such is the influence of a tea-gown. However, he forgave her, in consideration of her immense audacity.)

'What can we do?' she almost whispered.

Her confidence in him affected him.

'Wait till it gets light,' said he.

So they waited, amid the waste of waters. In a hot July it is not unpleasant to dangle one's feet in water during the sultry dark hours. She told him more and more.

When the inspiring grey preliminaries of the dawn began, Denry saw that at the back of the pantechnicon the waste of waters extended for at most a yard, and that it was easy, by climbing on to the roof, to jump therefrom to the wharf. He did so, and then fixed a plank so that Ruth could get ashore. Relieved of their weight the table floated out after them. Denry seized it, and set about smashing it to pieces with his feet.

'What *are* you doing?' she asked faintly. She was too enfeebled to protest more vigorously.

'Leave it to me,' said Denry. 'This table is the only thing that can give your show away. We can't carry it back. We might meet some one.'

He tied the fragments of the table together with rope that was afloat in the van, and attached the heavy iron bar whose function was to keep the doors closed. Then he sank the faggot of wood and iron in a distant corner of the basin.

'There!' he said. 'Now you understand. Nothing's happened except that a furniture van's run off and fallen into the canal owing to the men's carelessness. We can settle the rest later – I mean about the rent and so on.'

They looked at each other.

Her skirts were nearly dry. Her nose showed no trace of bleeding, but there was a bluish lump over her left eye. Save that he was hatless, and that his trousers clung, he was not utterly unpresentable.

They were alone in the silent dawn.

'You'd better go home by Acre Lane, not up Brougham Street,' he said. 'I'll come in during the morning.'

It was a parting in which more was felt than said.

They went one after the other through the devastated gateway, baptizing the path as they walked. The Town Hall clock struck three as Denry crept up his mother's stairs. He had seen not a soul.

IV

The exact truth in its details was never known to more than two inhabitants of Bursley. The one thing clear certainly appeared to be that Denry, in endeavouring to prevent a runaway pantechnicon from destroying the town, had travelled with it into the canal. The romantic trip was accepted as perfectly characteristic of Denry. Around this island of fact washed a fabulous sea of uninformed gossip, in which assertion conflicted with assertion, and the names of Denry and Ruth were continually bumping against each other.

Mr Herbert Calvert glanced queerly and perhaps sardonically at Denry when Denry called and handed over ten pounds (less commission) which he said Miss Earp had paid on account.

'Look here,' said the little Calvert, his mean little eyes gleaming. 'You must get in the balance at once.'

'That's all right,' said Denry. 'I shall.'

'Was she trying to hook it on the q.t.?' Calvert demanded.

'Oh, no!' said Denry. 'That was a very funny misunderstanding. The only explanation I can think of is that that van must have come to the wrong house.'

'Are you engaged to her?' Calvert asked, with amazing effrontery.

Denry paused. 'Yes,' he said. 'Are you?'

Mr Calvert wondered what he meant.

He admitted to himself that the courtship had begun in a manner surpassingly strange.

CHAPTER 4

Wrecking of a Life

I

In the Five Towns, and perhaps elsewhere, there exists a custom in virtue of which a couple who have become engaged in the early summer find themselves by a most curious coincidence at the same seaside resort, and often in the same street thereof, during August. Thus it happened to Denry and to Ruth Earp. There had been difficulties – there always are. A business man who lives by collecting weekly rents obviously cannot go away for an indefinite period. And a young woman who lives alone in the world is bound to respect public opinion. However, Ruth arranged that her girlish friend, Nellie Cotterill, who had generous parents, should accompany her. And the North Staffordshire Railway's philanthropic scheme of issuing four-shilling tourist return tickets to the seaside enabled Denry to persuade himself that he was not absolutely mad in contemplating a fortnight on the shores of England.

Ruth chose Llandudno, Llandudno being more stylish than either Rhyl or Blackpool, and not dearer. Ruth and Nellie had a double room in a boarding-house, No. 26 St Asaph's Road (off the Marine Parade), and Denry had a small single room in another boarding-house, No. 28 St Asaph's Road. The ideal could scarcely have been approached more nearly.

Denry had never seen the sea before. As, in his gayest clothes, he strolled along the esplanade or on the pier between those two girls in their gayest clothes, and mingled with the immense crowd of pleasure-seekers and money-spenders, he was undoubtedly much impressed by the beauty and grandeur of the sea. But what impressed him far more than the beauty and grandeur of the sea was the field for profitable commercial enterprise which a place like Llandudno presented. He had not only his first vision of the sea, but his first genuine vision of the possibilities of amassing wealth by honest ingenuity. On the morning after his arrival he went out for a walk and lost himself near the Great Orme, and had to return hurriedly along the whole length of the Parade about nine o'clock. And through every ground-floor window of every house he saw a long table full of people eating and drinking the same kinds of food. In Llandudno fifty thousand souls desired always to perform the same act at the same time; they wanted to be distracted and they would do anything for the sake of distraction, and would pay for the privilege. And they would all pay at once.

This great thought was more majestic to him than the sea, or the Great Orme, or the Little Orme.

It stuck in his head because he had suddenly grown into a very serious person. He had now something to live for, something on which to lavish his energy. He was happy in being affianced, and more proud than happy, and more startled than proud. The manner and method of his courtship had sharply differed from his previous conception of what such an affair would be. He had not passed through the sensations which he would have expected to pass through. And then this question was continually presenting itself : *What could she see in him?* She must have got a notion that he was far more wonderful than he really was. Could it be true that she, his superior in experience and in splendour of person, had kissed him? *Him!* He felt that it would be his duty to live up to this exaggerated notion which she had of him. But how?

II

They had not yet discussed finance at all, though Denry would have liked to discuss it. Evidently she regarded him as a man of means. This became clear during the progress of the journey to Llandudno. Denry was flattered, but the next day he had slight misgivings, and on the following day he was alarmed; and on the day after that his state resembled terror. It is truer to say that she regarded him less as a man of means than as a magic and inexhaustible siphon of money.

He simply could not stir out of the house without spending money, and often in ways quite unforeseen. Pier, minstrels,

Punch and Judy, bathing, buns, ices, canes, fruit, chairs, row-boats, concerts, toffee, photographs, char-à-bancs: any of these expenditures was likely to happen whenever they went forth for a simple stroll. One might think that strolls were gratis, that the air was free! Error! If he had had the courage he would have left his purse in the house as Ruth invariably did. But men are moral cowards.

He had calculated thus: Return fare, four shillings a week. Agreed terms at boarding-house, twenty-five shillings a week. Total expenses per week, twenty-nine shillings – say thirty!

On the first day he spent fourteen shillings on nothing whatever – which was at the rate of five pounds a week of sup-plementary estimates! On the second day he spent nineteen shil-lings on nothing whatever, and Ruth insisted on his having tea with herself and Nellie at their boarding-house; for which of course he had to pay, while his own tea was wasting next door. So the figures ran on, jumping up each day. Mercifully, when Sunday dawned the open wound in his pocket was temporarily staunched. Ruth wished him to come in for tea again. He re-fused – at any rate he did not come – and the exquisite placidity of the stream of their love was slightly disturbed.

Nobody could have guessed that she was in monetary difficul-ties on her own account. Denry, as a chivalrous lover, had assis-ted her out of the fearful quagmire of her rent; but she owed much beyond rent. Yet, when some of her quarterly fees had come in, her thoughts had instantly run to Llandudno, joy, and frocks. She did not know what money was, and she never would. This was, perhaps, part of her superior splendour. The gentle, timid, silent Nellie occasionally let Denry see that she, too, was scandalized by her bosom friend's recklessness. Often Nellie would modestly beg for permission to pay her share of the cost for an amusement. And it seemed just to Denry that she should pay her share, and he violently wished to accept her money, but he could not. He would even get quite curt with her when she insisted. From this it will be seen how absurdly and irrationally different he was from the rest of us.

Nellie was continually with them, except just before they sepa-rated for the night. So that Denry paid consistently for three.

But he liked Nellie Cotterill. She blushed so easily, and she so obviously worshipped Ruth and admired himself, and there was a marked vein of common-sense in her ingenuous composition.

On the Monday morning he was up early and off to Bursley to collect rents and manage estates. He had spent nearly five pounds beyond his expectation. Indeed, if by chance he had not gone to Llandudno with a portion of the previous week's rents in his pockets, he would have been in what the Five Towns call a fix.

While in Bursley he thought a good deal. Bursley in August encourages nothing but thought. His mother was working as usual. His recitals to her of the existence led by betrothed lovers at Llandudno were vague.

On the Tuesday evening he returned to Llandudno, and, despite the general trend of his thoughts, it once more occurred that his pockets were loaded with a portion of the week's rents. He did not know precisely what was going to happen, but he knew that something was going to happen; for the sufficient reason that his career could not continue unless something did happen. Without either a quarrel, an understanding, or a miracle, three months of affianced bliss with Ruth Earp would exhaust his resources and ruin his reputation as one who was ever equal to a crisis.

III

What immediately happened was a storm at sea. He heard it mentioned at Rhyl, and he saw, in the deep night, the foam of breakers at Prestatyn. And when the train reached Llandudno, those two girls in ulsters and caps greeted him with wondrous tales of the storm at sea, and of wrecks, and of lifeboats. And they were so jolly, and so welcoming, so plainly glad to see their cavalier again, that Denry instantly discovered himself to be in the highest spirits. He put away the dark and brooding thoughts which had disfigured his journey, and became the gay Denry of his own dreams. The very wind intoxicated him. There was no rain.

It was half-past nine, and half Llandudno was afoot on the Parade and discussing the storm — a storm unparalleled, it seemed, in the month of August. At any rate, people who had visited Llandudno yearly for twenty-five years declared that never had they witnessed such a storm. The new lifeboat had gone forth, amid cheers, about six o'clock to a schooner in distress near Rhos, and at eight o'clock a second lifeboat (an old one which the new one had replaced and which had been bought for a floating warehouse by an aged fisherman) had departed to the rescue of a Norwegian barque, the *Hjalmar*, round the bend of the Little Orme.

'Let's go on the pier,' said Denry. 'It will be splendid.'

He was not an hour in the town, and yet was already hanging expense !

'They've closed the pier,' the girls told him.

But when in the course of their meanderings among the excited crowd under the gas-lamps they arrived at the pier-gates, Denry perceived figures on the pier.

'They're sailors and things, and the Mayor,' the girls explained.

'Pooh !' said Denry, fired.

He approached the turnstile and handed a card to the official. It was the card of an advertisement agent of the *Staffordshire Signal*, who had called at Brougham Street in Denry's absence about the renewal of Denry's advertisement.

'Press,' said Denry to the guardian at the turnstile, and went through with the ease of a bird on the wing.

'Come along,' he cried to the girls.

The guardian seemed to hesitate.

'These ladies are with me,' he said.

The guardian yielded.

It was a triumph for Denry. He could read his triumph in the eyes of his companions. When she looked at him like that, Ruth was assuredly marvellous among women, and any ideas derogatory to her marvellousness which he might have had at Bursley and in the train were false ideas.

At the head of the pier beyond the pavilion, there were gathered together some fifty people, and the tale ran that the second lifeboat had successfully accomplished its mission and was approaching the pier.

'I shall write an account of this for the *Signal*,' said Denry, whose thoughts were excusably on the Press.

'Oh, do!' exclaimed Nellie.

'They have the *Signal* at all the newspaper shops here,' said Ruth.

Then they seemed to be merged in the storm. The pier shook and trembled under the shock of the waves, and occasionally, though the tide was very low, a sprinkle of water flew up and caught their faces. The eyes could see nothing save the passing glitter of the foam on the crest of a breaker. It was the most thrilling situation that any of them had ever been in.

And at last came word from the mouths of men who could apparently see as well in the dark as in daylight, that the second lifeboat was close to the pier. And then everybody momentarily saw it – a ghostly thing that heaved up pale out of the murk for an instant, and was lost again. And the little crowd cheered.

The next moment a Bengal light illuminated the pier, and the lifeboat was silhouetted with strange effectiveness against the storm. And some one flung a rope, and then another rope arrived out of the sea, and fell on Denry's shoulder.

'Haul on there!' yelled a hoarse voice. The Bengal light expired.

Denry hauled with a will. The occasion was unique. And those few seconds were worth to him the whole of Denry's precious life – yes, not excluding the seconds in which he had kissed Ruth and the minutes in which he had danced with the Countess of Chell. Then two men with beards took the rope from his hands. The air was now alive with shoutings. Finally there was a rush of men down the iron stairway to the lower part of the pier, ten feet nearer the water.

'You stay here, you two!' Denry ordered.

'But, Denry –'

'Stay here, I tell you!' All the male in him was aroused. He was off, after the rush of men. 'Half a jiffy,' he said, coming back. 'Just take charge of this, will you?' And he poured into their hands about twelve shillings' worth of copper, small change of rents, from his hip-pocket. 'If anything happened, that might sink me,' he said, and vanished.

It was very characteristic of him, that effusion of calm sagacity in a supreme emergency.

IV

Beyond getting his feet wet Denry accomplished but little in the dark basement of the pier. In spite of his success in hauling in the thrown rope, he seemed to be classed at once down there by the experts assembled as an eager and useless person who had no right to the space which he occupied. However, he witnessed the heaving arrival of the lifeboat and the disembarking of the rescued crew of the Norwegian barque, and he was more than ever decided to compose a descriptive article for the *Staffordshire Signal*. The rescued and the rescuing crews disappeared in single file to the upper floor of the pier, with the exception of the coxswain, a man with a spreading red beard, who stayed behind to inspect the lifeboat, of which indeed he was the absolute owner. As a journalist Denry did the correct thing and engaged him in conversation. Meanwhile, cheering could be heard above. The coxswain, who stated that his name was Cregeen, and that he was a Manxman, seemed to regret the entire expedition. He seemed to be unaware that it was his duty now to play the part of the modest hero to Denry's interviewing. At every loose end of the chat he would say gloomily:

'And look at her now, I'm telling ye!' Meaning the battered craft, which rose and fell on the black waves.

Denry ran upstairs again, in search of more amenable material. Some twenty men in various sou'-westers and other headgear were eating thick slices of bread and butter and drinking hot coffee, which with foresight had been prepared for them in the pier buffet. A few had preferred whisky. The whole crowd was now under the lee of the pavilion, and it constituted a spectacle which Denry said to himself he should refer to in his articles as 'Rembrandtesque'. For a few moments he could not descry Ruth and Nellie in the gloom. Then he saw the indubitable form of his betrothed at a penny-in-the-slot machine, and the indubitable form of Nellie at another penny-in-the-slot machine. And then he could hear the click-click-click of the machines, working rapidly. And his thoughts took a new direction.

Presently Ruth ran with blithe gracefulness from her machine and commenced a generous distribution of packets to the members of the crews. There was neither calculation nor exact justice in her generosity. She dropped packets on to heroic knees with a splendid gesture of largesse. Some packets even fell on the floor. But she did not mind.

Denry could hear her saying:

'You must eat it. Chocolate is so sustaining. There's nothing like it.'

She ran back to the machines, and snatched more packets from Nellie, who under her orders had been industrious; and then began a second distribution.

A calm and disinterested observer would probably have been touched by this spectacle of impulsive womanly charity. He might even have decided that it was one of the most beautifully human things that he had ever seen. And the fact that the hardy heroes and Norsemen appeared scarcely to know what to do with the silver-wrapped bonbons would not have impaired his admiration for these two girlish figures of benevolence. Denry, too, was touched by the spectacle, but in another way. It was the rents of his clients that were being thus dissipated in a very luxury of needless benevolence. He muttered:

'Well, that's a bit thick, that is!' But of course he could do nothing.

As the process continued, the clicking of the machine exacerbated his ears.

'Idiotic!' he muttered.

The final annoyance to him was that everybody except himself seemed to consider that Ruth was displaying singular ingenuity, originality, enterprise, and goodness of heart.

In that moment he saw clearly for the first time that the marriage between himself and Ruth had not been arranged in Heaven. He admitted privately then that the saving of a young woman from violent death in a pantechnicon need not inevitably involve espousing her. She was without doubt a marvellous creature, but it was as wise to dream of keeping a carriage and pair as to dream of keeping Ruth. He grew suddenly cynical. His age leaped to fifty or so, and the curve of his lips changed.

Ruth, spying around, saw him and ran to him with a glad cry.

'Here!' she said, 'take these. They're no good.' She held out her hands.

'What are they?' he asked.

'They're the halfpennies.'

'So sorry!' he said, with an accent whose significance escaped her, and took the useless coins.

'We've exhausted all the chocolate,' said she. 'But there's butterscotch left – it's nearly as good – and gold-tipped cigarettes. I daresay some of them would enjoy a smoke. Have you got any more pennies?'

'No!' he replied. 'But I've got ten or a dozen half-crowns. They'll work the machine just as well, won't they?'

This time she did notice a certain unusualness in the flavour of his accent. And she hesitated.

'Don't be silly!' she said.

'I'll try not to be,' said Denry. So far as he could remember, he had never used such a tone before. Ruth swerved away to rejoin Nellie.

Denry surreptitiously counted the halfpennies. There were eighteen. She had fed those machines, then, with over a hundred and thirty pence.

He murmured, 'Thick, thick!'

Considering that he had returned to Llandudno in the full intention of putting his foot down, of clearly conveying to Ruth that his conception of finance differed from hers, the second sojourn had commenced badly. Still, he had promised to marry her, and he must marry her. Better a lifetime of misery and insolvency than a failure to behave as a gentleman should. Of course, if she chose to break it off . . . But he must be minutely careful to do nothing which might lead to a breach. Such was Denry's code. The walk home at midnight, amid the reverberations of the falling tempest, was marked by a slight pettishness on the part of Ruth, and by Denry's polite taciturnity.

Yet the next morning, as the three companions sat together under the striped awning of the buffet on the pier, nobody could have divined, by looking at them, that one of them at any rate was the most uncomfortable young man in all Llandudno. The sun was hotly shining on their bright attire and on the still turbulent waves. Ruth, thirsty after a breakfast of herrings and bacon, was sucking iced lemonade up a straw. Nellie was eating chocolate, undistributed remains of the night's benevolence. Denry was yawning, not in the least because the proceedings failed to excite his keen interest, but because he had been a journalist till three a.m. and had risen at six in order to dispatch a communication to the editor of the *Staffordshire Signal* by train. The girls were very playful. Nellie dropped a piece of chocolate into Ruth's glass, and Ruth fished it out, and bit at it.

'What a jolly taste!' she exclaimed.

And then Nellie bit at it.

'Oh, it's just lovely!' said Nellie, softly.

'Here, dear!' said Ruth, 'try it.'

And Denry had to try it, and to pronounce it a delicious novelty (which indeed it was) and generally to brighten himself up. And all the time he was murmuring in his heart, 'This can't go on.'

Nevertheless, he was obliged to admit that it was he who had invited Ruth to pass the rest of her earthly life with him, and not *vice versa*.

'Well, shall we go on somewhere else?' Ruth suggested.

And he paid yet again. He paid and smiled, he who had meant to be the masterful male, he who deemed himself always equal to a crisis. But in this crisis he was helpless.

They set off down the pier, brilliant in the brilliant crowd. Everybody was talking of wrecks and lifeboats. The new lifeboat had done nothing, having been forestalled by the Prestatyn boat; but Llandudno was apparently very proud of its brave old worn-out lifeboat which had brought ashore the entire crew of the *Hjalmar*, without casualty, in a terrific hurricane.

'Run along, child,' said Ruth to Nellie, 'while uncle and auntie talk to each other for a minute.'

Nellie stared, blushed, and walked forward in confusion. She was startled. And Denry was equally startled. Never before had Ruth so brazenly hinted that lovers must be left alone at intervals. In justice to her, it must be said that she was a mirror for all the proprieties. Denry had even reproached her, in his heart, for not sufficiently showing her desire for his exclusive society. He wondered, now, what was to be the next revelation of her surprising character.

'I had our bill this morning,' said Ruth.

She leaned gracefully on the handle of her sunshade, and they both stared at the sea. She was very elegant, with an aristocratic air. The bill, as she mentioned it, seemed a very negligible trifle. Nevertheless, Denry's heart quaked.

'Oh!' he said. 'Did you pay it?'

'Yes,' said she. 'The landlady wanted the money, she told me. So Nellie gave me her share, and I paid it at once.'

'Oh!' said Denry.

There was a silence. Denry felt as though he were defending a castle, or as though he were in a dark room and somebody was calling him, calling him, and he was pretending not to be there and holding his breath.

'But I've hardly enough money left,' said Ruth. 'The fact is, Nellie and I spent such a lot yesterday and the day before ... You've no idea how money goes!'

'Haven't I?' said Denry. But not to her – only to his own heart.

To her he said nothing.

'I suppose we shall have to go back home,' she ventured lightly. 'One can't run into debt here. They'd claim our luggage.'

'What a pity!' said Denry, sadly.

Just those few words – and the interesting part of the interview was over! All that followed counted not in the least. She had meant to induce him to offer to defray the whole of her expenses in Llandudno – no doubt in the form of a loan; and she had failed. She had intended him to repair the disaster

caused by her chronic extravagance. And he had only said:
'What a pity!'

'Yes, it is!' she agreed bravely, and with a finer disdain than
ever of petty financial troubles. 'Still, it can't be helped.'

'No, I suppose not,' said Denry.

There was undoubtedly something fine about Ruth. In that
moment she had it in her to kill Denry with a bodkin. But she
merely smiled. The situation was terribly strained, past all
Denry's previous conceptions of a strained situation; but she
deviated with superlative *sang-froid* into frothy small talk. A
proud and unconquerable woman! After all, what were men for,
if not to pay?

'I think I shall go home tonight,' she said, after the excursion
into prattle.

'I'm sorry,' said Denry.

He was not coming out of his castle.

At that moment a hand touched his shoulder. It was the hand
of Cregeen, the owner of the old lifeboat.

'Mister,' said Cregeen, too absorbed in his own welfare to
notice Ruth. 'It's now or never! Five-and-twenty'll buy the
Fleetwing, if ten's paid down this mornun.'

And Denry replied boldly:

'You shall have it in an hour. Where shall you be?'

'I'll be in John's cabin, under the pier,' said Cregeen, 'where
ye found me this mornun.'

'Right,' said Denry.

If Ruth had not been caracoling on her absurdly high horse,
she would have had the truth out of Denry in a moment concerning these early morning interviews and mysterious transactions in shipping. But from that height she could not deign to
be curious. And so she said naught. Denry had passed the whole
morning since breakfast and had uttered no word of pre-
prandial encounters with mariners, though he had talked a lot
about his article for the *Signal* and of how he had risen betimes
in order to dispatch it by the first train.

And as Ruth showed no curiosity Denry behaved on the as-
sumption that she felt none. And the situation grew even more
strained.

As they walked down the pier towards the beach, at the dinner-hour, Ruth bowed to a dandiacal man who obsequiously saluted her.

'Who's that?' asked Denry, instinctively.

'It's a gentleman that I was once engaged to,' answered Ruth, with cold, brief politeness.

Denry did not like this.

The situation almost creaked under the complicated stresses to which it was subject. The wonder was that it did not fly to pieces long before evening.

VI

The pride of the principal actors being now engaged, each person was compelled to carry out the intentions which he had expressed either in words or tacitly. Denry's silence had announced more efficiently than any words that he would under no inducement emerge from his castle. Ruth had stated plainly that there was nothing for it but to go home at once, that very night. Hence she arranged to go home, and hence Denry refrained from interfering with her arrangements. Ruth was lugubrious under a mask of gaiety; Nellie was lugubrious under no mask whatever. Nellie was merely the puppet of these betrothed players, her elders. She admired Ruth and she admired Denry, and between them they were spoiling the little thing's holiday for their own adult purposes. Nellie knew that dreadful occurrences were in the air – occurrences compared to which the storm at sea was a storm in a tea-cup. She knew partly because Ruth had been so queerly polite, and partly because they had come separately to St Asaph's Road and had not spent the entire afternoon together.

So quickly do great events loom up and happen that at six o'clock they had had tea and were on their way afoot to the station. The odd man of No. 26 St Asaph's Road had preceded them with the luggage. All the rest of Llandudno was joyously strolling home to its half-past-six high tea – grand people to whom weekly bills were as dust and who were in a position to stop in Llandudno for ever and ever, if they chose! And Ruth and Nellie were conscious of the shame which always afflicts those whom necessity forces to the railway station of a pleasure resort in the middle of the season. They saw omnibuses loaded with luggage and jolly souls were actually *coming*, whose holiday had not yet properly commenced. And this spectacle added to their humiliation and their disgust. They genuinely felt that they belonged to the lower orders.

Ruth, for the sake of effect, joked on the most solemn subjects. She even referred with giggling laughter to the fact that she had borrowed from Nellie in order to discharge her liabilities for the final twenty-four hours at the boarding-house. Giggling laughter being contagious, as they were walking side by side close together, they all laughed. And each one secretly thought how ridiculous was such behaviour, and how it failed to reach the standard of true worldliness.

Then, nearer the station, some sprightly caprice prompted Denry to raise his hat to two young women who were crossing the road in front of them. Neither of the two young women responded to the homage.

'Who are they?' asked Ruth, and the words were out of her mouth before she could remind herself that curiosity was beneath her.

'It's a young lady I was once engaged to,' said Denry.

'Which one?' asked the ninny, Nellie, astounded.

'I forget,' said Denry.

He considered this to be one of his greatest retorts – not to Nellie, but to Ruth. Nellie naturally did not appreciate its loveliness. But Ruth did. There was no facet of that retort that escaped Ruth's critical notice.

At length they arrived at the station, quite a quarter of an hour before the train was due, and half-an-hour before it came in.

Denry tipped the odd man for the transport of the luggage.

'Sure it's all there?' he asked the girls, embracing both of them in his gaze.

'Yes,' said Ruth, 'but where's yours?'

'Oh!' he said. 'I'm not going tonight. I've got some business to attend to here. I thought you understood. I expect you'll be all right, you two together.'

After a moment, Ruth said brightly: 'Oh yes! I was quite forgetting about your business.' Which was completely untrue, since she knew nothing of his business, and he had assuredly not informed her that he would not return with them.

But Ruth was being very brave, haughty, and queenlike, and for this the precise truth must sometimes be abandoned. The most precious thing in the world to Ruth was her dignity – and who can blame her? She meant to keep it at no matter what costs.

In a few minutes the bookstall on the platform attracted them as inevitably as a prone horse attracts a crowd. Other people were near the bookstall, and as these people were obviously leaving Llandudno, Ruth and Nellie felt a certain solace. The social outlook seemed brighter for them. Denry bought one or two penny papers, and then the newsboy began to paste up the contents poster of the *Staffordshire Signal*, which had just arrived. And on this poster, very prominent, were the words: 'The Great Storm in North Wales. Special Descriptive Report.' Denry snatched up one of the green papers and opened it, and on the first column of the news-page saw his wondrous description, including the word 'Rembrandtesque'. 'Graphic Account by a Bursley Gentleman of the Scene at Llandudno', said the sub-title. And the article was introduced by the phrase: 'We are indebted to Mr E. H. Machin, a prominent figure in Bursley,' etc.

It was like a miracle. Do what he would, Denry could not stop his face from glowing.

With false calm he gave the paper to Ruth. Her calmness in receiving it upset him.

'We'll read it in the train,' she said primly, and started to talk about something else. And she became most agreeable and companionable.

Mixed up with papers and sixpenny novels on the bookstall were a number of souvenirs of Llandudno – paper-knives, pens, paper-weights, watch-cases, pen-cases, all in light wood or glass, and ornamented with coloured views of Llandudno, and also the word 'Llandudno' in large German capitals, so that mistakes might not arise. Ruth remembered that she had even intended to buy a crystal paper-weight with a view of the Great Orme at the bottom. The bookstall clerk had several crystal paper-weights with views of the pier, the Hotel Majestic, the Esplanade, the Happy Valley, but none with a view of the Great Orme. He had also paper-knives and watch-cases with a view of the Great Orme. But Ruth wanted a combination of paper-weight and Great Orme, and nothing else would satisfy her. She was like that. The clerk admitted that such a combination existed, but he was sold 'out of it'.

'Couldn't you get one and send it to me?' said Ruth.

And Denry saw anew that she was incurable.

'Oh yes, miss,' said the clerk. 'Certainly, miss. Tomorrow at latest.' And he pulled out a book. 'What name?'

Ruth looked at Denry, as women do look on such occasions.

'Rothschild,' said Denry.

It may seem perhaps strange that that single word ended their engagement. But it did. She could not tolerate a rebuke. She walked away, flushing. The bookstall clerk received no order. Several persons in the vicinity dimly perceived that a domestic scene had occurred, in a flash, under their noses, on a platform of a railway station. Nellie was speedily aware that something very serious had happened, for the train took them off without Ruth speaking a syllable to Denry, though Denry raised his hat and was almost effusive.

The next afternoon Denry received by post a ring in a box. 'I will not submit to insult,' ran the brief letter.

'I only said "Rothschild"!' Denry murmured to himself. 'Can't a fellow say "Rothschild"?'

But secretly he was proud of himself.

CHAPTER 5

The Mercantile Marine

I

THE decisive-scene, henceforward historic, occurred in the shanty known as 'John's cabin' — John being the unacknowledged leader of the long-shore population under the tail of Llandudno pier. The cabin, festooned with cordage, was lighted by an oil-lamp of a primitive model and round the orange case on which the lamp was balanced sat Denry, Cregeen, the owner of the lifeboat, and John himself (to give, as it were, a semi-official character to whatever was afoot).

'Well, here you are,' said Denry, and handed to Cregeen a piece of paper.

'What's this, I'm asking ye?' said Cregeen, taking the paper in his large fingers and peering at it as though it had been a papyrus.

But he knew quite well what it was. It was a cheque for twenty-five pounds. What he did not know was that, with the ten pounds paid in cash earlier in the day, it represented a very large part indeed of such of Denry's savings as had survived his engagement to Ruth Earp. Cregeen took a pen as though it had been a match-end and wrote a receipt. Then, after finding a stamp in a pocket of his waistcoat under his jersey, he put it in his mouth and lost it there for a long time. Finally Denry got the receipt, certifying that he was the owner of the lifeboat formerly known as *Llandudno*, but momentarily without a name, together with all her gear and sails.

'Are ye going to live in her?' the rather curt John inquired.

'Not in her. On her,' said Denry.

And he went out on to the sand and shingle, leaving John and Cregeen to complete the sale to Cregeen of the *Fleetwing*, a small cutter specially designed to take twelve persons forth for 'a pleasant sail in the bay'. If Cregeen had not had a fancy for the *Fleetwing* and a perfect lack of the money to buy her,

78

Denry might never have been able to induce him to sell the life-boat.

Under another portion of the pier Denry met a sailor with a long white beard, the aged Simeon, who had been one of the crew that rescued the *Hjalmar,* but whom his colleagues appeared to regard rather as an ornament than a motive force.

'It's all right,' said Denry.

And Simeon, in silence, nodded his head slowly several times.

'I shall give you thirty shilling for the week,' said Denry.

And that venerable head oscillated again in the moon-lit gloom and rocked gradually to a standstill.

Presently the head said, in shrill, slow tones:

'I've seen three o' them Norwegian chaps. Two of 'em can no more speak English than a babe unborn; no, nor understand what ye say to 'em, though I fair bawled in their ear-holes.'

'So much the better,' said Denry.

'I showed 'em that sovereign,' said the bearded head, wagging again.

'Well,' said Denry, 'you won't forget. Six o'clock tomorrow morning.'

'Ye'd better say five,' the head suggested. 'Quieter like.'

'Five, then,' Denry agreed.

And he departed to St Asaph's Road burdened with a tremendous thought.

The thought was:

'I've gone and done it this time!'

Now that the transaction was accomplished and could not be undone, he admitted to himself that he had never been more mad. He could scarely comprehend what had led him to do that which he had done. But he obscurely imagined that his caprice for the possession of sea-going craft must somehow be the result of his singular adventure with the pantechnicon in the canal at Bursley.

He was so preoccupied with material interests as to be capable of forgetting, for a quarter of an hour at a stretch, that in all essential respects his life was wrecked, and that he had nothing to hope for save hollow worldly success. He knew that Ruth would return the ring. He could almost see the postman holding

79

the little cardboard cube which would contain the rendered ring. He had loved, and loved tragically. (That was how he put it – in his unspoken thoughts; but the truth was merely that he had loved something too expensive.) Now the dream was done. And a man of disillusion walked along the Parade towards St Asaph's Road among revellers, a man with a past, a man who had probed women, a man who had nothing to learn about the sex. And amid all the tragedy of his heart, and all his apprehensions concerning hollow, worldly success, little thoughts of absurd unimportance kept running about like clockwork mice in his head. Such as that it would be a bit of a bore to have to tell people at Bursley that his engagement, which truly had thrilled the town, was broken off. Humiliating, that! And, after all, Ruth was a glittering gem among women. Was there another girl in Bursley so smart, so effective, so truly ornate?

Then he comforted himself with the reflection: 'I'm certainly the only man that ever ended an engagement by just saying "Rothschild!"' This was probably true. But it did not help him to sleep.

II

The next morning at 5.20 the youthful sun was shining on the choppy water of the Irish Sea, just off the Little Orme, to the west of Llandudno Bay. Oscillating on the uneasy waves was Denry's lifeboat, manned by the nodding bearded head, three ordinary British longshoremen, a Norwegian who could speak English of two syllables, and two other Norwegians who by a strange neglect of education could speak nothing but Norwegian.

Close under the headland, near a morsel of beach lay the remains of the *Hjalmar* in an attitude of repose. It was as if the *Hjalmar*, after a long struggle, had lain down like a cab-horse and said to the tempest: 'Do what you like now!'

'Yes,' the venerable head was piping. 'Us can come out comfortable in twenty minutes, unless the tide be setting east strong. And, as for getting back, it'll be the same, other way round, if ye understand me.'

There could be no question that Simeon had come out

comfortable. But he was the coxwain. The rowers seemed to be perspiringly aware that the boat was vast and beamy.

'Shall we row up to it?' Simeon inquired, pointing to the wreck.

Then a pale face appeared above the gunwale, and an expiring, imploring voice said: 'No. We'll go back.' Whereupon the pale face vanished again.

Denry had never before been outside the bay. In the navigation of pantechnicons on the squall-swept basins of canals he might have been a great master, but he was unfitted for the open sea. At that moment he would have been almost ready to give the lifeboat and all that he owned for the privilege of returning to land by train. The inward journey was so long that Denry lost hope of ever touching his native island again. And then there was a bump. And he disembarked, with hope burning up again cheerfully in his bosom. And it was a quarter to six.

By the first post, which arrived at half-past seven, there came a brown package. 'The ring!' he thought, starting horribly. But the package was a cube of three inches, and would have held a hundred rings. He undid the cover, and saw on half a sheet of notepaper the words:

Thank you so much for the lovely time you gave me. I hope you will like this, Nellie.

He was touched. If Ruth was hard, mercenary, costly, her young and ingenuous companion could at any rate be grateful and sympathetic. Yes, he was touched. He had imagined himself to be dead to all human affections, but it was not so. The package contained chocolate, and his nose at once perceived that it was chocolate impregnated with lemon – the surprising but agreeable compound accidentally invented by Nellie on the previous day at the pier buffet. The little thing must have spent a part of the previous afternoon in preparing it, and she must have put the package in the post at Crewe. Secretive and delightful little thing! After his recent experience beyond the bay he had imagined himself to be incapable of ever eating again, but it was not so. The lemon gave a peculiar astringent, appetizing, *settling* quality to the chocolate. And he ate even with gusto.

The result was that, instead of waiting for the nine o'clock boarding-house breakfast, he hurried energetically into the streets and called on a jobbing printer whom he had seen on the previous evening. As Ruth had said, 'There is nothing like chocolate for sustaining you.'

III

At ten o'clock two Norwegian sailors, who could only smile in answer to the questions which assailed them, were distributing the following handbill on the Parade:

WRECK OF THE HJALMAR
HEROISM AT LLANDUDNO

Every hour, at 11, 12, 2, 3, 4, 5, and 6 o'clock, THE IDENTICAL (guaranteed) LIFEBOAT which rescued the crew of the

HJALMAR

will leave the beach for the scene of the wreck. Manned by Simeon Edwards, the oldest boatman in LLANDUDNO, and by members of the rescued crew, genuine Norwegians (guaranteed.)

SIMEON EDWARDS, Coxswain

Return Fare, with use of Cork Belt and Lifelines if desired, 2s. 6d.

A UNIQUE OPPORTUNITY
A UNIQUE EXPERIENCE

P.S. — The bravery of the lifeboatmen has been the theme of the Press throughout the Principality and neighbouring counties.

E. D. MACHIN

At eleven o'clock there was an eager crowd down on the beach where, with some planks and a piece of rock, Simeon had arranged an embarkation pier for the lifeboat. One man, in overalls, stood up to his knees in the water and escorted passengers up the planks, while Simeon's confidence-generating beard received them into the broad waist of the boat. The rowers wore sou'-westers and were secured to the craft by life-lines, and these conveniences were also offered, with life-belts, to the intrepid excursionists. A paper was pinned in the stern: 'Licensed to carry Fourteen.' (Denry had just paid the fee.) But quite forty people were anxious to make the first voyage.

'No more,' shrilled Simeon, solemnly. And the wader scrambled in and the boat slid away.

'Fares, please!' shrilled Simeon.

He collected one pound fifteen, and slowly buttoned it up in the right-hand pocket of his blue trousers.

'Now, my lads, with a will,' he gave the order. And then, with deliberate method, he lighted his pipe. And the lifeboat shot away.

Close by the planks stood a young man in a negligent attitude, and with a look on his face as if to say: 'Please do not imagine that I have the slightest interest in this affair.' He stared consistently out to sea until the boat had disappeared round the Little Orme, and then he took a few turns on the sands, in and out amid the castles. His heart was beating in a most disconcerting manner. After a time he resumed his perusal of the sea. And the lifeboat reappeared and grew larger and larger, and finally arrived at the spot from which it had departed, only higher up the beach because the tide was rising. And Simeon debarked first, and there was a small blue and red model of a lifeboat in his hand, which he shook to a sound of coins.

'*For* the Lifeboat Fund! *For* the Lifeboat Fund!' he gravely intoned.

Every debarking passenger dropped a coin into the slit.

In five minutes the boat was refilled, and Simeon had put the value of fourteen more half-crowns into his pocket.

The lips of the young man on the beach moved, and he murmured:

'That makes over three pounds! Well, I'm dashed!'

At the hour appointed for dinner he went to St Asaph's Road, but could eat nothing. He could only keep repeating very softly to himself, 'Well, I'm dashed!'

Throughout the afternoon the competition for places in the lifeboat grew keener and more dangerous. Denry's craft was by no means the sole craft engaged in carrying people to see the wreck. There were dozens of boats in the business, which had suddenly sprung up that morning, the sea being then fairly inoffensive for the first time since the height of the storm. But the other boats simply took what the lifeboat left. The guaranteed identity of the lifeboat, and of the Norsemen (who replied to questions in gibberish), and of Simeon himself; the sou'-westers, the life-belts and the lines; even the collection for the Lifeboat Fund at the close of the voyage: all these matters resolved themselves into a fascination which Llandudno could not resist.

And in regard to the collection, a remarkable crisis arose. The model of a lifeboat became full, gorged to the slot. And the Local Secretary of the Fund had the key. The model was dis-patched to him by special messenger to open and to empty, and in the meantime Simeon used his sou'-wester as a collecting-box. This contretemps was impressive. At night Denry received twelve pounds odd at the hands of Simeon Edwards. He show-ered the odd in largess on his heroic crew, who had also received many tips. By the evening post the fatal ring arrived from Ruth, as he anticipated. He was just about to throw it into the sea, when he thought better of the idea, and stuck it in his pocket. He tried still to feel that his life had been blighted by Ruth. But he could not. The twelve pounds, largely in silver, weighed so heavy in his pocket. He said to himself: 'Of course this can't last!'

IV

Then came the day when he first heard someone saying dis-creetly behind him:

'That's the lifeboat chap!'

Or more briefly:

'That's him!'

Implying that in all Llandudno 'him' could mean only one person.

And for a time he went about the streets self-consciously. However, that self-consciousness soon passed off, and he wore his fame as easily as he wore his collar.

The lifeboat trips to the *Hjalmar* became a feature of daily life in Llandudno. The pronunciation of the ship's name went through a troublous period. Some one said the 'j' ought to be pronounced to the exclusion of the 'h', and others maintained the contrary. In the end the first two letters were both abandoned utterly, also the last — but nobody had ever paid any attention to the last. The facetious had a trick of calling the wreck *Inkerman*. This definite settlement of the pronunciation of the name was a sign that the pleasure-seekers of Llandudno had definitely fallen in love with the lifeboat-trip habit. Denry's timid fear that the phenomenon which put money into his pocket could not continue, was quite falsified. It continued violently. Denry wished hat the *Hjalmar* had been wrecked a month earlier. He calculated that the tardiness of the *Hjalmar* in wrecking itself had involved him in a loss of some four hundred pounds. If only the catastrophe had happened early in July, instead of early in August, and he had been there. Why, if forty *Hjalmars* had been wrecked, and their forty crews saved by forty different lifeboats, and Denry had bought all the lifeboats, he could have filled them all!

Still, the regularity of his receipts was extremely satisfactory and comforting. The thing had somehow the air of being a miracle; at any rate of being connected with magic. It seemed to him that nothing could have stopped the visitors to Llandudno from fighting for places in his lifeboat and paying handsomely for the privilege. They had begun the practice, and they looked as if they meant to go on with the practice eternally. He thought that the monotony of it would strike them unfavourably. But no! He thought that they would revolt against doing what everyone had done. But no! Hundreds of persons arrived fresh from the railway station every day, and they all appeared to be drawn to that lifeboat as to a magnet. They all seemed to know instantly and instinctively that to be correct in Llandudno they must make at least one trip in Denry's lifeboat.

He was pocketing an income which far exceeded his most golden visions. And therefore naturally his first idea was to make that income larger and larger still. He commenced by putting up the price of the afternoon trips. There was a vast deal too much competition for seats in the afternoon. This competition led to quarrels, unseemly language, and deplorable loss of temper. It also led to loss of time. Denry was therefore benefiting humanity by charging three shillings after two o'clock. This simple and benign device equalized the competition throughout the day, and made Denry richer by seven or eight pounds a week.

But his fertility of invention did not stop there. One morning the earliest excursionists saw a sort of Robinson Crusoe marooned on the strip of beach near the wreck. All that heartless fate had left him appeared to be a machine on a tripod and a few black bags. And there was no shelter for him save a shallow cave. The poor fellow was quite respectably dressed. Simeon steered the boat round by the beach, which shelved down sharply, and as he did so the Robinson Crusoe hid his head in a cloth, as though ashamed, or as though he had gone mad and believed himself to be an ostrich. Then apparently he thought the better of it, and gazed boldly forth again. And the boat passed on its starboard side within a dozen feet of him and his machine. Then it put about and passed on the port side. And the same thing occurred on every trip. And the last trippers of the day left Robinson Crusoe on the strip of beach in his solitude.

The next morning a photographer's shop on the Parade pulled down its shutters and displayed posters all over the upper part of its windows. And the lower part of the windows held sixteen different large photographs of the lifeboat broadside on. The likenesses of over a hundred visitors, many of them with sou'-westers, cork belts, and life-lines, could be clearly distinguished in these picturesque groups. A notice said:

Copies of any of these magnificent permanent photographs can be supplied, handsomely mounted, at a charge of two shillings each. Orders executed in rotation, and delivered by post if necessary. It is respectfully requested that cash be paid with order. Otherwise orders cannot be accepted.

Very few of those who had made the trip could resist the fascination of a photograph of themselves in a real lifeboat, manned by real heroes and real Norwegians on real waves, especially if they had worn the gear appropriate to lifeboats. The windows of the shop were beset throughout the day with crowds anxious to see who was in the lifeboat, and who had come out well, and who was a perfect fright. The orders on the first day amounted to over fifteen pounds, for not everybody was content with one photograph. The novelty was acute and enchanting, and it renewed itself each day. 'Let's go down and look at the lifeboat photographs,' people would say, when they were wondering what to do next. Some persons who had not 'taken nicely' would perform a special trip in the lifeboat and would wear special clothes and compose special faces for the ordeal. The Mayor of Ashby-de-la-Zouch for that year ordered two hundred copies of a photograph which showed himself in the centre, for presentation as New Year's cards. On the mornings after very dull days or wet days, when photography had been impossible or unsatisfactory, Llandudno felt that something lacked. Here it may be mentioned that inclement weather (of which, for the rest, there was little) scarcely interfered with Denry's receipts. Imagine a lifeboat being deterred by rain or by a breath of wind! There were tarpaulins. When the tide was strong and adverse, male passengers were allowed to pull, without extra charge, though naturally they would give a trifle to this or that member of the professional crew.

Denry's arrangement with the photographer was so simple that a child could have grasped it. The photographer paid him sixpence on every photograph sold. This was Denry's only connection with the photographer. The sixpences totalled over a dozen pounds a week. Regardless of cost, Denry reprinted his article from the *Staffordshire Signal* descriptive of the night of the wreck, with a photograph of the lifeboat and its crew, and presented a copy to every client of his photographic department.

v

Llandudno was next titillated by the mysterious 'Chocolate Remedy', which made its first appearance in a small boat that plied off Robinson Crusoe's strip of beach. Not infrequently passengers in the lifeboat were inconvenienced by displeasing and even distressing sensations, as Denry had once been inconvenienced. He felt deeply for them. The Chocolate Remedy was designed to alleviate the symptoms while captivating the palate. It was one of the most agreeable remedies that the wit of man ever invented. It tasted like chocolate and yet there was an astringent flavour of lemon in it – a flavour that flattered the stomach into a good opinion of itself, and seemed to say, 'All's right with the world'. The stuff was retailed in sixpenny packets, and you were advised to eat only a very little of it at a time, and not to masticate, but merely to permit melting. Then the Chocolate Remedy came to be sold on the lifeboat itself, and you were informed that if you 'took' it before starting on the wave, no wave could disarrange you. And, indeed, many persons who followed this advice suffered no distress, and were proud accordingly, and duly informed the world. Then the Chocolate Remedy began to be sold everywhere. Young people bought it because they enjoyed it, and perfectly ignored the advice against over-indulgence and against mastication. The Chocolate Remedy penetrated like the refrain of a popular song to other seaside places. It was on sale from Morecambe to Barmouth, and at all the landing-stages of the steamers for the Isle of Man and Anglesey. Nothing surprised Denry so much as the vogue of the Chocolate Remedy. It was a serious anxiety to him, and he muddled both the manufacture and distribution of the remedy, from simple ignorance and inexperience. His chief difficulty at first had been to obtain small cakes of chocolate that were not stamped with the maker's name or mark. Chocolate manufacturers seemed to have a passion for imprinting their Quakerly names on every bit of stuff they sold. Having at length obtained a supply, he was silly enough to spend time in preparing the remedy himself in his bedroom! He might as well have tried to feed the British Army from his mother's kitchen. At length he went to a confectioner in Rhyl and a greengrocer in Llandudno, and by giving away half the secret to each, he contrived to keep the whole secret to himself. But even then he was manifestly unequal to the situation created by the demand for the Chocolate Remedy. It was a situation that needed the close attention of half a dozen men of business. It was quite different from the affair of the lifeboat.

One night a man who had been staying a day or two in the boarding-house in St Asaph's Road said to Denry:

'Look here, mister. I go straight to the point. What'll you take?'

And he explained what he meant. What would Denry take for the entire secret and rights of the Chocolate Remedy and the use of the name 'Machin' ('without which none was genuine').

'What do you offer?' Denry asked.

'Well, I'll give you a hundred pounds down, and that's my last word.'

Denry was staggered. A hundred pounds for simply nothing at all — for dipping bits of chocolate in lemon-juice!

He shook his head.

'I'll take two hundred,' he replied.

And he got two hundred. It was probably the worst bargain that he ever made in his life. For the Chocolate Remedy continued obstinately in demand for ten years afterwards. But he was glad to be rid of the thing; it was spoiling his sleep and wearing him out.

He had other worries. The boatmen of Llandudno regarded him as an enemy of the human race. If they had not been nature's gentlemen they would have burned him alive at a stake. Cregeen, in particular, consistently referred to him in terms which could not have been more severe had Denry been the assassin of Cregeen's wife and seven children. In daring to make over a hundred pounds a week out of a ramshackle old lifeboat that Cregeen had sold to him for thirty-five pounds, Denry was outraging Cregeen's moral code. Cregeen had paid thirty-five pounds for the *Fleetwing*, a craft immeasurably superior to Denry's nameless tub. And was Cregeen making a hundred pounds a week out of it? Not a hundred shillings! Cregeen genuinely thought that he had a right to half Denry's profits. Old Simeon, too, seemed to think that *he* had a right to a large percentage of the same profits. And the Corporation, though it was notorious that excursionists visited the town purposely to voyage in the lifeboat, the Corporation made difficulties — about the embarking and disembarking, about the photograph strip of beach, about the crowds on the pavement outside the photograph shop. Denry learnt that he had committed the sin of not being a native of Llandudno. He was a stranger, and he was taking money out of the town. At times he wished he could have been born again. His friend and saviour was the Local Secretary of the Lifeboat Institution, who happened to be a Town Councillor. This worthy man, to whom Denry paid over a pound a day, was invaluable to him. Further, Denry was invited – nay commanded – to contribute to nearly every church, chapel, mission, and charity in Carnarvonshire, Flintshire, and other counties. His youthfulness was not accepted as an excuse. And as his gross profits could be calculated by any dunce who chose to stand on the beach for half a day, it was not easy for him to pretend that he was on the brink of starvation. He could only ward off attacks by stating with vague, convinced sadness that his expenses were much greater than anyone could imagine.

In September, when the moon was red and full, and the sea glassy, he announced a series of nocturnal 'Rocket Fêtes'. The lifeboat, hung with Chinese lanterns, put out in the evening (charge five shillings) and, followed by half the harbour's fleet of rowing-boats and cutters, proceeded to the neighbourhood of the strip of beach, where a rocket apparatus had been installed by the help of the Lifeboat Secretary. The mortar was trained; there was a flash, a whizz, a line of fire, and a rope fell out of the sky across the lifeboat. The effect was thrilling and roused cheers. Never did the Lifeboat Institution receive such an advertisement as Denry gave it – gratis.

After the rocketing Denry stood alone on the slopes of the Little Orme and watched the lanterns floating home over the water, and heard the lusty mirth of his clients in the still air. It was an emotional experience for him.

'By Jove!' he said, 'I've wakened this town up!'

VI

One morning, in the very last sad days of the dying season, when his receipts had dropped to the miserable figure of about fifty pounds a week, Denry had a great and pleasing surprise. He met Nellie on the Parade. It was a fact that the recognition of that innocent, childlike blushing face gave him joy. Nellie was with her father, Councillor Cotterill, and her mother. The Councillor was a speculative builder, who was erecting several streets of British homes in the new quarter above the new municipal park at Bursley. Denry had already encountered him once or twice in the way of business. He was a big and portly man of forty-five, with a thin face and a consciousness of prosperity. At one moment you would think him a jolly, bluff fellow, and at the next you would be disconcerted by a note of cunning or of harshness. Mrs Councillor Cotterill was one of those women who fail to live up to the ever-increasing height of their husbands. Afflicted with an eternal stage-fright, she never opened her closed-pressed lips in society, though a few people knew that she could talk as fast and as effectively as anyone. Difficult to set in motion, her vocal machinery was equally difficult to stop. She generally wore a low bonnet and a mantle. The Cotterills had been spending a fortnight in the Isle of Man, and they had come direct from Douglas to Llandudno by steamer, where they meant to pass two or three days. They were staying at Craig-y-don, at the eastern end of the Parade.

'Well, young man!' said Councillor Cotterill.

And he kept on young-manning Denry with an easy patronage which Denry could scarcely approve of. 'I bet I've made more money this summer than you have with all your jerrying!' said Denry silently to the Councillor's back while the Cotterill family were inspecting the historic lifeboat on the beach. Councillor Cotterill said frankly that one reason for their calling at Llandudno was his desire to see this singular lifeboat, about which there had really been a very great deal of talk in the Five Towns. The admission comforted Denry. Then the Councillor recommenced his young-manning.

'Look here,' said Denry, carelessly, 'you must come and dine with me one night, all of you – will you?'

Nobody who has not passed at least twenty years in a district where people dine at one o'clock, and dining after dark is regarded as a wild idiosyncrasy of earls, can appreciate the effect of this speech.

The Councillor, when he had recovered himself, said that they would be pleased to dine with him; Mrs Cotterill's tight lips were seen to move, but not heard; and Nellie glowed.

'Yes,' said Denry, 'come and dine with me at the Majestic.'

The name of the Majestic put an end to the young-manning.

It was the new hotel by the pier, and advertised itself as the most luxurious hotel in the Principality. Which was bold of it, having regard to the magnificence of caravanserais at Cardiff. It had two hundred bedrooms, and waiters who talked English imperfectly; and its prices were supposed to be fantastic.

After all, the most startled and frightened person of the four was perhaps Denry. He had never given a dinner to anybody. He had never even dined at night. He had never been inside the Majestic. He had never had the courage to go inside the Majestic. He had no notion of the mysterious preliminaries to the offering of a dinner in a public place.

But the next morning he contracted to give away the lifeboat to a syndicate of boatmen, headed by John their leader, for thirty-five pounds. And he swore to himself that he would do that dinner properly, even if it cost him the whole price of the boat. Then he met Mrs Cotterill coming out of a shop. Mrs Cotterill, owing to a strange hazard of fate, began talking at once. And Denry, as an old shorthand writer, instinctively calculated that not Thomas Allen Reed himself could have taken Mrs Cotterill down verbatim. Her face tried to express pain, but pleasure shone out of it. For she found herself in an exciting contretemps which she could understand.

'Oh, Mr Machin,' she said, 'what *do* you think's happened? I don't know how to tell you, I'm sure. Here you've arranged for that dinner tomorrow and it's all settled, and now Miss Earp telegraphs to our Nellie to say she's coming tomorrow for a day or two with us. You know Ruth and Nellie are *such* friends. It's like as if what must be, isn't it? I don't know what to do, I do declare. What *ever* will Ruth say at us leaving her all alone the first night she comes? I really do think she might have –'

'You must bring her along with you,' said Denry.

'But won't you – shan't you – won't she – won't it –'

'Not at all,' said Denry. 'Speaking for myself, I shall be delighted.'

'Well, I'm sure you're very sensible,' said Mrs Cotterill. 'I was but saying to Mr Cotterill over breakfast – I said to him –'

'I shall ask Councillor Rhys-Jones to meet you,' said Denry. 'He's one of the principal members of the Town Council here;

Local Secretary of the Lifeboat Institution. Great friend of mine.'

'Oh!' exclaimed Mrs Cotterill, 'it'll be quite an affair.'

It was.

Denry found to his relief that the only difficult part of arranging a dinner at the Majestic was the steeling of yourself to enter the gorgeous portals of the hotel. After that, and after murmuring that you wished to fix up a little snack, you had nothing to do but listen to suggestions, each surpassing the rest in splendour, and say 'Yes'. Similarly with the greeting of a young woman who was once to you the jewel of the world. You simply said, 'Good afternoon, how are you?' And she said the same. And you shook hands. And there you were, still alive!

The one defect of the dinner was that the men were not in evening dress. (Denry registered a new rule of life: Never travel without your evening dress, because you never know what may turn up.) The girls were radiantly white. And after all there is nothing like white. Mrs Cotterill was in black silk and silence. And after all there is nothing like black silk. There was champagne. There were ices. Nellie, not being permitted champagne, took her revenge in ice. Denry had found an opportunity to relate to her the history of the Chocolate Remedy. She said, 'How wonderful you are!' And he said it was she who was wonderful. Denry gave no information about the Chocolate Remedy to her father. Neither did she. As for Ruth, indubitably she was responsible for the social success of the dinner. She seemed to have the habit of these affairs. She it was who loosed tongues. Nevertheless, Denry saw her now with different eyes, and it appeared incredible to him that he had once mistaken her for the jewel of the world.

At the end of the dinner Councillor Rhys-Jones produced a sensation by rising to propose the health of their host. He referred to the superb heroism of England's lifeboatmen, and in the name of the Institution thanked Denry for the fifty-three pounds which Denry's public had contributed to the funds. He said it was a noble contribution and that Denry was a philanthropist. And he called on Councillor Cotterill to second the toast. Which Councillor Cotterill did, in good set terms, the

93

result of long habit. And Denry stammered that he was much obliged, and that really it was nothing.

But when the toasting was finished, Councillor Cotterill lapsed somewhat into a patronizing irony, as if he were jealous of a youthful success. And he did not stop at 'young man'. He addressed Denry grandiosely as 'my boy'.

'This lifeboat – it was just an idea, my boy, just an idea,' he said.

'Yes,' said Denry, 'but I thought of it.'

'The question is,' said the Councillor, 'can you think of any more ideas as good?'

'Well,' said Denry, 'can *you*?'

With reluctance they left the luxury of the private dining-room, and Denry surreptitiously paid the bill with a pile of sovereigns, and Councillor Rhys-Jones parted from them with lively grief. The other five walked in a row along the Parade in the moonlight. And when they arrived in front of Craig-y-don, and the Cotterills were entering, Ruth, who loitered behind, said to Denry in a liquid voice:

'I don't feel a bit like going to sleep. I suppose you wouldn't care for a stroll?'

'Well –'

'I daresay you're very tired,' she said.

'No,' he replied, 'it's this moonlight I'm afraid of.'

And their eyes met under the door-lamp, and Ruth wished him pleasant dreams and vanished. It was exceedingly subtle.

VII

The next afternoon the Cotterills and Ruth Earp went home, and Denry with them. Llandudno was just settling into its winter sleep, and Denry's rather complex affairs had all been put in order. Though the others showed a certain lassitude, he himself was hilarious. Among his insignificant luggage was a new hat-box, which proved to be the origin of much gaiety.

'Just take this, will you?' he said to a porter on the platform at Llandudno Station, and held out the new hat-box with an air of calm. The porter innocently took it, and then, as the hat-box nearly jerked his arm out of the socket, gave vent to his astonishment after the manner of porters.

'By gum mister!' said he, 'that's heavy!'

It, in fact, weighed nearly two stone.

'Yes,' said Denry, 'it's full of sovereigns, of course.'

And everybody laughed.

At Crewe, where they had to change, and again at Knype and at Bursley, he produced astonishment in porters by concealing the effort with which he handed them the hat-box, as though its weight was ten ounces. And each time he made the same witticism about sovereigns.

'What *have* you got in that hat-box?' Ruth asked.

'Don't I tell you?' said Denry, laughing. 'Sovereigns!'

Lastly, he performed the same trick on his mother. Mrs Machin was working, as usual, in the cottage in Brougham Street. Perhaps the notion of going to Llandudno for a change had not occurred to her. In any case, her presence had been necessary in Bursley, for she had frequently collected Denry's rents for him, and collected them very well. Denry was glad to see her again, and she was glad to see him, but they concealed their feelings as much as possible. When he basely handed her the hat-box she dropped it, and roundly informed him that she was not going to have any of his pranks.

After tea, whose savouriness he enjoyed quite as much as his own state dinner, he gave her a key and asked her to open the hat-box, which he had placed on a chair.

'What is there in it?'

'A lot of jolly fine pebbles that I've been collecting on the beach,' he said.

She got the hat-box on to her knee, and unlocked it, and came to a thick cloth, which she partly withdrew, and then there was a scream from Mrs Machin, and the hat-box rolled with a terrific crash to the tiled floor, and she was ankle-deep in sovereigns. She could see sovereigns running about all over the parlour. Gradually even the most active sovereigns decided to lie down and be quiet, and a great silence ensued. Denry's heart was beating.

Mrs Machin merely shook her head. Not often did her son

deprive her of words, but this theatrical culmination of his home-coming really did leave her speechless.

Late that night rows of piles of sovereigns decorated the oval table in the parlour.

'A thousand and eleven,' said Denry, at length, beneath the lamp. 'There's fifteen missing yet. We'll look for 'em to-morrow.'

For several days afterwards Mrs Machin was still picking up sovereigns. Two had even gone outside the parlour, and down the two steps into the backyard, and finding themselves unable to get back, had remained there.

And all the town knew that the unique Denry had thought of the idea of returning home to his mother with a hat-box crammed with sovereigns. This was Denry's 'latest', and it em-ployed the conversation of the borough for I don't know how long.

CHAPTER 6

His Burglary

I

THE fact that Denry Machin decided not to drive behind his mule to Sneyd Hall showed in itself that the enterprise of interviewing the Countess of Chell was not quite the simple daily trifling matter that he strove to pretend it was.

The mule was a part of his more recent splendour. It was aged seven, and it had cost Denry ten pounds. He had bought it off a farmer whose wife 'stood' St Luke's Market. His excuse was that he needed help in getting about the Five Towns in pursuit of cottage rents, for his business of a rent-collector had grown. But for this purpose a bicycle would have served equally well, and would not have cost a shilling a day to feed, as the mule did, nor have shied at policemen, as the mule nearly always did. Denry had bought the mule simply because he had been struck all of a sudden with the idea of buying the mule. Some time previously Jos Curtenty (the Deputy-Mayor, who became Mayor of Bursley on the Earl of Chell being called away to govern an Australian colony) had made an enormous sensation by buying a flock of geese and driving them home himself. Denry did not like this. He was indeed jealous, if a large mind can be jealous. Jos Curtenty was old enough to be his grandfather, and had been a recognized 'card' and 'character' since before Denry's birth. But Denry, though so young, had made immense progress as a card, and had, perhaps justifiably, come to consider himself as the premier card, the very ace, of the town. He felt that some reply was needed to Curtenty's geese, and the mule was his reply. It served excellently. People were soon asking each other whether they had heard that Denry Machin's 'latest' was to buy a mule. He obtained a little old victoria for another ten pounds, and a good set of harness for three guineas. The carriage was low, which enabled him, as he said, to nip in and out much more easily than in and out of a trap. In his business you did

97

almost nothing but nip in and out. On the front seat he caused to be fitted a narrow box of japanned tin, with a formidable lock and slits on the top. This box was understood to receive the rents, as he collected them. It was always guarded on journeys by a cross between a mastiff and something unknown, whose growl would have terrorized a lion-tamer. Denry himself was afraid of Rajah, the dog, but he would not admit it. Rajah slept in the stable behind Mrs Machin's cottage, for which Denry paid a shilling a week. In the stable there was precisely room for Rajah, the mule and the carriage, and when Denry entered to groom or to harness, something had to go out.

The equipage quickly grew into a familiar sight in the streets of the district. Denry said that it was funny without being vulgar. Certainly it amounted to a continual advertisement for him; an infinitely more effective advertisement than, for instance, a sandwichman at eighteen-pence a day, and costing no more, even with the licence and the shoeing. Moreover, a sandwichman has this inferiority to a turnout: when you have done with him you cannot put him up to auction and sell him. Further, there are no sandwichmen in the Five Towns; in that democratic and independent neighbourhood nobody would deign to be a sandwichman.

The mulish vehicular display does not end the tale of Denry's splendour. He had an office in St Luke's Square, and in the office was an office-boy, small but genuine, and a real copying-press, and outside it was the little square signboard which in the days of his simplicity used to be screwed on to his mother's door. His mother's steely firmness of character had driven him into the extravagance of an office. Even after he had made over a thousand pounds out of the Llandudno lifeboat in less than three months, she would not listen to a proposal for going into a slightly larger house, of which one room might serve as an office. Nor would she abandon her own labours as a sempstress. She said that since her marriage she had always lived in that cottage and had always worked, and that meant to die there, working: and that Denry could do what he chose. He was a bold youth, but not bold enough to dream of quitting his mother; besides, his share of household expenses in the cottage was only ten shillings a week. So he rented the office; and he hired and office-boy, partly to convey to his mother that he *should* do what he chose, and partly for his own private amusement.

He was thus, at an age when fellows without imagination are fraying their cuffs for the enrichment of their elders and glad if they can afford a cigar once a month, in possession of a business, business premises, a clerical staff, and a private carriage drawn by an animal unique in the Five Towns. He was living on less than his income; and in the course of about two years, to a small extent by economies and to a large extent by injudicious but happy investments, he had doubled the Llandudno thousand and won the deference of the manager of the bank at the top of St Luke's Square – one of the most unsentimental men that ever wrote 'refer to drawer' on a cheque.

And yet Denry was not satisfied. He had a secret woe, due to the facts that he was gradually ceasing to be a card, and that he was not multiplying his capital by two every six months. He did not understand the money market, nor the stock market, nor even the financial article in the *Signal*; but he regarded himself as a financial genius, and deemed that as a financial genius he was vegetating. And as for setting the town on fire, or painting it scarlet, he seemed to have lost the trick of that.

II

And then one day the populace saw on his office door, beneath his name-board, another sign:

FIVE TOWNS UNIVERSAL THRIFT CLUB
Secretary and Manager – E. H. MACHIN

An idea had visited him.

Many tradesmen formed slate-clubs – goose-clubs, turkey-clubs, whisky-clubs – in the autumn, for Christmas. Their humble customers paid so much a week to the tradesmen, who charged them nothing for keeping it, and at the end of the agreed period they took out the total sum in goods – dead or alive; eatable, drinkable, or wearable. Denry conceived a universal slate-club. He meant it to embrace each of the Five Towns. He saw forty thousand industrial families paying weekly instalments into his slate-club. He saw his slate-club entering into contracts with all the principal tradesmen of the entire district, so that the members of the slate-club could shop with slate-club tickets practically where they chose. He saw his slate-club so powerful that no tradesman could afford not to be in relations with it. He had induced all Llandudno to perform the same act daily for nearly a whole season, and he now wished to induce all the vast Five Towns to perform the same act to his profit for all eternity.

And he would be a philanthropist into the bargain. He would encourage thrift in the working-man and the working-man's wife. He would guard the working-man's money for him; and to save trouble to the working-man he would call at the working-man's door for the working-man's money. Further, as a special inducement and to prove superior advantages to ordinary slate-clubs, he would allow the working-man to spend his full nominal subscription to the club as soon as he had actually paid only half of it. Thus, after paying ten shillings to Denry, the working-man could spend a pound in Denry's chosen shops, and Denry would settle with the shops at once, while collecting the balance weekly at the working-man's door. But this privilege of anticipation was to be forfeited or postponed if the working-man's earlier payments were irregular.

And Denry would bestow all these wondrous benefits on the working-man without any charge whatever. Every penny that members paid in, members would draw out. The affair was enormously philanthropic.

Denry's modest remuneration was to come from the shopkeepers upon whom his scheme would shower new custom. They were to allow him at least twopence in the shilling discount on all transactions, which would be more than 16 per cent on his capital; and he would turn over his capital three times a year. He calculated that out of 50 per cent per annum he would be able to cover working expenses and a little over.

Of course, he had to persuade the shopkeepers. He drove his mule to Hanbridge and began with Bostocks, the largest but not the most distinguished drapery house in the Five Towns. He succeeded in convincing them on every point except that of his own financial stability. Bostocks indicated their opinion that he looked far too much like a boy to be financially stable. His reply was to offer to deposit fifty pounds with them before starting business, and to renew the sum in advance as quickly as the members of his club should exhaust it. Cheques talk. He departed with Bostocks' name at the head of his list, and he used them as a clinching argument with other shops. But the prejudice against his youth was strong and general. 'Yes,' tradesmen would answer, 'what you say is all right, but you are so young.' As if to insinuate that a man must be either a rascal or a fool until he is thirty, just as he must be either a fool or a physician after he is forty. Nevertheless, he had soon compiled a list of several score shops.

His mother said:

'Why don't you grow a beard? Here you spend money on razors, strops, soaps, and brushes, besides a quarter of an hour of your time every day, and cutting yourself – all to keep yourself from having something that would be the greatest help to you in business! With a beard you'd look at least thirty-one. Your father had a splendid beard, and so could you if you chose.'

This was high wisdom. But he would not listen to it. The truth is, he was getting somewhat dandiacal.

At length his scheme lacked naught but what Denry called a 'right-down good starting shove'. In a word, a fine advertisement to fire it off. Now, he could have had the whole of the first page of the *Signal* (at that period) for five-and-twenty pounds. But he had been so accustomed to free advertisements of one sort or another that the notion of paying for one was loathsome to him. Then it was that he thought of the Countess of Chell, who happened to be staying at Knype. If he could obtain that great aristocrat, that ex-Mayoress, that lovely witch, that benefactor of the district, to honour his Thrift Club as patroness, success was certain. Everybody in the Five Towns sneered at the Countess and called her a busybody; she was even dubbed 'Interfering Iris' (Iris being one of her eleven Christian names); the Five Towns was fiercely democratic – in theory. In practice the Countess was worshipped; her smile was worth at least five pounds, and her invitation to tea was priceless. She could not have been more sincerely adulated in the United States, the home of social equality.

Denry said to himself:

'And why *shouldn't* I get her name as patroness? I will have her name as patroness.'

Hence the expedition to Sneyd Hall, one of the ancestral homes of the Earls of Chell.

III

He had been to Sneyd Hall before many times – like the majority of the inhabitants of the Five Towns – for, by the generosity of its owner, Sneyd Park was always open to the public. To picnic in Sneyd Park was one of the chief distractions of the Five Towns on Thursday and Saturday afternoons. But he had never entered the private gardens. In the midst of the private gardens stood the Hall, shut off by immense iron palisades, like a lion in a cage at the Zoo. On the autumn afternoon of his historic visit, Denry passed with qualms through the double gates of the palisade, and began to crunch the gravel of the broad drive that led in a straight line to the overwhelming Palladian façade of the Hall.

Yes, he was decidedly glad that he had not brought his mule. As he approached nearer and nearer to the Countess's front-door his arguments in favour of the visit grew more and more ridiculous. Useless to remind himself that he had once danced with the Countess at the municipal ball, and amused her to the giggling point, and restored her lost fan to her. Useless to remind himself that he was a quite exceptional young man, with a quite exceptional renown, and the equal of any man or woman on earth. Useless to remind himself that the Countess was notorious for her affability and also for her efforts to encourage the true welfare of the Five Towns. The visit was grotesque.

He ought to have written. He ought, at any rate, to have announced his visit by a note. Yet only an hour earlier he had been arguing that he could most easily capture the Countess by storm, with no warning or preparations of any kind.

Then, from a lateral path, a closed carriage and pair drove rapidly up to the Hall, and a footman bounced off the hammer-cloth. Denry could not see through the carriage, but under it he could distinguish the skirts of some one who got out of it. Evidently the Countess was just returning from a drive. He quickened his pace, for at heart he was an audacious boy.

'She can't eat me,' he said.

This assertion was absolutely irrefutable, and yet there remained in his bold heart an irrational fear that after all she *could* eat him. Such is the extraordinary influence of a Palladian façade!

After what seemed several hours of torture entirely novel in his experience, he skirted the back of the carriage and mounted the steps to the portal. And, although the coachman was innocuous, being apparently carved in stone, Denry would have given a ten-pound note to find himself suddenly in his club or even in church. The masonry of the Hall rose up above him like a precipice. He was searching for the bell-knob in the face of the precipice when a lady suddenly appeared at the doors. At first he thought it was the Countess, and that heart of his began to slip down the inside of his legs. But it was not the Countess.

'Well?' demanded the lady. She was dressed in black.

'Can I see the Countess?' he inquired.

The lady stared at him. He handed her his professional card which lay waiting all ready in his waistcoat pocket.

'I will ask my lady,' said the lady in black.

Denry perceived from her accent that she was not English.

She disappeared through a swinging door; and then Denry most clearly heard the Countess's own authentic voice saying in a pettish, disgusted tone:

'Oh! Bother!'

And he was chilled. He seriously wished that he had never thought of starting his confounded Universal Thrift Club.

After some time the carriage suddenly drove off, presumably to the stables. As he was now within the hollow of the porch, a sort of cave at the foot of the precipice, he could not see along the length of the façade. Nobody came to him. The lady who had promised to ask my lady whether the latter could see him did not return. He reflected that she had not promised to return; she had merely promised to ask a question. As the minutes passed he grew careless, or grew bolder, gradually dropping his correct attitude of a man-about-town paying an afternoon call, and peered through the glass of the doors that divided him from the Countess. He could distinguish nothing that had life. One of his preliminary tremors had been caused by a fanciful vision of multitudinous footmen, through a double line of whom he would be compelled to walk in order to reach the Countess. But there was not even one footman. This complete absence of indoor footmen seemed to him remiss, not in accordance with centuries of tradition concerning life at Sneyd.

Then he caught sight, through the door, of the back of Jock, the Countess's carriage footman and the son of his mother's old friend. Jock was standing motionless at a half-open door to the right of the space between Denry's double doors and the next pair of double doors. Denry tried to attract his attention by singular movements and strange noises of the mouth. But Jock, like his partner the coachman, appeared to be carven in stone. Denry decided that he would go in and have speech with Jock. They were on Christian-name terms, or had been a few years ago. He unobtrusively pushed at the doors, and at the very same moment Jock, with a start – as though released from some spell – vanished away from the door to the right.

Denry was now within.

'Jock!' He gave a whispering cry, rather conspiratorial in tone. And as Jock offered no response, he hurried after Jock through the door to the right. This door led to a large apartment which struck Denry as being an idealization of a first-class waiting-room at a highly important terminal station. In a wall to the left was a small door, half open. Jock must have gone through that door. Denry hesitated – he had not properly been invited into the Hall. But in hesitating he was wrong; he ought to have followed his prey without qualms. When he had conquered qualms and reached the further door, his eyes were met, to their amazement, by an immense perspective of great chambers. Denry had once seen a Pullman car, which had halted at Knype Station with a French actress on board. What he saw now presented itself to him as a train of Pullman cars, one opening into the other, constructed for giants. Each car was about as large as the large hall in Bursley Town Hall, and, like that auditorium, had a ceiling painted to represent blue sky, milk-white clouds, and birds. But in the corners were groups of naked Cupids, swimming joyously on the ceiling; in Bursley Town Hall there were no naked Cupids. He understood now that he had been quite wrong in his estimate of the room by which he had come into this Versailles. Instead of being large it was tiny, and instead of being luxurious it was merely furnished with miscellaneous odds and ends left over from far more important furnishings. It was indeed naught but a nondescript box of a hole insignificantly wedged between the state apartments and the outer lobby.

For an instant he forgot that he was in pursuit of Jock. Jock was perfectly invisible and inaudible. He must, however, have gone down the vista of the great chambers, and therefore Denry went down the vista of the great chambers after him, curiously expecting to have a glimpse of his long salmon-tinted coat or his cockaded hat popping up out of some corner. He reached the other end of the vista, having traversed three enormous chambers, of which the middle one was the most enormous and the most gorgeous. There were high windows everywhere to his right, and to his left, in every chamber, double doors with gilt handles of a peculiar shape. Windows and doors, with equal splendour, were draped in hangings of brocade. Through the windows he had glimpses of the gardens in their autumnal colours, but no glimpse of a gardener. Then a carriage flew past the windows at the end of the suite, and he had a very clear though a transient view of two menials on the box-seat; one of those menials he knew must be Jock. Hence Jock must have escaped from the state suite by one of the numerous doors.

Denry tried one door after another, and they were all fastened firmly on the outside. The gilded handles would turn, but the lofty and ornate portals would not yield to pressure. Mystified and startled, he went back to the place from which he had begun his explorations, and was even more seriously startled, and more deeply mystified to find nothing but a blank wall where he had entered. Obviously he could not have penetrated through a solid wall. A careful perusal of the wall showed him that there was indeed a door in it, but that the door was artfully disguised by painting and other devices so as to look like part of the wall. He had never seen such a phenomenon before. A very small glass knob was the door's sole fitting. Denry turned this crystal, but with no useful result. In the brief space of time since his entrance, that door, and the door by which Jock had gone, had been secured by unseen hands. Denry imagined sinister persons bolting all the multitudinous doors, and inimical eyes staring at him through many keyholes. He imagined himself to be the victim of some fearful and incomprehensible conspiracy.

Why, in the sacred name of common-sense, should he have been imprisoned in the state suite? The only answer to the conundrum was that nobody was aware of his quite unauthorized presence in the state suite. But then why should the state suite be so suddenly locked up, since the Countess had just come in from a drive? It then occurred to him that, instead of just coming in, the Countess had been just leaving. The carriage must have driven round from some humbler part of the Hall, with the lady in black in it, and the lady in black – perhaps a lady's-maid – alone had stepped out from it. The Countess had been waiting for the carriage in the porch, and had fled to avoid being forced to meet the unfortunate Denry. (Humiliating thought!) The carriage had then taken her up at a side door. And now she was gone. Possibly she had left Sneyd Hall not to return for months, and that was why the doors had been locked. Perhaps everybody had departed from the Hall save one aged and deaf retainer – he knew, from historical novels which he had glanced at in his youth, that in every Hall that respected itself an aged and deaf retainer was invariably left solitary during the absences of the noble owner. He knocked on the small disguised door. His unique purpose in knocking was naturally to make a noise, but something prevented him from making a noise. He felt that he must knock decently, discreetly; he felt that he must not outrage the conventions.

No result to this polite summoning.

He attacked other doors; he attacked every door he could put his hands on; and gradually he lost his respect for decency and the conventions proper to Halls, knocking loudly and more loudly. He banged. Nothing but sheer solidity stopped his sturdy hands from going through the panels. He so far forgot himself as to shake the doors with all his strength furiously.

And finally he shouted: 'Hi there! Hi! Can't you hear?'

Apparently the aged and deaf retainer could not hear. Apparently he was the deafest retainer that a peeress of the realm ever left in charge of a princely pile.

'Well, that's a nice thing!' Denry exclaimed, and he noticed that he was hot and angry. He took a certain pleasure in being angry. He considered that he had a right to be angry.

At this point he began to work himself up into the state of 'not caring', into the state of despising Sneyd Hall, and everything for which it stood. As for permitting himself to be impressed or intimidated by the lonely magnificence of his environment, he laughed at the idea; or, more accurately, he snorted at it. Scornfully he tramped up and down those immense interiors, doing the caged lion, and cogitating in quest of the right dramatic, effective act to perform in the singular crisis. Unhappily, the carpets were very thick, so that though he could tramp, he could not stamp; and he desired to stamp. But in the connecting doorways there were expanses of bare, highly polished oak floor, and here he did stamp.

The rooms were not furnished after the manner of ordinary rooms. There was no round or square table in the midst of each, with a checked cloth on it, and a plant in the centre. Nor in front of each window was there a small table with a large Bible thereupon. The middle parts of the rooms were empty, save for a group of statuary in the largest room. Great arm-chairs and double-ended sofas were ranged about in straight lines, and among these, here and there, were smaller chairs gilded from head to foot. Round the walls were placed long narrow tables with tops like glass-cases, and in the cases were all sorts of strange matters — such as coins, fans, daggers, snuff-boxes. In various corners white statues stood awaiting the day of doom without a rag to protect them from the winds of destiny. The walls were panelled in tremendous panels, and in each panel was a formidable dark oil-painting. The mantelpieces were so preposterously high that not even a giant could have sat at the fireplace and put his feet on them. And if they had held clocks, as mantelpieces do, a telescope would have been necessary to discern the hour. Above each mantelpiece, instead of a looking-glass, was a vast picture. The chandeliers were overpowering in glitter and in dimensions.

Near to a sofa Denry saw a pile of yellow linen things. He picked up the topmost article, and it assumed the form of a chair. Yes, these articles were furniture-covers. The Hall, then, was to be shut up. He argued from the furniture-covers that somebody must enter sooner or later to put the covers on the furniture.

Then he did a few more furlongs up and down the vista, and sat down at the far end, under a window. Anyhow, there were always the windows. High though they were from the floor, he could easily open one, spring out, and slip unostentatiously away. But he thought he would wait until dusk fell. Prudence is seldom misplaced. The windows, however, held a disappointment for him. A mere bar, padlocked, prevented each one of them from being opened; it was a simple device. He would be under the necessity of breaking a plate-glass pane. For this enterprise he thought he would wait until black night. He sat down again. Then he made a fresh and noisy assault on all the doors. No result. He sat down a third time, and gazed into the gardens where the shadows were creeping darkly. Not a soul in the gardens. Then he felt a draught on the crown of his head, and looking aloft he saw that the summit of the window had a transverse glazed flap, for ventilation, and that this flap had been left open. If he could have climbed up, he might have fallen out on the other side into the gardens and liberty. But the summit of the window was at least sixteen feet from the floor. Night descended.

IV

At a vague hour in the evening a stout woman dressed in black, with a black apron, a neat violet cap on her head, and a small lamp in her podgy hand, unlocked one of the doors giving entry to the state rooms. She was on her nightly round of inspection. The autumn moon, nearly at full, had risen and was shining into the great windows. And in front of the furthest window she perceived in the radiance of the moonshine a pyramidal group, somewhat in the style of a family of acrobats, dangerously arranged on the stage of a music-hall. The base of the pyramid comprised two settees; upon these were several arm-chairs laid flat, and on the arm-chairs two tables covered with cushions and rugs; lastly, in the way of inanimate nature, two gilt chairs. On the gilt chairs was something that unmistakably moved, and was fumbling with the top of the window. Being a stout woman with a tranquil and sagacious mind, her first act was not to drop the lamp. She courageously clung to the lamp.

'Who's there?' said a voice from the apex of the pyramid.

Then a subsidence began, followed by a crash and a multitudinous splintering of glass. The living form dropped on to one of the settees, rebounding like a football from its powerful springs. There was a hole as big as a coffin in the window. The living form collected itself, and then jumped wildly through that hole into the gardens.

Denry ran. The moment had not struck him as a moment propitious for explanation. In a flash he had seen the ridiculousness of endeavouring to convince a stout lady in black that he was a gentleman paying a call on the Countess. He simply scrambled to his legs and ran. He ran aimlessly in the darkness and sprawled over a hedge, after crossing various flower-beds. Then he saw the sheen of the moon on Sneyd Lake, and he could take his bearings. In winter all the Five Towns skate on Sneyd Lake if the ice will bear, and the geography of it was quite familiar to Denry. He skirted its east bank, plunged into Great Shendon Wood, and emerged near Great Shendon Station, on the line from Stafford to Knype. He inquired for the next train in the tones of innocency, and in half an hour was passing through Sneyd Station itself. In another fifty minutes he was at home. The clock showed ten-fifteen. His mother's cottage seemed amazingly small. He said that he had been detained in Hanbridge on business, that he had had neither tea nor supper, and that he was hungry. Next morning he could scarcely be sure that his visit to Sneyd Hall was not a dream. In any event it had been a complete failure.

V

It was on this untriumphant morning that one of the tenants under his control, calling at the cottage to pay some rent overdue, asked him when the Universal Thrift Club was going to commence its operations. He had talked of the enterprise to all his tenants, for it was precisely with his tenants that he hoped to make a beginning. He had there a *clientèle* ready to his hand, and as he was intimately acquainted with the circumstances of each, he could judge between those who would be reliable and those to whom he would be obliged to refuse membership. The tenants, conclaving together of an evening on doorsteps, had come to the conclusion that the Universal Thrift Club was the very contrivance which they had lacked for years. They saw in it a cure for all their economic ills, and the gate to Paradise. The dame who put the question to him on the morning after his defeat wanted to be the possessor of carpets, a new teapot, a silver brooch, and a cookery book; and she was evidently depending upon Denry. On consideration he saw no reason why the Universal Thrift Club should not be allowed to start itself by the impetus of its own intrinsic excellence. The dame was inscribed for three shares, paid eighteen-pence entrance fee, undertook to pay three shillings a week, and received a document entitling her to spend £3 18s. in sixty-five shops as soon as she had paid £1 19s. to Denry. It was a marvellous scheme. The rumour of it spread; before dinner Denry had visits from other aspirants to membership, and he had posted a cheque to Bostocks, but more from ostentation than necessity; for no member could possibly go into Bostocks with his coupons until at least two months had elapsed.

But immediately after dinner, when the posters of the early edition of the *Signal* waved in the streets, he had material for other thought. He saw a poster as he was walking across to his office. The awful legend ran:

ASTOUNDING ATTEMPTED BURGLARY
AT
SNEYD HALL

In buying the paper he was afflicted with a kind of ague. And the description of events at Sneyd Hall was enough to give ague to a negro. The account had been taken from the lips of Mrs Gater, housekeeper at Sneyd Hall. She had related to a reporter how, upon going into the state suite before retiring for the night, she had surprised a burglar of Herculean physique and Titanic proportions. Fortunately she knew her duty, and did not blench. The burglar had threatened her with a revolver, and then, finding such bluff futile, had deliberately jumped through a large plate-glass window and vanished. Mrs Gater could not conceive how the fellow had 'effected an entrance'. (According to the reporter, Mrs Gater said 'effected an entrance', not 'got in'. And here it may be mentioned that in the columns of the *Signal* burglars never get into a residence; without exception they invariably effect an entrance.) Mrs Gater explained further how the plans of the burglar must have been laid with the most diabolic skill; how he must have studied the daily life of the Hall patiently for weeks, if not months; how he must have known the habits and plans of every soul in the place, and the exact instant at which the Countess had arranged to drive to Stafford to catch the London express.

It appeared that save for four maidservants, a page, two dogs, three gardeners, and the kitchen-clerk, Mrs Gater was alone in the Hall. During the late afternoon and early evening they had all been to assist at a rat-catching in the stables, and the burglar must have been aware of this. It passed Mrs Gater's comprehension how the criminal had got clear away out of the gardens and park, for to set up a hue and cry had been with her the work of a moment. She could not be sure whether he had taken any valuable property, but the inventory was being checked. Though surely for her an inventory was scarcely necessary, as she had been housekeeper at Sneyd Hall for six-and-twenty years, and might be said to know the entire contents of the mansion by heart! The police were at work. They had studied footprints and *débris*. There was talk of obtaining detectives from London. Up to the time of going to press, no clue had been discovered, but Mrs Gater was confident that a clue would be discovered, and of her ability to recognize the burglar when he should be caught. His features, as seen in the moonlight, were imprinted on her mind for ever. He was a young man, well dressed. The Earl had telegraphed, offering a reward of £20 for the fellow's capture. A warrant was out.

So it ran on.

Denry saw clearly all the errors of tact which he had committed on the previous day. He ought not to have entered uninvited. But having entered, he ought to have held firm in quiet dignity until the housekeeper came, and then he ought to have gone into full details with the housekeeper, producing his credentials and showing her unmistakably that he was offended by the experience which somebody's gross carelessness had forced upon him.

Instead of all that, he had behaved with simple stupidity, and the result was that a price was upon his head. Far from acquiring moral impressiveness and influential aid by his journey to Sneyd Hall, he had utterly ruined himself as a founder of a Universal Thrift Club. You cannot conduct a thrift club from prison, and a sentence of ten years does not inspire confidence in the ignorant mob. He trembled at the thought of what would happen when the police learned from the Countess that a man with a card on which was the name of Machin had called at Sneyd just before her departure.

However, the police never did learn this from the Countess (who had gone to Rome for the autumn). It appeared that her maid had merely said to the Countess that 'a man' had called, and also that the maid had lost the card. Careful research showed that the burglar had been disturbed before he had had opportunity to burgle. And the affair, after raising a terrific bother in the district, died down.

Then it was that an article appeared in the *Signal*, signed by Denry, and giving a full picturesque description of the state apartments at Sneyd Hall. He had formed a habit of occasional contributions to the *Signal*. This article began:

The recent sensational burglary at Sneyd Hall has drawn attention to the magnificent state apartments of that unique mansion. As very few but the personal friends of the family are allowed a glimpse of these historic rooms, they being of course quite closed to the public, we have thought that some account of them might interest the readers of the *Signal*. On the occasion of our last visit . . ., etc.

He left out nothing of their splendour.

The article was quoted as far as Birmingham in the Midlands Press. People recalled Denry's famous waltz with the Countess at the memorable dance in Bursley Town Hall. And they were bound to assume that the relations thus begun had been more or less maintained. They were struck by Denry's amazing discreet self-denial in never boasting of them. Denry rose in the market of popular esteem. Talking of Denry, people talked of the Universal Thrift Club, which went quietly ahead, and they admitted that Denry was of the stuff which succeeds and deserves to succeed.

But only Denry himself could appreciate fully how great Denry was, to have snatched such a wondrous victory out of such a humiliating defeat!

His chin slowly disappeared from view under a quite presentable beard. But whether the beard was encouraged out of respect for his mother's sage advice, or with the object of putting the housekeeper of Sneyd Hall off the scent, if she should chance to meet Denry, who shall say?

CHAPTER 7

The Rescuer of Dames

I

It next happened that Denry began to suffer from the ravages of a malady which is almost worse than failure - namely, a surfeit of success. The success was that of his Universal Thrift Club. This device, by which members after subscribing one pound in weekly instalments could at once get two pounds' worth of goods at nearly any large shop in the district, appealed with enormous force to the democracy of the Five Towns. There was no need whatever for Denry to spend money on advertising. The first members of the club did all the advertising and made no charge for doing it. A stream of people anxious to deposit money with Denry in exchange for a card never ceased to flow into his little office in St Luke's Square. The stream, indeed, constantly thickened. It was a wonderful invention, the Universal Thrift Club. And Denry ought to have been happy, especially as his beard was growing strongly and evenly, and giving him the desired air of a man of wisdom and stability. But he was not happy. And the reason was that the popularity of the Thrift Club necessitated much book-keeping, which he hated.

He was an adventurer, in the old honest sense, and no clerk. And he found himself obliged not merely to buy large books of account, but to fill them with figures; and to do addition sums from page to page; and to fill up hundreds of cards; and to write out lists of shops, and to have long interviews with printers whose proofs made him dream of lunatic asylums; and to reckon innumerable piles of small coins; and to assist his small office-boy in the great task of licking envelopes and stamps. Moreover, he was worried by shopkeepers; every shopkeeper in the district now wanted to allow him twopence in the shilling on the purchases of club members. And he had to collect all the subscriptions, in addition to his rents; and also to make personal preliminary inquiries as to the reputation of intending members.

If he could have risen every day at 4 a.m. and stayed up working every night till 4 a.m. he might have got through most of the labour. He did, as a fact, come very near to this ideal. So near that one morning his mother said to him, at her driest:

'I suppose I may as well sell your bedstead, Denry?'

And there was no hope of improvement; instead of decreasing, the work multiplied.

What saved him was the fortunate death of Lawyer Lawton. The aged solicitor's death put the town into mourning and hung the church with black. But Denry as a citizen bravely bore the blow because he was able to secure the services of Penkethman, Lawyer Lawton's eldest clerk, who, after keeping the Lawton books and writing the Lawton letters for thirty-five years, was dismissed by young Lawton for being over fifty and behind the times. The desiccated bachelor was grateful to Denry. He called Denry 'Sir', or rather he called Denry's suit of clothes 'Sir', for he had a vast respect for a well-cut suit. On the other hand, he maltreated the little office-boy, for he had always been accustomed to maltreating little office-boys, not seriously, but just enough to give them an interest in life. Penkethman enjoyed desks, ledgers, pens, ink, rulers, and blotting-paper. He could run from bottom to top of a column of figures more quickly than the fire-engine could run up Oldcastle Street; and his totals were never wrong. His gesture with a piece of blotting-paper as he blotted off a total was magnificent. He liked long hours; he was thoroughly used to overtime, and his boredom in his lodgings was such that he would often arrive at the office before the appointed hour. He asked thirty shillings a week, and Denry in a mood of generosity gave him thirty-one. He gave Denry his whole life, and put a meticulous order into the establishment. Denry secretly thought him a miracle, but up at the club at Hillport he was content to call him 'the human machine'. 'I wind him up every Saturday night with a sovereign, half a sovereign, and a shilling,' said Denry, 'and he goes for a week. Compensated balance adjusted for all temperatures. No escapement. Jewelled in every hole. Ticks in any position. Made in England.'

This jocularity of Denry's was a symptom that Denry's spirits were rising. The bearded youth was seen oftener in the streets behind his mule and his dog. The adventurer had, indeed, taken to the road again. After an emaciating period he began once more to stouten. He was the image of success. He was the picturesque card, whom everybody knew and everybody had pleasure in greeting. In some sort he was rather like the flag on the Town Hall.

And then a graver misfortune threatened.

It arose out of the fact that, though Denry was a financial genius, he was in no sense qualified to be a Fellow of the Institute of Chartered Accountants. The notion that an excess of prosperity may bring ruin had never presented itself to him, until one day he discovered that out of over two thousand pounds there remained less than six hundred to his credit at the bank. This was at the stage of the Thrift Club when the founder of the Thrift Club was bound under the rules to give credit. When the original lady member had paid in her two pounds or so, she was entitled to spend four pounds or so at shops. She did spend found pounds or so at shops. And Denry had to pay the shops. He was thus temporarily nearly two pounds out of pocket, and he had to collect that sum by trifling instalments. Multiply this case by five hundred, and you will understand the drain on Denry's capital. Multiply it by a thousand, and you will understand the very serious peril which overhung Denry. Multiply it by fifteen hundred and you will understand that Denry had been culpably silly to inaugurate a mighty scheme like the Universal Thrift Club on a paltry capital of two thousand pounds. He had. In his simplicity he had regarded two thousand pounds as boundless wealth.

Although new subscriptions poured in, the drain grew more distressing. Yet he could not persuade himself to refuse new members. He stiffened his rules, and compelled members to pay at his office instead of on their own doorsteps; he instituted fines for irregularity. But nothing could stop the progress of the Universal Thrift Club. And disaster approached. Denry felt as though he were being pushed nearer and nearer to the edge of a precipice by a tremendous multitude of people. At length, very much against his inclination, he put up a card in his window that no new members could be accepted until further notice, pending the acquisition of larger offices and other arrangements. For the shrewd, it was a confession of failure, and he knew it.

Then the rumour began to form, and to thicken, and to spread, that Denry's famous Universal Thrift Club was unsound at the core, and that the teeth of those who had bitten the apple would be set on edge.

And Denry saw that something great, something decisive, must be done and done with rapidity.

II

His thoughts turned to the Countess of Chell. The original attempt to engage her moral support in aid of the Thrift Club had ended in a dangerous fiasco. Denry had been beaten by circumstances. And though he had emerged from the defeat with credit, he had no taste for defeat. He disliked defeat even when it was served with jam. And his indomitable thoughts turned to the Countess again. He put it to himself in this way, scratching his head:

'I've got to get hold of that woman, and that's all about it!'

The Countess at this period was busying herself with the policemen of the Five Towns. In her exhaustless passion for philanthropy, bazaars, and platforms, she had already dealt with orphans, the aged, the blind, potter's asthma, crèches, churches, chapels, schools, economic cookery, the smoke-nuisance, country holidays, Christmas puddings and blankets, healthy musical entertainments, and barmaids. The excellent and beautiful creature was suffering from a dearth of subjects when the policemen occurred to her. She made the benevolent discovery that policemen were overworked, underpaid, courteous, and trustworthy public servants, and that our lives depended on them. And from this discovery it naturally followed that policemen deserved her energetic assistance. Which assistance resulted in the erection of a Policemen's Institute at Hanbridge, the chief of the Five Towns. At the Institute policemen would be able to play at draughts, read the papers, and drink everything non-alcoholic at prices that defied competition. And the Institute also conferred other benefits on those whom all the five Mayors of the Five Towns fell into the way of describing as 'the stalwart guardians of the law'. The Institute, having been built, had to be opened with due splendour and ceremony. And naturally the Countess of Chell was the person to open it, since without her it would never have existed.

The solemn day was a day in March, and the hour was fixed for three o'clock, and the place was the large hall of the Institute itself, behind Crown Square, which is the Trafalgar Square of Hanbridge. The Countess was to drive over from Sneyd. Had the epoch been ten years later she would have motored over. But probably that would not have made any difference to what happened.

In relating what did happen, I confine myself to facts, eschewing imputations. It is a truism that life is full of coincidences, but whether these events comprised a coincidence, or not, each reader must decide for himself, according to his cynicism or his faith in human nature.

The facts are: First, that Denry called one day at the house of Mrs Kemp a little lower down Brougham Street, Mrs Kemp being friendly with Mrs Machin, and the mother of Jock, the Countess's carriage-footman, whom Denry had known from boyhood. Second, that a few days later, when Jock came over to see his mother, Denry was present, and that subsequently Denry and Jock went for a stroll together in the cemetery, the principal resort of strollers in Bursley. Third, that on the afternoon of the opening ceremony the Countess's carriage broke down in Sneyd Vale, two miles from Sneyd and three miles from Hanbridge. Fourth, that five minutes later Denry, all in his best clothes, drove up behind his mule. Fifth, that Denry drove right past the breakdown, apparently not noticing it. Sixth, that Jock, touching his hat to Denry as if to a stranger (for, of course, while on duty a footman must be dead to all humanities), said: 'Excuse me, sir,' and so caused Denry to stop.

These are the simple facts.

Denry looked round with that careless half-turn of the upper part of the body which drivers of elegant equipages affect when their attention is called to something trifling behind them. The mule also looked round – it was a habit of the mule's and if the dog had been there the dog would have shown an even livelier inquisitiveness; but Denry had left the faithful animal at home.

'Good-afternoon, Countess,' he said, raising his hat, and trying to express surprise, pleasure, and imperturbability all at once.

The Countess of Chell, who was standing in the road, raised her lorgnon, which was attached to the end of a tortoiseshell pole about a foot long, and regarded Denry. This lorgnon was a new device of hers, and it was already having the happy effect of increasing the sale of longhandled lorgnons throughout the Five Towns.

'Oh! it's you, is it?' said the Countess. 'I see you've grown a beard.'

It was just this easy familiarity that endeared her to the district. As observant people put it, you never knew what she would say next, and yet she never compromised her dignity.

'Yes,' said Denry. 'Have you had an accident?'

'No,' said the Countess, bitterly: 'I'm doing this for idle amusement.'

The horses had been taken out, and were grazing by the roadside like common horses. The coachman was dipping his skirts in the mud as he bent down in front of the carriage and twisted the pole to and fro and round about and round about. The footman, Jock, was industriously watching him.

'It's the pole-pin, sir,' said Jock.

Denry descended from his own hammercloth. The Countess was not smiling. It was the first time that Denry had ever seen her without an efficient smile on her face.

'Have you got to be anywhere particular?' he asked. Many ladies would not have understood what he meant. But the Countess was used to the Five Towns.

'Yes,' said she. 'I have got to be somewhere particular. I've got to be at the Police Institute at three o'clock particular, Mr Machin. And I shan't be. I'm late now. We've been here ten minutes.'

The Countess was rather too often late for public ceremonies.

Nobody informed her of the fact. Everybody, on the contrary, assiduously pretended that she had arrived to the very second. But she was well aware that she had a reputation for unpunctuality. Ordinarily, being too hurried to invent a really clever excuse, she would assert lightly that something had happened to her carriage. And now something in truth had happened to her carriage – but who would believe it at the Police Institute?

'If you'll come with me, I'll guarantee to get you there by three o'clock,' said Denry.

The road thereabouts was lonely. A canal ran parallel with it at a distance of fifty yards, and on the canal a boat was moving in the direction of Hanbridge at the rate of a mile an hour. Such was the only other vehicle in sight. The outskirts of Knype, the nearest town, did not begin until at least a mile further on; and the Countess, dressed for the undoing of mayors and other unimpressionable functionaries, could not possibly have walked even half a mile in that rich dark mud. She thanked him, and without a word to her servants took the seat beside him.

III

Immediately the mule began to trot the Countess began to smile again. Relief and content were painted upon her handsome features. Denry soon learnt that she knew all about mules – or almost all. She told him how she had ridden hundreds of miles on mules in the Apennines, where there were no roads, and only mules, goats, and flies could keep their feet on the steep, stony paths. She said that a good mule was worth forty pounds in the Apennines, more than a horse of similar quality. In fact, she was very sympathetic about mules. Denry saw that he must drive with as much style as possible, and he tried to remember all that he had picked up from a book concerning the proper manner of holding the reins. For in everything that appertained to riding and driving the Countess was an expert. In the season she hunted once or twice a week with the North Staffordshire Hounds, and the *Signal* had stated that she was a fearless horsewoman. It made this statement one day when she had been thrown and carried to Sneyd senseless.

The mule, too, seemingly conscious of its responsibilities and its high destiny, put its best foot foremost and behaved in general like a mule that knew the name of its great-grandfather. It went through Knype in admirable style, not swerving at the steam-cars nor exciting itself about the railway bridge. A photographer who stood at his door manoeuvring a large camera startled it momentarily, until it remembered that it had seen a camera before. The Countess, who wondered why on earth a photographer should be capering round a tripod in a doorway, turned to inspect the man with her lorgnon.

They were now coursing up the Cauldon Bank towards Hanbridge. They were already within the boundaries of Hanbridge, and a pedestrian here and there recognized the Countess. You can hide nothing from the quidnunc of Hanbridge. Moreover, when a quidnunc in the streets of Hanbridge sees somebody famous or striking, or notorious, he does not pretend that he has seen nobody. He points unmistakably to what he has observed, if he has a companion, and if he has no companion he stands still and stares with such honest intensity that the entire street stands and stares too. Occasionally you may see an entire street standing and staring without any idea of what it is staring at. As the equipage dashingly approached the busy centre of Hanbridge, the region of fine shops, public-houses, hotels, halls, and theatres, more and more of the inhabitants knew that Iris (as they affectionately called her) was driving with a young man in a tumble-down little victoria behind a mule whose ears flapped like an elephant's. Denry being far less renowned in Hanbridge than in his native Bursley, few persons recognized him. After the victoria had gone by people who had heard the news too late rushed from shops and gazed at the Countess's back as at a fading dream until the insistent clang of a car-bell made them jump again to the footpath.

At length Denry and the Countess could see the clock of the Old Town Hall in Crown Square and it was a minute to three. They were less than a minute off the Institute.

'There you are!' said Denry, proudly. 'Three miles if it's a yard, in seventeen minutes. For a mule it's none so dusty.'

And such was the Countess's knowledge of the language of

the Five Towns that she instantly divined the meaning of even that phrase, 'none so dusty'.

They swept into Crown Square grandly.

And then, with no warning, the mule suddenly applied all the automatic brakes which a mule has, and stopped.

'Oh Lor!' sighed Denry. He knew the cause of that arresting.

A large squad of policemen, a perfect regiment of policemen, was moving across the north side of the square in the direction of the Institute. Nothing could have seemed more reassuring, less harmful, than that band of policemen, off duty for the afternoon and collected together for the purpose of giving a hearty and policemanly welcome to their benefactress the Countess. But the mule had his own views about policemen. In the early days of Denry's ownership of him he had nearly always shied at the spectacle of a policeman. He would tolerate steam-rollers, and even falling kites, but a policeman had ever been antipathetic to him. Denry, by patience and punishment, had gradually brought him round almost to the Countess's views of policemen – namely, that they were a courteous and trustworthy body of public servants, not to be treated as scarecrows or the dregs of society. At any rate, the mule had of late months practically ceased to set his face against the policing of the Five Towns. And when he was on his best behaviour he would ignore a policeman completely.

But there were several hundreds of policemen in that squad, the majority of all the policemen in the Five Towns. And clearly the mule considered that Denry, in confronting him with several hundred policemen simultaneously, had been presuming upon his good-nature.

The mule's ears were saying agitatedly:

'A line must be drawn somewhere, and I have drawn it where my forefeet now are.'

The mule's ears soon drew together a little crowd.

It occurred to Denry that if mules were so wonderful in the Apennines the reason must be that there are no policemen in the Apennines. It also occurred to him that something must be done to this mule.

'Well?' said the Countess, inquiringly.

It was a challenge to him to prove that he and not the mule was in charge of the expedition.

He briefly explained the mule's idiosyncrasy, as it were apologizing for its bad taste in objecting to public servants whom the Countess cherished.

'They'll be out of sight in a moment,' said the Countess. And both she and Denry tried to look as if the victoria had stopped in that special spot for a special reason, and that the mule was a pattern of obedience. Nevertheless, the little crowd was growing a little larger.

'Now,' said the Countess, encouragingly. The tail of the regiment of policemen had vanished towards the Institute.

'Tchk! Tchk!' Denry persuaded the mule.

No response from those forefeet!

'Perhaps I'd better get out and walk,' the Countess suggested. The crowd was becoming inconvenient, and had even begun to offer unsolicited hints as to the proper management of mules. The crowd was also saying to itself: 'It's her! It's her! It's her!' Meaning that it was the Countess.

'Oh no,' said Denry, 'it's all right.'

And he caught the mule 'one' over the head with his whip.

The mule, stung into action, dashed away, and the crowd scattered as if blown to pieces by the explosion of a bomb. Instead of pursuing a right line the mule turned within a radius of its own length, swinging the victoria round after it as though the victoria had been a kettle attached to it with string. And Countess, Denry, and victoria were rapt with miraculous swiftness away — not at all towards the Policemen's Institute, but down Longshaw Road, which is tolerably steep. They were pursued, but ineffectually. For the mule had bolted and was winged. They fortunately came into contact with nothing except a large barrow of carrots, turnips, and cabbages which an old woman was wheeling up Longshaw Road. The concussion upset the barrow, half filled the victoria with vegetables, and for a second stayed the mule; but no real harm seemed to have been done, and the mule proceeded with vigour. Then the Countess noticed that Denry was not using his right arm, which swung about rather uselessly.

'I must have knocked my elbow against the barrow,' he muttered. His face was pale.

'Give me the reins,' said the Countess.

'I think I can turn the brute up here,' he said.

And he did in fact neatly divert the mule up Birches Street, which is steeper even than Longshaw Road. The mule for a few instants pretended that all gradients, up or down, were equal before its angry might. But Birches Street has the slope of a house-roof. Presently the mule walked, and then it stood still. And half Birches Street emerged to gaze, for the Countess's attire was really very splendid.

'I'll leave this here, and we'll walk back,' said Denry. 'You won't be late – that is, nothing to speak of. The Institute is just round the top here.'

'You don't mean to say you're going to let that mule beat you?' exclaimed the Countess.

'I was only thinking of your being late.'

'Oh, bother !' said she. 'Your mule may be ruined.' The horse-trainer in her was aroused.

'And then my arm?' said Denry.

'Shall I drive back ?' the Countess suggested.

'Oh, do,' said Denry. 'Keep on up the street, and then to the left.'

They changed places, and two minutes later she brought the mule to an obedient rest in front of the Police Institute, which was all newly red with terracotta. The main body of policemen had passed into the building, but two remained at the door, and the mule haughtily tolerated them. The Countess dispatched one to Longshaw Road to settle with the old woman whose vegetables they had brought away with them. The other policeman, who, owing to the Countess's philanthropic energy, had received a course of instruction in first aid, arranged a sling for Denry's arm. And then the Countess said that Denry ought certainly to go with her to the inauguraion ceremony. The policeman whistled a boy to hold the mule. Denry picked a carrot out of the complex folds of the Countess's rich costume. And the Countess and her saviour entered the portico and were therein met by an imposing group of important male personages, several of whom wore mayoral chains. Strange tales of what had happened to the Countess had already flown up to the Institute, and the chief expression on the faces of the group seemed to be one of astonishment that she still lived.

IV

Denry observed that the Countess was now a different woman. She had suddenly put on a manner to match her costume, which in certain parts was stiff with embroidery. From the informal companion and the tamer of mules she had miraculously developed into the public celebrity, the peeress of the realm, and the inaugurator-general of philanthropic schemes and buildings. Not one of the important male personages but would have looked down on Denry! And yet, while treating Denry as a jolly equal, the Countess with all her embroidered and stiff politeness somehow looked down on the important male personages – and they knew it. And the most curious thing was that they seemed rather to enjoy it. The one who seemed to enjoy it the least was Sir Jehoshophat Dain, a white-bearded pillar of terrific imposingness.

Sir Jee – as he was then beginning to be called – had recently been knighted, by way of reward for his enormous benefactions to the community. In the *rôle* of philanthropist he was really much more effective than the Countess. But he was not young, he was not pretty, he was not a woman, and his family had not helped to rule England for generations – at any rate, so far as anybody knew. He had made more money than had ever before been made by a single brain in the manufacture of earthenware, and he had given more money to public causes than a single pocket had ever before given in the Five Towns. He had never sought municipal honours, considering himself to be somewhat above such trifles. He was the first purely local man to be knighted in the Five Towns. Even before the bestowal of the knighthood his sense of humour had been deficient, and immediately afterwards it had vanished entirely. Indeed, he did not miss it. He divided the population of the kingdom into two classes – the titled and the untitled. With Sir Jee, either you

125

were titled, or you weren't. He lumped all the untitled together; and to be just to his logical faculty, he lumped all the titled together. There were various titles – Sir Jee admitted that – but a title was a title, and therefore all titles were practically equal. The Duke of Norfolk was one titled individual, and Sir Jee was another. The fine difference between them might be perceptible to the titled, and might properly be recognized by the titled when the titled were among themselves, but for the untitled such a difference ought not to exist and could not exist.

Thus for Sir Jee there were two titled beings in the group – the Countess and himself. The Countess and himself formed one caste in the group, and the rest another caste. And although the Countess, in her punctilious demeanour towards him, gave due emphasis to his title (he returning more than due emphasis to hers), he was not precisely pleased by the undertones of suave condescension that characterized her greeting of him as well as her greeting of the others. Moreover, he had known Denry as a clerk of Mr Duncalf's, for Mr Duncalf had done a lot of legal work for him in the past. He looked upon Denry as an upstart, a capering mountebank, and he strongly resented Denry's familiarity with the Countess. He further resented Denry's sling, which gave to Denry an interesting romantic aspect (despite his beard), and he more than all resented that Denry should have rescued the Countess from a carriage accident by means of his preposterous mule. Whenever the Countess, in the preliminary chatter, referred to Denry or looked at Denry, in recounting the history of her adventures, Sir Jee's soul squirmed, and his body sympathized with his soul. Something in him that was more powerful than himself compelled him to do his utmost to reduce Denry to a moral pulp, to flatten him, to ignore him, or to exterminate him by the application of ice. This tactic was no more lost on the Countess than it was on Denry. And the Countess foiled it at every instant. In truth, there existed between the Countess and Sir Jee a rather hot rivalry in philanthropy and the cultivation of the higher welfare of the district. He regarded himself, and she regarded herself, as the most brightly glittering star of the Five Towns.

When the Countess had finished the recital of her journey,

Quid nunc

page 121

```
LAFAYETTE
COLLEGE STORE          12/15/98

                         ###1
TRADE BOOK    17000000   5756
SUBTOTAL                 7.95
TAX                      7.95
TOTAL                     .48
                         8.43

CASH                    20.00

CHANGE                  11.57

THANK YOU
#300860 0009 R09 T16:25
```

and the faces of the group had gone through all the contortions proper to express terror, amazement, admiration, and manly sympathy, Sir Jee took the lead, coughed, and said in his elaborate style:

'Before we adjourn to the hall, will not your ladyship take a little refreshment?'

'Oh no, thanks,' said the Countess. 'I'm not a bit upset.' Then she turned to the enslinged Denry and with concern added: 'But will *you* have something?'

If she could have foreseen the consequences of her question, she might never have put it. Still, she might have put it just the same.

Denry paused an instant, and an old habit rose up in him.

'Oh no, thanks,' he said, and turning deliberately to Sir Jee, he added: 'Will *you*?'

This, of course, was mere crude insolence to the titled philanthropic white-beard. But it was by no means the worst of Denry's behaviour. The group – every member of the group – distinctly perceived a movement of Denry's left hand towards Sir Jee. It was the very slightest movement, a wavering, a nothing. It would have had no significance whatever, but for one fact. Denry's left hand still held the carrot.

Everybody exhibited the most marvellous self-control. And everybody except Sir Jee was secretly charmed, for Sir Jee had never inspired love. It is remarkable how local philanthropists are unloved, locally. The Countess, without blenching, gave the signal for what Sir Jee called the 'adjournment' to the hall. Nothing might have happened, yet everything had happened.

v

Next, Denry found himself seated on the temporary platform which had been erected in the large games hall of the Policemen's Institute. The Mayor of Hanbridge was in the chair, and he had the Countess on his right and the Mayoress of Bursley on his left. Other mayoral chains blazed in the centre of the platform, together with fine hats of mayoresses and uniforms of police-superintendents and captains of fire-brigades. Denry's sling also contributed to the effectiveness; he was placed behind the Countess. Policemen (looking strange without helmets) and their wives, sweethearts, and friends, filled the hall to its fullest; enthusiasm was rife and strident; and there was only one little sign that the untoward had occurred. That little sign was an empty chair in the first row near the Countess. Sir Jee, a prey to a sudden indisposition, had departed. He had somehow faded away, while the personages were climbing the stairs. He had faded away amid the expressed regrets of those few who by chance saw him in the act of fading. But even these bore up manfully. The high humour of the gathering was not eclipsed.

Towards the end of the ceremony came the votes of thanks, and the principal of these was the vote of thanks to the Countess, prime cause of the Institute. It was proposed by the Superintendent of the Hanbridge Police. Other personages had wished to propose it, but the stronger right of the Hanbridge Superintendent, as chief officer of the largest force of constables in the Five Towns, could not be disputed. He made a few facetious references to the episode of the Countess's arrival, and brought the house down by saying that if he did his duty he would arrest both the Countess and Denry for driving to the common danger. When he sat down, amid tempestuous applause, there was a hitch. According to the official programme Sir Jehoshophat Dain was to have seconded the vote, and Sir Jee was not there. All that remained of Sir Jee was his chair. The Mayor of Hanbridge looked round about, trying swiftly to make up his mind what was to be done, and Denry heard him whisper to another mayor for advice.

'Shall I do it?' Denry whispered, and by at once rising relieved the Mayor from the necessity of coming to a decision.

Impossible to say why Denry should have risen as he did, without any warning. Ten seconds before, five seconds before, he himself had not the dimmest idea that he was about to address the meeting. All that can be said is that he was subject to these attacks of the unexpected.

Once on his legs he began to suffer, for he had never before been on his legs on a platform, or even on a platform at all. He could see nothing whatever except a cloud that had mysteriously and with frightful suddenness filled the room. And through this cloud he could feel that hundreds and hundreds of eyes were piercingly fixed upon him. A voice was saying inside him – 'What a fool you are! What a fool you are! I always told you you were a fool!' And his heart was beating as it had never beat, and his forehead was damp, his throat distressingly dry, and one foot nervously tap-tapping on the floor. This condition lasted for something like ten hours, during which time the eyes continued to pierce the cloud and him with patient, obstinate cruelty.

Denry heard some one talking. It was himself.

The Superintendent had said: 'I have very great pleasure in proposing the vote of thanks to the Countess of Chell.'

And so Denry heard himself saying: 'I have very great pleasure in seconding the vote of thanks to the Countess of Chell.'

He could not think of anything else to say. And there was a pause, a real pause, not a pause merely in Denry's sick imagination.

Then the cloud was dissipated. And Denry himself said to the audience of policemen, with his own natural tone, smile and gesture, colloquially, informally, comically:

'Now then! Move along there, please! I'm not going to say any more!'

And for a signal he put his hands in the position for applauding. And sat down.

He had tickled the stout ribs of every bobby in the place. The applause surpassed all previous applause. The most staid ornaments of the platform had to laugh. People nudged each other and explained that it was 'that chap Machin from Bursley', as if to imply that that chap Machin from Bursley never let a day pass without doing something striking and humorous. The Mayor was still smiling when he put the vote to the meeting, and the Countess was still smiling when she responded.

Afterwards in the portico, when everything was over, Denry exercised his right to remain in charge of the Countess. They escaped from the personages by going out to look for her carriage and neglecting to return. There was no sign of the

Countess's carriage, but Denry's mule and victoria were waiting in a quiet corner.

'May I drive you home?' he suggested.

But she would not. She said that she had a call to pay before dinner, and that her brougham would surely arrive the very next minute.

'Will you come and have tea at the Sub Rosa?' Denry next asked.

'The Sub Rosa?' questioned the Countess.

'Well,' said Denry, 'that's what we call the new tea-room that's just been opened round here.' He indicated a direction. 'It's quite a novelty in the Five Towns.'

The Countess had a passion for tea.

'They have splendid China tea,' said Denry.

'Well,' said the Countess, 'I suppose I may as well go through with it.'

At the moment her brougham drove up. She instructed her coachman to wait next to the mule and victoria. Her demeanour had cast off all its similarity to her dress: it appeared to imply that, as she had begun with a mad escapade, she ought to finish with another one.

Thus the Countess and Denry went to the tea-shop, and Denry ordered tea and paid for it. There was scarcely a customer in the place, and the few who were fortunate enough to be present had not the wit to recognize the Countess. The proprietress did not recognize the Countess. (Later, when it became known that the Countess had actually patronized the Sub Rosa, half the ladies of Hanbridge were almost ill from sheer disgust that they had not heard of it in time. It would have been so easy for them to be there, taking tea at the next table to the Countess, and observing her choice of cakes, and her manner of holding a spoon, and whether she removed her gloves or retained them in the case of a meringue. It was an opportunity lost that would in all human probability never occur again.)

And in the discreet corner which she had selected the Countess fired a sudden shot at Denry.

'How did you get all those details about the state rooms at Sneyd?' she asked.

Upon which opening the conversation became lively.

The same evening Denry called at the *Signal* office and gave an order for a half-page advertisement of the Five Towns Universal Thrift Club — 'Patroness, the Countess of Chell'. The advertisement informed the public that the club had now made arrangements to accept new members. Besides the order for a half-page advertisement, Denry also gave many interesting and authentic details about the historic drive from Sneyd Vale to Hanbridge. The next day the *Signal* was simply full of Denry and the Countess. It had a large photograph, taken by a photographer on Cauldon Bank, which showed Denry actually driving the Countess, and the Countess's face was full in the picture. It presented, too, an excellently appreciative account of Denry's speech, and it congratulated Denry on his first appearance in the public life of the Five Towns. (In parenthesis it sympathized with Sir Jee in his indisposition.) In short, Denry's triumph obliterated the memory of his previous triumphs. It obliterated, too, all rumours adverse to the Thrift Club. In a few days he had a thousand new members. Of course, this addition only increased his liabilities; but now he could obtain capital on fair terms, and he did obtain it. A company was formed. The Countess had a few shares in this company. So (strangely) had Jock and his companion the coachman. Not the least of the mysteries was that when Denry reached his mother's cottage on the night of the tea with the Countess, his arm was not in a sling, and showed no symptom of having been damaged.

CHAPTER 8

Raising a Wigwam

I

A STILL young man – his age was thirty – with a short, strong beard peeping out over the fur collar of a vast overcoat, emerged from a cab at the snowy corner of St Luke's Square and Brougham Street, and paid the cabman with a gesture that indicated both wealth and the habit of command. And the cabman, who had driven him over from Hanbridge through the winter night, responded accordingly. Few people take cabs in the Five Towns. There are few cabs to take. If you are going to a party you may order one in advance by telephone, reconciling yourself also in advance to the expense, but to hail a cab in the street without forethought and jump into it as carelessly as you would jump into a tram – this is by very few done. The young man with the beard did it frequently, which proved that he was fundamentally ducal.

He was encumbered with a large and rather heavy parcel as he walked down Brougham Street, and, moreover, the footpath of Brougham Street was exceedingly dirty. And yet no one acquainted with the circumstances of his life would have asked why he had dismissed the cab before arriving at his destination, because every one knew. The reason was that this ducal person, with the gestures of command, dared not drive up to his mother's door in a cab oftener than about once a month. He opened that door with a latch-key (a modern lock was almost the only innovation that he had succeeded in fixing on his mother), and stumbled with his unwieldy parcel into the exceedingly narrow lobby.

'Is that you, Denry?' called a feeble voice from the parlour.

'Yes,' said he, and went into the parlour, hat, fur coat, parcel, and all.

Mrs Machin, in a shawl and an antimacassar over the shawl, sat close to the fire and leaning towards it. She looked cold and ill. Although the parlour was very tiny and the fire comparatively large, the structure of the grate made it impossible that the room should be warm, as all the heat went up the chimney. If Mrs Machin had sat on the roof and put her hands over the top of the chimney, she would have been much warmer than at the grate.

'You aren't in bed?' Denry queried.

'Can't you see?' said his mother. And, indeed, to ask a woman who was obviously sitting up in a chair whether she was in bed, did seem somewhat absurd. She added, less sarcastically: 'I was expecting ye every minute. Where have ye had your tea?'

'Oh!' he said lightly, 'in Hanbridge.'

An untruth! He had not had his tea anywhere. But he had dined richly at the new Hôtel Métropole, Hanbridge.

'What have ye got there?' asked his mother.

'A present for you,' said Denry. 'It's your birthday tomorrow.'

'I don't know as I want reminding of that,' murmured Mrs Machin.

But when he had undone the parcel and held up the contents before her, she exclaimed:

'Bless us!'

The staggered tone was an admission that for once in a way he had impressed her.

It was a magnificent sealskin mantle, longer than sealskin mantles usually are. It was one of those articles the owner of which can say: 'Nobody can have a better than this – I don't care who she is.' It was worth in monetary value all the plain, shabby clothes on Mrs Machin's back, and all her very ordinary best clothes upstairs, and all the furniture in the entire house, and perhaps all Denry's dandiacal wardrobe too, except his fur coat. If the entire contents of the cottage, with the aforesaid exception, had been put up to auction, they would not have realized enough to pay for that sealskin mantle.

Had it been anything but a sealskin mantle, and equally costly, Mrs Machin would have upbraided. But a sealskin mantle is not 'showy'. It 'goes with' any and every dress and bonnet. And the most respectable, the most conservative, the most austere woman may find legitimate pleasure in wearing it. A sealskin mantle is the sole luxurious ostentation that a woman of Mrs Machin's temperament – and there are many such in the Five Towns and elsewhere – will conscientiously permit herself.

'Try it on,' said Denry.

She rose weakly and tried it on. It fitted as well as a sealskin mantle can fit.

'My word – it's warm!' she said. This was her sole comment.

'Keep it on,' said Denry.

His mother's glance withered the suggestion.

'Where are you going?' he asked, as she left the room.

'To put it away,' said she. 'I must get some moth-powder to-morrow.'

He protested with inarticulate noises, removed his own furs, which he threw down on to the old worn-out sofa, and drew a windsor chair up to the fire. After a while his mother returned, and sat down in her rocking-chair, and began to shiver again under the shawl and the antimacassar. The lamp on the table lighted up the left side of her face and the right side of his.

'Look here, mother,' said he, 'you must have a doctor.'

'I shall have no doctor.'

'You've got influenza, and it's a very tricky business – influenza is; you never know where you are with it.'

'Ye can call it influenza if ye like,' said Mrs Machin. 'There was no influenza in my young days. We called a cold a cold.'

'Well,' said Denry, 'you aren't well, are you?'

'I never said I was,' she answered grimly.

'No,' said Denry, with the triumphant ring of one who is about to devastate an enemy. 'And you never will be in this rotten old cottage.'

'This was reckoned a very good class of house when your father and I came into it. And it's always been kept in repair. It was good enough for your father, and it's good enough for me. I don't see myself flitting. But some folks have gotten so grand. As for health, old Reuben next door is ninety-one. How many people over ninety are there in those gimcrack houses up by the Park, I should like to know?'

Denry could argue with any one save his mother. Always, when he was about to reduce her to impotence, she fell on him thus and rolled him in the dust. Still, he began again.

'Do we pay four-and-sixpence a week for this cottage, or don't we?' he demanded.

'And always have done,' said Mrs Machin. 'I should like to see the landlord put it up,' she added, formidably, as if to say: 'I'd landlord him, if he tried to put *my* rent up!'

'Well,' said Denry, 'here we are living in a four-and-six-a-week cottage, and do you know how much I'm making? I'm making two thousand pounds a year. That's what I'm making.'

A second wilful deception of his mother! As Managing Director of the Five Towns Universal Thrift Club, as proprietor of the majority of its shares, as its absolute autocrat, he was making very nearly four thousand a year. Why could he not as easily have said four as two to his mother? The simple answer is that he was afraid to say four. It was as if he ought to blush before his mother for being so plutocratic, his mother who had passed most of her life in hard toil to gain a few shillings a week. Four thousand seemed so fantastic! And in fact the Thrift Club, which he had invented in a moment, had arrived at a prodigious success, with its central offices in Hanbridge and its branch offices in the other four towns, and its scores of clerks and collectors presided over by Mr Penkethman. It had met with opposition. The mighty said that Denry was making an unholy fortune under the guise of philanthropy. And to be on the safe side the Countess of Chell had resigned her official patronage of the club and given her shares to the Pirehill Infirmary, which had accepted the high dividends on them without the least protest. As for Denry, he said that he had never set out to be a philanthropist nor posed as one, and that his unique intention was to grow rich by supplying a want, like the rest of them, and that anyhow there was no compulsion to belong to his Thrift Club. Then letters in his defence from representatives of the thousands and thousands of members of the club rained into the columns of the *Signal*, and Denry was the most discussed personage in the county. It was stated that such thrift clubs, under various names, existed in several large towns in Yorkshire and

Lancashire. This disclosure rehabilitated Denry completely in general esteem, for whatever obtains in Yorkshire and Lancashire must be right for Staffordshire; but it rather dashed Denry, who was obliged to admit to himself that after all he had not invented the Thrift Club. Finally the hundreds of tradesmen who had bound themselves to allow a discount of twopence in the shilling to the club (sole source of the club's dividends) had endeavoured to revolt. Denry effectually cowed them by threatening to establish cooperative stores – there was not a single cooperative store in the Five Towns. They knew he would have the wild audacity to do it.

Thenceforward the progress of the Thrift Club had been unruffled. Denry waxed amazingly in importance. His mule died. He dared not buy a proper horse and dogcart, because he dared not bring such an equipage to the front door of his mother's four-and-sixpenny cottage. So he had taken to cabs. In all exterior magnificence and lavishness he equalled even the great Harold Etches, of whom he had once been afraid; and like Etches he became a famous *habitué* of Llandudno pier. But whereas Etches lived with his wife in a superb house at Bleakridge, Denry lived with his mother in a ridiculous cottage in ridiculous Brougham Street. He had a regiment of acquaintances and he accepted a lot of hospitality, but he could not return it at Brougham Street. His greatness fizzled into nothing in Brougham Street. It stopped short and sharp at the corner of St Luke's Square, where he left his cabs. He could do nothing with his mother. If she was not still going out as a sempstress the reason was, not that she was not ready to go out, but that her old clients had ceased to send for her. And could they be blamed for not employing at three shillings a day the mother of a young man who wallowed in thousands sterling? Denry had essayed over and over again to instil reason into his mother, and he had invariably failed. She was too independent, too profoundly rooted in her habits; and her character had more force than his. Of course, he might have left her and set up a suitably gorgeous house of his own.

But he would not.

In fact, they were a remarkable pair.

On this eve of her birthday he had meant to cajole her into some step, to win her by an appeal, basing his argument on her indisposition. But he was being beaten off once more. The truth was that a cajoling, caressing tone could not be long employed towards Mrs Machin. She was not persuasive herself, nor favourable to persuasiveness in others.

'Well,' said she, 'if you're making two thousand a year, ye can spend it or save it as ye like, though ye'd better save it. Ye never know what may happen in these days. There was a man dropped half-a-crown down a grid opposite only the day before yesterday.'

Denry laughed.

'Ay!' she said; 'ye can laugh.'

'There's no doubt about one thing,' he said, 'you ought to be in bed. You ought to stay in bed for two or three days at least.'

'Yes,' she said. 'And who's going to look after the house while I'm moping between blankets?'

'You can have Rose Chudd in,' he said.

'No,' said she. 'I'm not going to have any woman rummaging about my house, and me in bed.'

'You know perfectly well she's been practically starving since her husband died, and as she's going out charing, why can't you have her and put a bit of bread into her mouth?'

'Because I won't have her! Neither her nor any one. There's naught to prevent you giving her some o' your two thousand a year if you've a mind. But I see no reason for my house being turned upside down by her, even if I *have* got a bit of a cold.'

'You're an unreasonable old woman,' said Denry.

'Happen I am!' said she. 'There can't be two wise ones in a family. But I'm not going to give up this cottage, and as long as I am standing on my feet I'm not going to pay any one for doing what I can do better myself.' A pause. 'And so you needn't think it! You can't come round me with a fur mantle.' She retired to rest. On the following morning he was very glum.

'You needn't be so glum,' she said.

But she was rather pleased at his glumness. For in him glumness was a sign that he recognized defeat.

137

The next episode between them was curiously brief. Denry had influenza. He said that naturally he had caught hers.

He went to bed and stayed there. She nursed him all day, and grew angry in a vain attempt to force him to eat. Towards night he tossed furiously on the little bed in the little bedroom, complaining of fearful headaches. She remained by his side most of the night. In the morning he was easier. Neither of them mentioned the word 'doctor'. She spent the day largely on the stairs. Once more towards night he grew worse, and she remained most of the second night by his side.

In the sinister winter dawn Denry murmured in a feeble tone :

'Mother, you'd better send for him.'

'Doctor?' she said. And secretly she thought that she *had* better send for the doctor, and that there must be after all some difference between influenza and a cold.

'No,' said Denry ; 'send for young Lawton.'

'Young Lawton !' she exclaimed. 'What do you want young Lawton to come *here* for?'

'I haven't made my will,' Denry answered.

'Pooh !' she retorted.

Nevertheless she was the least bit in the world frightened. And she sent for Dr Stirling, the aged Harrop's Scotch partner.

Dr Stirling, who was full-bodied and left little space for anybody else in the tiny, shabby bedroom of the man with four thousand a year, gazed at Mrs Machin, and he gazed also at Denry.

'Ye must go to bed this minute,' said he.

'But he's *in* bed,' cried Mrs Machin.

'I mean yerself,' said Dr Stirling.

She was very nearly at the end of her resources. And the proof was that she had no strength left to fight Dr Stirling. She did go to bed. And shortly afterwards Denry got up. And a little later, Rose Chudd, that prim and efficient young widow from lower down the street, came into the house and controlled it as if it had been her own. Mrs Machin, whose constitution was hardy, arose in about a week, cured, and duly dismissed Rose with wages and without thanks. But Rose had been. Like the *Signal*'s burglars, she had 'effected an entrance'. And the house had not been turned upside down. Mrs Machin, though she tried, could not find fault with the result of Rose's uncontrolled activities.

III

One morning – and not very long afterwards, in such wise did Fate seem to favour the young at the expense of the old – Mrs Machin received two letters which alarmed and disgusted her. One was from her landlord, announcing that he had sold the house in which she lived to a Mr Wilbraham of London, and that in future she must pay the rent to the said Mr Wilbraham or his legal representatives. The other was from a firm of London solicitors announcing that their client, Mr Wilbraham, had bought the house, and that the rent must be paid to their agent, whom they would name later.

Mrs Machin gave vent to her emotion in her customary manner: 'Bless us!'

And she showed the impudent letters to Denry.

'Oh!' said Denry. 'So he has bought them, has he? I heard he was going to.'

'Them?' exclaimed Mrs Machin. 'What else has he bought?'

'I expect he's bought all the five – this and the four below, as far as Downes's. I expect you'll find that the other four have had notices just like these. You know all this row used to belong to the Wilbrahams. You surely must remember that, mother?'

'Is he one of the Wilbrahams of Hillport, then?'

'Yes, of course he is.'

'I thought the last of 'em was Cecil, and when he'd beggared himself here he went to Australia and died of drink. That's what I always heard. We always used to say as there wasn't a Wilbraham left.'

'He did go to Australia, but he didn't die of drink. He disappeared, and when he'd made a fortune he turned up again in Sydney, so it seems. I heard he's thinking of coming back here to settle. Anyhow, he's buying up a lot of the Wilbraham property. I should have thought you'd have heard of it. Why, lots of people have been talking about it.'

'Well,' said Mrs Machin, 'I don't like it.'

She objected to a law which permitted a landlord to sell a house over the head of a tenant who had occupied it for more than thirty years. In the course of the morning she discovered that Denry was right – the other tenants had received notices exactly similar to hers.

Two days later Denry arrived home for tea with a most surprising article of news. Mr Cecil Wilbraham had been down to Bursley from London, and had visited him, Denry. Mr Cecil Wilbraham's local information was evidently quite out of date, for he had imagined Denry to be a rent-collector and estate agent, whereas the fact was that Denry had abandoned this minor vocation years ago. His desire had been that Denry should collect his rents and watch over his growing interests in the district.

'So what did you tell him?' asked Mrs Machin.

'I told him I'd do it,' said Denry.

'Why?'

'I thought it might be safer for *you*,' said Denry, with a certain emphasis. 'And, besides, it looked as if it might be a bit of a lark. He's a very peculiar chap.'

'Peculiar?'

'For one thing, he's got the largest moustaches of any man I ever saw. And there's something up with his left eye. And then I think he's a bit mad.'

'Mad?'

'Well, touched. He's got a notion about building a funny sort of a house for himself on a plot of land at Bleakridge. It appears he's fond of living alone, and he's collected all kinds of dodges for doing without servants and still being comfortable.'

'Ay! But he's right there!' breathed Mrs Machin in deep sympathy. As she said about once a week, 'She never could abide the idea of servants.' 'He's not married, then?' she added

'He told me he'd been a widower three times, but he'd never had any children,' said Denry.

'Bless us!' murmured Mrs Machin.

Denry was the one person in the town who enjoyed the acquaintance and the confidence of the thrice-widowed stranger with long moustaches. He had descended without notice on Bursley, seen Denry (at the branch office of the Thrift Club), and then departed. It was understood that later he would permanently settle in the district. Then the wonderful house began to rise on the plot of land at Bleakridge. Denry had general charge of it, but always subject to erratic and autocratic instructions from London. Thanks to Denry, who, since the historic episode at Llandudno, had remained very friendly with the Cotterill family, Mr Cotterill had the job of building the house; the plans came from London. And though Mr Cecil Wilbraham proved to be exceedingly watchful against any form of imposition, the job was a remunerative one for Mr Cotterill, who talked a great deal about the originality of the residence. The town judged of the wealth and importance of Mr Cecil Wilbraham by the fact that a person so wealthy and important as Denry should be content to act as his agent. But then the Wilbrahams had been magnates in the Bursley region for generations, up till the final Wilbraham smash in the late seventies. The town hungered to see those huge moustaches and that peculiar eye. In addition to Denry, only one person had seen the madman, and that person was Nellie Cotterill, who had been viewing the half-built house with Denry one Sunday morning when the madman had most astonishingly arrived upon the scene, and after a few minutes vanished. The building of the house strengthened greatly the friendship between Denry and the Cotterills. Yet Denry neither liked Mr Cotterill nor trusted him.

The next incident in these happenings was that Mrs Machin received notice from the London firm to quit her four-and-sixpence-a-week cottage. It seemed to her that not merely Brougham Street, but the world, was coming to an end. She was very angry with Denry for not protecting her more successfully. He was Mr Wilbraham's agent, he collected the rent, and it was his duty to guard his mother from unpleasantness. She observed, however, that he was remarkably disturbed by the notice, and he assured her that Mr Wilbraham had not consulted him in the matter at all. He wrote a letter to London, which she signed, demanding the reason of this absurd notice flung at an ancient and perfect tenant. The reply was that Mr Wilbraham intended to pull the houses down, beginning with Mrs Machin's, and rebuild.

'Pooh!' said Denry. 'Don't you worry your head, mother; I shall arrange it. He'll be down here soon to see his new house – it's practically finished, and the furniture is coming in – and I'll just talk to him.'

But Mr Wilbraham did not come, the explanation doubtless being that he was mad. On the other hand, fresh notices came with amazing frequency. Mrs Machin just handed them over to Denry. And then Denry received a telegram to say that Mr Wilbraham would be at his new house that night and wished to see Denry there. Unfortunately, on the same day, by the afternoon post, while Denry was at his offices, there arrived a sort of supreme and ultimate notice from London to Mrs Machin, and it was on blue paper. It stated, baldly, that as Mrs Machin had failed to comply with all the previous notices, had, indeed, ignored them, she and her goods would now be ejected into the street, according to the law. It gave her twenty-four hours to flit. Never had a respectable dame been so insulted as Mrs Machin was insulted by that notice. The prospect of camping out in Brougham Street confronted her. When Denry reached home that evening, Mrs Machin, as the phrase is, 'gave it him'.

Denry admitted frankly that he was nonplussed, staggered, and outraged. But the thing was simply another proof of Mr Wilbraham's madness. After tea he decided that his mother must put on her best clothes, and go up with him to see Mr Wilbraham and firmly expostulate – in fact, they would arrange the situation between them; and if Mr Wilbraham was obstinate they would defy Mr Wilbraham. Denry explained to his mother that an Englishwoman's cottage was her castle, that a landlord's minions had no right to force an entrance, and that the one thing that Mr Wilbraham could do was to begin unbuilding the cottage from the top outside ... And he would like to see Mr Wilbraham try it on!

So the sealskin mantle (for it was spring again) went up with Denry to Bleakridge.

The moon shone in the chill night. The house stood back from Trafalgar Road in the moonlight – a squarish block of a building.

'Oh!' said Mrs Machin, 'it isn't so large.'

'No! He didn't want it large. He only wanted it large enough,' said Denry, and pushed a button to the right of the front door. There was no reply, though they heard the ringing of the bell inside. They waited. Mrs Machin was very nervous, but thanks to her sealskin mantle she was not cold.

'This is a funny doorstep,' she remarked, to kill time.

'It's of marble,' said Denry.

'What's that for?' asked his mother.

'So much easier to keep clean,' said Denry.

'Well,' said Mrs Machin, 'it's pretty dirty now, anyway.'

It was.

'Quite simple to clean,' said Denry, bending down. 'You just turn this tap at the side. You see, it's so arranged that it sends a flat jet along the step. Stand off a second.'

He turned the tap, and the step was washed pure in a moment.

'How is it that that water steams?' Mrs Machin demanded.

'Because it's hot,' said Denry. 'Did you ever know water steam for any other reason?'

'Hot water outside?'

'Just as easy to have hot water outside as inside, isn't it?' said Denry.

'Well, I never!' exclaimed Mrs Machin. She was impressed.

'That's how everything's dodged up in this house,' said Denry. He shut off the water.

And he rang once again. No answer! No illumination within the abode!

'I'll tell you what I shall do,' said Denry at length. 'I shall let myself in. I've got a key of the back door.'

'Are you sure it's all right?'

'I don't care if it isn't all right,' said Denry, defiantly. 'He asked me to be up here, and he ought to be here to meet me. I'm not going to stand any nonsense from anybody.'

In they went, having skirted round the walls of the house.

Denry closed the door, pushed a switch, and the electric light shone. Electric light was then quite a novelty in Bursley. Mrs Machin had never seen it in action. She had to admit that it was less complicated than oil-lamps. In the kitchen the electric light blazed upon walls tiled in grey and a floor tiled in black and white. There was a gas range and a marble slopstone with two taps. The woodwork was dark. Earthenware saucepans stood on a shelf. The cupboards were full of gear chiefly in earthenware. Denry began to exhibit to his mother a tank provided with ledges and shelves and grooves, in which he said that everything except knives could be washed and dried automatically.

'Hadn't you better go and find your Mr Wilbraham?' she interrupted.

'So I had,' said Denry; 'I was forgetting him.'

She heard him wandering over the house and calling in divers tones upon Mr Wilbraham. But she heard no other voice. Meanwhile she examined the kitchen in detail, appreciating some of its devices and failing to comprehend others.

'I expect he's missed the train,' said Denry, coming back. 'Anyhow, he isn't here. I may as well show you the rest of the house now.'

He led her into the hall, which was radiantly lighted.

'It's quite warm here,' said Mrs Machin.

'The whole house is heated by steam,' said Denry. 'No fireplaces.'

'No fireplaces!'

'No! No fireplaces. No grates to polish, ashes to carry down, coals to carry up, mantelpieces to dust, fire-irons to clean, fenders to polish, chimneys to sweep.'

'And suppose he wants a bit of fire all of a sudden in summer?'

'Gas stove in every room for emergencies,' said Denry.

She glanced into a room.

'But,' she cried, 'it's all complete, ready! And as warm as toast.'

'Yes,' said Denry, 'he gave orders. I can't think why on earth he isn't here.'

At that moment an electric bell rang loud and sharp, and Mrs Machin jumped.

'There he is!' said Denry, moving to the door.

'Bless us! What will he think of us being here like?' Mrs Machin mumbled.

'Pooh!' said Denry, carelessly. And he opened the door.

v

Three persons stood on the newly-washed marble step – Mr and Mrs Cotterill and their daughter.

'Oh! Come in! Come in! Make yourselves quite at home. That's what *we're* doing,' said Denry in blithe greeting and added, 'I suppose he's invited you too?'

And it appeared that Mr Cecil Wilbraham had indeed invited them too. He had written from London saying that he would be glad if Mr and Mrs Cotterill would 'drop in' on this particular evening. Further, he had mentioned that, as he had already had the pleasure of meeting Miss Cotterill, perhaps she would accompany her parents.

'Well, he isn't here,' said Denry, shaking hands. 'He must have missed his train or something. He can't possibly be here now till tomorrow. But the house seems to be all ready for him ...'

'Yes, my word! And how's yourself, Mrs Cotterill?' put in Mrs Machin.

'So we may as well look over it in its finished state. I suppose that's what he asked us up for,' Denry concluded.

Mrs Machin explained quickly and nervously that she had not been comprised in any invitation; that her errand was pure business.

'Come on upstairs,' Denry called out, turning switches and adding radiance to radiance.

'Denry!' his mother protested, 'I'm sure I don't know what Mr and Mrs Cotterill will think of you! You carry on as if you owned everything in the place. I wonder *at* you!'

'Well,' said Denry, 'if anybody in this town is the owner's agent I am. And Mr Cotterill has built the blessed house. If Wilbraham wanted to keep his old shanty to himself, he shouldn't send out invitations. It's simple enough not to send out invitations. Now, Nellie!'

He was hanging over the balustrade at the curve of the stairs.

The familiar ease with which he said, 'Now, Nellie,' and especially the spontaneity of Nellie's instant response, put new thoughts into the mind of Mrs Machin. But she neither pricked up her ears, nor started back, nor accomplished any of the acrobatic feats which an ordinary mother of a wealthy son would have performed under similar circumstances. Her ears did not even tremble. And she just said:

'I like this balustrade knob being of black china.'

'Every knob in the house is of black china,' said Denry. 'Never shows dirt. But if you should take it into your head to clean it, you can do it with a damp cloth in a second.'

Nellie now stood beside him. Nellie had grown up since the Llandudno episode. She did not blush at a glance. When spoken to suddenly she could answer without torture to herself. She could, in fact, maintain a conversation without breaking down for a much longer time than, a few years ago, she had been able to skip without breaking down. She no longer imagined that all the people in the street were staring at her, anxious to find faults in her appearance. She had temporarily ruined the lives of several amiable and fairly innocent young men by refusing to marry them. (For she was pretty, and her father cut a figure in the town, though her mother did not.) And yet, despite the immense accumulation of her experiences and the weight of her varied knowledge of human nature, there was something very girlish and timidly roguish about her as she stood on the stairs near Denry, waiting for the elder generation to follow. The old Nellie still lived in her.

The party passed to the first floor.

And the first floor exceeded the ground floor in marvels. In each bedroom two aluminium taps poured hot and cold water respectively into a marble basin, and below the marble basin was a sink. No porterage of water anywhere in the house. The water

146

came to you, and every room consumed its own slops. The bedsteads were of black enamelled iron and very light. The floors were covered with linoleum, with a few rugs that could be shaken with one hand. The walls were painted with grey enamel. Mrs Cotterill, with her all-seeing eye, observed a detail that Mrs Machin had missed. There were no sharp corners anywhere. Every corner, every angle between wall and floor or wall and wall, was rounded, to facilitate cleaning. And every wall, floor, ceiling, and fixture could be washed, and all the furniture was enamelled and could be wiped with a cloth in a moment instead of having to be polished with three cloths and many odours in a day and a half. The bathroom was absolutely waterproof; you could spray it with a hose, and by means of a gas apparatus you could produce an endless supply of hot water independent of the general supply. Denry was apparently familiar with each detail of Mr Wilbraham's manifold contrivances, and he explained them with an enormous gusto.

'Bless us!' said Mrs Machin.

'Bless us!' said Mrs Cotterill (doubtless the force of example).

They descended to the dining-room, where a supper-table had been laid by order of the invisible Mr Cecil Wilbraham. And there the ladies lauded Mr Wilbraham's wisdom in eschewing silver. Everything of the table service that could be of earthenware was of earthenware. The forks and spoons were electroplate.

'Why,' Mrs Cotterill said, 'I could run this house without a servant and have myself tidy by ten o'clock in a morning.'

And Mrs Machin nodded.

'And then when you want a regular turn-out, as you call it,' said Denry, 'there's the vacuum-cleaner.'

The vacuum-cleaner was at that period the last word of civilization, and the first agency for it was being set up in Bursley. Denry explained the vacuum-cleaner to the housewives, who had got no further than a Ewbank. And they again called down blessings on themselves.

'What price this supper?' Denry exclaimed. 'We ought to eat it. I'm sure he'd like us to eat it. Do sit down, all of you. I'll take the consequences.'

Mrs Machin hesitated even more than the other ladies.

'It's really very strange, him not being here.' She shook her head.

'Don't I tell you he's quite mad,' said Denry.

'I shouldn't think he was so mad as all that,' said Mrs Machin, dryly. 'This is the most sensible kind of a house I've ever seen.'

'Oh! Is it?' Denry answered. 'Great Scott! I never noticed those three bottles of wine on the sideboard.'

At length he succeeded in seating them at the table. Thenceforward there was no difficulty. The ample and diversified cold supper began to disappear steadily, and the wine with it. And as the wine disappeared so did Mr Cotterill (who had been pompous and taciturn) grow talkative, offering to the company the exact figures of the cost of the house, and so forth. But ultimately the sheer joy of life killed arithmetic.

Mrs Machin, however, could not quite rid herself of the notion that she was in a dream that outraged the proprieties. The entire affair, for an unromantic spot like Bursley, was too fantastically and wickedly romantic.

'We must be thinking about home, Denry,' said she.

'Plenty of time,' Denry replied. 'What! All that wine gone! I'll see if there's any more in the sideboard.'

He emerged, with a red face, from bending into the deeps of the enamelled sideboard, and a wine-bottle was in his triumphant hand. It had already been opened.

'Hooray!' he proclaimed, pouring a white wine into his glass and raising the glass: 'here's to the health of Mr Cecil Wilbraham.'

He made a brave tableau in the brightness of the electric light.

Then he drank. Then he dropped the glass, which broke.

'Ugh! What's that?' he demanded, with the distorted features of a gargoyle.

His mother, who was seated next to him, seized the bottle. Denry's hand, in clasping the bottle, had hidden a small label, which said:

*POISON. – Nettleship's Patent Enamel-
Cleaning Fluid. One wipe does it.*

Confusion! Only Nellie Cotterill seemed to be incapable of
realizing that a grave accident had occurred. She had laughed
throughout the supper, and she still laughed, hysterically,
though she had drunk scarcely any wine. Her mother silenced
her.

Denry was the first to recover.

'It'll be all right,' said he, leaning back in his chair. 'They
always put a bit of poison in those things. It can't hurt me,
really. I never noticed the label.'

Mrs Machin smelt at the bottle. She could detect no odour, but
the fact that she could detect no odour appeared only to increase
her alarm.

'You must have an emetic instantly,' she said.

'Oh no!' said Denry. 'I shall be all right.' And he did seem to
be suddenly restored.

'You must have an emetic instantly,' she repeated.

'What can I have?' he grumbled. 'You can't expect to find
emetics here.'

'Oh yes, I can,' said she. 'I saw a mustard tin in a cupboard in
the kitchen. Come along now, and don't be silly.'

Nellie's hysteric mirth surged up again.

Denry objected to accompanying his mother into the kitchen.
But he was forced to submit. She shut the door on both of them.
It is probable that during the seven minutes which they spent
mysteriously together in the kitchen, the practicability of the
kitchen apparatus for carrying off waste products was duly
tested. Denry came forth, very pale and very cross, on his
mother's arm.

'There's no danger now,' said his mother, easily.

Naturally the party was at an end. The Cotterills sympathized, and prepared to depart, and inquired whether Denry
could walk home.

Denry replied, from a sofa, in a weak, expiring voice, that he
was perfectly incapable of walking home, that his sensations
were in the highest degree disconcerting, that he should sleep in

that house, as the bedrooms were ready for occupation, and that he should expect his mother to remain also.

And Mrs Machin had to concur. Mrs Machin sped the Cotterills from the door as though it had been her own door. She was exceedingly angry and agitated. But she could not impart her feelings to the suffering Denry. He moaned on a bed for about half-an-hour, and then fell asleep. And in the middle of the night, in the dark, strange house, she also fell asleep.

VI

The next morning she arose and went forth, and in about half-an-hour returned. Denry was still in bed, but his health seemed to have resumed its normal excellence. Mrs Machin burst upon him in such a state of complicated excitement as he had never before seen her in.

'Denry,' she cried, 'what do you think?'

'What?' said he.

'I've just been down home, and they're – they're pulling the house down. All the furniture's out, and they've got all the tiles off the roof, and the windows out. And there's a regular crowd watching.'

Denry sat up.

'And I can tell you another piece of news,' said he. 'Mr Cecil Wilbraham is dead.'

'Dead!' she breathed.

'Yes,' said Denry. *'I think he's served his purpose.* As we're here, we'll stop here. Don't forget it's the most sensible kind of a house you've ever seen. Don't forget that Mrs Cotterill could run it without a servant and have herself tidy by ten o'clock in a morning.'

Mrs Machin perceived then, in a flash of terrible illumination, that there never had been any Cecil Wilbraham; that Denry had merely invented him and his long moustaches and his wall eye for the purpose of getting the better of his mother. The whole affair was an immense swindle upon her. Not a Mr Cecil Wilbraham, but her own son had bought her cottage over her head and jockeyed her out of it beyond any chance of getting into it

150

again. And to defeat his mother the rascal had not simply perverted the innocent Nellie Cotterill to some cooperation in his scheme, but he had actually bought four other cottages, because the landlord would not sell one alone, and he was actually demolishing property to the sole end of stopping her from re-entering it!

Of course, the entire town soon knew of the upshot of the battle, of the year-long battle, between Denry and his mother, and the means adopted by Denry to win. The town also had been hoodwinked, but it did not mind that. It loved its Denry the more, and seeing that he was now properly established in the most remarkable house in the district, it soon afterwards made him a Town Councillor as some reward for his talent in amusing it.

And Denry would say to himself:

'Everything went like clockwork, except the mustard and water. I didn't bargain for the mustard and water. And yet, if I was clever enough to think of putting a label on the bottle and to have the beds prepared, I ought to have been clever enough to keep mustard out of the house.' It would be wrong to mince the unpleasant fact that the sham poisoning which he had arranged to the end that he and his mother should pass the night in the house had finished in a manner much too realistic for Denry's pleasure. Mustard and water, particularly when mixed by Mrs Machin, is mustard and water.

She had that consolation.

CHAPTER 9

The Great Newspaper War

I

WHEN Denry and his mother had been established a year and a
month in the new house at Bleakridge, Denry received a visit
one evening which perhaps flattered him more than anything
had ever flattered him. The visitor was Mr Myson. Now Mr
Myson was the founder, proprietor and editor of the *Five
Towns Weekly*, a new organ of public opinion which had been
in existence about a year; and Denry thought that Mr Myson
had popped in to see him in pursuit of an advertisement of the
Thrift Club, and at first he was not at all flattered.

But Mr Myson was not hunting for advertisements, and
Denry soon saw him to be the kind of man who would be likely
to depute that work to others. Of middle height, well and
quietly dressed, with a sober, assured deportment, he spoke in a
voice and accent that were not of the Five Towns; they were
superior to the Five Towns. And in fact Mr Myson originated in
Manchester and had seen London. He was not provincial, and
he beheld the Five Towns as part of the provinces; which no
native of the Five Towns ever succeeds in doing. Nevertheless,
his manner to Denry was the summit of easy and yet deferential
politeness.

He asked permission 'to put something before' Denry. And
when, rather taken aback by such smooth phrases, Denry had
graciously accorded the permission, he gave a brief history of the
Five Towns Weekly, showing how its circulation had grown,
and definitely stating that at that moment it was yielding a
profit. Then he said:

'Now my scheme is to turn it into a daily.'

'Very good notion,' said Denry, instinctively.

'I'm glad you think so,' said Mr Myson. 'Because I've come
here in the hope of getting your assistance. I'm a stranger to the
district, and I want the cooperation of some one who isn't. So

152

I've come to you. I need money, of course, though I have myself what most people would consider sufficient capital. But what I need more than money is – well – moral support.'

'And who put you on to me?' asked Denry.

Mr Myson smiled. 'I put myself on to you,' said he. 'I think I may say I've got my bearings in the Five Towns, after over a year's journalism in it, and it appeared to me that you were the best man I could approach. I always believe in flying high.'

Therein was Denry flattered. The visit seemed to him to seal his position in the district in a way in which his election to the Bursley Town Council had failed to do. He had been somehow disappointed with that election. He had desired to display his interest in the serious welfare of the town, and to answer his opponent's arguments with better ones. But the burgesses of his ward appeared to have no passionate love of logic. They just cried 'Good old Denry!' and elected him – with a majority of only forty-one votes. He had expected to feel a different Denry when he could put 'Councillor' before his name. It was not so. He had been solemnly in the mayoral procession to church, he had attended meetings of the council, he had been nominated to the Watch Committee. But he was still precisely the same Denry, though the youngest member of the council. But now he was being recognized from the outside. Mr Myson's keen Manchester eye, ranging over the quarter of a million inhabitants of the Five Towns in search of a representative individual force, had settled on Denry Machin. Yes, he was flattered. Mr Myson's choice threw a rose-light on all Denry's career: his wealth and its origin; his house and stable, which were the astonishment and the admiration of the town; his Universal Thrift Club; yea, and his councillorship! After all, these *were* marvels. (And possibly the greatest marvel was the resigned presence of his mother in that wondrous house, and the fact that she consented to employ Rose Chudd, the incomparable Sappho of charwomen, for three hours every day.)

In fine, he perceived from Mr Myson's eyes that his position was unique.

And after they had chatted a little, and the conversation had deviated momentarily from journalism to house property, he offered to display Machin House (as he had christened it) to Mr Myson, and Mr Myson was really impressed beyond the ordinary. Mr Myson's homage to Mrs Machin, whom they chanced on in the paradise of the bathroom, was the polished mirror of courtesy. How Denry wished that he could behave like that when he happened to meet countesses.

Then, once more in the drawing-room, they resumed the subject of newspapers.

'You know,' said Mr Myson, 'it's really a very bad thing indeed for a district to have only one daily newspaper. I've nothing myself to say against *The Staffordshire Signal*, but you'd perhaps be astonished' – this in a confidential tone – 'at the feeling there is against the *Signal* in many quarters.'

'Really!' said Denry.

'Of course its fault is that it isn't sufficiently interested in the great public questions of the district. And it can't be. Because it can't take a definite side. It must try to please all parties. At any rate it must offend none. That is the great evil of a journalistic monopoly ... Two hundred and fifty thousand people – why! there is an ample public for two first-class papers. Look at Nottingham! Look at Bristol! Look at Leeds! Look at Sheffield! ... and *their* newspapers.'

And Denry endeavoured to look at these great cities! Truly the Five Towns was just about as big.

The dizzy journalistic intoxication seized him. He did not give Mr Myson an answer at once, but he gave himself an answer at once. He would go into the immense adventure. He was very friendly with the *Signal* people – certainly; but business was business, and the highest welfare of the Five Towns was the highest welfare of the Five Towns.

Soon afterwards all the hoardings of the district spoke with one blue voice, and said that the *Five Towns Weekly* was to be transformed into the *Five Towns Daily*, with four editions, beginning each day at noon, and that the new organ would be conducted on the lines of a first-class evening paper.

The inner ring of knowing ones knew that a company entitled 'The Five Towns Newspapers, Limited', had been formed, with a capital of ten thousand pounds, and that Mr Myson held three thousand pounds' worth of shares, and the great Denry Machin one thousand five hundred, and that the remainder were to be sold and allotted as occasion demanded. The inner ring said that nothing would ever be able to stand up against the *Signal*. On the other hand, it admitted that Denry, the most prodigious card ever born into the Five Towns, had never been floored by anything. The inner ring anticipated the future with glee. Denry and Mr Myson anticipated the future with righteous confidence. As for the *Signal*, it went on its august way, blind to sensational hoardings.

II

On the day of the appearance of the first issue of the *Five Towns Daily*, the offices of the new paper at Hanbridge gave proof of their excellent organization, working in all details with an admirable smoothness. In the basement a Marinoni machine thundered like a sucking dove to produce fifteen thousand copies an hour. On the ground floor ingenious arrangements had been made for publishing the paper; in particular, the iron railings to keep the boys in order in front of the publishing counter had been imitated from the *Signal*. On the first floor was the editor and founder with his staff, and above that the composing department. The number of stairs that separated the composing department from the machine-room was not a positive advantage, but bricks and mortar are inelastic, and one does what one can. The offices looked very well from the outside, and they compared passably with the offices of the *Signal* close by. The posters were duly in the ground-floor windows, and gold signs, one above another to the roof, produced an air of lucrative success.

Denry happened to be in the *Daily* offices that afternoon. He had had nothing to do with the details of organization, for details of organization were not his speciality. His speciality was large, leading ideas. He knew almost nothing of the agreements with correspondents and Press Association and Central News, and the racing services and the fiction syndicates, nor of the difficulties with the Compositors' Union, nor of the struggle to lower the price of paper by the twentieth of a penny per pound, nor of the awful discounts allowed to certain advertisers, nor of the friction with the railway company, nor of the sickening adulation that had been lavished on quite unimportant newsagents, nor – worst of all – of the dearth of newsboys. These matters did not attract him. He could not stoop to them. But when Mr Myson, calm and proud, escorted him down to the machine-room, and the Marinoni threw a folded pink *Daily* almost into his hands, and it looked exactly like a real newspaper, and he saw one of his own descriptive articles in it, and he reflected that he was an owner of it – then Denry was attracted and delighted, and his heart beat. For this pink thing was the symbol and result of the whole affair, and had the effect of a miracle on him.

And he said to himself, never guessing how many thousands of men had said it before him, that a newspaper was the finest toy in the world.

About four o'clock the publisher, in shirt sleeves and an apron, came up to Mr Myson and respectfully asked him to step into the publishing office. Mr Myson stepped into the publishing office and Denry with him, and they there beheld a small ragged boy with a bleeding nose and a bundle of *Dailys* in his wounded hand.

'Yes,' the boy sobbed; 'and they said they'd cut my eyes out and plee [play] marbles wi' 'em, if they cotched me in Crown Square agen.' And he threw down the papers with a final yell.

The two directors learnt that the delicate threat had been uttered by four *Signal* boys, who had objected to any fellow-boys offering any paper other than the *Signal* for sale in Crown Square or anywhere else.

Of course, it was absurd.

Still, absurd as it was, it continued. The central publishing offices of the *Daily* at Hanbridge, and its branch offices in the neighbouring towns, were like military hospitals, and the truth appeared to the directors that while the public was panting to buy copies of the *Daily*, the sale of the *Daily* was being prevented by means of a scandalous conspiracy on the part of *Signal* boys. For it must be understood that in the Five Towns people prefer to catch their newspaper in the street as it flies and cries.

The *Signal* had a vast army of boys, to whom every year it gave a great *fête*. Indeed, the *Signal* possessed nearly all the available boys, and assuredly all the most pugilistic and strongest boys. Mr Myson had obtained boys only after persistent inquiry and demand, and such as he had found were not the fittest, and therefore were unlikely to survive. You would have supposed that in a district that never ceases to grumble about bad trade and unemployment, thousands of boys would have been delighted to buy the *Daily* at fourpence a dozen and sell it at sixpence. But it was not so.

On the second day the dearth of boys at the offices of the *Daily* was painful. There was that magnificent, enterprising newspaper waiting to be sold, and there was the great enlightened public waiting to buy; and scarcely any business could be done because the *Signal* boys had established a reign of terror over their puny and upstart rivals!

The situation was unthinkable.

Still, unthinkable as it was, it continued. Mr Myson had thought of everything except this. Naturally it had not occurred to him that an immense and serious effort for the general weal was going to be blocked by a gang of tatterdemalions.

He complained with dignity to the *Signal*, and was informed with dignity by the *Signal* that the *Signal* could not be responsible for the playful antics of its boys in the streets; that, in short, the Five Towns was a free country. In the latter propositions Mr Myson did not concur.

After trouble in the persuasion of parents – astonishing how indifferent the Five Towns' parent was to the loss of blood by his offspring! – a case reached the police-court. At the hearing the *Signal* gave a solicitor a watching brief, and that solicitor expressed the *Signal*'s horror of carnage. The evidence was excessively contradictory, and the Stipendiary dismissed the summons with a good joke. The sole definite result was that the boy whose father had ostensibly brought the summons, got his ear torn within a quarter of an hour of leaving the court. Boys will be boys.

Still, the *Daily* had so little faith in human nature that it could not believe that the *Signal* was not secretly encouraging its boys to be boys. It could not believe that the *Signal*, out of a sincere desire for fair play and for the highest welfare of the district, would willingly sacrifice nearly half its circulation and a portion of its advertisement revenue. And the hurt tone of Mr Myson's leading articles seemed to indicate that in Mr Myson's opinion his older rival *ought* to do everything in its power to ruin itself. The *Signal* never spoke of the fight. The *Daily* gave shocking details of it every day.

The struggle trailed on through the weeks.

Then Denry had one of his ideas. An advertisement was printed in the *Daily* for two hundred able-bodied men to earn two shillings for working six hours a day. An address different from the address of the *Daily* was given. By a ruse Denry procured the insertion of the advertisement in the *Signal* also.

'We must expend our capital on getting the paper on to the streets,' said Denry. 'That's evident. We'll have it sold by men. We'll soon see if the *Signal* ragamuffins will attack *them*. And we wont pay 'em by results; we'll pay 'em a fixed wage; that'll fetch 'em. And a commission on sales into the bargain. Why! I wouldn't mind engaging *five* hundred men. Swamp the streets! That's it! Hang expense. And when we've done the trick, then we can go back to the boys; they'll have learnt their lesson.'

And Mr Myson agreed and was pleased that Denry was living up to his reputation.

The state of the earthenware trade was supposed that summer to be worse than it had been since 1869, and the grumblings of the unemployed were prodigious, even seditious. Mr Myson therefore, as a measure of precaution, engaged a couple of policemen to ensure order at the address, and during the hours, named in the advertisement as a rendezvous for respectable men in search of a well-paid job. Having regard to the thousands of perishing families in the Five Towns, he foresaw a rush and a crush of eager breadwinners. Indeed, the arrangements were elaborate.

Forty minutes after the advertised time for the opening of the reception of respectable men in search of money, four men had arrived. Mr Myson, mystified, thought that there had been a mistake in the advertisement, but there was no mistake in the advertisement. A little later two more men came. Of the six, three were tipsy, and the other three absolutely declined to be seen selling papers in the streets. Two were abusive, one facetious. Mr Myson did not know his Five Towns; nor did Denry. A Five Towns' man, when he can get neither bread nor beer, will keep himself and his family on pride and water. The policemen went off to more serious duties.

III

Then came the announcement of the thirty-fifth anniversary of the *Signal*, and of the processional *fête* by which the *Signal* was at once to give itself a splendid spectacular advertisement and to reward and enhearten its boys. The *Signal* meant to liven up the streets of the Five Towns on that great day by means of a display of all the gilt chariots of Snape's Circus in the main thoroughfare. Many of the boys would be in the gilt chariots. Copies of the anniversary number of the *Signal* would be sold from the gilt chariots. The idea was excellent, and it showed that after all the *Signal* was getting just a little more afraid of its young rival than it had pretended to be.

For, strange to say, after a trying period of hesitation, the *Five Towns Daily* was slightly on the upward curve – thanks to Denry. Denry did not mean to be beaten by the puzzle which the *Daily* offered to his intelligence. There the *Daily* was, full of news, and with quite an encouraging show of advertisements, printed on real paper with real ink – and yet it would not 'go'. Notoriously the *Signal* earned a net profit of at the very least five thousand a year, whereas the *Daily* earned a net loss of at the very least sixty pounds a week – and of that sixty quite a third was Denry's money. He could not explain it. Mr Myson tried to rouse the public by passionately stirring up extremely urgent matters – such as the smoke nuisance, the increase of the rates, the park question, German competition, technical education for apprentices; but the public obstinately would not be roused concerning its highest welfare to the point of insisting on a regular supply of the *Daily*. If a mere five thousand souls had positively demanded daily a copy of the *Daily* and not slept till boys or agents had responded to their wish, the troubles of the *Daily* would soon have vanished. But this ridiculous public did not seem to care which paper was put into its hand in exchange for its halfpenny, so long as the sporting news was put there. It simply was indifferent. It failed to see the importance to such an immense district of having two flourishing and mutually-opposing daily organs. The fundamental boy difficulty remained ever present.

And it was the boy difficulty that Denry perseveringly and ingeniously attacked, until at length the *Daily* did indeed possess some sort of a brigade of its own, and the bullying and slaughter in the streets (so amusing to the inhabitants) grew a little less one-sided.

A week or more before the *Signal*'s anniversary day, Denry heard that the *Signal* was secretly afraid lest the *Daily*'s brigade might accomplish the marring of its gorgeous procession, and that the *Signal* was ready to do anything to smash the *Daily*'s brigade. He laughed; he said he did not mind. About that time hostilities were rather acute; blood was warming, and both papers, in the excitation of rivalry, had partially lost the sense of what was due to the dignity of great organs. By chance a tremendous football match – Knype *v.* Bursley – fell on the very Saturday of the procession. The rival arrangements for the reporting of the match were as tremendous as the match itself, and somehow the match seemed to add keenness to the journalistic struggle, especially as the *Daily* favoured Bursley and the *Signal* was therefore forced to favour Knype.

By all the laws of hazard there ought to have been a hitch on that historic Saturday. Telephone or telegraph ought to have broken down, or rain ought to have made play impossible, but no hitch occurred. And at five-thirty o'clock of a glorious afternoon in earliest November the *Daily* went to press with a truly brilliant account of the manner in which Bursley (for the first and last time in its history) had defeated Knype by one goal to none. Mr Myson was proud. Mr Myson defied the *Signal* to beat his descriptive report. As for the *Signal*'s procession – well, Mr Myson and the chief sub-editor of the *Daily* glanced at each other and smiled.

And a few minutes later the *Daily* boys were rushing out of the publishing room with bundles of papers – assuredly in advance of the *Signal*.

It was at this juncture that the unexpected began to occur to the *Daily* boys. The publishing door of the *Daily* opened into Stanway Rents, a narrow alley in a maze of mean streets behind Crown Square. In Stanway Rents was a small warehouse in which, according to rumours of the afternoon, a free soup kitchen was to be opened. And just before the football edition of the *Daily* came off the Marinoni, it emphatically was opened, and there issued from its inviting gate an odour – not, to be sure, of soup, but of toasted cheese and hot jam – such an odour as had never before tempted the nostrils of a *Daily* boy; a unique and omnipotent odour. Several boys (who, I may state frankly, were traitors to the *Daily* cause, spies and mischief-makers from elsewhere) raced unhesitatingly in, crying that toasted cheese sandwiches and jam tarts were to be distributed like lightning to all authentic newspaper lads.

The entire gang followed – scores, over a hundred – inwardly expecting to emerge instantly with teeth fully employed, followed like sheep into a fold.

And the gate was shut.

Toasted cheese and hot jammy pastry were faithfully served to the ragged host – but with no breathless haste. And when, loaded, the boys struggled to depart, they were instructed by the kind philanthropist who had fed them to depart by another exit, and they discovered themselves in an enclosed yard, of which the double doors were apparently unyielding. And the warehouse door was shut also. And as the cheese and jam disappeared, shouts of fury arose on the air. The yard was so close to the offices of the *Daily* that the chimneypots of those offices could actually be seen. And yet the shouting brought no answer from the lords of the *Daily*, congratulating themselves up there on their fine account of the football match, and on their celerity in going to press and on the loyalty of their brigade.

The *Signal*, it need not be said, disavowed complicity in this extraordinary entrapping of the *Daily* brigade by means of an odour. Could it be held responsible for the excess of its disinterested sympathizers? ... Still, the appalling trick showed the high temperature to which blood had risen in the genial battle between great rival organs. Persons in the inmost ring whispered that Denry Machin had at length been bested on this critically important day.

IV

Snape's Circus used to be one of the great shining institutions of North Staffordshire, trailing its magnificence on sculptured wheels from town to town, and occupying the dreams of boys from one generation to another. Its headquarters were at Axe, in the Moorlands, ten miles away from Hanbridge, but the riches of old Snape had chiefly come from the Five Towns. At the time of the struggle between the *Signal* and the *Daily* its decline had already begun. The aged proprietor had recently died, and the name, and the horses, and the chariots, and the carefully-repaired tents had been sold to strangers. On the Saturday of the anniversary and the football match (which was also Martinmas Saturday) the circus was set up at Oldcastle, on the edge of the Five Towns, and was giving its final performances of the season. Even boys will not go to circuses in the middle of a Five Towns' winter. The *Signal* people had hired the processional portion of Snape's for the late afternoon and early evening. And the instructions were that the entire *cortège* should be round about the *Signal* offices, in marching order, not later than five o'clock.

But at four o'clock several gentlemen with rosettes in their button-holes and *Signal* posters in their hands arrived important and panting at the fair-ground at Oldcastle, and announced that the programme had been altered at the last moment, in order to defeat certain feared machinations of the unscrupulous *Daily*. The cavalcade was to be split into three groups, one of which, the chief, was to enter Hanbridge by a 'back road', and the other two were to go to Bursley and Longshaw respectively. In this manner the forces of advertisement would be distributed, and the chief parts of the district equally honoured.

The special linen banners, pennons, and ribbons – bearing the words –

had already been hung and planted and draped about the gilded summits of the chariots. And after some delay the processions were started, separating at the bottom of the Cattle Market. The head of the Hanbridge part of the procession consisted of an enormous car of Jupiter, with six wheels and thirty-six paregorical figures (as the clown used to say), and drawn by six piebald steeds guided by white reins. This coach had a windowed interior (at the greater fairs it sometimes served as a box-office) and in the interior one of the delegates of the *Signal* had fixed himself; from it he directed the paths of the procession.

It would be futile longer to conceal that the delegate of the *Signal* in the bowels of the car of Jupiter was not honestly a delegate of the *Signal* at all. He was, indeed, Denry Machin, and none other. From this single fact it will be seen to what extent the representatives of great organs had forgotten what was due to their dignity and to public decency. Ensconced in his lair Denry directed the main portion of the *Signal*'s advertising procession by all manner of discreet lanes round the skirts of Hanbridge and so into the town from the hilly side. And ultimately the ten vehicles halted in Crapper Street, to the joy of the simple inhabitants.

Denry emerged and wandered innocently towards the offices of his paper, which were close by. It was getting late. The first yelling of the imprisoned *Daily* boys was just beginning to rise on the autumn air.

Suddenly Denry was accosted by a young man.

'Hello, Machin!' cried the young man. 'What have you shaved your beard off, for? I scarcely knew you.'

'I just thought I would, Swetnam,' said Denry, who was obviously discomposed.

It was the youngest of the Swetnam boys; he and Denry had taken a sort of curt fancy to one another.

'I say,' said Swetnam, confidentially, as if obeying a swift impulse, 'I did hear that the *Signal* people meant to collar all your chaps this afternoon, and I believe they have done. Hear that now?' (Swetnam's father was intimate with the *Signal* people.)

'I know,' Denry replied.

'But I mean – papers and all.'

'I know,' said Denry.

'Oh!' murmured Swetnam.

'But I'll tell you a secret,' Denry added. 'They aren't today's papers. They're yesterday's, and last week's and last month's. We've been collecting them specially and keeping them nice and new-looking.'

'Well, you're a caution!' murmured Swetnam.

'I am,' Denry agreed.

A number of men rushed at that instant with bundles of the genuine football edition from the offices of the *Daily*.

'Come on!' Denry cried to them. 'Come on! This way! By-by, Swetnam.'

And the whole file vanished round a corner. The yelling of imprisoned cheese-fed boys grew louder.

v

In the meantime at the *Signal* office (which was not three hundred yards away, but on the other side of Crown Square) apprehension had deepened into anxiety as the minutes passed and the Snape Circus procession persisted in not appearing on the horizon of the Oldcastle Road. The *Signal* would have telephoned to Snape's, but for the fact that a circus is never on the telephone. It then telephoned to its Oldcastle agent, who, after a long delay, was able to reply that the cavalcade had left Oldcastle at the appointed hour, with every sign of health and energy. Then the *Signal* sent forth scouts all down the Oldcastle Road to put spurs into the procession, and the scouts returned, having seen nothing. Pessimists glanced at the possibility of the whole procession having fallen into the canal at Caulron Bridge. The paper was printed, the train-parcels for Knype, Longshaw, Bursley, and Turnhill were dispatched; the boys were waiting; the fingers of the clock in the publishing department were simply flying. It had been arranged that the bulk of the Hanbridge edition, and in particular the first copies of it, should be sold by boys from the gilt chariots themselves. The publisher hesitated for an awful moment, and then decided that he could wait no more, and that the boys must sell the papers in the usual way from the pavements and gutters. There was no knowing what the *Daily* might not be doing.

And then *Signal* boys in dozens rushed forth paper-laden, but they were disappointed boys; they had thought to ride in gilt chariots, not to paddle in mud. And almost the first thing they saw in Crown Square was the car of Jupiter in its glory, flying all the *Signal* colours; and other cars behind. They did not rush now; they sprang, as from a catapult; and alighted like flies on the vehicles. Men insisted on taking their papers from them and paying for them on the spot. The boys were startled; they were entirely puzzled; but they had not the habit of refusing money. And off went the procession to the music of its own band down the road to Knype, and perhaps a hundred boys on board, cheering. The men in charge then performed a curious act: they tore down all the *Signal* flagging, and replaced it with the emblem of the *Daily*.

So that all the great and enlightened public wandering home in crowds from the football match at Knype, had the spectacle of a *Daily* procession instead of a *Signal* procession, and could scarce believe their eyes. And *Dailys* were sold in quantities from the cars. At Knype Station the procession curved and returned to Hanbridge, and finally, after a multitudinous triumph, came to a stand with all its *Daily* bunting in front of the *Signal* offices; and Denry appeared from his lair. Denry's men fled with bundles.

'They're an hour and a half late,' said Denry calmly to one of the proprietors of the *Signal*, who was on the pavement. 'But I've managed to get them here. I thought I'd just look in to thank you for giving such a good feed to our lads.'

The telephones hummed with news of similar *Daily* processions in Longshaw and Bursley. And there was not a high-class private bar in the district that did not tinkle with delighted astonishment at the brazen, the inconceivable effrontery of that card, Denry Machin. Many people foresaw law suits, but it was agreed that the *Signal* had begun the game of impudence in trapping the *Daily* lads so as to secure a holy calm for its much trumpeted procession.

And Denry had not finished with the *Signal*.

In the special football edition of the *Daily* was an announcement, the first, of special Martinmas *fêtes* organized by the *Five Towns Daily*. And on the same morning every member of the Universal Thrift Club had received an invitation to the said *fêtes*. They were three – held on public ground at Hanbridge, Bursley, and Longshaw. They were in the style of the usual Five Towns 'wakes'; that is to say, roundabouts, shows, gingerbread stalls, swings, coconut shies. But at each *fête* a new and very simple form of 'shy' had been erected. It consisted of a row of small railway signals.

'March up! March up!' cried the shy-men. 'Knock down the signal! Knock down the signal! And a packet of Turkish delight is yours. Knock down the signal!'

And when you had knocked down the signal the men cried:

'We wrap it up for you in the special Anniversary Number of the *Signal*.'

And they disdainfully tore into suitable fragments copies of the *Signal* which had cost Denry & Co. a halfpenny each, and enfolded the Turkish delight therein, and handed it to you with a smack.

And all the fair-grounds were carpeted with draggled and muddy *Signals*. People were up to the ankles in *Signals*.

The affair was the talk of Sunday. Few matters in the Five Towns have raised more gossip than did that enormous escapade which Denry invented and conducted. The moral damage to the *Signal* was held to approach the disastrous. And now not the possibility but the probability of law-suits was incessantly discussed.

On the Monday both papers were bought with anxiety. Everybody was frothing to know what the respective editors would say.

But in neither sheet was there a single word as to the affair. Both had determined to be discreet; both were afraid. The *Signal* feared lest it might not, if the pinch came, be able to prove its innocence of the crime of luring boys into confinement by means of toasted cheese and hot jam. The *Signal* had also to consider its seriously damaged dignity; for such wounds silence is the best dressing. The *Daily* was comprehensively afraid. It had practically driven its gilded chariots through the entire Decalogue. Moreover, it had won easily in the grand altercation. It was exquisitely conscious of glory.

Denry went away to Blackpool, doubtless to grow his beard.

The proof of the *Daily*'s moral and material victory was that soon afterwards there were four applicants, men of substance, for shares in the *Daily* company. And this, by the way, was the end of the tale. For these applicants, who secured options on a majority of the shares, were emissaries of the *Signal*. Armed with options, the *Signal* made terms with its rival, and then by mutual agreement killed it. The price of its death was no trifle, but it was less than a year's profits of the *Signal*. Denry considered that he had been 'done'. But in the depths of his heart he was glad that he had been done. He had had too disconcerting a glimpse of the rigours and perils of journalism to wish to continue it. He had scored supremely and, for him, to score was life itself. His reputation as a card was far, far higher than ever. Had he so desired, he could have been elected to the House of Commons on the strength of his procession and *fête*.

Mr Myson, somewhat scandalized by the exuberance of his partner, returned to Manchester.

And the *Signal*, subsequently often referred to as 'The Old Lady', resumed its monopolistic sway over the opinions of a quarter of a million of people, and has never since been attacked.

CHAPTER 10

His Infamy

I

WHEN Denry at a single stroke 'wherreted' his mother and proved his adventurous spirit by becoming the possessor of one of the first motor-cars ever owned in Bursley, his instinct naturally was to run up to Councillor Cotterill's in it. Not that he loved Councillor Cotterill, and therefore wished to make him a partaker in his joy; for he did not love Councillor Cotterill. He had never been able to forgive Nellie's father for those patronizing airs years and years before at Llandudno, airs indeed which had not even yet disappeared from Cotterill's attitude towards Denry. Though they were Councillors on the same Town Council, though Denry was getting richer and Cotterill was assuredly not getting richer, the latter's face and tone always seemed to be saying to Denry: 'Well, you are not doing so badly for a beginner.' So Denry did not care to lose an opportunity of impressing Councillor Cotterill. Moreover, Denry had other reasons for going up to the Cotterills. There existed a sympathetic bond between him and Mrs Cotterill, despite her prim taciturnity and her exasperating habit of sitting with her hands pressed tight against her body and one over the other. Occasionally he teased her – and she liked being teased. He had glimpses now and then of her secret soul; he was perhaps the only person in Bursley thus privileged. Then there was Nellie. Denry and Nellie were great friends. For the rest of the world she had grown up, but not for Denry, who treated her as the chocolate child; while she, if she called him anything, called him respectfully 'Mr'.

The Cotterills had a fairly large old house with a good garden 'up Bycars Lane', above the new park and above all those red streets which Mr Cotterill had helped to bring into being. Mr Cotterill built new houses with terra-cotta facings for others, but preferred an old one in stucco for himself. His abode had been saved from the parcelling out of several Georgian estates. It was dignified. It had a double entrance gate, and from this portal the drive started off for the house door, but deliberately avoided reaching the house door until it had wandered in curves over the entire garden. That was the Georgian touch! The modern touch was shown in Councillor Cotterill's bay windows, bathroom and garden squirter. There was stabling, in which were kept a Victorian dogcart and a Georgian horse, used by the Councillor in his business. As sure as ever his wife or daughter wanted the dogcart, it was either out or just going out, or the Georgian horse was fatigued and needed repose. The man who groomed the Georgian also ploughed the flowerbeds, broke the windows in cleaning them, and put blacking on brown boots. Two indoor servants had differing views as to the frontier between the kingdom of his duties and the kingdom of theirs. In fact, it was the usual spacious household of successful trade in a provincial town.

Denry got to Bycars Lane without a breakdown. This was in the days, quite thirteen years ago, when automobilists made their wills and took food supplies when setting forth. Hence Denry was pleased. The small but useful fund of prudence in him, however, forbade him to run the car along the unending sinuous drive. The May night was fine, and he left the loved vehicle with his new furs in the shadow of a monkey-tree near the gate.

As he was crunching towards the door, he had a beautiful idea: 'I'll take 'em all out for a spin. There'll just be room!' he said.

Now even today, when the very cabman drives his automobile, a man who buys a motor cannot say to a friend: 'I've bought a motor. Come for a spin,' in the same self-unconscious accents as he would say: 'I've bought a boat. Come for a sail,' or 'I've bought a house. Come and look at it.' Even today and in the centre of London there is still something about a motor — well something ... Everybody who has bought a motor, and everybody who has dreamed of buying a motor, will comprehend me. Useless to feign that a motor is the most banal thing imaginable. It is not. It remains the supreme symbol of swagger.

If such is the effect of a motor in these days and in Berkeley Square, what must it have been in that dim past, and in that dim town three hours by the fastest express from Euston? The imagination must be forced to the task of answering this question. Then will it be understood that Denry was simply tingling with pride.

'Master in?' he demanded of the servant, who was correctly starched, but unkempt in detail.

'No, sir. He ain't been in for tea.'

('I shall take the women out then,' said Denry to himself.)

'Come in! Come in!' cried a voice from the other side of the open door of the drawing-room, Nellie's voice! The manners and state of a family that has industrially risen combine the spectacular grandeur of the caste to which it has climbed with the ease and freedom of the caste which it has quitted.

'Such a surprise!' said the voice. Nellie appeared, rosy.

Denry threw his new motoring cap hastily on to the hall-stand. No! He did not hope that Nellie would see it. He hoped that she would not see it. Now that the moment was really come to declare himself the owner of a motor-car, he grew timid and nervous. He would have liked to hide his hat. But then Denry was quite different from our common humanity. He was capable even of feeling awkward in a new suit of clothes. A singular person.

'Hello!' she greeted him.

'Hello!' he greeted her.

Their hands touched.

'Father hasn't come yet,' she added. He fancied she was not quite at ease.

'Well,' he said, 'what's this surprise.'

She motioned him into the drawing-room.

The surprise was a wonderful woman, brilliant in black – not black silk, but a softer, delicate stuff. She reclined in an easy-chair with surpassing grace and self-possession. A black Egyptian shawl, spangled with silver, was slipping off her shoulders. Her hair was dressed – that is to say, it was *dressed*; it was obviously and thrillingly a work of elaborate art. He could see her two feet and one of her ankles. The boots, the open-work stocking – such boots, such an open-work stocking, had never been seen in Bursley, not even at a ball! She was in mourning, and wore scarcely any jewellery, but there was a gleaming tint of gold here and there among the black, which resulted in a marvellous effect of richness. The least experienced would have said, and said rightly: 'This must be a woman of wealth and fashion.' It was the detail that finished the demonstration. The detail was incredible. There might have been ten million stitches in the dress. Ten sempstresses might have worked on the dress for ten years. An examination of it under a microscope could but have deepened one's amazement at it.

She was something new in the Five Towns, something quite new.

Denry was not equal to the situation. He seldom was equal to a small situation. And although he had latterly acquired a considerable amount of social *savoir*, he was constantly mislaying it, so that he could not put his hand on it at the moment when he most required it, as now.

'Well, Denry!' said the wondrous creature in black, softly.

And he collected himself as though for a plunge, and said:

'Well, Ruth!'

This was the woman whom he had once loved, kissed, and engaged himself to marry. He was relieved that she had begun with Christian names, because he could not recall her surname. He could not even remember whether he had ever heard it. All he knew was that, after leaving Bursley to join her father in Birmingham, she had married somebody with a double name, somebody well off, somebody older than herself; somebody apparently of high social standing; and that this somebody had died.

She made no fuss. There was no implication in her demeanour that she expected to be wept over as a lone widow; or that because she and he had on a time been betrothed, therefore they could never speak naturally to each other again. She just talked as if nothing had ever happened to her, and as if about twenty-four hours had elapsed since she had last seen him. He felt that she must have picked up this most useful diplomatic calmness in her contacts with her late husband's class. It was a valuable lesson to him: 'Always behave as if nothing had happened – no matter what has happened.'

To himself he was saying:

'I'm glad I came up in my motor.'

He seemed to need something in self-defence against the sudden attack of all this wealth and all this superior social tact, and the motor-car served excellently.

'I've been hearing a great deal about you lately,' said she with a soft smile, unobtrusively rearranging a fold of her skirt.

'Well,' he replied, 'I'm sorry I can't say the same of you.'

Slightly perilous perhaps, but still he thought it rather neat.

'Oh!' she said. 'You see I've been so much out of England. We were just talking about holidays. I was saying to Mrs Cotterill they certainly ought to go to Switzerland this year for a change.'

'Yes, Mrs Capron-Smith was just saying –' Mrs Cotterill put in.

(So that was her name.)

'It would be something too lovely!' said Nellie in ecstasy.

Switzerland! Astonishing how with a single word she had marked the gulf between Bursley people and herself. The Cotterills had never been out of England. Not merely that, but the Cotterills had never dreamt of going out of England. Denry had once been to Dieppe, and had come back as though from Timbuctoo with a traveller's renown. And she talked of Switzerland easily!

'I suppose it is very jolly,' he said.

'Yes,' she said, 'it's splendid in summer. But, of course, *the* time is winter, for the sports. Naturally, when you aren't free to take a bit of a holiday in winter, you must be content with summer, and very splendid it is. I'm sure you'd enjoy it frightfully, Nell.'

'I'm sure I should – frightfully!' Nellie agreed. 'I shall speak to father. I shall make him –'

'Now, Nellie –' her mother warned her.

'Yes, I shall, mother,' Nellie insisted.

'There *is* your father!' observed Mrs Cotterill, after listening.

Footsteps crossed the hall, and died away into the dining-room.

'I wonder why on earth father doesn't come in here. He must have heard us talking,' said Nellie, like a tyrant crossed in some trifle.

A bell rang, and then the servant came into the drawing-room and remarked: 'If you please, mum,' at Mrs Cotterill, and Mrs Cotterill disappeared, closing the door after her.

'What are they up to, between them?' Nellie demanded, and she, too, departed, with wrinkled brow, leaving Denry and Ruth together. It could be perceived on Nellie's brow that her father was going 'to catch it'.

'I haven't seen Mr Cotterill yet,' said Mrs Capron-Smith.

'When did you come?' Denry asked.

'Only this afternoon.'

She continued to talk.

As he looked at her, listening and responding intelligently now and then, he saw that Mrs Capron-Smith was in truth the woman that Ruth had so cleverly imitated ten years before. The imitation had deceived him then; he had accepted it for genuine. It would not have deceived him now – he knew that. Oh yes! This was the real article that could hold its own anywhere ... Switzerland! And not simply Switzerland, but a refinement on Switzerland! Switzerland in winter! He divined that in her opinion Switzerland in summer was not worth doing – in the way of correctness. But in winter ...

II

Nellie had announced a surprise for Denry as he entered the house, but Nellie's surprise for Denry, startling and successful though it proved, was as naught to the surprise which Mr Cotterill had in hand for Nellie, her mother, Denry, the town of Bursley, and various persons up and down the country.

Mrs Cotterill came hysterically in upon the duologue between Denry and Ruth in the drawing-room. From the activity of her hands, which, instead of being decently folded one over the other, were waving round her head in the strangest way, it was clear that Mrs Cotterill was indeed under the stress of a very unusual emotion.

'It's those creditors – at last! I knew it would be! It's all those creditors! They won't let him alone, and now they've *done* it.'

So Mrs Cotterill! She dropped into a chair. She had no longer any sense of shame, of what was due to her dignity. She seemed to have forgotten that certain matters are not proper to be discussed in drawing-rooms. She had left the room Mrs Councillor Cotterill; she returned to it nobody in particular, the personification of defeat. The change had operated in five minutes.

Mrs Capron-Smith and Denry glanced at each other, and even Mrs Capron-Smith was at a loss for a moment. Then Ruth approached Mrs Cotterill and took her hand. Perhaps Mrs Capron-Smith was not so astonished after all. She and Nellie's mother had always been 'very friendly'. And in the Five Towns 'very friendly' means a lot.

'Perhaps if you were to leave us,' Ruth suggested, twisting her head to glance at Denry.

It was exactly what he desired to do. There could be no doubt that Ruth was supremely a woman of the world. Her tact was faultless.

He left them, saying to himself: 'Well, here's a go!'

In the hall, through an open door, he saw Councillor Cotterill standing against the dining-room mantelpiece.

When Cotterill caught sight of Denry he straightened himself into a certain uneasy perkiness.

'Young man,' he said in a counterfeit of his old patronizing tone, 'come in here. You may as well hear about it. You're a friend of ours. Come in and shut the door.'

Nellie was not in view.

Denry went in and shut the door.

'Sit down,' said Cotterill.

And it was just as if he had said: 'Now, you're a fairly bright sort of youth, and you haven't done so badly in life; and as a reward I mean to admit you to the privilege of hearing about our ill-luck, which for some mysterious reason reflects more credit on me than your good luck reflects on you, young man.'

And he stroked his straggling grey beard.

'I'm going to file my petition tomorrow,' said he, and gave a short laugh.

'Really!' said Denry, who could think of nothing else to say. His name was not Capron-Smith.

'Yes; they won't leave me any alternative,' said Mr Cotterill. Then he gave a brief history of his late commercial career to the young man. And he seemed to figure it as a sort of tug-of-war between his creditors and his debtors, he himself being the rope. He seemed to imply that he had always done his sincere best to attain the greatest good of the greatest number, but that those wrong-headed creditors had consistently thwarted him. However, he bore them no grudge. It was the fortune of the tug-of-war. He pretended, with shabby magnificence of spirit, that a bankruptcy at the age of near sixty, in a community where one has cut a figure, is a mere passing episode.

'Are you surprised?' he asked foolishly, with a sheepish smile.

Denry took vengeance for all the patronage that he had received during a decade.

'No!' he said. 'Are you?'

Instead of kicking Denry out of the house for an impudent young jackanapes, Mr Cotterill simply resumed his sheepish smile.

Denry had been surprised for a moment, but he had quickly recovered. Cotterill's downfall was one of those events which any person of acute intelligence can foretell after they have happened. Cotterill had run the risks of the speculative builder, built and mortgaged, built and mortgaged, sold at a profit, sold without profit, sold at a loss, and failed to sell, given bills, second mortgages, and third mortgages; and because he was a builder and could do nothing but build, he had continued to build in defiance of Bursley's lack of enthusiasm for his erections. If rich gold deposits had been discovered in Bursley Municipal Park, Cotterill would have owned a mining camp and amassed immense wealth; but unfortunately gold deposits were not discovered in the Park. Nobody knew his position; nobody ever does know the position of a speculative builder. He did not know it himself. There had been rumours, but they had been contradicted in an adequate way. His recent refusal of the mayoral chain, due to lack of spare coin, had been attributed to prudence. His domestic existence had always been conducted on the same moderately lavish scale. He had always paid the baker, the butcher, the tailor, the dressmaker.

And now he was to file his petition in bankruptcy, and tomorrow the entire town would have 'been seeing it coming' for years.

'What shall you do?' Denry inquired in amicable curiosity.

'Well,' said Cotterill, 'that's the point. I've got a brother a builder in Toronto, you know. He's doing very well; building *is* building over there. I wrote to him a bit since, and he replied by the next mail – by the next mail – that what he wanted was just a man like me to overlook things. He's getting an old man now, is John. So, you see, there's an opening waiting for me.'

As if to say, 'The righteous are never forsaken.'

'I tell you all this as you're a friend of the family like,' he added.

Then, after an expanse of vagueness, he began hopefully, cheerfully, undauntedly:

'Even *now* if I could get hold of a couple of thousand I could pull through handsome – and there's plenty of security for it.'

'Bit late now, isn't it?'

'Not it. If only some one who really knows the town, and has faith in the property market, would come down with a couple of thousand – well, he might double it in five years.'

'Really!'

'Yes,' said Cotterill. 'Look at Clare Street.'

Clare Street was one of his terra-cotta masterpieces.

'You, now,' said Cotterill, insinuating. 'I don't expect anyone can teach *you* much about the value of property in this town. You know as well as I do. If you happen to have a couple of thousand loose – by gosh! it's a chance in a million.'

'Yes,' said Denry. 'I should say that was just about what it was.'

'I put it before you,' Cotterill proceeded, gathering way, and missing the flavour of Denry's remark. 'Because you're a friend of the family. You're so often here. Why, it's pretty near ten years . . .'

Denry sighed: 'I expect I come and see you all about once a

fortnight fairly regular. That makes two hundred and fifty times in ten years. Yes . . .'

'A couple of thou',' said Cotterill, reflectively.

'Two hundred and fifty into two thousand – eight. Eight pounds a visit. A shade thick, Cotterill, a shade thick. You might be half a dozen fashionable physicians rolled into one.'

Never before had he called the Councillor 'Cotterill' unadorned. Mr Cotterill flushed and rose.

Denry does not appear to advantage in this interview. He failed in magnanimity. The only excuse that can be offered for him is that Mr Cotterill had called him 'young man' once or twice too often in the course of ten years. It is subtle.

III

'No,' whispered Ruth, in all her wraps. 'Don't bring it up to the door. I'll walk down with you to the gate, and get in there.'

He nodded.

They were off, together. Ruth, it had appeared, was actually staying at the Five Towns Hotel at Knype, which at that epoch was the only hotel in the Five Towns seriously pretending to be 'first-class' in the full-page advertisement sense. The fact that Ruth was staying at the Five Towns Hotel impressed Denry anew. Assuredly she did things in the grand manner. She had meant to walk down by the Park to Bursley Station and catch the last loop-line train to Knype, and when Denry suddenly disclosed the existence of his motor-car, and proposed to see her to her hotel in it, she in her turn had been impressed. The astonishment in her tone as she exclaimed: 'Have you got a *motor*?' was the least in the world naïve.

Thus they departed together from the stricken house, Ruth saying brightly to Nellie, who had reappeared in a painful state of demoralization, that she should return on the morrow.

And Denry went down the obscure drive with a final vision of the poor child, Nellie, as she stood at the door to speed them. It was extraordinary how that child had remained a child. He knew that she must be more than half-way through her twenties, and yet she persisted in being the merest girl. A delightful little thing; but no *savoir vivre*, no equality to a situation, no spectacular pride. Just a nice, bright girl, strangely girl-ish ... The Cotterills had managed that bad evening badly. They had shown no dignity, no reserve, no discretion; and old Cotterill had been simply fatuous in his suggestion. As for Mrs Cotterill, she was completely overcome, and it was due solely to Ruth's calm, managing influence that Nellie, nervous and whimpering, had wound herself up to come and shut the front door after the guests.

It was all very sad.

When he had successfully started the car, and they were sliding down the Moorthorne hill together, side by side, their shoulders touching, Denry threw off the nightmarish effect of the bankrupt household. After all, there was no reason why he should be depressed. He was not a bankrupt. He was steadily adding riches to riches. He acquired wealth mechanically now. Owing to the habits of his mother, he never came within miles of living up to his income. And Ruth – she, too, was wealthy. He felt that she must be wealthy in the strict significance of the term. And she completed wealth by experience of the world. She was his equal. She understood things in general. She had lived, travelled, suffered, reflected – in short, she was a completed article of manufacture. She was no little, clinging, raw girl. Further, she was less hard than of yore. Her voice and gestures had a different quality. The world had softened her. And it occurred to him suddenly that her sole fault – extravagance – had no importance now that she was wealthy.

He told her all that Mr Cotterill had said about Canada. And she told him all that Mrs Cotterill had said about Canada. And they agreed that Mr Cotterill had got his deserts, and that, in its own interest, Canada was the only thing for the Cotterill family; and the sooner the better. People must accept the consequences of bankruptcy. Nothing could be done.

'I think it's a pity Nellie should have to go,' said Denry.

'Oh! *Do* you?' replied Ruth.

'Yes; going out to a strange country like that. She's not what you may call the Canadian kind of girl. If she could only get something to do here ... If something could be found for her.'

'Oh, I don't agree with you at *all*,' said Ruth. 'Do you really think she ought to leave her parents just *now*? Her place is with her parents. And besides, between you and me, she'll have a much better chance of marrying there than in *this* town – after all this. Of course I shall be very sorry to lose her – and Mrs Cotterill, too. But . . .'

'I expect you're right,' Denry concurred.

And they sped on luxuriously through the lamp-lit night of the Five Towns. And Denry pointed out his house as they passed it. And they both thought much of the security of their positions in the world, and of their incomes; and of the honeyed deference of their bankers; and also of the mistake of being a failure . . . You could do nothing with a failure.

IV

On a frosty morning in early winter you might have seen them together in a different vehicle – a first-class compartment of the express from Knype to Liverpool. They had the compartment to themselves, and they were installed therein with every circumstance of luxury. Both were enwrapped in furs, and a fur rug united their knees in its shelter. Magazines and newspapers were scattered about to the value of a labourer's hire for a whole day; and when Denry's eye met the guard's it said 'shilling'. In short, nobody could possibly be more superb than they were on that morning in that compartment.

The journey was the result of peculiar events.

Mr Cotterill had made himself a bankrupt, and cast away the robe of a Town Councillor. He had submitted to the inquisitiveness of the Official Receiver, and to the harsh prying of those rampant baying beasts, his creditors. He had laid bare his books, his correspondence, his lack of method, his domestic extravagance, and the distressing fact that he had continued to trade long after he knew himself to be insolvent. He had for several months, in the interests of the said beasts, carried on his own business as manager at a nominal salary. And gradually everything that was his had been sold. And during the final weeks the Cotterill family had been obliged to quit their dismantled house and exist in lodgings. It had been arranged that they should go to Canada by way of Liverpool, and on the day before the journey of Denry and Ruth to Liverpool they had departed from the borough of Bursley (which Mr Cotterill had so extensively faced with terra-cotta) unhonoured and unsung. Even Denry, though he had visited them in their lodgings to say good-bye, had not seen them off at the station; but Ruth Capron-Smith had seen them off at the station. She had interrupted a sojourn to Southport in order to come to Bursley, and dispatch them therefrom with due friendliness. Certain matters had to be attended to after their departure, and Ruth had promised to attend to them.

Now immediately after seeing them off Ruth had met Denry in the street.

'Do you know,' she said brusquely, 'those people are actually going steerage? I'd no idea of it. Mr and Mrs Cotterill kept it from me, and I should not have heard of it only from something Nellie said. That's why they've gone today. The boat doesn't sail till tomorrow afternoon.'

'Steerage?' and Denry whistled.

'Yes,' said Ruth. 'Nothing but pride, of course. Old Cotterill wanted to have every penny he could scrape, so as to be able to make the least tiny bit of show when he gets to Toronto, and so – steerage! Just think of Mrs Cotterill and Nellie in the steerage. If I'd known of it I should have altered that, I can tell you, and pretty quickly too; and now it's too late.'

'No, it isn't,' Denry contradicted her flatly.

'But they've gone.'

'I could telegraph to Liverpool for saloon berths – there's bound to be plenty at this time of year – and I could run over to Liverpool tomorrow and catch 'em on the boat, and make 'em change.'

She asked him whether he really thought he could, and he assured her.

'Second-cabin berths would be better,' said she.

'Why?'

'Well, because of dressing for dinner, and so on. They haven't got the clothes, you know.'

'Of course,' said Denry.

'Listen,' she said, with an enchanting smile. 'Let's halve the cost, you and I. And let's go to Liverpool together, and – er – make the little gift, and arrange things. I'm leaving for Southport tomorrow, and Liverpool's on my way.'

Denry was delighted by the suggestion, and telegraphed to Liverpool with success.

Thus they found themselves on that morning in the Liverpool express together. The work of benevolence in which they were engaged had a powerful influence on their mood, which grew both intimate and tender. Ruth made no concealment of her regard for Denry; and as he gazed across the compartment at her, exquisitely mature (she was slightly older than himself), dressed to a marvel, perfect in every detail of manner, knowing all that was to be known about life, and secure in a handsome fortune – as he gazed, Denry reflected, joyously, victoriously:

'I've got the dibs, of course. But she's got 'em too – perhaps more. Therefore she must like me for myself alone. This brilliant creature has been everywhere and seen everything, and she comes back to the Five Towns and comes back to *me*.'

It was his proudest moment. And in it he saw his future far more glorious than he had dreamt.

'When shall you be out of mourning?' he inquired.

'In two months,' said she.

This was not a proposal and acceptance, but it was very nearly one. They were silent, and happy.

Then she said:

'Do you ever have business at Southport?'

And he said, in a unique manner:

'I shall have.'

Another silence. This time he felt he *would* marry her.

v

The White Star liner, *Titubic*, stuck out of the water like a row of houses against the landing-stage. There was a large crowd on her promenade-deck, and a still larger crowd on the landing-stage. Above the promenade-deck officers paced on the navigating deck, and above that was the airy bridge, and above that the funnels, smoking, and somewhere still higher a flag or two fluttering in the icy breeze. And behind the crown on the landing-stage stretched a row of four-wheeled cabs and rickety horses. The landing-stage swayed ever so slightly on the tide. Only the ship was apparently solid, apparently cemented in foundations of concrete.

On the starboard side of the promenade-deck, among a hundred other small groups, was a group consisting of Mr and Mrs Cotterill and Ruth and Denry. Nellie stood a few feet apart. Mrs Cotterill was crying. People naturally thought she was crying because of the adieux; but she was not. She wept because Denry and Ruth, by sheer force of will, had compelled them to come out of the steerage and occupy beautiful and commodious berths in the second cabin, where the manner of the stewards was quite different. She wept because they had been caught in the steerage. She wept because she was ashamed, and because people were too kind. She was at once delighted and desolated. She wanted to outpour psalms of gratitude, and also she wanted to curse.

Mr Cotterill said stiffly that he should repay – and that soon.

An immense bell sounded impatiently.

'We'd better be shunting,' said Denry. 'That's the second.'

In exciting crises he sometimes employed such peculiar language as this. And he was very excited. He had done a great deal of rushing about. The upraising of the Cotterill family from the social Hades of the steerage to the respectability of the second cabin had demanded all his energy, and a lot of Ruth's.

Ruth kissed Mrs Cotterill and then Nellie. And Mrs Cotterill and Nellie acquired rank and importance for the whole voyage by reason of being kissed in public by a woman so elegant and aristocratic as Ruth Capron-Smith.

And Denry shook hands. He looked brightly at the parents, but he could not look at Nellie; nor could she look at him; their handshaking was perfunctory. For months their playful intimacy had been in abeyance.

'Good-bye.'

'Good luck.'

'Thanks. Good-bye.'

'Good-bye.'

The horrible bell continued to insist.

'All non-passengers ashore! All ashore!'

The numerous gangways were thronged with people obeying the call, and handkerchiefs began to wave. And there was a regular vibrating tremor through the ship.

Mr and Mrs Cotterill turned away.

Ruth and Denry approached the nearest gangway, and Denry stood aside, and made a place for her to pass. And, as always, a number of women pushed into the gangways immediately after her, and Denry had to wait, being a perfect gentleman.

His eye caught Nellie's. She had not moved.

He felt then as he had never felt in his life. No, absolutely never. Her sad, her tragic glance rendered him so uncomfortable, and yet so deliciously uncomfortable, that the symptoms startled him. He wondered what would happen to his legs. He was not sure that he had legs.

However, he demonstrated the existence of his legs by running up to Nellie. Ruth was by this time swallowed in the crowd on the landing-stage. He looked at Nellie. Nellie looked at him. Her lips twitched.

'What am I doing here?' he asked of his soul.

She was not at all well dressed. She was indeed shabby – in a steerage style. Her hat was awry; her gloves miserable. No girlish pride in her distraught face. No determination to overcome Fate. No consciousness of ability to meet a bad situation. Just those sad eyes and those twitching lips.

'Look here,' Denry whispered, 'you must come ashore for a second. I've something I want to give you, and I've left it in the cab.'

'But there's no time. The bell's . . .'

'Bosh!' he exclaimed gruffly, extinguishing her timid, childish voice. 'You won't go for at least a quarter of an hour. All that's only a dodge to get people off in plenty of time. Come on, I tell you.'

And in a sort of hysteria he seized her thin, long hand and dragged her along the deck to another gangway, down whose steep slope they stumbled together. The crowd of sightseers and handkerchief-wavers jostled them. They could see nothing but heads and shoulders, and the great side of the ship rising above. Denry turned her back on the ship.

'This way.' He still held her hand.

He struggled to the cab-rank.

'Which one is it?' she asked.

'Any one. Never mind which. Jump in.' And to the first driver whose eye met his, he said : 'Lime Street Station.'

The gangways were being drawn away. A hoarse boom filled the air, and then a cheer.

'But I shall miss the boat,' the dazed girl protested.

'Jump in.'

He pushed her in.

'But I shall miss the . . .'

'I know you will,' he replied, as if angrily. 'Do you suppose I was going to let you go by that steamer? Not much.'

'But mother and father . . .'

'I'll telegraph. They'll get it on landing.'

'And where's Ruth?'

'*Be hanged to Ruth!*' he shouted furiously.

As the cab rattled over the cobbles the *Titubic* slipped away from the landing-stage. The irretrievable had happened.

Nellie burst into tears.

'Look here,' Denry said savagely. 'If you don't dry up, I shall have to cry myself.'

'What are you going to do with me?' she whimpered.

'Well, what do *you* think? I'm going to marry you, of course.'

His aggrieved tone might have been supposed to imply that people had tried to thwart him, but that he had no intention of being thwarted, nor of asking permissions, nor of conducting himself as anything but a fierce tyrant.

As for Nellie, she seemed to surrender.

Then he kissed her – also angrily. He kissed her several times – yes, even in Lord Street itself – less and less angrily.

'Where are you taking me to?' she inquired humbly, as a captive.

'I shall take you to my mother's,' he said.

'Will she like it?'

'She'll either like it or lump it,' said Denry. 'It'll take a fortnight.'

'What?'

'The notice, and things.'

In the train, in the midst of a great submissive silence, she
murmured:

'It'll be simply awful for father and mother.'

'That can't be helped,' said he. 'And they'll be far too sea-sick
to bother their heads about you.'

'You can't think how you've staggered me,' said she.

'You can't think how I've staggered myself,' said he.

'When did you decide to ...'

'When I was standing at the gangway, and you looked at me,'
he answered.

'But ...'

'It's no use butting,' he said. 'I'm like that ... That's me,
that is.'

It was the bare truth that he had staggered himself. But he
had staggered himself into a miraculous, ecstatic happiness. She
had no money, no clothes, no style, no experience, no particular
gifts. But she was she. And when he looked at her, calmed, he
knew that he had done well for himself. He knew that if he had
not yielded to that terrific impulse he would have done badly for
himself. Mrs Machin had what she called a ticklish night of it.

VI

The next day he received a note from Ruth, dated Southport,
inquiring how he came to lose her on the landing-stage, and
expressing concern. It took him three days to reply, and even
then the reply was a bad one. He had behaved infamously to
Ruth; so much could not be denied. Within three hours of
practically proposing to her, he had run off with a simple girl,
who was not fit to hold a candle to her. And he did not care.
That was the worst of it; he did not care.

Of course the facts reached her. The facts reached everybody;
for the singular reappearance of Nellie in the streets of Bursley

immediately after her departure for Canada had to be explained. Moreover, the infamous Denry was rather proud of the facts. And the town inevitably said: 'Machin all over, that! Snatching the girl off the blooming lugger. Machin all over.' And Denry agreed privately that it was Machin all over.

'What other chap,' he demanded of the air, 'would have thought of it? Or had the pluck? ...'

It was mere malice on the part of destiny that caused Denry to run across Mrs Capron-Smith at Euston some weeks later. Happily they both had immense nerve.

'Dear me,' said she. 'What are *you* doing here?'

'Only honeymooning,' he said.

CHAPTER II

In the Alps

ALTHOUGH Denry was extremely happy as a bridegroom, and capable of the most foolish symptoms of affection in private, he said to himself, and he said to Nellie (and she sturdily agreed with him): 'We aren't going to be the ordinary silly honeymooners.' By which, of course, he meant that they would behave so as to be taken for staid married persons. They failed thoroughly in this enterprise as far as London, where they spent a couple of nights, but on leaving Charing Cross they made a new and a better start, in the light of experience.

Their destination, it need hardly be said, was Switzerland. After Mrs Capron-Smith's remarks on the necessity of going to Switzerland in winter if one wished to respect one's self, there was really no alternative to Switzerland. Thus it was announced in the *Signal* (which had reported the wedding in ten lines, owing to the excessive quietude of the wedding) that Mr and Mrs Councillor Machin were spending a month at Mont Pridoux, sur Montreux, on the Lake of Geneva. And the announcement looked very well.

At Dieppe they got a through carriage. There were several through carriages for Switzerland on the train. In walking through the corridors from one to another Denry and Nellie had their first glimpse of the world which travels and which runs off for a holiday whenever it feels in the mood. The idea of going for a holiday in any month but August seemed odd to both of them. Denry was very bold and would insist on talking in a naturally loud voice. Nellie was timid and clinging. 'What do you say?' Denry would roar at her when she half-whispered something, and she had to repeat it so that all could hear. It was part of their plan to address each other curtly, brusquely, and to frown, and to pretend to be slightly bored by each other.

They were outclassed by the world which travels. Try as they might, even Denry was morally intimidated. He had managed his clothes fairly correctly; he was not ashamed of them; and Nellie's were by no means the worst in the compartment; indeed, according to the standard of some of the most intimidating women, Nellie's costume erred in not being quite sufficiently negligent, sufficiently 'anyhow'. And they had plenty, and ten times plenty of money, and the consciousness of it. Expense was not being spared on that honeymoon. And yet ... Well, all that can be said is that the company was imposing. The company, which was entirely English, seemed to be unaware that anyone ever did anything else but travel luxuriously to places mentioned in second-year geographies. It astounded Nellie that there should be so many people in the world with nothing to do but spend. And they were constantly saying the strangest things with an air of perfect calm.

'How much did you pay for the excess luggage?' an untidy young woman asked of an old man.

'Oh! Thirteen pounds,' answered the old man, carelessly.

And not long before Nellie had scarcely escaped ten days in the steerage of an Atlantic liner.

After dinner in the restaurant car – no champagne, because it was vulgar, but a good sound, expensive wine – they felt more equal to the situation, more like part-owners of the train. Nellie prudently went to bed ere the triumphant feeling wore off. But Denry stayed up smoking in the corridor. He stayed up very late, being too proud and happy and too avid of new sensations to be able to think of sleep. It was a match which led to a conversation between himself and a thin, drawling, overbearing fellow with an eyeglass. Denry had hated this lordly creature all the way from Dieppe. In presenting him with a match he felt that he was somehow getting the better of him, for the match was precious in the nocturnal solitude of the vibrating corridor. The mere fact that two people are alone together and awake, divided from a sleeping or sleepy population only by a row of closed, mysterious doors, will do much to break down social barriers. The excellence of Denry's cigar also helped. It atoned for the breadth of his accent.

He said to himself:

'I'll have a bit of a chat with this johnny.'

And then he said aloud:

'Not a bad train this!'

'No!' the eyeglass agreed languidly. 'Pity they give you such a beastly dinner!'

And Denry agreed hastily that it was.

Soon they were chatting of places, and somehow it came out of Denry that he was going to Montreux. The eyeglass professed its indifference to Montreux in winter, but said the resorts above Montreux were all right, such as Caux or Pridoux.

And Denry said:

'Well, of course, shouldn't think of stopping *in* Montreux. Going to try Pridoux.'

The eyeglass said it wasn't going so far as Switzerland yet; it meant to stop in the Jura.

'Geneva's a pretty deadly place, ain't it?' said the eyeglass after a pause.

'Ye-es,' said Denry.

'Been there since that new esplanade was finished?'

'No,' said Denry. 'I saw nothing of it.'

'When were you there?'

'Oh! A couple of years ago.'

'Ah! It wasn't started then. Comic thing! Of course they're awfully proud in Geneva of the view of Mont Blanc.'

'Yes,' said Denry.

'Ever noticed how queer women are about that view? They're no end keen on it at first, but after a day or two it gets on their nerves.'

'Yes,' said Denry. 'I've noticed that myself. My wife . . .'

He stopped, because he didn't know what he was going to say. The eyeglass nodded understandingly.

'All alike,' it said. 'Odd thing!'

When Denry introduced himself into the two-berth compartment which he had managed to secure at the end of the carriage for himself and Nellie, the poor tired child was as wakeful as an owl.

'Who have you been talking to?' she yawned.

'The eyeglass johnny.'

189

'Oh! Really,' Nellie murmured, interested and impressed. 'With him, have you? I could hear voices. What sort of a man is he?'

'He seems to be an ass,' said Denry. 'Fearfully haw-haw. Couldn't stand him for long. I've made him believe we've been married for two years.'

II

They stood on the balcony of the Hôtel Beau-Site of Mont Pridoux. A little below, to the right, was the other hotel, the Métropole, with the red-and-white Swiss flag waving over its central tower. A little below that was the terminal station of the funicular railway from Montreux. The railway ran down the sheer of the mountain into the roofs of Montreux, like a wire. On it, two toy trains crawled towards each other, like flies climbing and descending a wall. Beyond the fringe of hotels that constituted Montreux was a strip of water, and beyond the water a range of hills white at the top.

'So these are the Alps!' Nellie exclaimed.

She was disappointed; he also. But when Denry learnt from the guidebook and by inquiry that the strip of lake was seven miles across, and the highest notched peaks ten thousand feet above the sea and twenty-five miles off, Nellie gasped and was content.

They liked the Hôtel Beau-Site. It had been recommended to Denry, by a man who knew what was what, as the best hotel in Switzerland. 'Don't you be misled by prices,' the man had said. And Denry was not. He paid sixteen francs a day for the two of them at the Beau-Site, and was rather relieved than otherwise by the absence of finger-bowls. Everything was very good, except sometimes the hot water. The hot-water cans bore the legend 'hot water', but these two words were occasionally the only evidence of heat in the water. On the other hand, the bedrooms could be made sultry by merely turning a handle; and the windows were double. Nellie was wondrously inventive. They breakfasted in bed, and she would save butter and honey from the breakfast to furnish forth afternoon tea, which was not included in the terms. She served the butter freshly with ice by the simple expedient of leaving it outside the window of a night. And Denry was struck by this house-wifery.

The other guests appeared to be of a comfortable, companionable class, with, as Denry said, 'no frills'. They were amazed to learn that a chattering little woman of thirty-five, who gossiped with everybody, and soon invited Denry and Nellie to have tea in her room, was an authentic Russian Countess, inscribed in the visitors' lists as 'Comtesse Ruhl (with maid), Moscow'. Her room was the untidiest that Nellie had ever seen, and the tea a picnic. Still, it was thrilling to have had tea with a Russian Countess ... (Plots! Nihilism! Secret police! Marble-palaces!) ... Those visitors' lists were breath-taking. Pages and pages of them; scores of hotels, thousands of names, nearly all English – and all people who came to Switzerland in winter, having naught else to do. Denry and Nellie bathed in correctness as in a bath.

The only persons in the hotel with whom they did not 'get on' nor 'hit it off' were a military party, chiefly named Clutterbuck, and presided over by a Major Clutterbuck and his wife. They sat at a large table in a corner – father, mother, several children, a sister-in-law, a sister, a governess – eight heads in all; and while utterly polite they seemed to draw a ring round themselves. They grumbled at the hotel; they played bridge (then a newish game); and once, when Denry and the Countess played with them (Denry being an adept card-player) for shilling points, Denry overheard the sister-in-law say that she was sure Captain Deverax wouldn't play for shilling points. This was the first rumour of the existence of Captain Deverax; but afterwards Captain Deverax began to be mentioned several times a day. Captain Deverax was coming to join them, and it seemed that he was a very particular man. Soon all the rest of the hotel had got its back up against this arriving Captain Deverax. Then a Clutterbuck cousin came, a smiling, hard, fluffy woman, and pronounced definitely that the Hôtel Beau-Site would never do for Captain Deverax. This cousin aroused Denry's hostility in a strange way. She imparted to the Countess (who united all sects) her opinion that Denry and Nellie were on their honeymoon. At night in a corner of the drawing-room the Countess delicately but bluntly asked Nellie if she had been married long. 'No,' said Nellie. 'A month?' asked the Countess, smiling. 'N-no,' said Nellie.

The next day all the hotel knew. The vast edifice of make-believe that Denry and Nellie had laboriously erected crumbled at a word, and they stood forth, those two, blushing for the criminals they were.

The hotel was delighted. There is more rejoicing in a hotel over one honeymoon couple than over fifty families with children.

But the hotel had a shock the same day. The Clutterbuck cousin had proclaimed that owing to the inadequacy of the bedroom furniture she had been obliged to employ a sofa as a wardrobe. Then there were more references to Captain Deverax. And then at dinner it became known – Heaven knows how! – that the entire Clutterbuck party had given notice and was seceding to the Hôtel Métropole. Also they had tried to carry the Countess with them, but had failed.

Now, among the guests of the Hôtel Beau-Site there had always been a professed scorn of the rival Hôtel Métropole, which was a franc a day dearer, and famous for its new and rich furniture. The Métropole had an orchestra twice a week, and the English Church services were held in its drawing-room; and it was larger than the Beau-Site. In spite of these facts the clients of the Beau-Site affected to despise it, saying that the food was inferior and that the guests were snobbish. It was an article of faith in the Beau-Site that the Beau-Site was the best hotel on the mountain-side, if not in Switzerland.

The insolence of this defection on the part of the Clutterbucks! How on earth *could* people have the face to go to a landlord and say to him that they meant to desert him in favour of his rival?

Another detail: the secession of nine or ten people from one hotel to the other meant that the Métropole would decidedly be more populous than the Beau-Site, and on the point of numbers the emulation was very keen. 'Well,' said the Beau-Site, 'let 'em go! With their Captain Deverax! We shall be better without 'em!' And that deadliest of all feuds sprang up – a rivalry between the guests of rival hotels. The Métropole had issued a general invitation to a dance, and after the monstrous conduct of the Clutterbucks the question arose whether the Beau-Site should not boycott the dance. However, it was settled that the truly effective course would be to go with critical noses in the air, and emit unfavourable comparisons with the Beau-Site. The Beau-Site suddenly became perfect in the esteem of its patrons. Not another word was heard on the subject of hot water being coated with ice. And the Clutterbucks, with incredible assurance, slid their luggage off in a sleigh to the Métropole, in the full light of day, amid the contempt of the faithful.

<h2 style="text-align:center">III</h2>

Under the stars the dancing section of the Beau-Site went off in jingling sleighs over the snow to the ball at the Métropole. The distance was not great, but it was great enough to show the inadequacy of furs against twenty degrees of mountain frost, and it was also great enough to allow the party to come to a general final understanding that its demeanour must be cold and critical in the gilded halls of the Métropole. The rumour ran that Captain Deverax had arrived, and everyone agreed that he must be an insufferable booby, except the Countess Ruhl, who never used her fluent exotic English to say ill of anybody.

The gilded halls of the Métropole certainly were imposing. The hotel was incontestably larger than the Beau-Site, newer, more richly furnished. Its occupants, too, had a lordly way with them, trying to others, but inimitable. Hence the visitors from the Beau-Site, as they moved to and fro beneath those crystal chandeliers from Tottenham Court Road, had their work cut out to maintain the mien of haughty indifference. Nellie, for instance, frankly could not do it. And Denry did not do it very well. Denry, nevertheless, did score one point over Mrs Clutterbuck's fussy cousin.

'Captain Deverax has come,' said this latter. 'He was very late. He'll be downstairs in a few minutes. We shall get him to lead the cotillon.'

'Captain Deverax?' Denry questioned.

'Yes. You've heard us mention him,' said the cousin, affronted.

'Possibly,' said Denry. 'I don't remember.'

On hearing this brief colloquy the cohorts of the Beau-Site felt that in Denry they possessed the making of a champion.

There was a disturbing surprise, however, waiting for Denry.

The lift descended, and with a peculiar double action of his arms on the doors, like a pantomime fairy emerging from an enchanted castle, a tall thin man stepped elegantly out of the lift and approached the company with a certain mincingness. But before he could reach the company several young women had rushed towards him, as though with the intention of committing suicide by hanging themselves from his neck. He was in an evening suit so perfect in detail that it might have sustained comparison with the costume of the head waiter. And he wore an eyeglass in his left eye. It was the eyeglass that made Denry jump. For two seconds he dismissed the notion . . . But another two seconds of examination showed beyond doubt that this eyeglass was the eyeglass of the train. And Denry had apprehensions . . .

'Captain Deverax !' exclaimed several voices.

The manner in which the youthful and the mature fair clustered around the Captain, aged forty (and not handsome) was really extraordinary, to the males of the Hôtel Beau-Site. Even the little Russian Countess attached herself to him at once. And by reason of her title, her social energy, and her personal distinction, she took natural precedence of the others.

'Recognize him ?' Denry whispered to his wife.

Nellie nodded. 'He seems rather nice,' she said diffidently.

'Nice!' Denry repeated the adjective. 'The man's an ass!'

And the majority of the Beau-Site party agreed with Denry's verdict either by word or gesture.

Captain Deverax stared fixedly at Denry; then smiled vaguely and drawled, 'Hullo! How d' do?'

And they shook hands.

'So you know him?' some one murmured to Denry.

'Know him? . . . Since infancy.'

The inquirer scented facetiousness, but he was somehow impressed. The remarkable thing was that though he regarded Captain Deverax as a popinjay, he could not help feeling a certain slight satisfaction in the fact that they were in some sort acquaintances ... Mystery of the human heart! ... He wished sincerely that he had not, in his conversation with the Captain in the train, talked about previous visits to Switzerland. It was dangerous.

The dance achieved that brightness and joviality which entitle a dance to call itself a success. The cotillon reached brilliance, owing to the captaincy of Captain Deverax. Several score opprobrious epithets were applied to the Captain in the course of the night, but it was agreed *nemine contradicente* that, whatever he would have done in front of a Light Brigade at Balaclava, as a leader of cotillons he was terrific. Many men, however, seemed to argue that if a man who *was* a man led a cotillon, he ought not to lead it too well, on pain of being considered a coxcomb.

At the close, during the hot soup, the worst happened. Denry had known that it would.

Captain Deverax was talking to Nellie, who was respectfully listening, about the scenery, when the Countess came up, plate in hand.

'No, no,' the Countess protested. 'As for me, I hate your mountains. I was born in the steppe where it is all level – level! Your mountains close me in. I am only here by order of my doctor. Your mountains get on my nerves.' She shrugged her shoulders.

Captain Deverax smiled.

'It is the same with you, isn't it?' he said, turning to Nellie.

'Oh, no,' said Nellie, simply.

'But your husband told me the other day that when you and he were in Geneva a couple of years ago, the view of Mont Blanc used to – er – upset you.'

'View of Mont Blanc?' Nellie stammered.

Everybody was aware that she and Denry had never been in Switzerland before, and that their marriage was indeed less than a month old.

'You misunderstood me,' said Denry, gruffly. 'My wife hasn't been to Geneva.'

'Oh!' drawled Captain Deverax.

His 'Oh!' contained so much of insinuation, disdain, and lofty amusement that Denry blushed, and when Nellie saw her husband's cheek she blushed in competition and defeated him easily. It was felt that either Denry had been romancing to the Captain, or that he had been married before, unknown to his Nellie, and had been 'carrying on' at Geneva. The situation, though it dissolved of itself in a brief space, was awkward. It discredited the Hôtel Beau-Site. It was in the nature of a repulse for he Hôtel Beau-Site (franc a day cheaper than the Métropole) and of a triumph for the popinjay. The fault was utterly Denry's. Yet he said to himself:

'I'll be even with that chap.'

On the drive home he was silent. The theme of conversation in the sleighs which did not contain the Countess was that the Captain had flirted tremendously with the Countess, and that it amounted to an affair.

IV

Captain Deverax was equally salient in the department of sports. There was a fair sheet of ice, obtained by cutting into the side of the mountain, and a very good tobogganing track, about half a mile in length and full of fine curves, common to the two hotels. Denry's predilection was for the track. He would lie on his stomach on the little contrivance which the Swiss call a luge, and which consists of naught but three bits of wood and two steel-clad runners, and would course down the perilous curves at twenty miles an hour. Until the Captain came, this was regarded as dashing, because most people were content to sit on the luge and travel legs-foremost instead of head-foremost. But the Captain, after a few eights on the ice, intimated that for the rest no sport was true sport save the sport of ski-running. He allowed it to be understood that luges were for infants. He had brought his skis, and these instruments of locomotion, some six feet in length, made a sensation among the inexperienced. For when he had strapped them to his feet the Captain, while stating candidly that his skill was as nothing to that of the Swedish professionals at St Moritz, could assuredly slide over snow in manner prodigious and beautiful. And he was exquisitely clothed for the part. His knickerbockers, in the elegance of their lines, were the delight of beholders. Ski-ing became the rage. Even Nellie insisted on hiring a pair. And the pronunciation of the word 'ski' aroused long discussions and was never definitely settled by anybody. The Captain said 'skee', but he did not object to 'shee', which was said to be the more strictly correct by a lady who knew some one who had been to Norway. People with no shame and no feeling for correctness said brazenly, 'sky'. Denry, whom nothing could induce to desert his luge, said that obviously 's-k-i' could only spell 'planks'. And thanks to his inspiration this version was adopted by the majority.

On the second day of Nellie's struggle with her skis she had more success than she either anticipated or desired. She had been making experiments at the summit of the track, slithering about, falling, and being restored to uprightness by as many persons as happened to be near. Skis seemed to her to be the most ungovernable and least practical means of travel that the madness of man had ever concocted. Skates were well-behaved old horses compared to these long, untamed fiends, and a luge was like a tricycle. Then suddenly a friendly starting push drove her a yard or two, and she glided past the level on to the first imperceptible slope of the track. By some hazard her two planks were exactly parallel, as they ought to be, and she glided forward miraculously. And people heard her say:

'How lovely!'

And then people heard her say:

'Oh!... Oh!'

For her pace was increasing. And she dared not strike her pole into the ground. She had, in fact, no control whatever over those two planks to which her feet were strapped. She might have been Mazeppa and they mustangs. She could not even fall. So she fled down the preliminary straight of the track, and ecstatic spectators cried: 'Look how *well* Mrs Machin is doing!'

Mrs Machin would have given all her furs to be anywhere off those planks. On the adjacent fields of glittering snow the Captain had been giving his adored Countess a lesson in the use of skis; and they stood together, the Countess somewhat insecure, by the side of the track at its first curve.

Nellie, dumb with excitement and amazement, swept towards them.

'Look out!' cried the Captain.

In vain! He himself might perhaps have escaped, but he could not abandon his Countess in the moment of peril, and the Countess could only move after much thought and many efforts, being scarce more advanced than Nellie. Nellie's wilful planks quite ignored the curve, and, as it were afloat on them, she charged off the track, and into the Captain and the Countess. The impact was tremendous. Six skis waved like semaphores in the air. Then all was still. Then, as the beholders hastened to the scene of the disaster, the Countess laughed and Nellie laughed. The laugh of the Captain was not heard. The sole casualty was a wound about a foot long in the hinterland of the Captain's unique knickerbockers. And as threads of that beautiful check pattern were afterwards found attached to the wheel of Nellie's pole, the cause of the wound was indisputable. The Captain departed home, chiefly backwards, but with great rapidity.

In the afternoon Denry went down to Montreux and returned with an opal bracelet, which Nellie wore at dinner.

'Oh! What a ripping bracelet!' said a girl.

'Yes,' said Nellie. 'My husband gave it me only today.'

'I suppose it's your birthday or something,' the inquisitive girl ventured.

'No,' said Nellie.

'How nice of him!' said the girl.

The next day Captain Deverax appeared in riding breeches. They were not correct for ski-running, but they were the best he could do. He visited a tailor's in Montreux.

v

The Countess Ruhl had a large sleigh of her own, also a horse; both were hired from Montreux. In this vehicle, sometimes alone, sometimes with a male servant, she would drive at Russian speed over the undulating mountain roads; and for such expeditions she always wore a large red cloak with a hood. Often she was thus seen, in the afternoon; the scarlet made a bright moving patch on the vast expanses of snow. Once, at some distance from the village, two tale-tellers observed a man on skis careering in the neighbourhood of the sleigh. It was Captain Deverax. The flirtation, therefore, was growing warmer and warmer. The hotels hummed with the tidings of it. But the Countess never said anything; nor could anything be extracted from her by even the most experienced gossips. She was an agreeable but a mysterious woman, as befitted a Russian Countess. Again and again were she and the Captain seen together afar off in the landscape. Certainly it was a novelty in flirtations. People wondered what might happen between the two at the fancy-dress ball which the Hôtel Beau-Site was to give in return for the hospitality of the Hôtel Métropole. The ball was offered not in love, but in emulation, almost in hate; for the jealousy displayed by the Beau-Site against the increasing insolence of the Métropole had become acute. The airs of the Captain and his lieges, the Clutterbuck party, had reached the limit of the Beau-Site's endurance. The Métropole seemed to take it for granted that the Captain would lead the cotillon at the Beau-Site's ball as he had led it at the Métropole's.

And then, on the very afternoon of the ball, the Countess received a telegram – it was said from St Petersburg – which necessitated her instant departure. And she went, in an hour, down to Montreux by the funicular railway, and was lost to the Beau-Site. This was a blow to the prestige of the Beau-Site. For the Countess was its chief star, and, moreover, much loved by her fellow-guests, despite her curious weakness for the popinjay, and the mystery of her outings with him.

In the stables Denry saw the Countess's hired sleigh and horse, and in the sleigh her glowing red cloak. And he had one of his ideas, which he executed, although snow was beginning to fall. In ten minutes he and Nellie were driving forth, and Nellie in the red cloak held the reins. Denry, in a coachman's furs, sat behind. They whirled past the Hôtel Métropole. And shortly afterwards, on the wild road towards Attalens, Denry saw a pair of skis scudding as quickly as skis can scud in their rear. It was astonishing how the sleigh, with all the merry jingle of its bells, kept that pair of skis at a distance of about a hundred yards. It seemed to invite the skis to overtake it, and then to regret the invitation and flee further. Up the hills it would crawl, for the skis climbed slowly. Down them it galloped, for the skis slid on the slopes at a dizzy pace. Occasionally a shout came from the skis. And the snow fell thicker and thicker. So for four or five miles. Starlight commenced. Then the road made a huge descending curve round a hollowed meadow, and the horse galloped its best. But the skis, making a straight line down the snow, acquired the speed of an express, and gained on the sleigh one yard in every three. At the bottom, where the curve met the straight line, was a farmhouse and outbuildings and a hedge and a stone wall and other matters. The sleigh arrived at the point first, but only by a trifle. 'Mind your toes,' Denry muttered to himself, meaning an injunction to the skis, whose toes were three feet long. The skis, through the eddying snow, yelled frantically to the sleigh to give room. The skis shot up into the road, and in swerving aside swerved into a snow-laden hedge, and clean over it into the farmyard, where they stuck themselves up in the air, as skis will when the person to whose feet they are attached is lying prone. The door of the farm opened and a woman appeared.

She saw the skis at her doorstep. She heard the sleigh-bells, but the sleigh had already vanished into the dusk.

'Well, that was a bit of a lark, that was, Countess!' said Denry to Nellie. 'That will be something to talk about. We'd better drive home through Corsier, and quick too! It'll be quite dark soon.'

'Supposing he's dead!' Nellie breathed, aghast, reining in the horse.

'Not he!' said Denry. 'I saw him beginning to sit up.'

'But how will he get home?'

'It looks a very nice farmhouse,' said Denry. 'I should think he'd be sorry to leave it.'

VI

When Denry entered the dining-room of the Beau-Site, which had been cleared for the ball, his costume drew attention not so much by its splendour or ingenuity as by its peculiarity. He wore a short Chinese-shaped jacket, which his wife had made out of blue linen, and a flat Chinese hat to match, which they had constructed together on a basis of cardboard. But his thighs were enclosed in a pair of absurdly ample riding-breeches of an impressive check and cut to a comic exaggeration of the English pattern. He had bought the cloth for these at the tailor's in Montreux. Below them were very tight leggings, also English. In reply to a question as to what or whom he supposed himself to represent, he replied:

'A Captain of Chinese cavalry, of course.'

And he put an eyeglass into his left eye and stared.

Now it had been understood that Nellie was to appear as Lady Jane Grey. But she appeared as Little Red Riding-Hood, wearing over her frock the forgotten cloak of the Countess Ruhl.

Instantly he saw her, Denry hurried towards her, with a movement of the legs and a flourish of the eyeglass in his left hand which powerfully suggested a figure familiar to every member of the company. There was laughter. People saw that the idea was immensely funny and clever, and the laughter ran about like fire. At the same time some persons were not quite sure whether Denry had not lapsed a little from the finest taste in this caricature. And all of them were secretly afraid that the uncomfortable might happen when Captain Deverax arrived.

However, Captain Deverax did not arrive. The party from the Métropole came with the news that he had not been seen at the hotel for dinner; it was assumed that he had been to Montreux and missed the funicular back.

'Our two stars simultaneously eclipsed!' said Denry, as the Clutterbucks (representing all the history of England) stared at him curiously.

'Why?' exclaimed the Clutterbuck cousin, 'who's the other?'

'The Countess,' said Denry. 'She went this afternoon — three o'clock.'

And all the Métropole party fell into grief.

'It's a world of coincidences,' said Denry, with emphasis.

'You don't mean to insinuate,' said Mrs Clutterbuck, with a nervous laugh, 'that Captain Deverax has – er – gone after the Countess?'

'Oh no!' said Denry, with unction. 'Such a thought never entered my head.'

'I think you're a very strange man, Mr Machin,' retorted Mrs Clutterbuck, hostile and not a bit reassured. 'May one ask what that costume is supposed to be?'

'A Captain of Chinese cavalry,' said Denry, lifting his eyeglass.

Nevertheless, the dance was a remarkable success, and little by little even the sternest adherents of the absent Captain Deverax deigned to be amused by Denry's Chinese gestures. Also, Denry led the cotillon, and was thereafter greatly applauded by the Beau-Site. The visitors agreed among themselves that, considering that his name was not Deverax, Denry acquitted himself honourably. Later he went to the bureau, and, returning, whispered to his wife:

'It's all right. He's come back safe.'

'How do you know?'

'I've just telephoned to ask.'

Denry's subsequent humour was wildly gay. And for some reason which nobody could comprehend, he put a sling round his left arm. His efforts to insert the eyeglass into his left eye with his right hand were insistently ludicrous and became a sure source of laughter for all beholders. When the Métropole party were getting into their sleighs to go home – it had ceased snowing – Denry was still trying to insert his eyeglass into his left eye with his right hand, to the universal joy.

VII

But the joy of the night was feeble in comparison with the violent joy of the next morning. Denry was wandering, apparently aimless, between the finish of the tobogganing track and the portals of the Métropole. The snowfall had repaired the defects of the worn track, but it needed to be flattened down by use, and a number of conscientious *lugeurs* were flattening it by frequent descents, which grew faster at each repetition. Other holiday-makers were idling about in the sunshine. A page-boy of the Métropole departed in the direction of the Beau-Site with a note.

At length – the hour was nearing eleven – Captain Deverax, languid, put his head out of the Métropole and sniffed the air. Finding the air sufferable, he came forth on to the steps. His left arm was in a sling. He was wearing the new knickerbockers which he had ordered at Montreux, and which were of precisely the same vast check as had ornamented Denry's legs on the previous night.

'Hullo !' said Denry, sympathetically. 'What's this ?'

The Captain needed sympathy.

'Ski-ing yesterday afternoon,' said he, with a little laugh. 'Hasn't the Countess told any of you?'

'No,' said Denry, 'not a word.'

The Captain seemed to pause a moment.

'Yes,' said he. 'A trifling accident. I was ski-ing with the Countess. That is, I was ski-ing and she was in her sleigh.'

'Then this is why you didn't turn up at the dance?'

'Yes,' said the Captain.

'Well,' said Denry, 'I hope it's not serious. I can tell you one thing, the cotillon was a most fearful frost without you.' The Captain seemed grateful.

They strolled together towards the track.

The first group of people that caught sight of the Captain with his checked legs and his arm in a sling began to smile. Observing this smile, and fancying himself deceived, the Captain attempted to put his eyeglass into his left eye with his right hand, and regularly failed. His efforts towards this feat changed the smiles to enormous laughter.

'I daresay it's awfully funny,' said he. 'But what can a fellow do with one arm in a sling?'

The laughter was merely intensified. And the group, growing as luge after luge arrived at the end of the track, seemed to give itself up to mirth, to the exclusion of even a proper curiosity about the nature of the Captain's damage. Each fresh attempt to put the eyeglass to his eye was coal on the crackling fire. The Clutterbucks alone seemed glum.

'What on earth is the joke?' Denry asked primly. 'Captain Deverax came to grief late yesterday afternoon, ski-ing with the Countess Ruhl. That's why he didn't turn up last night. By the way, where was it, Captain?'

'On the mountain, near Attalens,' Deverax answered gloomily. 'Happily there was a farmhouse near – it was almost dark.'

'With the Countess?' demanded a young impulsive schoolgirl.

'You did say the Countess, didn't you?' Denry asked.

'Why, certainly,' said the Captain, testily.

'Well,' said the schoolgirl with the nonchalant thoughtless cruelty of youth, 'considering that we all saw the Countess off in the funicular at three o'clock, I don't see how you could have been ski-ing with her when it was nearly dark.' And the child turned up the hill with her luge, leaving her elders to unknot the situation.

'Oh, yes!' said Denry. 'I forgot to tell you that the Countess left yesterday after lunch.'

At the same moment the page-boy, reappearing, touched his cap and placed a note in the Captain's only free hand.

'Couldn't deliver it, sir. The Comtesse left early yesterday afternoon.'

Convicted of imaginary adventure with noble ladies, the Captain made his retreat, muttering, back to the hotel. At lunch Denry related the exact circumstances to a delighted table, and the exact circumstances soon reached the Clutterbuck faction at the Métropole. On the following day the Clutterbuck faction and Captain Deverax (now fully enlightened) left Mont Pridoux for some paradise unknown. If murderous thoughts could kill, Denry would have lain dead. But he survived to go with about half the Beau-Site guests to the funicular station to wish the Clutterbucks a pleasant journey. The Captain might have challenged him to a duel, but a haughty and icy ceremoniousness was deemed the best treatment for Denry. 'Never show a wound' must have been the Captain's motto.

The Beau-Site had scored effectively. And, now that its rival had lost eleven clients by one single train, it beat the Métropole even in vulgar numbers.

Denry had an embryo of a conscience somewhere, and Nellie's was fully developed.

'Well,' said Denry, in reply to Nellie's conscience, 'it serves him right for making me look a fool over that Geneva business. And besides, I can't stand uppishness, and I won't. I'm from the Five Towns, I am.'

Upon which singular utterance the incident closed.

CHAPTER 12

The Supreme Honour

I

DENRY was not as regular in his goings and comings as the generality of business men in the Five Towns; no doubt because he was not by nature a business man at all, but an adventurous spirit who happened to be in a business which was much too good to leave. He was continually, as they say there, 'up to something' that caused changes in daily habits. Moreover, the Universal Thrift Club (Limited) was so automatic and self-winding that Denry ran no risks in leaving it often to the care of his highly drilled staff. Still, he did usually come home to his tea about six o'clock of an evening, like the rest, and like the rest, he brought with him a copy of the *Signal* to glance at during tea.

One afternoon in July he arrived thus upon his waiting wife at Machin House, Bleakridge. And she could see that an idea was fermenting in his head. Nellie understood him. One of the most delightful and reassuring things about his married life was Nellie's instinctive comprehension of him. His mother understood him profoundly. But she understood him in a manner sardonic, slightly malicious and even hostile, whereas Nellie understood him with her absurd love. According to his mother's attitude, Denry was guilty till he had proved himself innocent. According to Nellie's, he was always right and always clever in what he did, until he himself said that he had been wrong and stupid — and not always then. Nevertheless, his mother was just as ridiculously proud of him as Nellie was; but she would have perished on the scaffold rather than admit that Denry differed in any detail from the common run of sons. Mrs Machin had departed from Machin House without waiting to be asked. It was characteristic of her that she had returned to Brougham Street and rented there an out-of-date cottage without a single one of the labour-saving contrivances that distinguished the residence which her son had originally built for her.

It was still delicious for Denry to sit down to tea in the dining-room, that miracle of conveniences, opposite the smile of his wife, which told him (a) that he was wonderful, (b) that she was enchanted to be alive, and (c) that he had deserved her particular caressing attentions and would receive them. On the afternoon in July the smile told him (d) that he was possessed by one of his ideas.

'Extraordinary how she tumbles to things!' he reflected.

Nellie's new fox-terrier had come in from the garden through the French window, and eaten part of a muffin, and Denry had eaten a muffin and a half, before Nellie, straightening herself proudly and putting her shoulders back (a gesture of hers) thought fit to murmur:

'Well, anything thrilling happened today?'

Denry opened the green sheet and read:

'"Sudden death of Alderman Bloor in London." What price that?'

'Oh!' exclaimed Nellie. 'How shocked father will be! They were always rather friendly. By the way, I had a letter from mother this morning. It appears as if Toronto was a sort of paradise. But you can see the old thing prefers Bursley. Father's had a boil on his neck, just at the edge of his collar. He says it's because he's too well. What did Mr Bloor die of?'

'He was in the fashion,' said Denry.

'How?'

'Appendicitis, of course. Operation – domino! All over in three days.'

'Poor man!' Nellie murmured, trying to feel sad for a change and not succeeding. 'And he was to have been mayor in November, wasn't he? How disappointing for him.'

'I expect he's got something else to think about,' said Denry.

After a pause Nellie asked suddenly:

'Who'll be mayor – now?'

'Well,' said Denry, 'his Worship Councillor Barlow, J.P., will be extremely cross if *he* isn't.'

'How horrid!' said Nellie, frankly. 'And he's got nobody at all to be mayoress.'

'Mrs Prettyman would be mayoress,' said Denry. 'When there's no wife or daughter, it's always a sister if there is one.'

'But can you *imagine* Mrs Prettyman as mayoress? Why, they say she scrubs her own doorstep – after dark. They ought to make you mayor.'

'Do you fancy yourself as mayoress?' he inquired.

'I should be better than Mrs Prettyman, anyhow.'

'I believe you'd make an A1 mayoress,' said Denry.

'I should be frightfully nervous,' she confidentially admitted.

'I doubt it,' said he.

The fact was, that since her return to Bursley from the honeymoon, Nellie was an altered woman. She had acquired, as it were in a day, to an astonishing extent, what in the Five Towns is called 'a nerve'.

'I should like to try it,' said she.

'One day you'll have to try it, whether you want to or not.'

'When will that be?'

'Don't know. Might be next year but one. Old Barlow's pretty certain to be chosen for next November. It's looked on as his turn next. I know there's been a good bit of talk about me for the year after Barlow. Of course, Bloor's death will advance everything by a year. But even if I come next after Barlow it'll be too late.'

'Too late? Too late for what?'

'I'll tell you,' said Denry. 'I wanted to be the youngest mayor that Bursley's ever had. It was only a kind of notion I had a long time ago. I'd given it up, because I knew there was no chance unless I came before Bloor, which of course I couldn't do. Now he's dead. If I could upset old Barlow's apple-cart I should just be the youngest mayor by the skin of my teeth. Huskinson, the mayor in 1884, was aged thirty-four and six months. I've looked it all up this afternoon.'

'How lovely if you *could* be the youngest mayor!'

'Yes. I'll tell you how I feel. I feel as though I didn't want to be mayor at all if I can't be the youngest mayor . . . you know.'

She knew.

'Oh!' she cried, 'do upset Mr Barlow's apple-cart. He's a horrid old thing. Should I be the youngest mayoress?'

'Not by chalks,' said he. 'Huskinson's sister was only sixteen.'

'But that's only playing at being mayoress!' Nellie protested.

'Anyhow, I do think you might be youngest mayor. Who settles it?'

'The Council, of course.'

'Nobody likes Councillor Barlow.'

'He'll be still less liked when he's wound up the Bursley Football Club.'

'Well, urge him on to wind it up, then. But I don't see what football has got to do with being mayor.'

She endeavoured to look like a serious politician.

'You are nothing but a cuckoo,' Denry pleasantly informed her. 'Football has got to do with everything. And it's been a disastrous mistake in my career that I've never taken any interest in football. Old Barlow wants no urging on to wind up the Football Club. He's absolutely set on it. He's lost too much over it. If I could stop him from winding it up I might...'

'What?'

'I dunno.'

She perceived that his idea was yet vague.

II

Not very many days afterwards the walls of Bursley called attention, by small blue and red posters (blue and red being the historic colours of the Bursley Football Club), to a public meeting, which was to be held in the Town Hall, under the presidency of the Mayor, to consider what steps could be taken to secure the future of the Bursley Football Club.

There were two 'great' football clubs in the Five Towns – Knype, one of the oldest clubs in England, and Bursley. Both were in the League, though Knype was in the first division while Bursley was only in the second. Both were, in fact, limited companies, engaged as much in the pursuit of dividends as in the practice of the one ancient and glorious sport which appeals to the reason and the heart of England. (Neither ever paid a dividend.) Both employed professionals, who, by a strange chance, were nearly all born in Scotland; and both also employed trainers who, before an important match, took the teams off to a hydropathic establishment far, far distant from any public-house. (This was called 'training'.) Now, whereas the Knype Club was struggling along fairly well, the Bursley Club had come to the end of its resources. The great football public had practically deserted it. The explanation, of course, was that Bursley had been losing too many matches. The great football public had no use for anything but victories. It would treat its players like gods – so long as they won. But when they happened to lose, the great football public simply sulked. It did not kick a man that was down; it merely ignored him, well knowing that the man could not get up without help. It cared nothing whatever for fidelity, municipal patriotism, fair play, the chances of war, or dividends on capital. If it could see victories it would pay sixpence, but it would not pay sixpence to assist at defeats.

Still, when at a special general meeting of the Bursley Football Club Limited, held at the registered office, the Coffee House, Bursley, Councillor Barlow, J.P., Chairman of the Company since the creation of the League, announced that the Directors had reluctantly come to the conclusion that they could not conscientiously embark on the dangerous risks of the approaching season, and that it was the intention of the Directors to wind up the club, in default of adequate public interest – when Bursley read this in the *Signal*, the town was certainly shocked. Was the famous club, then, to disappear for ever, and the football ground to be sold in plots, and the grand stand for firewood? The shock was so severe that the death of Alderman Bloor (none the less a mighty figure in Bursley) had passed as a minor event.

Hence the advertisement of the meeting in the Town Hall caused joy and hope, and people said to themselves: 'Something's bound to be done; the old club can't go out like that.' And everybody grew quite sentimental. And although nothing is supposed to be capable of filling Bursley Town Hall except a political meeting and an old folk's treat, Bursley Town Hall was as near full as made no matter for the football question. Many men had cheerfully sacrificed a game of billiards and a glass of beer in order to attend it.

The Mayor, in the chair, was a mild old gentleman who knew nothing whatever about football and had probably never seen a football match; but it was essential that the meeting should have august patronage, and so the Mayor had been trapped and tamed. On the mere fact that he paid an annual subscription to the golf club, certain parties built up the legend that he was a true sportsman, with the true interests of sport in his soul.

He uttered a few phrases, such as 'the manly game', 'old associations', 'bound up with the history of England', 'splendid fellows', 'indomitable pluck', 'dogged by misfortune' (indeed, he produced quite an impression on the rude and grim audience), and then he called upon Councillor Barlow to make a statement.

Councillor Barlow, on the Mayor's right, was a different kind of man from the Mayor. He was fifty and iron-grey, with whiskers, but no moustache; short, stoutish, raspish.

He said nothing about manliness, pluck, history, or Auld Lang Syne.

He said he had given his services as Chairman to the football club for thirteen years; that he had taken up £2000 worth of shares in the Company; and that as at that moment the Company's liabilities would exactly absorb its assets, his £2000 was worth exactly nothing. 'You may say,' he said, 'I've lost that £2000 in thirteen years. That is, it's the same as if I'd been steadily paying three pun' a week out of my own pocket to provide football matches that you chaps wouldn't take the trouble to go and see. That's the straight of it! What have I got for my pains? Nothing but worries and these!' (He pointed to his grey hairs.) 'And I'm not alone; there's others; and now I have to come and defend myself at a public meeting. I'm supposed not to have the best interests of football at heart. Me and my co-Directors,' he proceeded, with even a rougher raspishness, 'have warned the town again and again what would happen if the matches weren't better patronized. And now it's happened, and now it's too late, you want to *do* something! You can't! It's too late. There's only one thing the matter with first-class football in Bursley,' he concluded, 'and it isn't the players. It's the public — it's yourselves. You're the most craven lot of tom-fools that ever a big football club had to do with. When we lose a match, what do you do? Do you come and encourage us next time? No, you stop away, and leave us fifty or sixty pound out of pocket on a match, just to teach us better ! Do you expect us to win every match ? Why, Preston North End itself' – here he spoke solemnly, of heroes – 'Preston North End itself in its great days didn't win every match – it lost to Accrington. But did the Preston public desert it? No ! *You* – you haven't got the pluck of a louse, nor the faithfulness of a cat. You've starved your football club to death, and now you call a meeting to weep and grumble. And you have the insolence to write letters to the *Signal* about bad management, forsooth ! If anybody in the hall thinks he can manage this club better than me and my co-Directors have done, I may say that we hold a majority of the shares, and we'll part with the whole show to any clever person or persons who care to take it off our hands at a bargain price. That's talking.'

He sat down.

Silence fell. Even in the Five Towns a public meeting is seldom bullied as Councillor Barlow had bullied that meeting. It was aghast. Councillor Barlow had never been popular: he had merely been respected; but thenceforward he became even less popular than before.

'I'm sure we shall all find Councillor Barlow's heat quite excusable –' the Mayor diplomatically began.

'No heat at all,' the Councillor interrupted. 'Simply cold truth ! '

A number of speakers followed, and nearly all of them were against the Directors. Some, with prodigious memories for every combination of players in every match that had ever been played, sought to prove by detailed instances that Councillor Barlow and his co-Directors had persistently and regularly muddled their work during thirteen industrious years. And they defended the insulted public by asserting that no public that respected itself would pay sixpence to watch the wretched football provided by Councillor Barlow. They shouted that the team wanted reconstituting, wanted new blood.

'Yes,' shouted Councillor Barlow in reply. 'And how are you going to get new blood, with transfer fees as high as they are now? You can't get even an average good player for less than

£200. Where's the money to come from? Anybody want to lend a thousand or so on second debentures?'

He laughed sneeringly.

No one showed a desire to invest in second debentures of the Bursley F.C. Ltd.

Still, speakers kept harping on the necessity of new blood in the team, and then others, bolder, harped on the necessity of new blood on the board.

'Shares on sale!' cried the Councillor. 'Any buyers? Or,' he added, 'do you want something for nothing – as usual?'

At length a gentleman rose at the back of the hall.

'I don't pretend to be an expert on football,' said he, 'though I think it's a great game, but I should like to say a few words as to this question of new blood.'

The audience craned its neck.

'Will Mr Councillor Machin kindly step up to the platform?' the Mayor suggested.

And up Denry stepped.

The thought in every mind was: 'What's he going to do? What's he got up his sleeve – this time?'

'Three cheers for Machin!' people chanted gaily.

'Order!' said the Mayor.

Denry faced the audience. He was now accustomed to audiences. He said:

'If I'm not mistaken, one of the greatest modern footballers is a native of this town.'

And scores of voices yelled: 'Ay! Callear! Callear! Greatest centre forward in England!'

'Yes,' said Denry. 'Callear is the man I mean. Callear left the district, unfortunately for the district, at the age of nineteen for Liverpool. And it was not till after he left that his astounding abilities were perceived. It isn't too much to say that he made the fortune of Liverpool City. And I believe it is the fact that he scored more goals in three seasons than any other player has ever done in the League. Then, York County, which was in a tight place last year, bought him from Liverpool for a high price, and, as all the world knows, Callear had his leg broken in the first match he played for his new club. That just happened to be the ruin of the York Club, which is now quite suddenly in bankruptcy (which happily we are not), and which is disposing of its players. Gentlemen, I say that Callear ought to come back to his native town. He is fitter than ever he was, and his proper place is in his native town.'

Loud cheers.

'As captain and centre forward of the club of the Mother of the Five Towns, he would be an immense acquisition and attraction, and he would lead us to victory.'

Renewed cheers.

'And how,' demanded Councillor Barlow, jumping up angrily, 'are we to get him back to his precious native town? Councillor Machin admits that he is not an expert on football. It will probably be news to him that Aston Villa have offered £700 to York for the transfer of Callear, and Blackburn Rovers have offered £750, and they're fighting it out between 'em. Any gentleman willing to put down £800 to buy Callear for Bursley?' he sneered. 'I don't mind telling you that steam-engines and the King himself couldn't get Callear into our club.'

'Quite finished?' Denry inquired, still standing.

Laughter, overtopped by Councillor Barlow's snort as he sat down.

Denry lifted his voice.

'Mr Callear, will you be good enough to step forward and let us all have a look at you?'

The effect of these apparently simple words surpassed any effect previously obtained by the most complex flights of oratory in that hall. A young, blushing, clumsy, long-limbed, small-bodied giant stumbled along the central aisle and climbed the steps to the platform, where Denry pointed him to a seat. He was recognized by all the true votaries of the game. And everybody said to everybody: 'By Gosh! It's him, right enough. It's Callear!' And a vast astonishment and expectation of good fortune filled the hall. Applause burst forth, and though no one knew what the appearance of Callear signified, the applause continued and waxed.

'Good old Callear!' The hoarse shouts succeeded each other. 'Good old Machin!'

'Anyhow,' said Denry, when the storm was stilled, 'we've got him here, without either steam-engines or His Majesty. Will the Directors of the club accept him?'

'And what about the transfer?' Councillor Barlow demanded.

'Would you accept him and try another season if you could get him free?' Denry retorted.

Councillor Barlow always knew his mind, and was never afraid to let other people share that knowledge.

'Yes,' he said.

'Then I will see that you have the transfer free.'

'But what about York?'

'I have settled with York provisionally,' said Denry. 'That is my affair. I have returned from York today. Leave all that to me. This town has had many benefactors far more important than myself. But I shall be able to claim this originality: I'm the first to make a present of a live man to the town. Gentlemen – Mr Mayor – I venture to call for three cheers for the greatest centre forward in England, our fellow-townsman.'

The scene, as the *Signal* said, was unique.

And at the Sports Club and the other clubs afterwards, men said to each other: 'No one but him would have thought of bringing Callear over specially and showing him on the platform ... That's cost him above twopence, that has!'

Two days later a letter appeared in the *Signal* (signed 'Fiat Justitia'), suggesting that Denry, as some reward for his public spirit, ought to be the next mayor of Bursley, in place of Alderman Bloor deceased. The letter urged that he would make an admirable mayor, the sort of mayor the old town wanted in order to wake it up. And also it pointed out that Denry would be the youngest mayor that Bursley had ever had, and probably the youngest mayor in England that year. The sentiment in the last idea appealed to the town. The town decided that it would positively *like* to have the youngest mayor it had ever had, and probably the youngest mayor in England that year. The *Signal* printed dozens of letters on the subject. When the Council met, more informally than formally, to choose a chief magistrate in place of the dead alderman, several councillors urged that what Bursley wanted was a young and *popular* mayor. And, in fine,

Councillor Barlow was shelved for a year. On the choice being published the entire town said: 'Now we *shall* have a mayoralty and don't you forget it!'

And Denry said to Nellie: 'You'll be mayoress to the youngest mayor, etc., my child. And it's cost me, including hotel and travelling expenses, eight hundred and eleven pounds six and sevenpence.'

III

The rightness of the Council in selecting Denry as mayor was confirmed in a singular manner by the behaviour of the football and of Callear at the opening match of the season.

It was a philanthropic match, between Bursley and Axe, for the benefit of a county orphanage, and, according to the custom of such matches, the ball was formally kicked off by a celebrity, a pillar of society. The ceremony of kicking off has no sporting significance; the celebrity merely with gentleness propels the ball out of the white circle and then flies for his life from the *mêlée*; but it is supposed to add to the moral splendour of the game. In the present instance the posters said: 'Kick-off at 3.45 by Councillor E. H. Machin, Mayor-designate.' And, indeed, no other celebrity could have been decently selected. On the fine afternoon of the match Denry therefore discovered himself with a new football at his toes, a silk hat on his head, and twenty-two Herculean players menacing him in attitudes expressive of an intention to murder him. Bursley had lost the toss, and hence Denry had to kick towards the Bursley goal. As the *Signal* said, he 'dispatched the sphere' straight into the keeping of Callear, who as centre forward was facing him, and Callear was dodging down the field with it before the Axe players had finished admiring Denry's effrontery. Every reader will remember with a thrill the historic match in which the immortal Jimmy Brown, on the last occasion when he captained Blackburn Rovers, dribbled the ball himself down the length of the field, scored a goal, and went home with the English Cup under his arm. Callear evidently intended to imitate the feat. He was entirely wrong. Dribbling tactics had been killed for ever, years before, by Preston North End, who invented the 'passing' game. Yet Callear went on, and good luck seemed to float over him like a cherub. Finally he shot; a wild, high shot; but there was an adverse wind which dragged the ball down, swept it round, and blew it into the net. The first goal had been scored in twenty seconds! (It was also the last in the match.) Callear's reputation was established. Useless for solemn experts to point out that he had simply been larking for the gallery, and that the result was a shocking fluke – Callear's reputation was established. He became at once the idol of the populace. As Denry walked gingerly off the field to the grand stand he, too, was loudly cheered, and he could not help feeling that, somehow, it was he who had scored that goal. And although nobody uttered the precise thought, most people did secretly think, as they gazed at the triumphant Denry, that a man who triumphed like that, because he triumphed like that, was the right sort of man to be mayor, the kind of man they needed.

Denry became identified with the highest class of local football. This fact led to a curious crisis in the history of municipal manners. On Corporation Sunday the mayor walks to church, preceded by the mace, and followed by the aldermen and councillors, the borough officials, the Volunteers and the Fire Brigade; after all these, in the procession, come individuals known as prominent citizens. Now the first and second elevens of the Bursley Football Club, headed by Callear, expressed their desire to occupy a place in Denry's mayoral procession; they felt that some public acknowledgement was due to the Mayor for his services to the national sport. Denry instantly agreed, with thanks: the notion seemed to him entirely admirable. Then some unfortunately-inspired parson wrote to the *Signal* to protest against professional footballers following the chief magistrate of the borough to church. His arguments were that such a thing was unheard-of, and that football was the cause of a great deal of evil gambling. Some people were inclined to agree with the protest, until Denry wrote to the *Signal* and put a few questions: Was Bursley proud of its football team? Or was Bursley ashamed of its football team? Was the practice of football incompatible with good citizenship? Was there anything dishonourable in playing football? Ought professional footballers to be considered as social pariahs? Was there any class of beings to whom the churches ought to be closed?

The parson foundered in a storm of opprobrium, scorn, and ironic laughter. Though the town laughed, it only laughed to hide its disgust of the parson.

People began to wonder whether the teams would attend in costume, carrying the football between them on a charger as a symbol. No such multitudes ever greeted a mayoral procession in Bursley before. The footballers, however, appeared in ordinary costume (many of them in frock-coats); but they wore neckties of the club colours, a device which was agreed to be in the nicest taste. St Luke's Church was crowded; and, what is stranger, the churchyard was also crowded. The church barely held the procession itself and the ladies who, by influence, had been accommodated with seats in advance. Thousands of persons filled the churchyard, and to prevent them from crushing into the packed fane and bursting it at its weakest point, the apse, the doors had to be locked and guarded. Four women swooned during the service; neither Mrs Machin, senior, nor Nellie, was among the four. It was the first time that anyone had been known to swoon at a religious service held in November. This fact alone gave a tremendous prestige to Denry's mayoralty. When, with Nellie on his arm, he emerged from the church to the thunders of the organ, the greeting which he received in the churchyard, though the solemnity of the occasion forbade clapping, lacked naught in brilliance and efficacy.

The real point and delight of that Corporation Sunday was not fully appreciated till later. It had been expected that the collection after the sermon would be much larger than usual, because the congregation was much larger than usual. But the church-wardens were startled to find it four times as large as usual. They were further startled to find only three threepenny-bits among all the coins. This singularity led to comment and to note-comparing. Everybody had noticed for weeks past a growing dearth of threepenny-bits. Indeed, threepenny-bits had practically vanished from circulation in the Five Towns. On the Monday it became known that the clerks of the various branches of the Universal Thrift Club, Limited, had paid into the banks enormous and unparalleled quantities of threepenny-bits, and for at least a week afterwards everybody paid for everything in threepenny-bits. And the piquant news passed from mouth to mouth that Denry, to the simple end of ensuring a thumping collection for charities on Corporation Sunday, had used the vast organization of the Thrift Club to bring about a famine of threepenny-bits. In the annals of the town that Sunday is referred to as 'Threepenny-bit Sunday', because it was so happily devoid of threepenny-bits.

A little group of councillors were discussing Denry.

'What a card!' said one, laughing joyously. 'He's a rare 'un, no mistake.'

'Of course, this'll make him more popular than ever,' said another. 'We've never had a man to touch him for that.'

'And yet,' demanded Councillor Barlow, 'what's he done? Has he ever done a day's work in his life? What great cause is he identified with?'

'He's identified,' said the speaker, 'with the great cause of cheering us all up.'

Clayhanger

Arnold Bennett's careful evocation of a boy growing to manhood during the last quarter of the nineteenth century, with its superb portrait of an autocratic father, stands on a literary level with *The Old Wives' Tale*. Set, like its successful predecessor, in the Five Towns, *Clayhanger* was destined to be the first novel in a trilogy.

Of the book and its hero Walter Allen has written in *The English Novel*: 'He is one of the most attractive heroes in twentieth-century fiction.' Bennett, who believed inordinately in the 'interestingness' of ordinary things and ordinary people, was never more successful in revealing the 'interestingness', of an apparently ordinary man in Edwin Clayhanger.

The Grim Smile of the Five Towns

In the short stories which make up *The Grim Smile of the Five Towns*, Arnold Bennett caught some of the manner of Maupassant, one of the French writers on whom he modelled his writing. The redolent tale of the coffin and the cheese, 'In a New Bottle', and 'The Silent Brothers' (who have not addressed one another for ten years) possess the true ring.

The pride, pretensions and provincial snobbery of the Potteries are handled by Arnold Bennett with amused tolerance. Most of his stories, like the four linked adventures of Vera Cheswardine, set the home life of the middle-class manufacturers of earthenware and porcelain against a 'singular scenery of coaldust, potsherds, flame and steam'. But Bennett never ignores the less successful members of families in a region where 'clogs to clogs is only three generations'.

Anna of the Five Towns

This is one of the finest of Arnold Bennett's novels, a brilliantly detailed picture of life in the Potteries; a tightly knit story of the destructive forces of evangelism and industrial expansion at work in a small community.

Arnold Bennett understood well the self-sufficiency of the people of Staffordshire. He sympathized with it and detested it. 'We are of the North, outwardly brusque, stoical, undemonstrative, scornful of the impulsive; inwardly all sentiment and crushed tenderness.' His work is filled with that secret and impulsive tenderness, and in *Anna of the Five Towns*, his central character attempts to respond to the emotions she feels but, preoccupied with sin and duty, salvation and savings, she ultimately submits to the world in which she lives.

Hilda Lessways

The second volume in Bennett's Clayhanger trilogy relates the early life of Hilda Lessways, before her marriage to Edwin Clayhanger. Her involvement with the enigmatic, self-made man, George Cannon, and his enterprises takes her from the offices of an embryo newspaper in the Five Towns to a venture into the guest-house business in Brighton.

As in *Clayhanger* Bennett, in Walter Allen's words, 'follows the grain of life'. Hilda, in her guilt at having failed her mother, in her relationship with Cannon, in her growing fascination for young Clayhanger, in the reality of her hopes and tragedies, is one of Bennett's most living heroines.

These Twain

The final volume in the Clayhanger trilogy is in many ways the most accomplished of the three novels, as Bennett, drawing together the threads, presents already-established personalities in confrontation.

Hilda is now married to Edwin Clayhanger and the two, with Hilda's son by her disastrous 'marriage' to George Cannon, are living in Bursley. As they cope with immediate tensions and with old wounds they are forced continually to reassess their relationship.

Bennett is at his best here, recreating a society and its characters – Auntie Hamps and Tertius Ingpen among them – and achieving a remarkably subtle and biting portrait of a marriage.